This book is due for return on or before the last date shown below.

D1356455

ARMEN T. MARSOOBIAN

FRAGMENTS OF A LOST HOMELAND

Remembering Armenia

I.B. TAURIS

LONDON · NEW YORK

This publication was made possible
by a generous grant from the
Dolores Zohrab Liebmann Fund

Published in 2015 by
I.B.Tauris & Co. Ltd
London • New York
www.ibtauris.com

ISBN: 978 1 78453 211 6
eISBN: 978 0 85773 701 4

A full CIP record for this book is available from the British Library
A full CIP record is available from the Library of Congress

Library of Congress Catalog Card Number: available

Typeset in Berthold Baskerville Book by Free Range Book Design & Production Limited
Printed and bound in Great Britain by T.J. International, Padstow, Cornwall

MIX
Paper from
responsible sources
FSC® C013056

This book is dedicated to
my grandparents Tsolag and Mariam,
my parents Alice and Michael
and my brother Gary.
Though no longer with us,
their spirits live on in all the work that I do.

CONTENTS

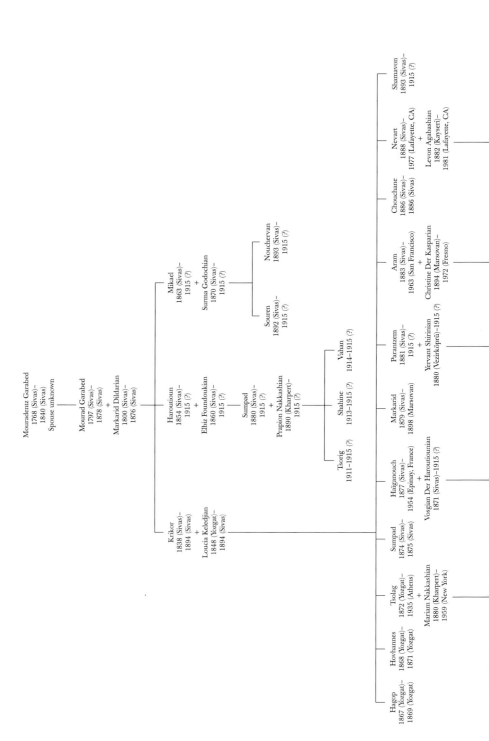

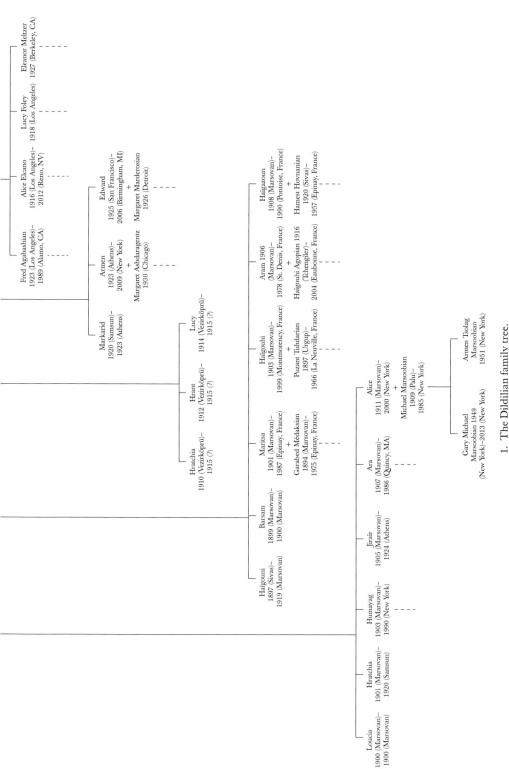

1. The Dildilian family tree.

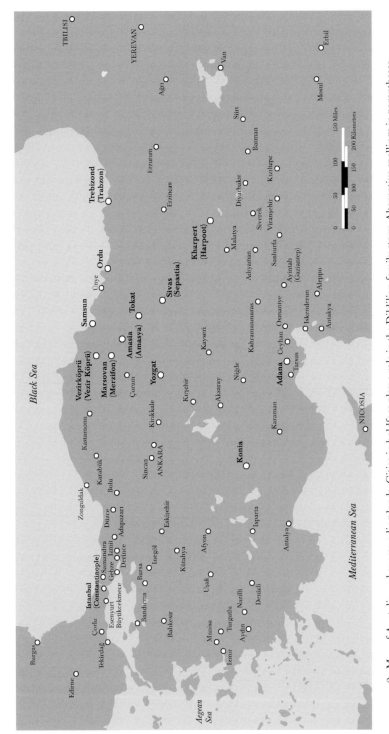

2. Map of Anatolia and surrounding lands. Cities in boldface play a role in the Dildilian family story. Alternative spellings in parentheses.

For everything, in time, gets lost … But for a little while some of that can be rescued, if only, faced with the vastness of all that is and all that there ever was, somebody makes the decision to look back, to have one last look, to search for a while in the debris of the past and to see not only what was lost but what there is still to be found.

Daniel Mendelsohn, *The Lost: A Search for Six of Six Million*

PREFACE

This book fulfills an unspoken promise I made over a quarter of a century ago. In the mid-1980s my two uncles, Humayag and Ara Dildilian, were working together to write the family story, including the important role that photography had played in many of its members' lives. Between my mother's generation and my grandfather's generation, I count six Dildilians who practiced the art of photography. Humayag was one of them and stewarded a significant collection of the family's photographs. The sudden death of Ara and the declining health and capabilities of Humayag made their dream impossible to fulfill. The two brothers had gathered together documents, letters, and memoirs over many years for the purpose of telling this story. These materials and the family photography collection were entrusted to me by my uncle Humayag shortly before his death in 1990. I began this preface by acknowledging an "unspoken promise" because, while my uncles never explicitly asked me to carry on their work, I knew in my heart that I had a moral obligation that I someday must fulfill. Publishing this book and organizing photography exhibitions in Turkey and in various cities around the world are my way of meeting this obligation.

One might ask why it took me over 20 years to write this book. Establishing my career as an academic philosopher and beginning a family both played a role in the delay. But I also suppose that I felt some trepidation in delving deeply into my family's story, for I suspected that much of it would be emotionally quite painful. I knew some aspects of the survival stories of both my mother's family, the Dildilians, and my father's family, the Marsoobians. My parents often openly talked about their lives in the "old country." Only after I dug much deeper into the trove of Dildilian material did I realize how utterly amazing was their story of survival. My family's story shares many themes common to those of countless Armenians in the diaspora. All are forever marked by the genocide that began in 1915. But much in the Dildilian story you are about to read is unique. I knew that my grandfather Tsolag's photography played a role in the family's survival. I was told that his skills were needed by the government and thus he and his immediate family, including my mother Alice, were saved from the death marches that took place in the summer of 1915. But I did not know that the family had to convert to Islam and adopt Turkish identities in order to avoid deportation and certain death. This last-minute, life-or-death decision saved the immediate family members in Marsovan, though nearly all family members in other Anatolian towns and cities perished. Thus my family remained in Marsovan during the whole course of the First World War and the years of turmoil that followed. But the story is not merely one of their own survival. They used their ingenuity to courageously rescue and hide upwards of 30 young men and women during those war years. While they continued to work as photographers, they soon took up important work in saving orphans and establishing orphanages. They did much to rebuild the lives of the few Armenians who survived the genocide. Their efforts were ultimately not rewarded, for they were forced to flee their homes and their homeland by 1923. Thus they began the slow process of rebuilding their shattered lives in Greece, France, England, and the United States.

In writing this book and organizing the exhibitions, I see myself as bearing witness to my family's story. Yet it is my grandfather, his siblings, and their children who have done the bulk of the work of bearing witness. Aside from the more than 800 Ottoman-era photographs I have received from them, hundreds and hundreds of pages of memoirs, speeches, and letters have survived that provide a truly fascinating account of what their lives were like in the decades that span both sides of the turn of the twentieth century. This wealth of visual and textual material makes the Dildilian story unique and unlike most diasporan Armenian stories. Many Armenian families count themselves lucky to have a few photographs and orally conveyed stories snatched from the catastrophe that marked the end of Armenian life in their historic homeland. Our family has more, much more, that allows us to understand what their lives were like in historic Armenia. The words and images in this book testify to all that was lost and also bear witness to the indestructible will of the Armenian people to survive, thus denying the genocide perpetrators their ultimate goal.

ACKNOWLEDGMENTS

Some of the early work on this project began when I was a Dukakis Fellow at the American College of Thessaloniki (ACT), the university division of Anatolia College. The then-president of the college Richard Jackson and his faculty and staff did much to create an ideal setting for me to begin the journey that would become this book. The Trustees of Anatolia College, as digital rights holders of some of the photographs, granted me permission to use them. I single out Stella Asderi of ACT's Bissell Library, who greatly facilitated my use of their archive. The many exchanges with Bill McGrew, a historian and former president of Anatolia College greatly enhanced my research.

Once I decided to write this book, I began the search for models that I might emulate. Two works stand out as early inspirations for the memory work in which I immersed myself, Daniel Mendelsohn's *The Lost: A Search for Six of Six Million* and Peter Singer's *Pushing Time Away: My Grandfather and the Tragedy of Jewish Vienna*. Though neither one resembles the style or structure of my book, reading them gave me the freedom to step outside my normal academic comfort zone. I also have found important philosophical validation for my work in Jeffrey Blustein's *The Moral Demands of Memory*.

My university, Southern Connecticut State University, is gratefully acknowledged for providing small research grants to facilitate my research. Additionally, the Dolores Zohrab Liebmann Fund provided generous publication funding.

My friends in Turkey, both those of Armenian origin and those not, have helped me make sense of the land of my origins. The wise guidance of Asena Günal, Murat Çelikkan, Osman Koker and Kirkor Sahakoglu must be noted. Most importantly I must thank Osman Kavala whose strong commitment to my work has been unwavering. Osman has been a true friend and partner, encouraging me at every turn. Finally, a most heartfelt thanks must be given to Ferda Keskin, whose friendship started during my first very cautious visit to Turkey in 2003. Whatever anxiety I may have felt as an Armenian visiting Turkey was alleviated by Ferda's warm and welcoming manner. He shared with me the experience of visiting the home that my grandfather built in Marsovan, the home of my mother's birth. Our visit was a moving experience for us both, a true sign of our friendship's depth.

My cousin Haïk Der Haroutiounian began his journey into the family story much earlier than I. His explorations led him to physically traverse the Anatolian landscape where once the family had lived. He refashioned himself into a first-class historian, and I have relied upon his language skills and detective-like intelligence to unravel many puzzling aspects of the family story. Haïk recovered, translated, and edited the memoir of his aunt Maritsa Médaksian, which plays a central role in my book. His brother Edouard furnished the English translation. For this assistance and the generous hospitality of all my French cousins, I am forever grateful.

All members of my extended family have been truly supportive of my work but I must single out the late Armen Dildilian and his wife Margaret for special thanks. Armen was the son of Aram, one of the Dildilian Brothers photographers, and shared with me many of his father's photographs and stories. His daughter Karen Tartell took time out from her busy schedule and read the complete manuscript. Her critical comments did much to improve the focus and readability of the book.

Two colleagues, Michael Shea and Renée Harlow, whose judgments I value highly, have greatly aided the progress of my work. Renée was the final reader of the manuscript. Her guidance as I struggled to tame a sometimes rambling monster of a manuscript will never be forgotten.

Finally, but not least importantly, I must thank my wife Fulvia and my daughter Sarah for the patience and understanding they have shown me over the years of this project. They have had to indulge my absences, both physical and temporal. I often traveled far afield pursuing this story, but even when I was home, I was sometimes living in the past while physically inhabiting the present. A loving thanks they justly deserve.

INTRODUCTION

Telling Our Story – How It All Began

I recall as a young child often entering my grandmother's dimly lit and sparingly furnished bedroom. Sitting on the small nightstand next to her tiny bed was a little wooden-framed photograph of a handsome bearded man, a man with very beautiful and penetrating eyes. This was my grandfather, Tsolag Dildilian, a grandfather I never knew. He had died many years before in some far-off land. He was seldom talked about, at least in front of my brother and me. Did I ask *mez mayrig* – the Armenian word for grandmother – about the photo? I do not recall. My child's curiosity did sometimes make me wonder about the photos of adults. What did these people look like as children? What did a beardless grandfather look like in his childhood? More than 50 years later, I still cannot answer this question. Yet I do know more, a lot more about my grandfather. I shall tell you his story and the story of my Armenian family.

I first began hearing fragments of this story as a child growing up in an immigrant Armenian family in New York City. The story was conveyed to me not in a typical narrative with a beginning, middle and end. Often these stories weren't being told to me at all. They were overheard snippets of conversations. At first they were words and phrases spoken at odd moments, sometimes with odd names, and often about unknown yet exotic-sounding places: Marsovan, Turkya, Bolis, Hratchia, Samsun, Palu, Yozgat, Haleb, Jiraïr, Aksoar, the orphans, the college, the studio, or as my mother used to say, the *atelier*. Words spoken in English, in Armenian, and in a language I was not meant to understand: Turkish. There were also photographs – a few, not many. There was that bearded man, distinguished-looking, my grandfather, whose photograph had rested for a brief time in the twilight of my grandmother's bedroom. There was also my grandmother whose presence animated our household, for she lived with us during the last years of her life. She was a living, though often silent, reminder of a time long past. The mysterious scar on her arm that she bore with dignity told a story that I was only to learn years later: the story of her terrifying escape from the roof of her burning home during the Hamidian Massacres of 1895. As I grew older some of these fragments slowly began to come together. They were snapshots into a distant time and place whose boundaries remained indistinct for me.

I am a first-generation American who as a child struggled with typical issues of assimilation. I grew up among families of Italian and Irish descent, while at the same time being exposed through school and play to African American and Jewish children. Yet most of these second- and third-generation children seldom faced those awkward public moments when their parents addressed them in a strange-sounding language, a language unfamiliar to most people. For those who were curious enough to inquire about the language that was spoken, the response "Armenian" inevitably led to further questions: "So, where is Armenia?" "Are your parents from this place called Armenia?" At that time, during the height of the Cold War, decades before the breakup of the Soviet Union, these were tricky questions to answer. Yes, I could locate for them the Soviet Republic of Armenia, that sliver of land-locked territory wedged between the Black and Caspian Seas, but this was only a half-truth. Such a response would inevitably lead to more confusing dialogue:

"Do you have relatives there in Armenia?"
"Well no, my parents did not come from there."
"So where were they from?"

Responding with the name "Anatolia" would not suffice since this word was as opaque as "Armenia." "Turkey," a much more familiar word, would create even more awkward moments, often leading to a pair of questions that had to be answered in the negative: "Are you then Turkish?" "Do you still have relatives in Turkey?" I cannot recall at what age I was able to answer these questions in a sensibly informed manner. I became aware of the rudiments of the events of 1915 well before reaching my teenage years. My awareness resulted from having attended an Armenian church and participating in Armenian youth organizations. On April 24, 1965 at the age of 14, I carried a memorial wreath in the commemorative procession marking the 50th anniversary of the Armenian Genocide in New York City's Madison Square Park. Yet even then I knew very little of the story you are about to read.

The story that follows incorporates large portions of two family memoirs. Additional material is quoted from other written family sources including letters and speeches, as well as oral testimony that was recorded on audio and videotape. The most frequently quoted sources are a book-length memoir and family history written by my great-uncle Aram Dildilian, a lengthy speech written by my grandfather Tsolag Dildilian, in which he tells the story of his love affair with photography, and a memoir written by my grandfather's niece, Maritsa Médaksian (née Der Haroutiounian), who often retells the stories her mother, Haïganouch, told her. The first was written in English, the latter two in Armenian. The photographs were taken by Tsolag and Aram, brothers who had established the Dildilian Brothers photography studios in Marsovan, Amasia, Samsun, Konia, and Adana.

3. Tsolag Dildilian (left), Aram Dildilian (standing), and
Haïganouch Der Haroutiounian, née Dildilian (right).

1

The Dildilians of Sivas

How the Family Got its Name

The Dildilian family story begins in the mid-eighteenth century. I say "story" because what we know about my family in those early years was shared orally by one generation with the next. I do not know when these stories were first written down, but in a speech my grandfather Tsolag tells us that his grandfather, Mourad, often read aloud family stories from what he calls "a book of dreams." This book has long been lost, but decades later these stories appeared in the memoirs of both Aram and Maritsa.

The Dildilian family name has long been associated with photography but much before the invention of photography in 1839, the Dildilians were practicing a variety of skilled crafts in the Anatolian city of Sivas, known to many Armenians by its earlier name, Sebastia. One of these crafts, blacksmithing, accounts for the creation of the family surname, Dildilian, a name unique among Armenian surnames. Unlike most Armenian surnames shared by many unrelated families, the Dildilian name is found only among Armenians who are members of our extended family. Aram begins his memoir with a description of one of his earliest known ancestors: "My great-grandfather, Garabed, was a blacksmith. He was born and lived and died in Sivas, Asia Minor, which is situated on a high plateau by the Alice River (Kuzul), which was once the capital city of an Armenian king, Senekereme. That is why that western section [of the Armenian Highlands] is called *Poker Haigks*, 'Minor Armenia'."

As I discovered only recently, the Dildilians were not always called "Dildilian," but at one time went by the surname Keledjian. My great-great-great-grandfather, Mouradentz Garabed Keledjian, born in Sivas in 1768, was the talented blacksmith identified above whose act of skill caused the surname change. My grandfather Tsolag, the eldest of his siblings, provides the first known record of this event in a speech given to family and friends in January of 1928:

> My grandfather Mourad had a "Book of Dreams" in which it was recorded that
> 150 years ago a military Pasha came to Sebastia and sent for a farrier, commanding

5

that his 400 horses be shod with new horseshoes within four days. "If you cannot fill the order, your head will be off." The poor craftsman, driven by the fear of losing his head, with an unbelievable speed finishes the task, puts the pincers and the hammer at the Pasha's feet and salutes him. The Pasha lifts his head and asks, "What do you want?" The master craftsman replies, "Sir, your command has been completed." The surprised Pasha says, *"Aferim, usta duel duel mi oldun."* (Bravo, master, you are the master duel duel.) Duel Duel is a small fast-moving horse from Mytilene [a Greek island in the Aegean off the west coast of Turkey, in Turkish called Midillisi]. Thus, as a result of grandfather's saving his head, today, I, his grandson – I do not know by how many generations – keep his respectable surname, Dildilian. I, too, have saved my head by a hair's breadth from Pashas.[1]

Aram's memoir includes a slightly different version but still involves the family being named after a fast horse.

4. A pair of Midilli/Mytiline ponies in a stable.

Maritsa many years later recounts the story of this defining event but gives a different version of the specific origin of the name "Dildilian." There is no fast Mytilene pony referenced in this story:

This is how the Keledjians became the Dildilians.
    A long time ago, when the beys had armed escorts of men on horseback or on foot and could thus rob, abduct and ransom ... a bey brings, I don't know how many horses to be re-shoed ... instructing him to have the job completed before

daybreak or he would be beheaded. Begging, or imploring the implacable bey would be futile. The bey knows it is an impossible task.

The blacksmith sets to work. When the bey comes the next morning, the blacksmith is distraught, and having just finished the job, he presents his tools at the bey's feet. But weariness and awe are such that he is unable to speak. Surprised at his silence, the bey asks him: "*Dilinle mi nallatın?*" (Did you shoe them with your tongue?) But the master still cannot utter a word, so the bey cries: "*Dil, dil!*" (Your tongue, your tongue!) In other words, "Speak up!"

These words remained and the blacksmith was called *dildil*, which became Dildilian.

Whether named in honor of a fast pony or a tongue-tied blacksmith, the Dildilian name stuck.

My Great-Great-Grandfather: The Successful Merchant or the Loafing Man of Leisure?

For those fortunate to have a family memoir that tells stories about ancestors and events long since past, the reader is usually given a singular perspective. The memoirist controls the space of memory. Characters may be sugar-coated or demonized. In the case of the Dildilian family story, we have multiple perspectives, both written and oral, male and female. Sometimes they may disagree about the facts, though more often they color those facts with their own meanings. Differences about religion will come to play a profound role in our memoirists' judgments about these facts. A more benign disagreement, one not based on religion, is evidenced in the portrayal of my great-great-grandfather, Mourad Garabed Dildilian. Mourad, unlike his ancestors in the blacksmithing trade, was a grocer. Aram briefly describes his "great-grandpa" without making any judgment as to his character. But as we will see, Aram's sister Haïganouch certainly had a different opinion. Aram writes:

> My great-grandpa, Garabed, had only one son, who was my grandfather, Mourad, and two daughters, Karan and Yeva. Grandpa Mourad was a tall, strong man. He had a grocery store. He married a very rich man's only daughter, Margaret Dildarian, a very short lady. They were blessed with three sons. My father, Krikor, was the first-born in 1838 in Sivas. He was fair complexioned, hazel eyed, and had black hair. My dearest uncle Haroutioun, was born in 1854 in Sivas, and was fair, with blue eyes and brown hair. My youngest uncle Mikael was born 1863 in Sivas and was fair with brown eyes and black hair.

To give you a flavor of what a grocery store would look like in mid-nineteenth-century Sivas, Aram drew a sketch.

GRAND·FOTHER'S GROCERY STORE

5. Mourad Garabed Dildilian's grocery store drawn by Aram Dildilian.

Now Haïganouch had a starkly negative opinion of her grandfather, whom she chooses to call by his second name, Garabed. She conveyed her unflattering view of her grandfather to her daughter Maritsa, whose words capture her mother's perspective:

Garabed is a handsome young man with delicate features, nice-looking but almost penniless. But he is probably a lucky man.

He marries the daughter of Dildarian, a wealthy and well-known man. The girl was of short height but this was offset by many qualities. She had a sharp mind and a sure taste, she was active, hard-working and full of common sense, in one word she was a pearl as her name said: Markarid, the pearl.

She had no money problems as a married woman. She lived a quiet and serene life with her three children, Krikor, Haroutioun and Mikael. It may be said that the children were brought up by the sole care of their mother, as Garabed did not work and had progressively become a perfect loafer. My mother used to say, when speaking of him: "My lazy grandfather." While his wife knitted stockings, or embroidered crepe cloth ornate with gold or silver

8

threads or velvet cloth for the trousseaus of Turkish girls while at the same time bringing up her children.

Maritsa describes how Markarid and her children were often very busy with household chores and activities in order to bring in more household income. Yet Mourad Garabed seemed oblivious: "And while these activities were going on, the father carelessly was playing knucklebones on the house terrace."

Knucklebones, or what is more commonly called the game of jacks, has a venerable history which some have traced to Asia Minor. Knucklebones is a very ancient game usually played with five small objects, originally the "knucklebones" or hocks of a sheep, that are thrown up and caught in various ways. Sophocles, in a fragment, ascribed the invention of knucklebones to Palamedes, who taught the pastime to his Greek countrymen during the Trojan War. Maybe the game was then picked up by the locals and spread across Anatolia, finding itself in the DNA of Mourad Garabed! Successful merchant or a lazy loafer who loved to play jacks and lived off his wife's money and hard work – we will never know for sure.

Great-Grandfather Krikor: A Son Who Chooses a Different Path

Krikor Dildilian, my great-grandfather, was a man much admired by all members of the family. He was born in Sivas in 1838. The eldest of three siblings, he eventually chose not to follow his father into the grocery business. This last statement must be qualified because he did make an unsuccessful childhood attempt at being a grocer. Aram relates the following about his father:

> One day when he was about four or five years old, he suggested to his cousin to play grocery store in the basement where his father stored his extra supplies. In the olden times, grocery men used to display all their merchandise in the open on big round wooden or straw trays, side-by-side and in rows … So, to imitate the grocery store, my father gets a bright idea. He takes his father's gold-embroidered Sunday blue jacket and cuts it in small square pieces, puts them side-by-side in rows and uses them as trays. On each square he puts some raisins, nuts, candy, and other dried fruits, etc. Soon they get tired of playing grocery store and want to drink sherbet but instead of mixing it in a small bowl, they pour the readymade candies into the upper small basin of the running fountain with the expectation of drinking sweet sherbet from the faucet. Fortunately, a passerby neighbor notices some candy floating on the river in front of our house as the drain was connected to the river (I should add that in those days candies were very expensive). So he follows [the trail of candies] up the river and notices that it is coming out of our house. He knocks on the door and warns of what is going on, but by that time the candy sack was half

full. Maybe his rich grandfather, Dildarian, saw in his grandchild some business ability in that childish but costly grocery game. Maybe that was the incentive for him to send father to Constantinople in his early youth to manage his business ... and surely he became a real success there.

Despite this early business failure, if you could call it that, Krikor did develop his skills as a merchant and businessman. His grandfather employed him in the family business and sent him to Constantinople and to other cities. Aram writes admiringly of his father: "My father was a smart man, quite well-informed and educated for his time. He was wise, prudent, progressive, diplomatic, good-natured, influential, and he knew how to make friends. I suppose he was a born businessman too."

Even as a very young man, Krikor seemed to have a bright future in Sivas. Maritsa also describes how he assisted his mother in her various home textile activities and soon found himself in the family business: "In the course of selling objects made by his mother and of making purchases, Krikor gained experience in the art of trade, which did not escape the attention of his uncle who took him as an apprentice at the age of 14." This entrepreneurial trait not only characterized Krikor but was passed down to the next generation, for my grandfather's generation was highly successful in a variety of endeavors even in the midst of some very difficult economic times.

Mid-nineteenth-century Ottoman city centers, such as the one in which the family home was located, often had houses constructed close together with walled courtyards in the rear. Such close-in construction provided a degree of security, that is, if one could trust one's neighbors. Both Aram and Maritsa tell a story in which such proximity may well have encouraged a crime. Aram writes:

In those days there were no banks or safes and safe deposit vaults to keep money in as there are now, so businessmen used to keep the daily earned money at home or put it in the bedroom in money sacks made of goat's hair. One night while father Krikor was sleeping in his room, he wakes up to some noise and sees in the dark a man across his room's window trying to put a plank to the window. So, in fear, he cries for help. The man must have been scared and ran back to his room. Next day, father goes to a Turkish friend, a very influential man, and he, in turn, said not to worry and not to tell anyone else about it. He tells father to go to his room at night as if nothing had happened, put the candle light on, pour out all his money and count it, and take his time in counting, put the money back into the sack and put it next to his bed and go to bed pretending sleep. In the meantime, he [the Turkish friend] sends his guard to take care of Krikor. The guard comes to the room beforehand and hides himself next to the window. Father goes to bed as if nothing had happened, putting the money sack near his pillow. Sure enough, about midnight the man puts a plank across the window again and walks towards father's window and tries to open the window latch. By the time he stretched his arm, bang! The sharp sword of the guard comes down in force. He misses the thief's arm, but two of his fingers fall on the floor (I remember very well that my father used to keep those fingers in his desk as a souvenir).

Maritsa relays a similar story but with a slightly different twist. Justice was meted out not by a Turkish guard, but by Krikor himself, and the culprit was a "turbaned mullah." The upshot was the same: "a number of fingers fell onto the floor." No mention is made here of souvenirs.

Krikor was young, ambitious and with the help of his mother's family seemed well on the road to a successful business career in his ancestral hometown of Sivas. With these bright prospects, it was natural that marriage should come into the picture. Markarid, Krikor's mother, would be the matchmaker as was the custom in those days:

> After a few years, the uncle [the wealthy Dildarian brother of his mother] wanted to send Krikor to some other place. Krikor's mother thought it would be better if he were engaged first and she started to look for a suitable girl. One day, as she was coming back from a girl-viewing visit [that is, match-making visit], the young girl who had just been placed with her as an apprentice seamstress came running to welcome her. As usual, the girl had taken off the veil covering her head that she wore as a sign of deference and, for the first time, Markarid closely observed the girl. She thought: "Why a far-flung quest? This girl is quite all right" and she had her engaged to her son. After that, Krikor went to work as a migrant trader or merchant [*bantoukht*]. He succeeded in his ventures and earned much money for his uncle.

Krikor's youthful days of success in Sivas were not to last. In Maritsa's account, passed on to her by her mother, Krikor's travels to Constantinople and beyond were not all a result of being brought into his maternal grandfather and uncle's business. Quite the opposite, as we will see, some of these travels found their origins in the greed of family and neighbors and the slanders made against him by those jealous of his success.

A Sojourn in Yozgat: The Dildilians Start Over Again

"Yozgat," another strange-sounding name from my youth. I remember as a young teenager seeing this name for the first time on a fancy hand-drawn family tree that was being passed around at one of our family reunions. Every autumn we would make the long journey up from New York City to Broadalbin, or in later years to Fonda, in upstate New York to attend the Dildilian–Sisson family reunion. Ara Dildilian, my mother's brother and the grandson of Krikor, would host this annual event. He had married a New England Yankee, Martha Sisson, whose roots could be traced back to the Pilgrims on the *Mayflower*. My brother and I would always look forward to these weekends in the country. Sometimes there was the added excitement of a "real" train journey on the old New York Central Railroad – a far cry from the subway rides we were accustomed to from Queens into Manhattan in order to attend our Armenian church. Uncle Ara and Aunt Martha's house was always part of the attraction. Their large house had many rooms and corridors, places to explore and to hide. This was quite a contrast from the bungalow in which we lived in the New York City borough of Queens. Uncle's house, with its many twists and turns, somehow became intertwined with the image of that colorful and intricately drawn family tree, the one that I was later to learn was drawn by my great-uncle, Aram Dildilian. He was a relative about whom I knew little at that time. What fascinated me the most about this document was the fact that there on a tiny branch at the far end of this tree was my name along with my brother's. Following the lines and the swirls of the tree took me back in time to that distant ancestor born in Sivas in 1768. Two hundred years of history separated me from him, two hundred years I knew little about. Connecting me to that distant ancestor was my grandfather, Tsolag Dildilian, born in 1872 in that unfamiliar city called Yozgat.

How did my grandfather come to be born in Yozgat given the fact that the ancestral home had always been Sivas? Aram explains that the success of his father spawned jealousy among his grandfather Dildarian's business acquaintances. Slanderous and accusatory letters convinced his grandfather to demand Krikor's return from Constantinople to Sivas. Aram writes: "That hasty action hurt my father's dignity, he being very sensitive, so he decides not to go back to Sivas and see his grandfather's face. Instead he goes to Yozgat with a friend. There he learns how to become a first-class shoemaker … and soon starts a business of his own. Later he sends for his father, mother, and two brothers."

Maritsa gives us a much more detailed account of the motivation behind this move to Yozgat. Krikor was recently engaged and appeared to be in line to inherit the Dildarian family business. A jealous uncle slanders Krikor, resulting in his fiancée's father calling off the engagement. Maritsa continues:

> Well, at that time [around 1860], a broken engagement was no small matter. So Krikor decided he would not return to Sivas and, as the business was not his and he had not the money to start up a new venture, he chose to become a shoemaker.
>
> He went to Bolis [Constantinople], and from there to Izmir, learning the shoemaking trade. He was dead set against returning to Sivas. He knew that Yozgat was at that time a new town where it was easier to earn a living. So he goes there and then has his family come and join him.

The family closes up the house and secures the household valuables, including Markarid's beautiful jewelry, in a chest that is nailed shut and sealed. Yozgat will be their new home.

Within a short period of time the Dildilians begin to prosper again. Krikor and his brothers are all busily engaged in building their shoe business. Krikor was soon to be married, the failed Sivas engagement well behind him. Aram writes:

> In Yozgat, my father became quite successful and married my mother Miss Loucia Kullijian, tall, blue eyed, light brown hair and fair complexion, in 1865. She was sweet, tenderhearted, and prayerful. Her father and three brothers were candy makers. She had three sisters, one is still alive in Egypt (95 years old and blind).
>
> There in Yozgat my parents were blessed with three boys. The first two died before they were three years old, but the third son, my loving brother Tsolag survived, blue eyed, blond, with lovely features – born May 1, 1872 in Yozgat.

So here is that name, "Yozgat," that I saw years ago on that branch of the family tree under my grandfather's name.

Maritsa continues her description of the events in Yozgat, picking up her narrative with a story about Krikor's in-laws, the Keledjians (the Kullijians of Aram's narrative). Unlike Aram's brief remark about his parents' marriage, Maritsa's account has a darker side, one that reflects the difficulties Armenians often faced in the Ottoman system that deprived them of many civil rights. The Keledjians had invested their fortune in a flour mill:

> But even before the first bag of flour is ground, a Turkish agha comes and seizes the mill … It is a severe blow. Keledjian was left hopeless. It is said that he kept sitting prostrated on his chair. He died shortly after, leaving five orphans, one of them being Loucia whom the Dildilians chose as a bride for Krikor.
>
> To this end, Garabed [Krikor's father] paid a visit to the Keledjians. Loucia, with her skirt folded up above her ankles, was pressing grapes with her feet. "What are you doing?" asked Garabed. "I am pressing the wine you'll drink," [literally she said: "I want to give you the juice (in Armenian: the "water") of my feet to drink"] answered Loucia candidly, which was indeed true. Water, wine, banquet, toasts … and Loucia became a Dildilian spouse and the Keledjians escaped poverty.

Mourad Garabed, though long retired from the grocery business, was able to pass on his confectionary skills to his daughter-in-law's orphaned brothers. They soon opened a shop, one specializing in *loukoums* – Turkish Delights. The Keledjians and the Dildilians prospered together. Krikor and Loucia soon began their own family: "The first three sons of Krikor and Loucia were born in Yozgat. The third was, by the godfather's will, christened Kantipios [Kantigianos], a curious name which the parents had never heard before it was pronounced by the godfather at the christening ceremony. Subsequently, the child was called Tsolag. The other two boys, Avedis and Hovhannes, died young."

The early death of children was not an uncommon occurrence in those times. Krikor's loss of his first two sons, Hagop – not Avedis as Maritsa incorrectly states – and Hovhannes, must have been a blow but in the next 26 years Loucia would go on to bear nine more children, seven of whom would live to adulthood.

Starting Over Yet Again: Returning Home to Sivas

The ten-year sojourn in Yozgat came to an end in 1873 for the Dildilians. Nature conspired to bring an end to their prosperity and forced them to return to Sivas. Maritsa briefly mentions famine as the primary cause for the return to Sivas: "However, as happiness never lasts long, famine broke out after a few happy years. Krikor took his family back to Sivas, thinking that, at least, they had a house there and would not pay a rent. As he came from Yozgat, he became known in Sivas under the name of the '*Yozgatle ghondouradji* [*kunduraci*]' [the shoemaker from Yozgat]." The famine she mentions was chronicled in the Western press and led to one of the first of many humanitarian campaigns to alleviate the suffering of the subjects of Ottoman Turkish rule. According to the March 31, 1875 issue of *The Times* in London, the famine that had begun in 1873 was still severely affecting central Anatolia two years later. By then 150,000 had perished and more were soon to die. The report in *The Times* blamed the incompetence and indifference of the Sublime Porte (central government) as much as the weather for the severity of the famine. In addition to relief efforts from England, Scotland, Switzerland and America, the paper noted that "the Armenians too, and to a trifling extent, the Greeks, came forward to aid members of their own communities."[2] Aram adds his thoughts to the confluence of events that led to their decision to return:

> Ten years later, one night there was a big fire that consumed their shoe shop. My grandfather, Mourad, though retired because of his age yet strong and brave, a tall, husky, well-built man, he rushes through the fire, puts his long red woolen belt around the sewing machine, takes it on his back and brings it out of the fire safely – by the way, that was the only sewing machine in Yozgat at that time.
>
> Just about that time, 1872–1873, there was a countrywide famine in which poor people suffered much. Well, my folks had no shoe shop, no means of livelihood, no food, no wheat, and not much money either. At that time they had gotten news that their hometown of Sivas is in plenty and is supplying the whole country with wheat. So my father, Krikor, takes his family, that is, my mother Loucia, brother Tsolag (only a few months old), his parents, and two brothers, and started their journey back to Sivas, taking along their belongings on pack horses. It was a long, tiresome journey.

My great-great-grandfather Mourad Garabed, that selfsame knucklebones-playing "perfect loafer" of earlier times, seems to have come into his own during those years in Yozgat: first by helping build up the confectionery business of his sons-in-law and then at the age of 75 rescuing the family's sewing machine from the flames that consumed their shoe business. No photographs exist of my great-great-grandfather, but I can just picture him in 1878, the last year of his life at the ripe old age of 81. My "candy man" is sitting in his garden in the family home in Sivas, a plate of *loukoums* at his feet, surrounded by children, including his two grandkids, Tsolag and Haïganouch, a sly smile on his face, challenging all comers to a game of knucklebones!

2

Prosperity and Loss Soon to be Captured in the Dildilian Camera Lens

The Dildilians Rebuild their Lives in Sivas

As Aram had described, the journey from Yozgat to Sivas was "long" and "tiresome." Even though the distance was only 225 kilometers (140 miles), journeys such as these over the poor roads of central Anatolia would probably take five days, but in this case much longer given the loads they were carrying:

> Finally they reached their hometown of Sivas from the northern passage (Marekoun). There were no highways in those days. While they were coming down the mountain road my grandmother, Markarid, sees in the distance the steeple and the cross on the dome of Sourp Nishan, an ancient Armenian monastery … that has in one big building three different chapels, "Sourp Nishan," "Asdvadzadzin" and "Sourp Garabed." In the treasure room there were hidden the throne and the crown of King Senekerem. (I am told that in 1916, the Turks had taken them away with other treasures of historic value.) Grandmother, in her joy, raises her arms into the air to praise the Lord, loses her balance and falls off the horse. Both her arms were broken.
>
> After a ten-year sojourn, finally they are back to their ancestral home …
>
> Before the family left for Yozgat, they left the ancestral home for safekeeping to father's aunt Karan Horkour, including all the household goods, copper utensils, carpets, rugs, and grandmother Margaret's [Markarid] hope chest full of fine clothing, jewels, pearls. But now all were gone. In the meantime, during those long years that they were away, Karan Horkour's family had torn down all the closet doors, shelves, railings, and wooden ceilings of all rooms except one and used it as firewood during the long winter days. That was a terrible thing to face, especially it was a terrible blow to my father, he being the only responsible person as head of the family.

Rebuilding their lives was no easy feat. Starting a shoe business in Sivas ran up against the traditional guild system (*Gedik*). While the authority of the *Gedik* was

6. A drawing of the Sourp Nishan Monastery with its three chapels.

in theory legally abolished a decade earlier, the guild still played a controlling role among the tradesmen in much of Anatolia. Aram describes the difficulties his father encountered and how he eventually prevailed:

> Father manages to start a small shoe shop with his brothers but soon there comes the master of the shoemakers' guild who, with a stern face, orders father to close the shop because they were not authorized to open a shoe shop. I can very well imagine father's state of mind and feelings. Here, back in his hometown with no money, no work, no helping hand but, on the other hand, his wealthy grandfather, living a couple hundred yards down the same street with all his plenty and power, altogether indifferent while his family is left helpless, sick, and foodless.

Krikor's rich grandfather, Dildarian, had disowned his only daughter Markarid and her children ten years earlier when Krikor was slandered by jealous relations. Dildarian was not about to help them resettle in Sivas. Fortunately Krikor was able to persuade a very powerful notable to intercede on his behalf with the guild. Krikor, the master shoemaker, was allowed to open his shop but the guild leader had to be placated with two pairs of shoes while all the shoemakers of Sivas were to be feasted at a picnic in the garden of Sourp Nishan Monastery. Aram describes his father's humble beginnings and the success that was to come:

Though the family had hardly enough food, they had to consent to it [the picnic] and then started working in their little shoe shop. Soon their fame went all around the city and they were so successful that they were able to rent the corner store of the municipal Casino, right on the highway to Baghdad on the bridge (Karehe Gamourch on Moundar Ked). Soon father made an ideal shoe shop of it with upholstered armchairs, coffee tables, and beautiful showcases for finished shoes and a big storefront with arched windows and a big signboard painted with different shoe styles on it – the only store sign in the city in those days.

Aram's passing reference to the disappearance of his mother's "hope chest" is further elaborated upon by Maritsa. This was Markarid's dowry, the only wealth that they had obtained from their connection to the wealthy and influential Dildarian family. Recall that Markarid's jewelry was left in the care of Mourad Garabed's sister:

They arrive and settle in their house. The chest is still there with its seals. They remove the padlock, the seals, but … oh, surprise, the chest is empty! Then they see that a board has been removed from the bottom of the chest. This was how the beautiful jewels had been stolen. (In May 1967, when my aunt Nevart, née Dildilian in Sivas, and her husband Agabashian had come from the United States to visit France, Nevart confirmed to me that, the day before Krikor's return, her uncle had stolen the contents of the chest.)

A wrong done to a family, especially a wrong done by a member of one's own family, is often long remembered. In our case, the missing family jewels seem to have taken on a legendary status, one that obsessed some members of the family for almost a century. The discovery that the jewels had gone missing took place in 1873. In 1967 Maritsa and her aunt Nevart, Krikor's daughter, are discussing their disappearance, a disappearance that had happened well before either of them were born. Maritsa actually goes to great lengths to describe what had gone missing:

These jewels were really beautiful pieces. Markarid's mother, Dildar, was rich and had given many high-value jewels and parures to her daughter when she was still under age. The pendant, which ornamented Markarid's bosom, was so heavy that it was suspended to the garment with a hook to relieve its weight. This hook must have been a curious thing: so small a thing supporting so valuable an object!

Another parure also was remarkable: a woven belt, ornate with pearls, which, after a turn around the waist, hung down to the ground. Who has not the remembrance of Markarid at the *hammam* [communal bathhouse]? She was always dressed in beautiful garments, showing off in front of the others, dressing and

19

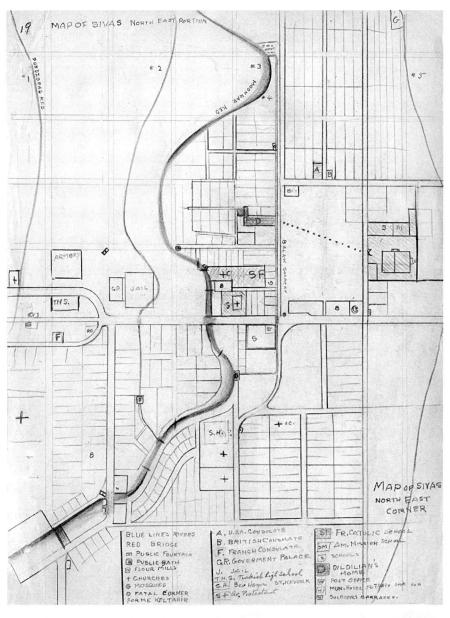

7. Aram's hand-drawn map of Sivas in the 1890s. The ancestral home is marked with a "D" in the upper center of the map.

undressing under the critical eyes of the other women. Women liked to show their best attire, their parures and jewels at the church, at the *hammam* and at weddings for these were the only occasions where they could show them.

It was not prudent, for one who possessed beautiful things, to leave them in a bag at the *hammam*. In Sivas, wealthy people booked a pool for their own use for a given day, and on that day, nobody else could gain access ... Thus, Dildar had had a hiding place prepared in the *hammam* where she left her jewels, and she kept the key attached with a knot in her *péchtimal* [apron]. Wasn't that absolute safety?

Maritsa describes these jewels and the flaunting of them, yet neither she, her mother, nor her grandmother could have witnessed a bejeweled Markarid in the *hammam* or anywhere else. "Who has not the remembrance of Markarid at the *hammam*?" Certainly Maritsa has this inherited remembrance, as did other members of the family who kept this story alive for over a century. A collective family memory has become a personal memory for Maritsa.

In the summer of 2012, I journeyed to Sivas in search of the ancestral home. After hours of searching using Aram's hand-drawn map, we found the street where the house should have been. Alas, the house was gone. What had once been a vibrant Armenian neighborhood had only a few Ottoman-era homes, most in run-down condition, but as I turned a corner onto a small square, a sight brought a wry smile to my face: Markarid's *hammam*.

8. The ruins today of the Sivas *hammam* where Markarid flaunted her jewelry.

21

The Vali *Loves the Dildilian Brothers' Shoes*

After overcoming the initial resistance of the local guild, the shoe business began to grow. Beginning with that one sewing machine rescued by his father in Yozgat, Krikor expanded the business from a small craftsman's shop into a factory and distribution center employing many workers. Krikor's brother Haroutioun played a crucial role in the business. He would continue the business after his brother's death in 1894. Despite the devastating losses in the Hamidian Massacres of 1894–96, the business continued on until 1915 when the remaining members of the family were deported. Maritsa gives a fascinating account of the workings of the family shoe business:

> Krikor's brother, Haroutioun, is a serious man, very kind, hard-working and it is he, in fact, who gets the business going. He supervises the back shop and the workers, leaving the care of clients and sales to his brother Krikor. For they are not only makers and sellers of shoes, they also supply leather and tools to other shoemakers.
>
> The shop is located in a select place in the bazaar, just next to the famous Stone Bridge. It has two windows with the entrance door in between. At the back, there is the workshop with windows and the warehouse extending by the riverside. The front shop windows as well as the back shop windows have white curtains and, in summer, they are decorated with geraniums. The shop's name is *"Tchitchekli Ghondouradji [Çiçekli Kunduracı]"* [The Flowered Shoemaker Shop]. In the nineteenth century, such a name in Anatolia is something! Materials arrive on camelback. Hides come in rolls. They are left to soak in vats to become tanned, supple and rot-proof leather. It is an on-going business with solid prospects ahead.

From all accounts Krikor appears to be very adept at handling all types of customers. His success with the many notables, both local and foreign, adds to his reputation. The story of the *vali*'s (provincial governor) love of Dildilian shoes is recounted by Maritsa:

> Shoemaker Krikor enjoys good reputation. He is the regular footwear supplier for good society and, as such, is a well-known character. One day a new *vali* is appointed. As it is the custom, the *vali* goes for a protocol visit, the so-called "welcome tour," around town. Krikor, seeing that the *vali* is wearing slippers, comes up to him and tactfully asks him why he does not wear shoes. "Shoes are too heavy," laments the *vali*. So Krikor manages to take measurements of the *vali*'s foot and he makes a pair of shoes that he presents to the *vali*. The *vali* tries them on; he finds them so light and so supple that he declares he will wear shoes from now on for he had never known such light shoes.
>
> Let me add that Krikor's seal mark, which was stamped on the shoe shank, was a weighing balance with two pans, one containing a shoe and the other a butterfly;

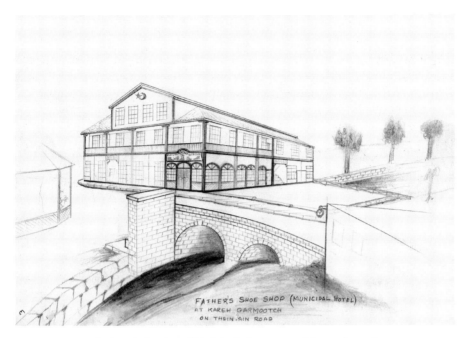

FATHER'S SHOE SHOP (MUNICIPAL HOTEL)
AT KAREH GARMOOTCH
ON THEIN-AIN ROAD

9. Aram's drawing of his father's shoe store and factory located
in the Municipal Hotel (Casino) in Sivas.

but the first pan was higher, indicating that the shoe was lighter than the butterfly.
I remember seeing that mark once on a shoe that my mother had shown to me.

The *vali's* friendship with the Dildilians and their important customers is also
recounted by Aram:

> My father's shop became the rendezvous of many government officials, especially
> the governor, the *vali* of Sivas, who often would come over after office hours, sit for
> awhile to have water pipe, drink coffee or tea and then go home. Later, father added
> a shoemaker's supply department as a side-line. He was the first to introduce rubber
> shoes in Sivas. I know that there was a time when he had 12 to 15 men working for
> him. He had two different types of shoemakers' sewing machines, presses, and all
> kinds of tools and novelties. The last making department had several hundred pairs
> of lasts to fit individual customers, especially some important people like Dr. Jewett,
> [the] U.S. Consul, Mr. Hubbard, Dr. Haroutune Shirinian, and others.

The governor of the vilayet (province) of Sivas referred to in these stories is not
identified and may well have been any one of a number of governors in the period
from the late 1870s to the 1890s. Consul Jewett and the American missionary,
Albert Hubbard, would have been neighbors of the Dildilians.[1]

The Vali *of Sivas:*
The Unanswerable Questions behind a Photograph

When I first began identifying and documenting the photographs in the Dildilian family collection, I came across a small portrait of a very distinguished-looking gentleman. Given his garb and medals, he was obviously an important Ottoman official. The photo was in a box with some of the oldest photos in the collection dating to the earliest years of the Dildilian photography business in Sivas. Krikor had rented studio space near his shoe store for his son Tsolag. Given the popularity of his shoes with the city's wealthy notables, the strategy may well have been to entice Krikor's customers to have their portraits taken at the nearby photo studio. If this marketing strategy worked, could this portrait be one of Krikor's notable customers, perhaps the *vali* himself, possibly the one with the need for lightweight footwear? An intriguing possibility, indeed. When I finally identified the portrait as that of Mamdouh Mehmet Pasha, *vali* of Sivas from April 1889 to November 1892, dates coinciding with the early years of the studio, I thought the mystery of the light-footed *vali* had been solved. Well, not quite.

Who was this Mamdouh Mehmet Pasha? From what I have learned, he was a central figure in the Ottoman administration under the sultan Abdul Hamid II. After first serving as *vali* of Konia, he was appointed to the same office in Sivas in April 1889, but was subsequently relieved of his duties in November 1892, after the sultan received complaints of the *vali's* "unjust and oppressive administration from the local Armenians." After "the establishment of his innocence in the Armenian affair," he was appointed *vali* of Ankara followed by a promotion to interior minister in November 1895, a position he held for 13 years. He remained a close confidant to the sultan for the duration of his reign.[2]

Here is a man accused by Armenians of oppression while governor of Sivas, who later becomes interior minister under Abdul Hamid II. On November 12, 1895, six days after being elevated to that post by the sultan, a government-instigated mob destroyed all the Armenian businesses in Sivas, including Krikor's shoe store and factory. Contemporary reports state that 1,500 Armenians and 10 Turks perished in the massacre. The family memoirs will describe these events in detail, but for now more questions than answers arise about this portrait found in a box of family photographs. Can one draw a connection between the events of the week of November 12, 1895 and Mamdouh's role as former governor of Sivas – a governor "falsely" accused of oppressing Armenians? May there have been some truth to the accusations? Was he the *vali* who patronized Krikor's store and helped Tsolag make a name for himself in the photography business? We will never know. Nor will we ever know what motivated Tsolag to save this photograph for posterity.

10. Mamdouh Mehmet Pasha, Governor of Sivas, April 1889–November 1892, built the high school that later served as the location of the Sivas Congress, September 4–11, 1919.

The Dildilians Grow and Prosper in Sivas

We jumped ahead by discussing photography, which does not enter our story until the next generation in 1888, and will play a central role in the family for the next 100 years. But for now, we remain in the 1870s and 1880s, a period of much change and intellectual ferment in the Ottoman Empire. A growing interaction between the educated classes of the empire, including its Armenian minority, and their counterparts in Western Europe led to demands for reform in the old system of governance. In 1876, the first constitution was introduced and resulted in the convening of an Ottoman Parliament (Meclis-i Mebusan – House of Deputies) for a brief period between 1877 and 1878. The majority of the deputies were non-Muslim, with a significant number of Armenians among them.[3] The Ottoman defeat in the Russo-Turkish War of 1877–78 and the subsequent Treaty of Berlin of 1878 led to an increased consular activity in the Anatolian interior. It is of interest to note that Aram identifies the locations of the French, British and American consulates on his map of Sivas, the latter two in close proximity to the Dildilian family home.

The 1870s also marked a period of growing prosperity and change in the Dildilian household. Krikor's business success was reflected in the improvements he was making in the ancestral home. Some changes did not sit well with Krikor's father, as related by Maritsa:

> Garabed has complaints and opens his heart to his friends. The boys have had a black chimney flue erected on the house front wall. In those times, people in Sivas used to get warm by huddling around the *t'onir* [clay oven]. Now the sons have installed a stove, the first one in town. Older people usually do not like novelties, notably Garabed, who never felt cold and used to laugh at people sensitive to cold. "I spit at the bum of the one who does not let his christening pants dry on him. I am cold only if I think of it," he used to say. In a town at 4,000 feet of altitude!

The change brought on by the talents of this new generation of Dildilians marked not only practical household matters but their business activities. Maritsa comments: "The sons also bought a special sewing machine for stitching the uppers and embroidering luxury shoes with silk threads of several colors, especially ladies' shoes." Krikor would soon buy a harmonium for his younger brother Haroutioun, who is described as having "an artist's soul and a refined taste." The culturally progressive atmosphere of the Dildilian home fostered a love of music and the arts that would play a prominent role in the next two generations. Haroutioun's son, Sumpad, would become a talented painter, photographer and civil engineer. Krikor's son Tsolag would become the pre-eminent art photographer in Anatolia, while his daughter Nevart would become a talented musician and singer.

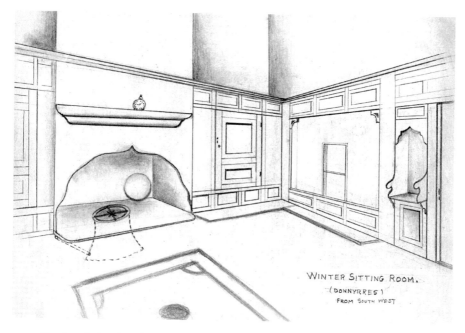

WINTER SITTING ROOM.
(DONNYRRES)
FROM SOUTH WEST

11. Aram's drawing of the winter sitting room, outlining the *t'onir* within the fireplace.

As we have already seen, travel in Anatolia was a difficult ordeal in this time period. Where there were roads, they were often in poor condition. In addition there was always the threat of brigands who would rob or hold travelers for ransom. Maritsa conveys one such story of highway robbery involving her grandmother Loucia's homesickness for the family she left beind in Yozgat:

> It was decided that Loucia would go to Yozgat to see her folks. Garabed embarked with his daughter-in-law and the children in a carriage and they set off. For that journey, they had to go through the Chamlebéli pass. Now, you must know what that pass was. In that time, travelers were ransomed everywhere. But ransoming was performed still better in Turkey where Christians were not allowed to have any sort of weapons with them. The Turks, in contrast, had full rights. Well, our travelers were robbed.
>
> When Garabed related the robbery, he used to say: "When they came out from under the pine trees one after the other, I then realized they were highwaymen." And the children used to laugh, saying: "Anybody would have realized that!"
>
> Haïganouch, who was still very young, remembered the journey as if in a dimmed dream.

This recollection was most likely a memory created by the constant retelling of her elders. Haïganouch would have been too young to recall the journey herself, being no more than two years old when her grandfather Mourad Garabed died in 1878. A collective family memory had been passed on as a personal dream-like memory.

The 1870s eventually saw the passing of my great-grandfather Krikor's parents, Markarid in 1876 and wily old Mourad Garabed in 1878. Aram writes of this transition from one generation to the next and the added responsibilities that fell upon the new patriarch of the family, Krikor:

> His first duty was to find a suitable wife for my uncle Haroutioun. Both father and mother were able to find a fine orphan girl, Elbiz Fundukian who was left in the care of her sister, Helline Potookian. My aunt Elbiz was slim and tall, had sweet and fine features, a brunette beauty, black hair, brown eyes. She was kind-hearted, sincere, unselfish and loving. A perfect match with my loving uncle as they both surpassed each other in Christian virtues. My uncle and aunt did not meet or see each other before they got married – they just trusted to the good judgment and arrangement of their elders.

A lack of intimate familiarity in courtship was certainly the norm, but in great-aunt Elbiz's case unfamiliarity marked the early months of her marriage:

> Even after they were married, they did not have much chance to see or converse with each other, as my dear uncle had to go to the shop to open the doors and provide work for the workers at daybreak and come home very late, after dark. By the time he came home everybody was busy preparing supper and table service, then cleaning up, dish washing, etc. Besides, in those days newlyweds were not supposed to show themselves and talk in the presence of the elders of the family ...
>
> One Sunday afternoon it happened that everybody in the family had gone out. My dear uncle and aunty were left at home all alone. Uncle asked for a cup of tea. While they were drinking tea side by side on the sofa, uncle lifted his head, looking out the window and sipping the tea, his big blue eyes shining like the open blue sky, my aunt cried out in amazement, "Oh dear, your eyes are blue!"

Aram does note that they were granted two children. The first-born, Vahan, died in infancy but the second, Sumpad, grew up to become a talented young man who would play an integral role in the Dildilian Brothers photography business.

Maritsa and Aram both clearly had a great fondness for their aunt Elbiz and her son, Sumpad. Maritsa describes in great detail the background of Elbiz's family, the Fundukians. Elbiz's brother's marriage brought the family connections to the sultan's court in Constantinople. While her sister married into the Potookian family, a prominent Amasia family whose head would briefly serve as the powerless lieutenant governor of Sivas during one of the ill-fated Western-inspired Armenian reforms, Elbiz, the second daughter, married Haroutioun, and would come to play an important role in the lives of the next two generations of the family. Maritsa refers to her as "our dear mamig" (our grandma) because she came to play that role upon the untimely death of Loucia in 1895. As for Elbiz's only son, Sumpad, Maritsa has the highest praise: "Then Sumpad was born, a boy full of fire and very smart. Oh, what a boy and what a man was he! God knows that I loved him more than my own uncles." Sumpad's many talents would make him a successful student and then art teacher at Anatolia College. He would join his talents with that of his uncle Tsolag, forming the Dildilian Brothers Art Photographers in Marsovan. Many pages in the memoirs are devoted to him.

The youngest of Krikor's brothers was Mikael. Unlike his older brothers, he resisted the traditional custom of arranged marriages. He was determined to choose his own bride and he did. Aram remarks, "Mikael did not wait for the elders to choose his life companion. He was modern – he married Surma Godoshian." Surprisingly – or maybe not – his marriage was the most troubled of the three Dildilian siblings and caused a major rift in the family: "But sorry to say, Uncle Mikael and his wife did not have family cooperative spirit so soon after they were married, they broke away from the family and in that way they broke my father's heart too." Aram was old enough to recall first-hand the parting of the ways. He describes the division of all the household goods into thirds and the departure of his uncle and aunt from the ancestral home. Mikael's ties to the family shoemaking business were also severed. As he often does, Aram concludes his accounts of family members with a reference to the future: "He was killed, his wife, his son, Suren, and daughter Nushervent, by the Turks in 1915 (we had unconfirmed news that Nushervent was alive in Constantinople)."

Nushervent would have been about 23 years old in 1915, so if she had survived the deportations or had been married off to a Turkish family, she may have been able to reconnect with the family after the Armistice in October 1918. But as we know from the stories of many survivors, there may have been a myriad of reasons not to try to reconnect with one's lost family.

Haïganouch, being six years older than her brother Aram, seems to have been privy to more details regarding the rocky marriage of her uncle Mikael and Surma. The account passed on to her daughter Maritsa, elaborates on just what was meant when Aram stated their marriage lacked a "cooperative spirit":

Alas, this Mikael! He is entirely different from his brothers. He is short, like his mother, but not at all like her in his character. He is lazy, sluggish and no good at anything.

Krikor finally finds a girl from a respectable family for Mikael, although the consent of the girl's family was hard to obtain. On the day of the engagement, everybody is busy. Elbiz is packing the pastries. Mikael shows up and asks: "Elbiz, what are you doing?" "What a question! We are going to the engagement party!" "What engagement?" asks Mikael. "Mégha! [God forgive!] As if you did not know! But *your* engagement!" "I do not want that girl. I love another one."

Loucia and Mikael's elder brothers were stunned by the news. On the girl's side however, this reversal was received with relief since the family had always been reluctant, and had accepted only because they could not turn down Krikor Agha.

The girl Mikael loved was Surma, daughter of the Godochians, who had given him an apple at a wedding party. She was taller than him and of a crude aspect. And she was of a lower social class. "The grass the donkey has sniffed is to be left in the bag" was his elder brother's comment. The couple was so badly suited that they were ashamed to celebrate the wedding in the cathedral church. The ceremony took place in the out-of-town monastery and a cushion was placed under Mikael's feet so that the two spouses' heads may stand at the same level. A very discreet ceremony, it was.

Anyway, the couple did not live in harmony and trouble started for Mikael. After her first son, Suren, was born, Surma went back to her father's house. Mikael succeeded in taking her back but quarrels were continuous. Mikael locked his wife's going-out shawl in a chest and kept the key. The wife took an iron pike which her mother-in-law used ... to draw sugar paste ... She was trying to pry open the chest when her husband came up and stopped her. She threatened him. Life was no longer bearable. Krikor gave Mikael his share and turned him out of the house and shop.

Some time later, a few friends pleaded with Krikor to have him back in the shop as he was in need and a second child was born, a girl named Nushervent. Krikor accepted to have Mikael back in the shop as a worker.

I feel slightly uncomfortable quoting at length this account of my ancestors' troubled marriage. Am I airing some of the family's dirty laundry, albeit 125 years after the fact? Maybe. My reason for doing so, I suppose, is a fascination with what our memoirists choose to tell us. This helps us appreciate their different sensibilities, prejudices and concerns. We learn who they are by what they tell us about others.

With the marriage of the three Dildilian brothers, Krikor, Haroutioun and Mikael, our narrative now begins to slowly shift into the next generation of the Dildilians. With 15 children born to the three siblings, 11 of whom were born to Krikor, this could get a little confusing. I have often struggled to sort out these relations, and I take comfort in the fact that even the generation before me had trouble doing so at times. Let me resolve one possible source of confusion below.

Infant mortality in the nineteenth century was extremely high, especially in the interior regions of the Ottoman Empire. Krikor's first two sons had died at an early age while the family was still in Yozgat. As was mentioned earlier, my grandfather Tsolag, who had been born in Yozgat, was one year old when the family returned to Sivas. I often recall having conversations with my mother (née Alice Dildilian) in which she struggled to keep straight the names and relative ages of her uncles and aunts. All very understandable given the fact that there were 11 of them and five of them had died well before she was born. This confusion with names was especially true in the case of Sumpad, who was the first child born to Krikor and Loucia upon their return to Sivas. This uncle Sumpad died as an infant decades before my mother was born in 1911. Yet there was often an "uncle" Sumpad around the household. This was the Sumpad we discussed earlier, the son of Krikor's younger brother Haroutioun, whose bright future was cut short in 1915. This Sumpad was the first boy born in the family after the death of the earlier Sumpad, and he may well have been named in his memory. In his memoir, Aram does us all a favor by identifying and briefly describing all 11 of his siblings before carrying on with his story:

> When my parents turned back from Yozgat to Sivas, my dearest brother was a year old [Tsolag], but they were granted two boys before him who died in Yozgat, so before going any further here, I'd better give the names and birthdays of my brothers and sisters and try to tell something about some of them that I know about personally:
>
> 1. Hagop, Vahan – born 1867 and died 1869 in Yozgat.
> 2. Hovhannes – born 1868 and died 1871 in Yozgat. He was blond and smart.
> 3. Tsolag (Kantigianos) – born May 1, 1872 in Yozgat. Blond, blue eyed, light complexioned, beautiful, fine features. He was smart, artistic, intelligent, industrious, loving, sacrificing and had business ability. He married Mariam Nakkashian of Harpoot in 1899 and was blessed with six children, four boys and two girls. He died of cancer in Athens, Greece, in 1935. His wife, Mariam, and sons, Humayag, Ara, and [daughter] Alice are now in the United States with their families and eight grandchildren.
> 4. Sumpad – born 1874 and died 1875 in Sivas.
> 5. Haïganouch – born 1877, July 9, in Sivas. She had light brown hair, blue eyes, full of love and tenderness. Dominating! She was fearless and heroic in every way. In 1896 in Sivas, she married Vosgian Der Haroutiounian, who was killed by Turks in 1915. She was blessed with six children, four boys and two girls. She is living in Paris, France, with her two boys and two daughters and their wives, husbands, and nine grandchildren.
> 6. Markarid [Margaret] – born April 4, 1879 in Sivas and died August 1898 of T.B. in Marsovan. She had black eyes, dark hair, white complexion. She was a beauty, bright, artistic, unassuming, enduring and very considerate.
> 7. Parantzem – born July 6, 1881 in Sivas and died in 1915. She had blue eyes, light brown hair and fair complexion. We grew up together and were playmates.

She was sweet, kind, loving, humble, sacrificing, bright, artistic, and a devoted Christian. In 1910 she married Yervant Shirinian in Vezir Köprü [present-day Vezirköprü], and was blessed with three children, two boys and one girl. All were killed by Turks in 1915.

8. Aram (that is I) – born September 18, 1883 in Sivas. Blue eyes, dark hair, fair complexion (lost right leg in 1897). Married Christine Der Kasparian in Marsovan, May 23, 1919. Blessed with three children, Margaret, born in Samsun, April 29, 1920, blue eyes, light brown hair, light complexion. She grew in grace and stature, was smart, sweet, and had all the promise of a fine life. God took her to Himself – she died in Athens on May 12, 1923.

   Armen – born January 28, 1923 in Athens, Greece, in a refugee camp without any doctors' or nurses' help. A beautiful child, blue eyes, light brown hair, and light complexion, we brought him to this blessed land. He married Margaret Ashdaragentz, June 26, 1948, in San Francisco in the little chapel of Lakeside Church.

   My son, Edward, was born July 11, 1925 in San Francisco, a native son of California. A sweet boy with brown eyes, dark brown hair, he married Margaret Marderosian June 29, 1946 in Detroit. They were granted a lovely girl, Denise, born June 19, 1950 in Detroit.

9. Shoushan – born 1886 in Sivas and died 1886 in Sivas.

10. Nevart (Mariam) – born May 28, 1888 in Sivas – blue eyes, light brown hair, fair complexion, she is bright, musical, artistic, loving, ambitious, dominating, and highly educated. She married Levon Agababashian, November 5, 1912 in Los Angeles, California and blessed with one boy, Fred (Vahram) and three girls, Alice, Lucy, Eleanor – all are married and have children – eight grandchildren altogether.

11. Shumavon [Shamavon or Chemavon] – born May 27, 1893 in Sivas, was left an orphan at age six months. Blue eyed, blond hair, white complexion, he was a talented poet, musician, and linguist. He was sweet, lovable, sentimental and trustful. He was killed in 1915 by the Turks.

In reading over Aram's account I am struck by the number of blue-eyed blond-haired girls and boys in the family – certainly not what one would think, having been conditioned to the stereotype of the dark-eyed and dark-haired Armenians. Two generations later I was born with blue eyes and blond hair. As often happens, a few years later my blue eyes turned hazel, the same color as my mother's. As for my blond hair, the only remnant to survive was pressed into a baby book by my mother 60 years ago. I dimly recall overhearing conversations at our family reunions in which various adults would put forward theories as to origins of the light complexions and blue eyes found in the Dildilian family. This may have been the moment when I first heard of the idea of our European origins. I guess this meant something for a child who saw some value in being identified with

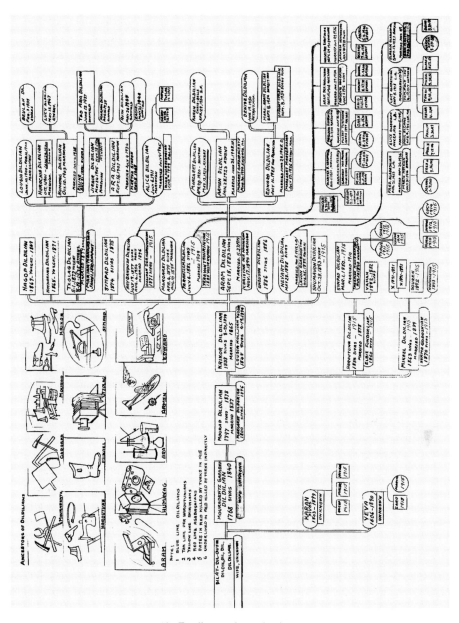

12. Family tree drawn by Aram.

the French, Germans, Greeks, and Italians, instead of some vaguely identified minority from Asia. Claims were made that many Armenians, especially those in the western Anatolian highlands, found their origins in the Phrygians, an Indo-European "racial" group closely akin to the Greeks. In Book 7 of his *History* (*c*.440 BC), Herodotus claims that the Armenians were Phrygian colonists and "were armed in the Phrygian fashion." Whatever may be the truth of such theories, the upshot of these conversations was the fact that Armenians should be identified with Europeans and not Asiatics, this despite the fact that much of historic Armenia falls within what was often called Asia Minor. As we will see, at least in the eyes of some, being closely identified with Europeans in the late Ottoman period was more often a curse than a blessing.

Daily Life in the Ancestral Home in Sivas

As the family business prospered into the 1880s, Krikor continued to restore and modernize the family's ancestral home. Ironically, although there are no photos of either the interior or the exterior of the house, we know many details of its appearance. Aram had vivid memories of his childhood home because many years later he reconstructed it both inside and out in both words and detailed pencil drawings. He also populated his sketches with many household items, displaying a particular fondness for his mother's kitchen utensils. This home comes alive in word and image:

> At the time of my birth, my father was in his glory. He was successful both financially and socially. As I said before, he was progressive, modern for his time, and had good taste. He repaired and modernized our ancestral home. We had five big rooms, the front room or parlor, where father used to stay, had an extended front with four big windows, two in front and two on each corner on the north and south, with double window sashes for the winter. The walls were painted with oil paint and there were soft cushioned sofas, upholstered chairs and ornamental wooden ceiling. The inner two rooms had open fireplaces with fancy front mantelpieces. The middle big room had a skylight in the center of heavy clear timbered ceiling, and the walls were fancy wooden panel. We had a sunken fireplace, "*t'onir*," where the food was cooked in wintertime. After the cooking was over, the opening was covered with a round and smooth stone slab, covered with pillows and carpets and used as sitting room to play games or tell stories on long winter nights. We had a basement with enough room for provisions, a bread-baking oven, a stable for cows and other animals that had two doors, one in the back street and the other on the main street. We had two running water fountains, one for drinking spring water and the other for general use.

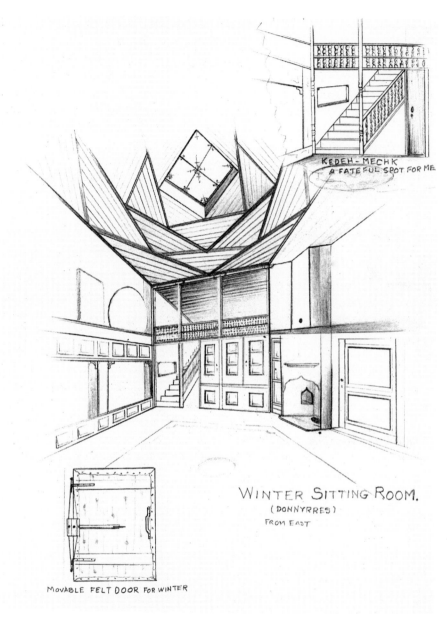

KEDEH—MECHK
A FATEFUL SPOT FOR ME

WINTER SITTING ROOM.
(DONNYRRES)
FROM EAST

MOVABLE FELT DOOR FOR WINTER

13. Aram's drawing of the winter sitting room from the east.

The main street (Balık Sokak) was a very busy road for horse caravans. Before the Samson–Baghdad highway was built, most of the traffic moved through the city's south side, but often the camel and fruit caravans passed by our house even though it was a hard-to-travel road but was much shorter. Besides all the flour-mill wagons

14. Aram's drawing of his father Krikor's parlor from the west.

15. Aram's drawing of his father Krikor's parlor from the east.

and quarry carts used to pass by and all the church and monastery pilgrims and Sunday picnickers. So we had plenty to see and enjoy looking out from our house windows. At our parlor, we had soft and comfortable sofas in front of the window and had upholstered armchairs and divans – something great in those days. We had carpets and rugs in every room. I remember well my father was one of the first ones to buy the kerosene lamps for the "burrow" dresser and chandelier lamp from the ceiling. Before that, we had several big and small fancy brass candleholders, stoves, and a brass portable charcoal fireplace. My father had a real taste for good things. Our house was a real old house but was well built so father, with his ingenuity and good taste, turned it into a lovely and cheerful place to live in.

Aram has lovingly drawn in both word and image a home that is especially inviting, richly filled with artifacts that were still etched in his memory decades later. As I mentioned earlier, in 2012 I journeyed to Sivas and embarked on a day-long quest in search of the Dildilian ancestral home. I knew beforehand the futility of such a quest given all the growth and development that has taken place in Sivas in the last 100 years. With the help of my Turkish friend Osman Koker and his local colleagues, we finally managed to locate the street that had once been named Balık Sokak. A few dilapidated Ottoman-era homes still remained on the street but no home that resembled the one found in the fine drawings Aram had left behind.

16. Aram's drawing of the family's ancestral home in Sivas.

A few of the brass kitchen items remain that were so fondly sketched by Aram so many years ago, not in Turkey, but in a vault in the basement of the Armenian Museum of America in Watertown, Massachusetts. To my mother's chagrin, these items were donated to the museum by my Yankee aunt upon the death of my uncle Ara, my mother's older brother.

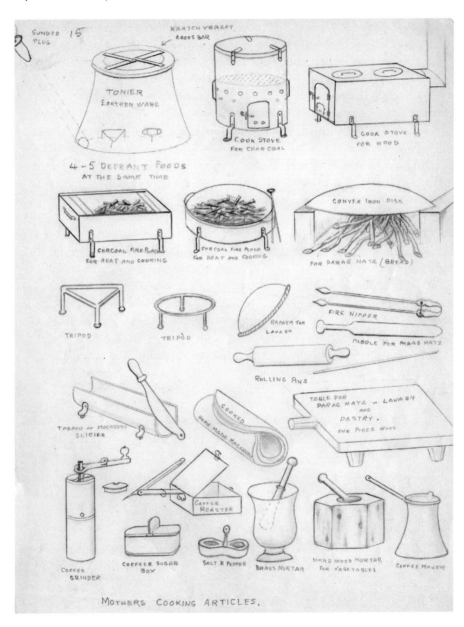

17. Aram's drawing of his mother's kitchen items.

As Aram indicates, my great-grandfather was "progressive and modern for his time." While the memoirs do not describe the level of education that he might have had, he was determined to make sure that all his children had schooling, even the girls. Maritsa describes the various schools her uncles and aunts attended:

> All the Dildilian children go to school. Tsolag attends the Varamian High School, Haïganouch the Azkayn High School. So does Sumpad. But Markarid and Parantzem go to the new school while Nevart is at the American nursery school. It is Haïganouch who takes them to school.
>
> One day when the winter cold was particularly intense, Haïganouch had her fingers frozen like bits of wood. So, when she reached the school door, she tried to move the knocker with her tongue but the tongue got stuck to it. Poor child!
>
> She was a good pupil, and her father was thinking of sending her to the American College in Marsovan when she is of age. In the meantime, while she attended school, she also went to the workshop of a carpet weaver. She was gifted and the craftsman asked her to create designs.

By the mid-1880s when Tsolag was old enough to attend high school, there were a number of alternatives available in Sivas. I cannot conclusively establish which high school my grandfather attended. There seem to be conflicting possibilities here. Maritsa identifies the school by name, the Varamian High School. The name is very similar to one of the ten schools run by the Armenian Apostolic Church, one of which is identified as the Aramian school.[4] Yet Aram's memoir mentions that Tsolag graduated from the American High School. This was most likely a school run by the American Protestant missionaries in Sivas. I know for certain that my grandfather Tsolag was a Protestant and went on to serve as a deacon in the Armenian Protestant church in Marsovan. Haïganouch remained a member of the Apostolic Church, sometimes referred to as the Gregorian Church after its founder Saint Gregory the Illuminator (c.257–c.331). Maritsa's memoir often refers to the tensions within the family regarding the fact that some members had become Protestants. Great-grandfather's religious affiliation is unclear, though most likely he had remained Apostolic. There is no definitive statement in the memoirs to settle the issue. Maritsa's remarks about her mother and uncle Sumpad seem also to indicate that they attended a co-educational high school. Since the Apostolic-organized schools were not co-educational, this may have been a school run by the missionaries. Even though boys and girls would be in the same building, at a certain age they would be segregated into separate classrooms by gender.

Aram remarks as to his father's interest in educational improvement and the progressive views he held:

He had been elected several times church trustee and councilman. Once he organized a group to start a university for higher education in Sivas and almost achieved that ideal. They had started a cooperative merchandise store to provide regular income and were about to succeed, but the Turkish government put a stop to it. With suspicious eyes, they saw a revolutionary tint back of that enterprise.

Also interesting to note is the fact that Krikor considered sending Haïganouch to the American Protestant-run college in Marsovan. This is most likely a reference to the Girls' Boarding School that had been operating in Marsovan since 1865. The Girls' School would eventually share the same campus as Anatolia College but was independently managed. Anatolia College would come to play a major, life-saving, role in the family's story in the decades to come.

Troubles in Sivas and Krikor's Arrest

As earlier noted, great social change and unrest marked the 1880s in parts of the Ottoman Empire. The sultan's failure to institute the reforms called for in the 1878 Treaty of Berlin led to a growing number of movements among the Armenian populace calling for varying degrees of self-determination. The resulting repression on the part of the Porte would soon directly impact the Dildilian family.

Besides the political tensions there were also religious tensions, some of them within the Christian Armenian community. Aram reports that "denominational movements" had just begun in Sivas, leading to competition and conflict. In one instance his father Krikor interceded to keep the religious peace. One of his apprentices was to be baptized by Baptist missionaries in a river near the local Protestant cemetery. A crowd had gathered and Krikor "was informed that some evil-minded, fanatic young men had come over to create a disturbance so father, with a stern face, orders them to go home. Soon all disappeared from the spot."

The "denominational movements" mentioned by Aram may be a reference to a new growing competition among Protestant missionaries – such as the Campbellites, reformed Baptists, and Mormons – rather than a reference to the longer-standing conflict with the Apostolic Church. The American Board of Commissioners for Foreign Missions (A.B.C.F.M.) had first established a mission in Sivas in 1851, but by the 1880s other non-Board missionaries had arrived, seeking converts. Over the prior 30 years the Apostolic Church had tried to suppress the growing Protestant movement in the empire, but by this period the suppression had turned into a healthier competition. The many competing Apostolic and Armenian Protestant and Missionary schools were a positive outgrowth of these tensions.

Krikor's peacemaking abilities were not as successful on another occasion. Tensions had risen in the city as a result of the governor's persecution of Armenians. Aram describes his father's failed attempt at peacemaking and the kind of justice – or lack thereof – that was evidenced in parts of the empire:

Early in the morning, a big group of Armenians gathered together to stone the Turkish governor's mansion because he was an unrighteous man and was persecuting Armenians. My father saw the crowd from his window and at once takes his briefcase and pretending he is going to his shop, pushed his way out to the crowd and with a murmuring voice pleads with them, "Boys, don't do this, don't be foolish, go home, go home … the consequences will be worse, don't do it." He keeps on going down towards the bridge (Lan Gamoorch) and he sees that they have not dispersed yet, so he makes the round of the big block and repeats the same plea, but no use … Finally, they start stoning and broke all the window glass and were about to break open the gate when a battalion of Turkish soldiers came and dispersed them all. But a few hours later, they arrested my father, Minassian of Gurum, and a few others, accusing them as the leaders … In jail, they gave him the third degree (an American expression). The Sivas jail was built on a small brook and in order to get forced confessions, they would make the accused stand up in that river, knee-deep, for hours. They punished my father and others the same way – no confession, no trial. He could not obtain outside help, so he was wise to make insider friends by feeding them plenty. Everyday either my brother Tsolag or one of his apprentices would carry two or three kinds of food to the jail. Those hungry jail keepers for once had plenty to eat, also some of his fellow jailmates. That way, he was able to get out to go to the Turkish bath every so often, then home for dinner and spend a few hours with us, and about 4 p.m., the guard jandarma would take him back to jail. They kept father in jail more than two years without any trial. He was a very sociable man and could make friends very easily.

Whether in his shoe shop or a prison cell, Krikor's social skills served him well. Personable and well-respected, he was often able to make the best of a bad situation.

Maritsa also describes the arrest and imprisonment of her grandfather, though in this case there seems to have been a trial: "Krikor was released on bail until the day of the trial. But, to gain his freedom, he had to waste a lot of money in the course of a few months, including the jewels belonging to Loucia and Elbiz. The jewels included necklaces in stepped rows which the two women wore at their necks or suspended to their headgears." A Turkish witness who had claimed that Krikor instigated the stoning had been found to suffer from hemeralopia, a condition that would have prevented him from seeing clearly in daylight. But as luck would have it, the witness died the night before the trial and his earlier testimony was accepted. Krikor was sentenced to prison. Maritsa reports that "bribery was required so that Krikor might have an individual, clean cell and food each day."

Bribery, not personality, seems to play the alleviating role in this account of Krikor's imprisonment. Though of course, the theme of the loss of jewelry that we have encountered before in Maritsa's stories recurs. Maritsa takes this opportunity to convey another important aspect of her grandfather's personality: "It was said that my grandfather Krikor used to talk in his sleep. His cell companions asked him questions and he answered. They even questioned him on his guiltiness, and he answered that he had done nothing. But one day, they asked him what it cost him to make a pair of shoes. He did not answer and woke up. There you have the tradesman, even in his sleep!" The shrewd businessman never reveals his trade secrets. Krikor's long incarceration took a toll on the family's fortunes. He was no longer involved in the day-to-day operation of the shoe business and had to rely on his younger brother and eldest son to keep the business going. Aram notes this fact: "While father was kept in jail his business went to pieces. Though my dear uncle Haroutioun had a heart of gold and was a wonderful craftsman, he was not a businessman as my father was. So it took some time to build up his business again." Such hardships were not new and unfortunately would be repeated again and again.

Let me close this section more positively by conveying a vignette by Aram about the introduction of the potato into Sivas. The Sivas region, as earlier remarked, was noted for its production of wheat and other grains and was often referred to as the grain bowl of Anatolia. Sources indicate that potatoes had been introduced from the Caucasus into Anatolia and the Black Sea coast earlier in the century, yet still may have been unknown in the Sivas region. Aram claims that his father Krikor played a major role in introducing the potato to the people of Sivas:[5]

Once my brother, Tsolag was sick and the doctor suggested feeding him potatoes. Potatoes? No one knew about potatoes and no one had any except for Mr. Hubbard, an American missionary. His cook, Cham Ovag was my father's friend, so through him, he was able to obtain some potatoes for seeding and finds out how to plant them. Our neighbor gardener, Soulayman, plants them for him. After eating, brother gets well and in that way, my father was the indirect means by which the potato was introduced to Sivas people.

The helpful gardener, Soulayman, reappears in our narrative, not in his role of gardening but as a killer of Armenians in the massacres of 1895.

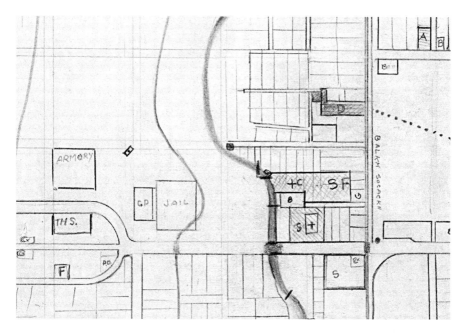

18. Aram's map showing the relation of the jail to the Dildilian home (D).
Note the small brook near the jail where confessions were coerced.

Tsolag's Photographic Career Begins

The year 1888 marked an important turning point in the life of the Dildilian family, though they were not aware of it at the time. In that year, photography entered into the family story. For the next 80 years photography was to play a central role in the lives of the family members and, in one instance, played a life-saving role. While Aram describes how his brother's path to a life of photography was somewhat trouble-free, we will shortly see in Tsolag's own words that this was not always the case:

> Soon after he [Krikor] built up his business, brother finished his schooling from the American High School and did not care to follow father's trade but wanted to be a photographer. Father was smart enough not to impose his will on him, as others used to do in the olden times. About that time, a traveling photographer, Jerahirjian, visited Sivas. My brother took advantage of that chance and took a few lessons in photography, something altogether new in that section of the country. Father bought him a 5x7 camera and brother started taking pictures. His first experiment was on me. I still have that picture with me. On the back, brother had written, "my first trial."

In this period there were no photographers with established studios in Sivas. The itinerant photographer was the custom. Photographers entered a town, set up shop for a few days, took photographs, developed and printed the results – often with the help of the local Armenian pharmacist – and then moved on. Most of these early photographers were Armenian, such as Jerahirjian. Aram describes the establishment of the first studio in Sivas. While other photographers had passed through Sivas at various times, my research has not uncovered a studio earlier than the one organized by the Dildilians. Aram describes how this came about:

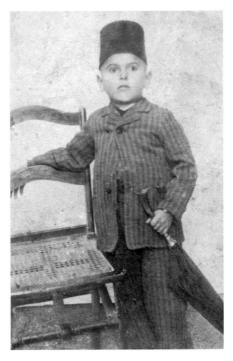

19. First photograph taken by Tsolag of his brother Aram. Late summer 1888.

Father rented a house near the Protestant church, with a big north-exposure yard suitable for picture taking ... About that time, a young man, Mikael Natourian, came from Constantinople pretending that he knew everything about photography ... So my father thought it would be a good idea to contract with him to organize a company of three, Natourian, Dildilian and Co. My father was to be president and brother and Natourian partners, with the understanding that after they are well-organized and well equipped, Sivas would be the headquarters, and one of the two would stay in Sivas and the other would go around to outside towns. So father mortgaged our ancestral home without telling my uncle anything about it, borrowed about $1,000 and ordered two wonderful sets of 10x12 cameras, rapid rectangular lenses and Voigtlander lenses, backgrounds, burnishers, trays, supplies and everything else, with the expectation of immediate success!

Aram's account of how my grandfather became a photographer is not based on first-hand recollections. Aram was five years old when his older brother first placed him before a camera and took his photograph. But in this instance we are fortunate to have my grandfather's own words, words spoken 40 years after the fact, as he tried to convey to his family the motivation and the circumstances behind his choice of photography as a career. Photography was an art for him. He always had a love for the visual. From his early days in primary school he was fascinated with "beautiful books," especially those such as "the large geography book of Boyajian" that had "full maps with lovely pictures" or books with illustrated Bible stories. His success with his lessons, "especially geography … awakened [his] drawing skills." In a humorous remark he reveals how he made art out of his lunch: "Mother used to give me walnuts for lunch. I used to squeeze them on a piece of paper to make them transparent and put them on pictures and trace them. Afterwards I put them on windowpanes, put a clean paper on them, retrace them and later shade them in." I suspect that there may have been times when he went hungry because of his artistic experiments – a youthful twist on the notion of the starving artist. He explains how he kept his artistic inclinations a secret:

> I used to do this secretly because my father did not permit me to do these things, thinking that if I would put my mind on these, then my lessons will suffer. In reality, that is the way it turned out. Successively, the schools changed but not my inclinations. They never changed, until the opening of Sepastia's well-organized Protestant school. My father sent me there. There, Professor Garabed Bilgoturian, now in America, encouraged my drawing aptitudes and advised my uncle to help me purchase paper and pencil. It was a very happy day when my uncle, keeping it a secret from my father, gave me 50 pennies to enable me to buy one sheet of drawing paper, one gum eraser and one pencil.

Tsolag then described how his talent expressed itself not in making of shoes as his father desired, but in taking photographs:

> My father at this time was the most skillful shoemaker and with my two uncles and 15 workers, worked in the same shop. It was my father's desire that I become a shoemaker, and an educated shoemaker, in order to bring European material directly [to Sivas]. I would thus add profit to the business. With that objective, he took me out of school. It is true that I helped father in the shop, cleaning, arranging, and organizing his correspondence, but I had no intention of becoming a shoemaker when this wonderful man [Uncle Haroutioun] mediated with my father with the following noteworthy saying, "Brother, you cannot force a dog to hunt." This saying, regardless of how old-fashioned it is, contains the unmatched soul of pedagogy. My uncle had seen in me the future Tsolag and successfully guided me.

Uncle Haroutioun successfully convinced his older brother, for Tsolag describes the day that his avocation was announced to the whole family. No longer was his art secret:

> 1888, June, Sunday evening after the family dinner, Oragim Emmin, a notable Sepastiatsi Protestant, unexpectedly announced that tomorrow I will go to do

45

photographic work. Oh, that day's good advice especially given to me by Oragim Emmin, I have never forgotten. I do not recall whether I slept that night or not but I do remember that early in the morning, prayerfully, I went to Saint Nishan Monastery to the altar of Abbot Mekhitar (the altar where he used to pray) and on my knees I pledged that if I learn this trade and become successful, I will keep 12 orphans. At that time at Saint Nishan Monastery they were keeping 24 orphans, children from the villages massacred by Mousa Bey. Black or dark-colored eyes, sad faces, they would bring tears to your eyes.

The reference to Mousa Bey must be a reference to the notorious Kurdish chieftain Musa Bey of Muş, who was put on trial in Constantinople the following year for a variety of crimes, mostly against Armenians. Though he was acquitted, he was sent into exile.[6] Little did Tsolag realize at the time, but his pledge to support 12 orphans would increase exponentially in 1918 when he and his brother Aram helped organize orphanages that supported nearly a thousand orphans.

Tsolag's initial training was not very successful. Though he does not mention him by name, Jerahirjian was probably the master referred to in the following passage:

By noon, I was at my master's studio but the master was never on his job. He was always eating and drinking with officers. My three months were finished. We gave him 30 red gold pieces, in return my master put in my hand a beautiful diploma declaring me a master. But where was photography? Where was I? After my first experiment, my father forbade me to go public. For almost a year I took pictures at home of my sisters and brothers and gained experience.

Tsolag's big break came the next year. The manuscript of the speech is somewhat corrupted at this point, but his success is clearly connected to his personal relationship with the governor of Sivas, identified here as Mamdouh Pasha. This Mamdouh Mehmet Pasha may have been the highly appreciative governor who patronized Krikor's shoe store. Tsolag appears to have been hired by the governor to travel around the province and to cities much further afield, such as Kastemoni, to take photographs of the antique monuments. The governor had also assigned him a guard for all his travels.

Tsolag describes the difficulties of being a photographer in Sivas, an important and ancient city but a far cry from the more cosmopolitan and forward-looking cities of Europe. By this time photography was a well-respected and flourishing profession in Constantinople. The Abdullah Frères studio in Constantinople, operated by three Armenian brothers, was internationally famous. They had gained the distinction of becoming court photographers to the sultan in 1862. A photograph taken by their studio topped the agendas of tourists who visited

Constantinople. But Sivas was still under the sway of a patriarchal and gendered system of prejudices. Tsolag describes the milieu:

> A few words about the psychology of photography at that time. Armenians were very jealous about their families. They would consider it immoral or immodest to have their women exposed to the photographer. Many would consider it belittlement to stand next to their women. My ears have heard many unkind remarks addressed to photographers … Let me not forget to say that there is some justification for people's criticism. Starting with my master, I have not seen a photographer who contradicted people's opinion. In this connection, my father gave strict instructions.

It is interesting to note that Tsolag does not tell us what those instructions were. A hint as to what Krikor's advice may have been is given to us by Maritsa, though she seems to restrict it to only his dealings with Turks and not Armenians:

> Tsolag is 17; he is fair-haired and blue-eyed like all his brothers and sisters. He is a handsome boy. His father knows that Tsolag will have to deal with Turkish women to picture them and, as a man of experience, he knows that a handsome man can be in danger when he approaches Turkish women. So the father calls Tsolag and asks him to swear that he will never bring a razor near his cheeks. From that day, Tsolag never touched his beard until his last day.

Though I have never been able to pinpoint the date on which Tsolag first grew his beard, we know from a group family photograph from November 1893 that he was clean-shaven at that point. Yet one can never know, youthful beards do tend to come and go. My first beard was grown in college but disappeared momentarily for my graduation photograph. I remember coming home from college during one of my breaks and encountering a split decision from my parents as to the suitability of my beard. My father found it outrageous and wouldn't stop complaining about my hippie looks, while my mother was much more sympathetic and told me how it brought back many lovely memories of her father, a man she always knew with a full beard. She reminisced about days long ago when as a small child she would sit in his lap and playfully run her fingers through his beard, sometimes weaving it into braids.

Tsolag was able to overcome the narrow-minded prejudices of the Armenians of Sivas with the help of the man who first opened the door of photography for him. He writes, "The above-mentioned Orag Emmin gave me a special rental of a renovated corner of a shop in which to open my first studio. Orag Emmin was a prominent man and had cast his shadow, and I, in the grace of that shadow, was successful in taking family group pictures of very strict, respectable Sepastia people." In the next sentence it is interesting to note that the subject shifts from the singular "I" to the plural "we." "Our fame in a short time spread even to

Marsovan. The second year of starting work, we received a welcome invitation which was repeated for three years." The welcome invitation was from Reverend Charles C. Tracy, the president of Anatolia College. As we already know from Aram's account, the "we" obliquely referred to here included Mikael Natourian. Natourian partnered with my grandfather for at least three years and was at this stage certainly the more experienced photographer. Why does my grandfather choose to omit all reference to him in his autobiographical speech? We need to dig deeper into the lacuna.

We know from the account given by Aram that Mikael Natourian lacked the resources to open a studio in Sivas. In a very telling turn of phrase Aram had remarked: "Mikael Natourian, came from Constantinople pretending that he knew everything about photography." Krikor had underwritten all the expenses of their studio by mortgaging the ancestral home. Maritsa had given a similar account, further noting that the costs of setting up the partnership were 200 Ottoman gold pounds.

From both Maritsa and Aram's accounts, we know that Krikor had a lot invested in his son's success. As was clear in the earlier excerpts, Krikor was a very influential citizen of Sivas. Maritsa reports that he had become the chairman of the Sénékérimian charity association and head of the shoemakers' guild, the same organization that had tried to prevent him from opening his business. Despite his stay in prison, he still seemed to have influence with the government. As "president" of the Natourian and Dildilian Studios, he was able to secure business for his photographer partners. In a curious story that is found in both Aram's and Maritsa's memoirs, we encounter a description of the photography business and an instance of Natourian's negligence mixed with an incidence of theft and a supernatural séance:

> My father was able to get a government order to take some official pictures in Zara, a big Armenian village. It was Natourian's turn to go out (before that, brother went to Gürün and was quite successful). On his way back home he falls asleep in the wagon. The driver takes the horses to the river for [them to] drink and when he comes back with the horses and hitched them to start the journey, he, Natourian wakes up and notices that the camera case is gone. At once they turn back and ask the people around the field but no one seems to know anything. So he comes back to Sivas and goes to his home. He does not even bother to inform father what had happened until the next afternoon. Naturally, father was not pleased after hearing all about it. Father takes some papers from the governor and goes to Zara. Next day was Sunday. My uncle asked our neighbor, Mugurdich Effendy, who was a magician, to try some of his tricks to locate the lost camera. He picked my sister, Parantzem as a medium. He said the medium must be pure in heart, simple minded and blue eyed. He put some water about an inch deep into a big white porcelain photographic tray, made her kneel down and covered her all over with a white

bed sheet. There was no other light in the room but the skylight. He asked her if she sees her father in the tray – she said, "No, but I see my brother coming down the steps." Then she said, "I see Natourian, he is sleeping wrapped in [a] woolen blanket. I see a village man take a shiny box and hide it under the wheat stack." Then she was asked what else she saw. She said, "He is digging the ground near a telegraph pole and hid the box there." Then she said, "Some man digs it out and hid it in the cow barn under the hay." Now let us come to father. He goes to the town master's home, gives him the governor's letter and tells him that though the box is shiny and fancy, it is not a money box, it is not valuable for anybody else but a photographer. Next day, the town master sends word around that whoever has that box and returns it tomorrow morning, will not be punished – but it will be harder later. Finally, the thief does not dare take it himself so he takes it to the priest and pleads not to press charges against the man. Father promises not to, but demands that he carry the box on his back and bring it to Sivas with him. So father puts the camera on the man's back and brings it back home ... When we told father that Mugurdich Effendy made Parantzem see what did happen, father was surprised as it was almost the identical actions the thief had done.

Natourian's negligence did not bode well for the future smooth operation of the business. His greed almost put an end to my grandfather's photographic career.

As Tsolag remarked earlier, the business had expanded to Marsovan by this time. Given the lucrative business in this college town and the steady stream of customers, they opened a permanent studio near the campus of Anatolia College. Maritsa describes the location's attraction:

> They settled in Marsovan, in Zéngoudjian's house that they converted into a studio. That house was located near the south gate of the American College compound. All the Americans patronized the studio, as well as the male and female boarding students who liked to send pictures to their parents, well-to-do people in general, especially the Greek boys and girls from Samsun. In addition, there were the class pictures shot on Commencement Day with the pupils and teachers, pictures of the music bands, and also individual pictures.

Many of the early photographs of Anatolia College from the early 1890s were taken by the partnership. The permanent studio opened in 1892 but soon the partnership soured. Tsolag chose to ignore the falling out in his speech, but Aram chronicled the events in his memoir:

> For a while this companionship went quite well. Later, Natourian went to Marsovan for one year, but he stayed there for three years contrary to their contract and understanding. Not only did he not come back to Sivas, but he did not even send father any report or send any money. Finally, father was about to go to Marsovan

personally to find out what is what when he got the bad news that Natourian was dead. So father put under court seal all the studio's belongings and was planning to go to Marsovan and attend personally whatever was necessary to do. Just about that time, Miss Willard, the girls' college president, tells Natourian's sister, Haïganouch, that "unless you pay your overdue boarding school dues, you can't stay in school." She starts crying and said, "How can I pay you, my brother is dead and Dildilians have put under government seal all my brother's belongings?" So Miss Willard, naturally, was terribly moved and asks famed Vosgerichian, to help free those sealed goods. So Vosgerichian goes to the house where his studio was and breaks the sealed door and sold everything to Soumbulian and gives the money to his sister, Haïganouch for her schooling.

Maritsa gives a somewhat different account but the culpability still lies with Mikael Natourian. Natourian was suffering from consumption and "when he felt his end coming, he had gone to the legal authorities and had the whole business registered in the name of his sister as if he had sole title," which accounted for his sister's ability to benefit from the sale of the studio and its contents. This financial loss almost ended Tsolag's career. Fortunately photography in Marsovan was in very great demand and with further assistance of his family, he resumed his work but now as the only photographer in the studio. This was the beginnings of the soon to be famous Dildilian Photography Studios.

The Death of my Great-Grandparents Loucia and Krikor

The new year of 1894 began with Tsolag busy with photography work for both Anatolia College and the government. He was making a name for himself and had a promising future ahead. He was 22 years old, independent and successful. But within a few months his life drastically changed. Tsolag was traveling when the first tragedy struck. He describes it with a saddened simplicity:

> In 1894, when I was returning home, I found that my mother had died from the cholera epidemic. Three brothers and four sisters had been orphaned and the eldest was 22 years old [Tsolag himself], the youngest 6 months. From this heavy sorrow, Father was not able to endure and six months later he, too, separated from us. My uncle and his wife took care of our needs like parents.

Aram vividly describes his brother's return to Sivas and the circumstances under which Tsolag learned of his mother's passing. Aram was ten years old at the time, and his memory of these events is a strange blend of boyish excitement and matter-of-fact reportage:

About that time, brother had gone on a tour for a government job to Kastamoni and surrounding towns, which proved to be a very profitable trip. Just about then, my mother died from a cholera epidemic that swept the country in April 1894. So father wired brother to come back home. He did not inform him of mother's passing. Father borrowed the governor's Landau and sent me, my younger uncle and our neighbor, Mugurdich Effendy, to meet brother at a certain place with "shish kebab," fruits, etc., so that he would be informed about mother's death before he comes home. For me it was fun and cause of great joy to have a ride in Pasha's Landau. O boy!

We arrived at a certain meeting spot and soon we saw his wagon coming and rushed to meet him. He jumped out, grabbed me, kissed me and hugged me in tears … He surely sensed what had happened as he asked where father and mother were and why they had not come. Well, it was time to tell him all. Mugurdich Effendy told him that father could not come because mother went to her rest … Soon we started to drive homeward. Everyone else was sobbing and eyes were wet but me, I was too busy with my brother's watch chain, his soft silky beard, artistic and stylish vest sweater or with the swift proceeding of the Landau wheels and trotting of the beautiful chestnut brown horses with their beautiful long manes floating in the air …

Soon we were home. I noticed almost all of our neighbors out in the street with sad and mournful looks on their faces. As soon as brother got into the house my older sister, Haïganouch, showed my youngest baby brother's cradle and said to him, "Here is what mother left for us, a beautiful, blond, blue-eyed Shamavon, only six months old."

Tsolag may not have even realized before this point that he now had a baby brother. Maritsa comments that the news of his mother's death must have been a shock to Tsolag because she was always "so healthy" and "so strong." My great-grandmother must have been a very healthy and strong woman, for by age 46 she had given birth to 11 children over a span of 26 years.

Cholera was common in the Ottoman Empire due to widespread unsanitary practices and ignorance of the transmission of the disease. An epidemic of cholera had arrived in Sivas on April 15. On June 29, 1894, the U.S. Consul, Milo A. Jewett, M.D. filed a report with his government detailing the epidemiology of the outbreak:

On the 12th of April, 20 women came from Tavra to a Turkish bath at Sivas. The next day a dozen of them were attacked with cholera, and on the 15th of April the malady burst out in epidemic form in all quarters of Sivas. I think that the women were all infected by the same source, perhaps at the bath, but however that may be, it is certain that after they were taken ill and the river contaminated by their choleraic dejections the disease appeared simultaneously in all parts of the city. During the first week of the epidemic there were about 500 cases.[7]

Tavra was a village in a predominantly Armenian area in the countryside, situated a mile north of the city on the banks of a small river, identified in Aram's map as the Moundar Ked. Consul Jewett stated that the sewage from this village flows into the same river that also "furnishes the fountains of the houses and flows in small streams through the streets of the city." On April 19, four days after the outbreak of the epidemic, my great-grandmother Loucia died. Maritsa relates the circumstances around her death: "The first one, and the only one, to be stricken is Loucia who is still breast-feeding her youngest child, Shamavon. Everybody in the house is busy helping. Day and night Loucia's naked body is kept wrapped up in hot towels. After a few days, her condition slowly improves. A permanent watch is kept at Loucia's bedside." At this point in the story there is a significant difference in the accounts given by Maritsa and Aram. Recall that Maritsa is conveying the account given to her by her mother Haïganouch, who at the time of her mother's death was 17 years old. Aram was 11 years old at the time and was an eyewitness to the event. He describes being in the same room with his mother:

> While I was sick in bed, a terrific cholera epidemic spread all over the country and thousands died … Though we, at our house, had taken all kinds of precautions and used only boiled water for drinking and used all kinds of medicines, somehow my dear mother was infected. She was almost well and we were happy. There was a terra cotta pitcher full of boiled water in the window to keep it cool and I was in the bed in the same room. She asked me to give her a drink and when I refused to do so, she got out of her bed and rushed to the window. By the time I let my sisters know, she drank and drank lots of cold water … she died that same night.

Maritsa does not mention Aram's presence and places her father Krikor in the room at the time. Haïganouch enters to relieve him and "sees her father by the window who implores with raised arms: 'Lord, you should not have done it. You had promised not to do it.' But Loucia was dead. During a moment when her husband was snoozing, she had got up to drink water … and that was that." Whether Haïganouch or Maritsa actually believed that somehow that last drink of water turned out to be fatal, the implication is that Krikor somehow blamed himself for his wife's death. Could this be the "heavy sorrow" that Krikor could no longer endure? The sorrow so simply and poignantly expressed by Tsolag? In the summer of 2012, I stood near that *hammam* off the street where my family had lived so very long ago. Flowing somewhere nearby was the small river, the one Aram calls the Moundar Ked, the dirty river. I could not help but think that there was some fatal connection between that *hammam* and the deaths that overtook my family in 1894.

Given the poor sanitary conditions in Sivas, outbreaks of both cholera and typhoid were not uncommon. Consul Jewett, in the same report quoted above, goes to great lengths in describing the system by which raw sewage flowed in the streets and alleys of the city. These were not the harmless "rivers of candy" from

Krikor's childhood game of grocer. Little effort was made in keeping the drinking water supply separate from sewage. Public health officials who were sent from Constantinople often arrived late and were ineffectual.

Soon after the death of my great-grandmother, the Dildilian household was struck by typhoid fever. Aram describes its arrival:

> About six months later there came an epidemic of typhoid fever into the city. One by one, every member of our family was infected. Our doctor, a family friend, said to my uncle, "I am sure everyone of them will pull through except Krikor Agha (father) because he is using alcohol."
>
> My brother was the last one to come down with it. While he was suffering in bed in the upper room, father passed away on August 20, 1894 and was buried. A few days later brother called me to his bedside, hugged me to his chest and said, "Aram, we are now left orphans but God is our Father and He will somehow take care of us." He gave me one silver mejidiah to take to Rev. Garabed Kullajian with a letter asking prayer for our family.

As was mentioned, all members of the family came down with typhoid fever. In reporting the progression of her mother Haïganouch's illness, Maritsa describes the classic symptoms of typhoid fever. Haïganouch experienced headaches and then a fever that left her in a state close to unconsciousness for 21 days. She lost weight and most of her hair but survived. The same claim that alcohol contributed to Krikor's death is also mentioned in Maritsa's account: "Haïganouch wept bitterly because she remembered her father's death. She asked the doctor how it was that her father died and her uncle not. 'Because,' said the doctor, 'Krikor Agha was used to liquor while his brother did not drink.' It is true that Krikor Agha had his glass of raki every evening when coming home, together with mezes, and it was his dinner." Alcohol is a stimulant and can aggravate the dehydration that accompanies typhoid fever but we know today that moderate alcohol consumption does not increase mortality. "Moderate," of course, is the key word here. Aram is also keen to point out that his father was not an alcoholic but he does draw a lesson about alcohol:

> My dear uncle, who was a prayerful and temperate man and who now became head of the family, called us all into the front room and said, "If my brother had not used alcohol regularly, he would not be dead. So now let us all vow not to use any kind of intoxicating liquor personally or in our homes." Thanks to God, up to this date neither my brother nor my family have become victims of that dreaded evil habit of mankind … It was stylish then and, sorry to say, it is stylish now with so-called civilized people to serve liquor to guests. It is my wish that my children would follow our family vow regarding the evil of drinking (Habakkuk 2:15, read it …).
>
> My father was not a drunkard but he used drinks extensively. He used to make his own wine expertly and had bottled, labeled, and sealed samples of

wine of 14 years dated 1880 up to his death. I do not know what became of that collection … Our parlor, rather father's room, was a pleasant place to be in. It was well lighted, well furnished and had an excellent view and scenery. Father was a man of pleasure (half-retired). He used to come home early in the afternoon. His refreshment or snack table would be set … it was some lovely sight. On it there were three beautiful cut glass vials, the big one for water and the smaller ones for drinks, and several cut glass dishes full of salads, cheese, abought, sujak, salted leblabu, and kinos besmet. He would have someone as companion to play tavloo [backgammon]. Poor uncle used to come home all tired and hungry but had to wait till their game was over to sit at the dinner table.

I must admit that on my recent trips to Turkey you will more often picture me following the example of my great-grandfather Krikor rather than his brother Haroutioun. Raki and meze have been my practice. Yet Aram has drawn more than a cautionary lesson on the health effects of alcohol. By bringing in religion and citing a verse from the Bible regarding the evils of serving alcohol to guests, he is equating this habit with sin.[8] Yet he is also keen not to condemn his much beloved father as is evidenced in the description of the rather benign manner in which Krikor mixed drinking with the pleasures of food and relaxation. Not serving alcohol to guests certainly became the rule in Aram's and Tsolag's households. My mother used to say that she never saw her father drink except on one occasion. In 1918 this rule was to be broken for a greater good, one that I will discuss later.

20. Dildilian family 1890. Mikael, Krikor and Haroutioun with their wives Surma, Loucia, Elbiz (first row, left to right). Clean-shaven Tsolag (center, back row) with his siblings and cousin.

3

The Childhood Recollections of Aram Dildilian

The Early Years of Joy and Adventure

Aram Dildilian's early years in Sivas were filled with childish adventures and play but were also marked by personal hardship and tragedy. Over 60 years later he wrote of this period in his life in amazingly rich detail. He vividly communicates what life was like for an Armenian boy growing up in Sivas. Aram's voice speaks with little interruption or comment in the pages that follow:

I was a welcome baby in the family, by everyone, after three girls. I was born, according to my birth certificate of baptism No. 270 and according to my father's handwriting on the back of the certificate, at 2 a.m. on September 18, 1883 (new calendar). My dear brother Tsolag was praying for a baby brother and as soon as I was born, early in the morning, he went to church to give thanks …

As I grew to self-consciousness I realized that I was the favorite of everyone in the family, especially my father. I do not remember that he ever punished me for my mischievous wrong doings and, as I remember, they were many. I guess I was my father's son! One day I got hold of father's shoemakers' perforated hammer and started to knock it here and there and when I hit on the plastered wall, I liked the design it made! I kept on hitting all over the newly painted walls until I was stopped … One cold morning, I was out in the street and I noticed the iron door knocker was covered with white thick frost. I used to like snow very much, so I tried to lick it. I did not get any snow in my mouth, but part of my tongue stuck to it … One hot day, I noticed some white stuff piled on a big log. I thought it was snow so I tried to put it in my mouth. Soon my fingers started bleeding as it was nothing else but crushed glass … Every time I did something like that my uncle used to say to me, "*Dzo* Boy, what kind of boy are you? If I tie your hands, your feet move. If I tie your feet, your tongue goes around. Can't you keep still a moment?"

Things that I remember of my childhood days are sweet and pleasant. Father used to bring me unavailable toys, chocolate and fancy candies that I could not see in the markets later when I grew bigger. I cannot understand where he could have bought those nice things in that backward country in those days ... My dear uncle, Haroutioun, used to teach me short poems and songs and each time we had visitors, he would ask me to say things by heart and sing for which he would give me money or candy. I don't know why, but I was not as strong bodily and often was sick, so I did not have much chance to play games with the boys, go swimming, or have any other kind of boyish fun. My only playmates were my sister, Parantzem, and my cousin, Sumpad, at home or in the backyard. We used to slide, jump, swing, and play in the snow. We used to make snowmen and snow houses. I remember well one year especially when it was so cold and there was lots of snow (each time it snowed they had to scrape the snow off the flat roofs so they would not cave in or cause them to leak when the snow melted). One day it snowed so much that everybody was locked in the house, so my uncle dug a tunnel to our neighbor's, Mugurdich Effendy's house and we had a wonderful time for weeks. We had plenty of provisions so all day long we used to play all kinds of games especially when Mugurdich Effendy would be willing to do all kinds of tricks in juggling. That Mugurdich Effendy was a wonderful man. A young Evangelical-minded Antranig Vartanian bought a complete set of printing presses and started publishing a weekly "Sivas," one side in Turkish and the other in Armenian. The Government sent him into exile and appointed our friend, Mugurdich Effendy, as government printer.

I have not been able to trace down this reference to Antranig Vartanian and the newspaper he had started in Sivas. There is one reference to an early attempt at starting a newspaper by the same name. A volume titled *History of the Armenians of Sebastia and Neighboring Villages* claims that in 1875 a native Armenian of Sebastia brought a printing press from Constantinople and began the publication of the *Sivas* weekly, half in Armenian and half Turkish.[1] We do know that after the restoration of the Ottoman Constitution in 1908, publishing flourished in Sivas with the emergence of two weekly newspapers in Armenian, *Andranig* (1909–12) and *Hoghtar* (1910–14).[2]

Let us return to Aram's remarkable account of his childhood days in Sivas, remarkable because these words were written by my great-uncle when he was in his sixties, an age that I have now reached. Are my childhood memories as vividly retrievable? I doubt it. Aram has set a high bar for any memoirist to reach:

In those days, children were somewhat neglected, but we were satisfied with what we had or could get. During long winter nights, we used to sit in the *t'onir* room and play by ourselves, "Mamoog Mamoog," "Jive Jive," "Alim Alim," etc., or tell and hear stories about "Adzoog Bouzoog," "Khlank Tavit," "Arch Marian" etc., or sit at the parlor windows with sister Parantzem, covering our heads with the heavy curtain, and watch the passers-by or count the people with the lanterns. The north side was mine and the south side was hers.

In those days, no one was allowed to go around at night without a lantern or some kind of identification. Once in awhile we would see some regular jandarma on patrol that would send waves of shivers through our bodies. We used to feel as if they would reach up to the window and grab us off, so we used to down our heads in great fear. I guess the fear of Turks has been crystallized in our whole being. Those occasional jandarma patrols were to arrest those who had no lantern or identification papers and those tobacco smugglers, "Kachakjis" who often would go around in secret, sneaking from house to house to deliver tobacco. Sometimes they would be acting boldly on horseback in one or in groups, shooting into the air and hollering and challenging the jandarmas to catch them. The tobacco business was franchised to European Régie [La Société de la régie co-intéressée des tabacs de l'empire Ottoman] to pay the foreign debts of the Turkish government, like the salt and other minerals. But the tobacco smugglers were making good money just the same. Usually, they would deliver first the cured tobacco leaves and another night they would bring the slicer wrapped around their leg and slice the tobacco enough for the year. The tobacco slicer is something like a paper trimmer but in half-cylinder shape. In the meantime, the housewife would take advantage and have him slice the homemade macaroni. My mother used to make some thick dough mixed with beaten eggs then she would open it into round sheets with rolling pins and dollies and half-bake it on a convex round metal disk 24" and pile the sheets on top of each other to keep them soft. The tobacco slicer would slice to the desired thickness. My mother used to make several different delicious dishes out of these home-made macaroni.

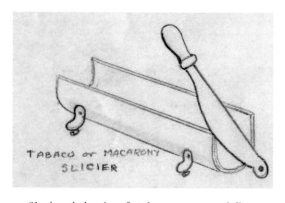

21. Aram's drawing of a tobacco or macaroni slicer.

To prepare the winter provisions would take many long and painstaking weeks and months but would provide much fun and amusement to us children as we had our share in it too. At least we had much excitement. First came the storing of wood for cooking and heating. In Sivas we did not have forests nearby. The woodcutter would cut big pine trees and roll them down from the hillside to the river. They would bind 5 or 6 of them together as a raft and steer it down the river at the bent bridge, "Dzoor Gamorch." There they would pull them out of the river to sell either for firewood or to lumbermen for building.

22. Egri Bridge (Bent Bridge) as it is today on the road from Sivas to Malatya.

Our greatest expectation was to ask for, and if we were not refused, to have a free ride on the empty ox carts for a few blocks and, naturally, walk back home! ... When the woodchopper would come to saw the big logs into small pieces and then into shreds, it was our lot to carry all the chopped wood into the basement, which we did not like so well, but it was fun to sit on the log and have a horsey ride with the rhythm of the saw, zig-zeb, zig-zeb, and sing with the saw.

Then it would be time for pickling of several kinds of ... fruits and vegetables, it was my mother's duty to go from garden to garden and bargain for the best buy with the least pay and it was for us children to watch at the rooftop under the hot sun so that the birds would not carry the fruits and vegetables away.

About flour, grain, wheat, and cereals, the wheat and all other grain used to come from the village. It was up to mother, Aunt Elbiz and my sisters to wash, clean, dry, and sift, and take them to the nearby flour mills right in the city. But most of the time father would rent one or two tents and take the whole family and set the tents on the meadows near Tarvar, an Armenian village which had several flour mills. There we would stay for several weeks and have a vacation in the meantime, while the flour, cereals, bulgur, gorgod, sermoag, and other foodstuffs are milled, processed and made ready ...

Almost every year, the whole family would go to either mill valley or some of the several mineral springs around Sivas such as "Dak Chermoog," "Bagh Chermoog" setting up tents or would go to one of the monastery's guest houses for vacation and either father or uncle would be with the family. One special year they took me to a mineral spring, "Yulanlik" where there were many water snakes. The idea was that the snakes would bite my wounds and cure me! It was a terrible and fearsome thing for me.

One hot summer Sunday, the whole family was invited by the governor, who was very friendly with my father, to his flour mill, "Pasha's Fabrica." I do not know what we ate but I was so pleased when they served us a cold pink sherbet drink and pink "Lokum" (Turkish Delight). The men folk were entertained on the meadow under a big shade tree, but I was with my mother and the womenfolk in the big solarium, "Keosak," with multicolored glass windows all around the room, which impressed me so much. Up to this day I do not forget it.

Another year we went to Khoner-Gudour, where at the door of the church, there was a rock with a deep footprint shape supposed to be made by the saint-healer of sicknesses. It was in a deep valley with pure drinking water and invigorating air. As I said before, to prepare provisions for the whole winter was a long and hard task for everybody. At wintertime, it was hard to buy freshly butchered meat. Therefore, father used to buy a fat steer and three or four lambs. The butcher used to come [to our] home and kill them and would cut into pieces certain sections for certain purposes, such as for abought (dried meat), saujaukt (sausage), Khuyma and Parag Khuyma, preserved meat in special molds or earthen jars which could be kept indefinitely for the whole winter long, and longer. For fresh vegetables, we used to dig a big hole in the ground, say 3 or 4 feet deep and cover the vegetables with earth, and then take them out anytime they were needed. That supply used to last a long time. The perishable fruits we used to hang in bunches or put on shelves. Sometimes it would be dehydrated but edible just the same. And for the bread, though we had a bread oven in the house, it was economical and tasty to make several kinds of dried bread, Kinoo basmet, Koundig basmet, Tzoghi-hatz, Patz-hatz, and Lavash, to keep in storage ...

Holidays such as New Year, Christmas, and Easter were days of real joy and fun. We used to celebrate for two or three days, visiting each other, especially the younger ones would visit and give greetings from one family head to the other family head, and were served [various] kinds of sweets.

I don't very well remember that we ever went to church in a group, yet we had our own space of seats. Often my uncle would take me with him on Sundays to the main mother church, which was a huge cathedral (one of the two in Armenia; the other built in Erzurum was bombed out of existence totally in 1951 by the Turks). My mother used to take me along with her ... to the main church, Sourp Asdvadzadzin on weekdays and to other churches nearby for prayer. I do not know why and I was too young to ask but she used to kneel down for hours and cry and pray. My little heart would be upset and I would cry with her. I do not know what she prayed for, maybe she was homesick. Her mother, three brothers and three sisters were in Yozgat. She used to express a deep desire to see her mother. Anyhow, my dear mother was a prayerful mother. Often in the afternoons, before father came home, she used to call us all into the inner room and we would pray standing in a straight row and in unison sing, "Praise ye the Lord, we passed the day in peace, Amen." Especially on Saturday afternoons, we, the children, would fumigate with incense all the nooks and corners of each room and then stand for prayer in preparation for Sunday. Often mother used to make up a lunch bundle, take me to one of those places of worship and with my Aunt Elbiz and sisters have a picnic in those places of worship and churches, and there were plenty in and around Sivas, such as "Sourp Nishan," three chapels in one; "Anabad," "Sourp Hagop," "Sourp Varvar," "Chatal Sourp Sarkis," "Ohan Osgi Peran," "Sourp Kevork" (part of which was given to the Greeks as a gift), "Sourp Sarkis," "Sourp Purgich," "Sourp Kar Soun Manoog," "Sourp Luvatz," etc.

As one of the leading families in Sivas, the Dildilians had dedicated seats in the main Apostolic Sourp Asdvadzadzin Cathedral in the city but often attended services in various different churches. During this period, the 1880s and early 1890s, some members of the Dildilian family began to identify themselves with the Protestant faith but may well have continued to attend Apostolic services. Aram's richly detailed description of Armenian life in Sivas continues:

> Our Sundays were never dull. We never went to picnics on Sundays but all the picnic goers had to pass by our house. It was some sight to watch them go up to Sourp Nishan, Anabad or Sourp Hagop, donned in their Sunday best, man, woman, and especially the young people. On the big plaza across from our house, young men, children, and even grown men would be playing all day long all kinds of games, or would have horse races or horse rides. Especially in the afternoon, the Army band would play to amuse the crowd about the plaza. We, the children, on nice summer days would go up on our house rooftop and play all kinds of games ...
>
> I don't know why I was weak in body and very delicate. I remember often I would wake up at night in a dizzy spell and with upset stomach. For that reason, I was not sent to regular schools though they were nearby our house. Instead, I was sent to Maron Varjouhi's private school, a next door neighbor. She was an old maid and used to work her gingham loom and in the meantime teach the little children, Aip, Pen, Kim (ABC) in unison and in rhythm. We had to repeat the same over and over and then kneel down on our little pillows, face down on folded arms. That was supposed to be our rest hour, yet we were much more tired than rested ...
>
> One very cold day, they were a little late to warm the room so when they brought in the big, portable charcoal fireplace with the blue and red flames on, at once all of us came around it with our little hands up over the fire to get warm. Just then, some boy pushed me over the fire and my little fingers went right into the red-hot fire. I do not remember what happened to me just then but I know that for many weeks later, mother used to doctor my hands with lime water and olive oil. After that, my father did not send me to that school anymore, or to any other school. He used to take me to his shop and one of his apprentices, Baron Vahan Tatarian, used to tutor me.

23. Camel caravans.

24. Mule caravans.

As I said before, my father's shop was a pleasant place to be in. There were nice seats and plenty of things to play with. It was situated on the main royal highway to Baghdad, on the corner of the bridge, Kare Gamoorch, and on the river, Moundar Ked. There were plenty of things to see and learn every day, for instance, the mail caravan, on packhorses in the winter, and with horse and wagon in the summer, with the tartar (the guard) leading the caravan on horseback, galloping down the hill chanting loudly like the town crier … Then there were the camel caravans passing by one after another … [a] sight to watch for hours, with their fancy headgear and multiple bell bands hanging on both sides and sometimes bellowing loudly in pain of I don't know why! Though I was safe inside the store window, often a shiver of a chill would pass through my little body when once in awhile a camel would turn his long neck towards me and look at me with a sad face as if I was the cause of his torture … Then would follow some horse or mule caravans loaded with merchandise, with fancy pack saddles and bells.

25. Springless cart.

Then in the afternoon, all kinds of covered and open horse wagons to transfer people from place to place. It was something to watch the village people with their oxcarts loaded with foodstuff, wood, charcoal, hay, barley, wheat, etc. Then the vegetable garden boys, carrying on their heads baskets full of fresh green onions, parsley, meat, cucumbers, carrots, etc., advertising their goods, chanting musically, naming their vegetables. The same way with all other kinds of foods and fancy-pastry peddlers; in fact, everyone who did sell anything would go around, hollering or chanting loud and harsh. Then, in the late afternoon, would come the travelers of all sorts, some with spring wagons, some springless, and yet others on horseback. Most of them would stop over at the top of my father's shop, which was a big municipal hotel, or across the street at Afton's Casino, which was an Armenian hotel. So all day long, I had all kinds of fun and amusement.

From Aram's description of life in Sivas and its environs, one realizes how centrally located, both geographically and socially, the Dildilian household and business were in the fabric of the city. Aram often had a bird's-eye view of the life around him. Years later he and his brother would be capturing similar images with their cameras.

Aram's Life-Changing Experience

The Dildilian family was prospering and still growing in the early 1890s. In 1888 Aram had welcomed a baby sister, Nevart, and five years later he was blessed with a baby brother, Shamavon. His older brother, Tsolag, whom he so admired, was establishing his career as a photographer. The shoemaking business was at its height financially and as a social hub for both the Turkish and Armenian notables of the city. Yet for Aram the decade ahead began inauspiciously. No date is given in his memoir, but an incident that would change his life forever took place sometime in 1891. He was not yet eight years old, but was brave enough to venture out into the city on his own. Aram describes what happened in a chapter of his memoir that he labels with the simple title, "I Become Sick."

One fateful morning, I was going happily to my father's shoe shop by myself, singing and jumping from one stepping-stone to the other. At the corner of Kel Tahir's Palace, the palace that was stoned years ago and for which my father was accused, they had laid big blocks of stones to let cartwheels pass in between and to let people step off the mud … I was not quite eight years old then and was crossing the corner singing and jumping. I did not notice that a Turkish mullah, a Mohammedan priest, with wide green turban wrapped over his red fez was walking with high wooden shoes and his long floating robe folded up on his back like the hump of load carriers so that it would not be splashed with mud. He pushed me aside with his strong arm and knocked me down to the ground saying in a harsh voice, "Get out of my way, you infidel's son, you spoiled my day" (a superstition like some people have here about the black cat, etc.). I fell down, hurt and scratched in the leg, so I turned back home and told my mother about what happened to me. She washed me and put clean clothes on me and told me, "Do not cry, you will forget all about it when you grow up."

Dear mother, she did not know and could not even imagine that I did not forget then and will not be able to forget till I close my eyes for the last time in this mortal life … as I have and feel that pain every minute of my life, in my aching body and soul, in joy and in sorrow, in want and in plenty.

Despite his sore leg, Aram continued to make his daily visits to the family shoe store until his uncle Haroutioun, noticed his pale and feverish countenance and sent him home.

Aram continues the narrative by describing the difficulties the family faced in obtaining proper medical care for him:

> That night I was not able to sleep at all. Next day our family doctor came, Haroutioun Shirinian, a fine kindhearted man. He gave me some medicine and put hot water bottles all around my body, and for days he kept doing the same, day in and day out. I was burning with fever ... In the meantime, when father was away, our well-meaning neighbors and friendly womenfolk would come and suggest all kinds of medicines, "old women's medicine" and treatments, and my mother obligingly did all that was suggested! Dear mother, maybe did not know how I was tortured ...
>
> Two or three weeks later, my leg had swelled 4 or 5 times its size and a small blister showed up where I was bruised in my fall ... so the doctor came and pierced it and lots of blood and pus came out. Gradually, the swelling came down somewhat, my high fever was gone, but I was in bed yet. Three or four months later, a small piece of bone came out through the opening where the doctor had pierced. Dr. Shirinian suggested to operate and clean it out, but because he could not do it all by himself, Dr. Karikin Sewny was to help him, but the Turks had put him in jail as supposed revolutionist. Being a U.S. citizen, he was released and at once left for America. Then father was planning to take me to Dr. Dad in Talas, the American Mission hospital, but the Turkish government did not permit father to go to Talas because of revolutionary movements.

For such an energetic child, Aram's confinement to his home must have been psychologically demoralizing. Yet this confinement may well have contributed to the keen photographic eye that he was to develop. He was now constantly creating images in his mind that half a century later would find their way into his memoir:

> I was confined to bed for several years. I was not cured, but there was gradual improvement. Often I could get around sore-footed. But day in and day out to be confined to bed was unbearable for me as a child, so they moved my bed to the corner by the windows so that I could enjoy the outside activities and surely there was plenty going on outside on both winter or summer days.
>
> Early in the morning I would wake up to the barking of street dogs, the crowing of cocks, or the constant bellowing or ba, ba, of the cows, sheep and goats, as in the morning, the shepherds of several sections of the city would gather the animals from different houses and take them in groups for grazing in the fields, through our street, Balık Sokak. It was some scene to watch them go out and return back

home in the evening in groups of 100 or more. Each animal quite well knows which street to turn or what door is hers ... It was interesting to watch the poor people following them closely to collect the manure or drop[ing]s. They would collect and put it in molds and dry it for fire[wood] substitute.

Again, early in the morning rain or sunshine, or on frozen snow, I would watch the old folks going to church murmuring, "Praise the Lord, praise the Lord." I used to wonder why they used to say, "Praise the Lord," all the time. Now that I am an old man myself, I can't do anything else but praise the Lord. It was a daily expectation for me to watch Bedros Surpazan Tahmigian going to his Vank Sourp Nishan (the monastery). He was a kind and sweet old bishop. Often, whenever I could, I used to go with my sister Parantzem to the door and stand for salute with folded arms and he would bless us with a sweet smile, riding on his chestnut color horse and maroon color "Damascus" saddle. Another daily joy was Tatos Aghbar (Cartozian). He used to haul rock from the quarry, especially when he was going up empty, he used to stand up on the planks and drive his beautiful white horses galloping with their long manes and tails floating in the air. Another real joy was to see Pasha's big sleigh going to his flour mill, his brown horses galloping, decorated with sweet-sounding bells and rattles. On Sunday mornings it was my delight to see the beautiful American flag on top of the U.S. Consulate building folding and unfolding as the wind blows up on high against the blue sky. I used to watch for hours, never knowing that some day that beautiful flag would be my flag and the flag of my children ...

On Sundays I used to enjoy watching the games, in different places, on the plaza across, [played] by children, young men, and even middle-aged men, and horse racing, horseback javelin-throwing and many other activities. In the afternoon, the army band used to drill and play wonderfully to amuse the people.

Aram experienced fevered nightmares that continued for years. During Aram's extended illness, both his mother and father died. Earlier in his memoir he described how his parents had been taken away from him by cholera and typhoid. The decade ahead was one of hardship and struggle.

In rereading his account of the years he spent confined to his home and often confined to his bed, I am suddenly reminded of a series of childhood illnesses that confined me to my bed and home. I can't recall at what age but sometime before I began school as a kindergartener, I developed rheumatic fever, followed by asthma and anemia. These diseases were ever-present in my earliest recollections. While in no sense equivalent in duration to Aram's condition, I distinctly remember weeks of never getting out of my pajamas. The rheumatic fever kept me at home for months on end. Like my great-uncle Aram, I spent hours staring out the windows of my house. My bedroom overlooked our garden, but since it was devoid of most human activity during the daylight hours – my brother was already in school and my father at work – I often placed myself in the front street-facing room, which had been a porch but was now enclosed though poorly heated. While 94th Street in East Elmhurst had its fair share of bustle with cars and people, it did not compare to Aram's account of a marching army band playing music, or instances of "horse racing" and "horseback javelin-throwing." Like Aram, I was allowed on occasion to leave the house but this was a mixed blessing. I was not to be on my feet for any length of time, so my parents put me in a stroller, which was humiliating, as I was too old to be pushed around in a stroller, especially by my brother who was only a year and a half my elder. My gangly body was too big for the stroller, and I felt that everyone was staring at me, thinking, this boy needs to grow up. I especially recall looking away when children my age were in the vicinity. Eye-balling dogs at their height level was not a pleasure either.

I realize now that this childhood illness must have been particularly troubling and embarrassing to my parents and grandmother. I have memories of sitting on the large leather upholstered chairs in Doctor Panvini's office listening to the conversations my mother had with the good doctor. He explained my anemia and the importance of bolstering my diet. I will never forget the pained expression on my poor mother's face. I can imagine what may have been going through her mind. I was skin and bones; she had survived untold hardships in Marsovan, Samsun and as a refugee in Greece. Though the memoirs do not overly dwell on the difficulties of obtaining food during the war years and its aftermath, there certainly were times when my family did not know where its next meal was coming from. There are a few photos of my mother taken during that period in which she is distinctly skinny, a condition she was never to emulate again. Having lost so much as a people, Armenians across the world pride themselves on their cuisine. Food, and lots of it, looms large in the Armenian cultural landscape. Here was my dear mother, now living in the land of plenty, being told that she must have her child eat more! While not given as an admonishment, these words must have cut very deeply into her Armenian soul. She had failed one of the supreme tests of Armenian motherhood: feeding, or should I say overfeeding, one's children. I recall her grieved responses to the doctor, "But he just won't eat anything we give him." The good doctor advised that it didn't matter what I ate, just as long as I ate something. I am embarrassed to say that my stubbornness with regard to food matters forced my parents to go to great lengths to indulge my narrowed culinary horizons. Apple pie and orange juice were my gastronomic universe. Not just any apple pie, for it had to be from a particular cafeteria-like establishment on 82nd Street near the Roosevelt Avenue elevated subway line. My father would gather me up and off we would go by bus to this emporium of bland, non-ethnic cuisine. Why was my food fixation not centered on paklava or bourma, foods plentiful in our household? Was I trying to be as American as apple pie even at the early age of five?

4

The Hamidian Massacres of 1894–96 and their Aftermath

The Background to the Events of November 1895

Despite the growing prosperity of the Dildilians of Sivas, the 1890s began with some ominous signs for the Armenian community. In 1890 Sultan Abdul Hamid II authorized the formation of a well-armed force of irregular cavalry consisting of tribesmen of the local Kurds, Turks, and Turkmens, ostensibly to provide security along the Ottoman border with Russia. Known as the Hamidiye Alaylari, these forces provided the sultan with a degree of control over the Kurdish tribes he had long tried to suppress and a weapon to wield against any Armenian attempts to assert rights long denied them.

Troubles had already been brewing in the countryside of the vilayet of Sivas prior to the full-scale massacres in the autumn of 1895. Aram describes a series of incidents that portend the evil that was to descend upon the Armenian provinces. He also attempts to provide some context for the fate of the Armenians under the sultan's yoke.

> When our last remaining Cilician kingdom was lost and the Armenians were subjugated to the Ottoman Turks, for a while they did treat the Armenians quite well and fairly, but for two reasons. First, they scattered the Armenians all over Asia Minor so that they would not be able to come together and revolt, and kept them also in the minority. Second, because Armenians were industrious people, they moved them all over to build up the country everywhere. They made them build mosques, minarets, bridges, fountains, flour mills, and palaces, especially on the shores of the Bosporus and Marmara seas. Everywhere they were good tailors, shoemakers, blacksmiths, carpenters, and all kinds of copper, silver, and goldsmiths. They made fine pottery and all kinds of household goods and war weapons for the army.
>
> On the other hand, the Turks were the landlords, government officials, fighting force ... These conditions in time became more accentuated so that there

were no craftsmen among the Turks. Armenians, being smart and progressive soon bettered themselves. Wherever they were taken or moved by force, soon they became rich and active in every business enterprise. Everywhere the Armenians had the best houses, best fruit gardens and best stores and shops. The Armenian quarters were in the finest sections and they were making a real comfortable living. So the orders always were to move them around to keep them under their thumb.

Later, the Sultans started a systematic and gradual annihilation of the Armenians by constant persecutions and other methods. The Sultans, in the past, established the "Yenicharies" [Janissaries] composed of rejected children of forced marriages of Armenian girls kidnapped or otherwise, as a fighting force. They were free to pillage, rob, and kill Armenians, but later, Sultan Asiz saw the folly and the danger of such irresponsible power and put an end to them.[1] Then, in my lifetime, Sultan Hamid [Abdul Hamid II] organized a regiment out of Caucasian refugees, bandits, and highwaymen called "Miralays" [*Hamidiye Alaylari*]. Their uniform was Circassian, a long coat with silver decorations with a black (papakh) hat made of newborn lambskin, and a silver emblem of Sultan Hamid. Their field of activities was around Sivas state where there were thousands of Armenian villages and farms. They robbed, killed and used all kinds of means to annihilate Armenians and took possession of those rich villages and farmlands.

In spite of all those systematic killings and persecutions, Armenians all over Asia Minor, especially in the last 100 years, were much more awake spiritually, financially and intellectually than any other people in the country, that is, Turks, Kurds, Greeks, and others. They had a better schooling system from kindergarten up to high school and college. They had the finest church buildings and church institutions like orphanages, hospitals, etc.

From what he has written, Aram clearly took great pride in the accomplishments of the Armenian people. A not-so-hidden assumption behind this account is the belief that both jealousy and resentment motivated the persecution of the Armenians of the empire. This common view persists among Armenians today. Many share another persistent belief that the Armenian minority was primarily urbanized. Aram's list of occupations is for the most part true, though he underemphasizes the large Armenian peasant population who pursued agricultural activities. This population received the greatest pressure from the more nomadic Kurdish tribes and felt the burden of the double taxation imposed by the Porte and local Kurdish chieftains.

Despite his description of a litany of evils perpetrated against the Armenian population, Aram does find the time to praise one Ottoman administrator who stood out as a morally upright individual, defending Armenian rights and lives. Rashid Pasha (Reshid Akif Pasha) was the *vali* (governor-general) of the vilayet of Sivas:[2]

"Miralay" [*Hamidiye Alaylari*] regiments of whom I wrote were authorized to destroy all the Armenian villages gradually. They were free to kill, rob, rape the women and subjugate them to forced labor and gradually got hold of their land and possessions. No one could complain about them as complaints were disregarded by high officials.

Finally, it was up to Rashid Pasha, the governor of Sivas state, who put an end to them. He sent those "Miralay" regiments in whole to Hijas to fight the Arabs, and not one single person came back. By the way, that Rashid Pasha was a singularly just and righteous governor who later became a member of the Turkish parliament. In 1915 during the Armenian deportation, he was the only high-standing person who dared to protest the wholesale destruction of Armenians in Asia Minor. In Marsovan, my brother and I had the honor to take his picture in our studio ... We made a big life-size enlargement, 3x6 feet, in a wide gold frame and presented it to him. He was very much pleased and ordered a royal medallion of merit, but, sorry to say, we never got it.

In those days, besides many untold atrocities that took place in the villages and countrywide, many terrible things happened right in Sivas. In our neighborhood, two strong young men were killed in the open by Turks. One day, there was an Armenian wedding near our house and after the church ceremony, the wedding party was coming back home in procession, playing and singing wedding songs according to Armenian custom. The Turks came in force, kidnapped the bride and went away on horseback. The bridegroom with others went after them, freed the bride, but soon after, the bridegroom died of his wounds.

Another time, the uncle of my father, Hadji Mourad, was butchered like cattle. They bound his arms and legs and cut off his head. No one did anything about it, and nobody was jailed. On the other hand, if an Armenian was suspected of any insignificant deed or action, it was enough to put him in jail for months without trial, as in my father's case.

The above account evidences an admirable trait in Aram's writing. He willingly praises Ottoman individuals who acted virtuously toward the Armenians while at the same time condemning the horrors perpetrated against his people.

Aram now takes up the issue of Armenian resistance to oppression. This issue lies at the heart of the Armenian Question as debated by historians to this day.

With constant murders, killings, and all sorts of molestations as everyday happenings, it was quite natural for Armenians to revolt ... Revolt, yes, the only way to be freed from Turkish yoke and rule. In the past the Greeks, Serbians, Romanians, and Bulgarians have been freed with the direct help and aid of England and Russia, so why not the Armenians? We did try, and failed, for a good many reasons: #1, we did not have the right type of leaders; #2, we did not have the sure promise or guarantee of either Russia or Great Britain; #3, the three big powers' interests were contrary to one another; #4, the geographical situation – Armenia being a land-locked country, we were not within easy reach of outside help; #5, we were scattered all over Asia Minor – we were not in the majority. So we did try, and failed … But I must state that it was not a general uprising either but a start of a movement. But before it got momentum, the Turkish government, being experienced, was quick to act. Besides jailing and hanging the leaders, the Sultan Hamid ordered a well-planned and systematic massacre, led by local authorities, inspiring the fanatic mob to kill, rob, and pillage the Armenians. Their password was, "The Gavoors (infidels) have trampled the main Mosque." This took place in 1894 and lasted up to 1896 in different towns and at different times, I guess to keep the Armenians in constant fear and anxiety. Those great Armenian massacres took place everywhere, always on Friday (their holy day). They killed more than 300,000 Armenians. Yes, here and there a few influential Turks kept and protected their neighboring Armenians, which I do consider a grace. Yet pillaging, ransacking, robbing, and plundering were general and the poverty that followed was indescribable.

Aram's interpretation of these events is interesting and rather controversial. While his account of the lack of Western support for the aspirations of the Armenians is defensible, the claim that Armenians were in "revolt" in the 1890s is not supportable by most historical accounts. Violent persecutions had already begun when the Armenian nationalist parties organized an armed resistance in Sassoun at the start of 1894. The scale and extent of Armenian resistance was not comparable to that of the Greeks, Serbs, Romanians and Bulgarians, though in the mind of Sultan Abdul Hamid the threat posed was certainly perceived as real.

The Massacres Arrive in Sivas

The massacres that had begun early in October 1895 in Constantinople quickly spread across the Armenian vilayets of the empire. They soon arrived in Sivas. Troubles in the countryside commenced in late October and by early November, consular reports by Dr. Milo Jewett confirmed the fact that whole villages and towns were being pillaged by bands of Dersim Kurds and others. Aram provides a harrowing account of the events in Sivas:

When … the Turks passed the word (rumor) that the Infidels (Gavoors) had attacked the Mosque … we heard gunshots far and near, right and left, everywhere. I was sick in bed. Soon, about 50 Turkish soldiers came from guardhouses and threw a chain from Mr. Hubbard's house to our door, across the plaza [blocking] the doorway of the Armenian quarters (see map of Sivas).

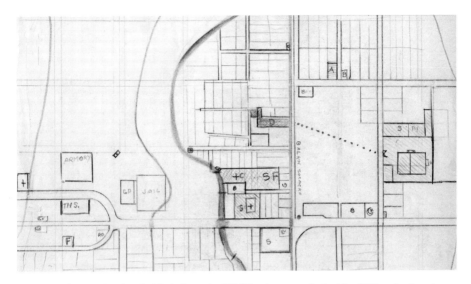

26. Aram's map showing the chain from the Dildilian home marked with a "D" to the American Mission compound of the Hubbards across the plaza. The Hubbards were not in residence, prevented from returning by the authorities in Constantinople. The American ("A") and British ("B") consulates were protected on the plaza's northern end.

The commander, Aly Bey, came and asked for a chair so my sister Haïganouch at once gave him a chair. Then he said, "My child, don't be scared, I am here to protect you, the Armenians." Yes, sure enough, that chain of soldiers did not let any Turks pass to the Armenian quarter, but they did not permit the Armenians to go to their homes either.

Just before the shooting started, a Turkish friend came to my uncle's shoe shop and told him, "Haroutioun, close the shop and hurry home." So uncle closed the shop, sent his help home, and hurries back home, but on the way, the shooting started. He goes on through the regular short road but when he sees some killing in the distance on the river bank, he turns to the main road. When he came to the river at the bridge "Lan Gamourge" he sees more killings in front of the Protestant school. He was so near home but he had to take another road to avoid killers, a longer road to our home. When he was about to turn into the street, he sees our gardener, Soulayman, a sharp yataghan knife in his hand and a revolver in his belt. Uncle wants to say hello but Soulayman, with a sharp and harsh voice, orders him to hurry and get out of his sight. So uncle hurries his steps. When he came to our backyard door, he was wondering how he would be able to get in. Just about that moment, my hero sister, Haïganouch, goes to the backyard to make sure that the backyard door is locked. Just at that time, uncle knocks at the door saying, "Haïganouch, it's me, open the door." You can imagine our great joy and praises. Just then, the commander, Aly Bey, knocked at the door and asked for a glass of water as it was a hot day. When sister gave him the water, Aly Bey sees the anguish

71

on her face. He repeats the same assurance saying, "My child, do not worry, as long as I am here nothing will happen to you." Then my sister said, "We have a back door, what if some people come over to the back door?" He said, "You just let me know, my child. I will take care of it." We had a window door in the inner room that opens onto the big balcony. The lock was inside and no one could open it from outside. Sister made sure to lock that window lock too. About that time the mob comes to the next door neighbor's, Khoigian's house. They all run to their garden at once and their older daughter, Haïganouch, puts a step-ladder to our balcony and starts hollering, but no use! We could not hear her as we were in the front room. She was a strong girl so, with a prayer in her heart, she gave a hard kick to the iron railing of the window … and the window was wide open. She rushed to the front room, half excited and said, "Turks are in our house." So my sister let Aly Bey know about it. By the time he took two soldiers and made the round of the block, they had already ransacked up to the second floor. Then sister Haïganouch, the only active mind and body, made a cup of Turkish coffee and served the commander with a piece of paklava. He was very pleased with that unexpected treat.

It was about 5:30 p.m. and my little sister, Nevart, had not come home yet from school. We were somewhat worried. A little later, the town crier announced that His Highness, His Majesty the King Sultan Hamid, had granted pardon to Armenians and there would be no more killings (yet killing continued that night and for several days and we did not feel safe for months). About 6 p.m., the Kavaz, the guard of the U.S. Consulate brought over my little sister, Mariam (later called Nevart as we had Mariam, my sister-in-law). When the shooting started, the Turkish officers took all the Protestant school children to Mr. Hubbard's house for safekeeping. On the way, my sister saw the Turks butchering an Armenian. Anyhow, we were glad and thankful to God that our family came out most fortunate out of all that killing. My uncle, Mikael and his family, were safe and all of our near and far relatives. Several months later, we were told that my dear brother, Tsolag, was safe in Marsovan. Our shoe shop, the only means for a living, was robbed and ruined and the benches, chairs, shelves, showcases were smashed to pieces. Uncle was not able to get any kind of job. The massacre happened at a time when we had no time to store our winter provisions, so for several months we had only brown, gritty bread given by the Turkish government, though it was not enough for all of us. Finally, one blessed day, we got $50 in money order from the American Mission, sent by dear brother from Marsovan, and later, a sewing machine so that uncle could restart his shoe making business.

From Aram's account it is clear that the Sivas massacres were selective in nature. The authorities appeared to exempt certain neighborhoods but not others. The commercial center of town, where the overwhelming majority of businesses were owned by Armenians, suffered the most. The Dildilian home was located near the American mission and the American and British consuls. Whether this proximity protected the Dildilian home is not clear. The past favorable relations with the governor or a personal connection to Aly Bey, enhanced by his love of paklava and coffee, may have been the cause. We will never know.

Maritsa provides a strikingly similar account of that day but with further gruesome details. As may be expected a reference to food introduces her report:

Krikor Agha had for a long time recommended that we always had at home enough reserves of biscuits, pancakes and *péksimits*. "One of those days, these dogs are going to turn evil, organize slaughters. Be careful to have food for at least some days. And if anything of that sort happens, get to the roof," he repeated.

One day, we hear the Turks shouting as if it were a password: "The mad buffalo is coming." And they repeat the phrase while running everywhere in the bazaar. Soon after, they show up with cudgels. The Armenians are terrified; they close their shops and workshops. They try to get back home.

An Armenian shoemaker thought he could enjoy the protection of a Turk, a bey, an influential gang leader with whom he had always had a deferential attitude. And that day, he was treating him with kebab. In view of the approaching danger, he prayed the Turk to leave for he had to close his workshop and go back home. "Have no fear, I am here," reassured the treacherous Turk who, after he had enjoyed his food, beheaded the Armenian himself on his own work bench.

Haïganouch hears shouts in the street: "*Mouslouman olan dépo-ya gèlsin Martini alsen.*" (That anyone who is a Muslim come to the weapons depot and take a Martini rifle.) The depot is very close, across the street. So she closes the doors and locks them as best as she can with whatever she finds. Soon after, a knock is heard at the back door. Anxiously, she goes to see what it is. My God, it is her uncle who came through the back and is begging: "Haïganouch, quick, open!" But she has pushed a lot of objects against the door and she must now remove them one by one, and in particular a big cask she had rolled to the door. At last, she can open the door. Her uncle falls inside. His first word is: "Is Sumpad home?" For he knew his son was often out in the streets. "He is home." So they blocked the door again and retired inside.

The police channel the crowd so that each one may have a weapon. Nearly all the consuls live in our part of the town. The police have the duty to protect them and their homes. A very tired policeman knocks at the main door. They recognize him and ask him what he wants. "Some water," he begs. They lower a mug of water to him with a string. "Don't be afraid," says the policeman, "there is no threat to you." And, in truth, nothing happened to them. How come the policeman asked for water from them? In fact, his beat was the Bézirdjoun sector, just across the street, and he knew our family. He always remained close to our house during the massacres.

The furious crowd is at work, killing unsparingly. Often, they break into houses to kill and loot. A Turk who had lost the use of his legs had attached pieces of wood to his knees and arms and he walked thus, on all fours, shouting and repeating: "Give me a *giaour* so that I, too, may go to heaven." A young boy of 18, a neighbor, had been beaten nearly to death; the crowd gave the boy to him so that he may finish him off, which he did by crushing his head with a large stone. Markarid, Haïganouch's younger sister, had observed that horrible scene. She never forgot it. Fear caused her a belly ache. Every now and then, her sister had to take her to the closet and this lasted for days.

Our neighbors, the Khelkheligians ... seeing that the crowd was furiously trying to break open their door and that the door would not hold much longer, climbed on their terrace, and from there passed over to ours. There, they tried to open our roof door. Their daughter-in-law ... gave such a blow with her feet, crying "Lord in Heaven!" that the door broke. They came in and stayed with us until the end of the massacre. When they went back home, their house had been looted.

Haïganouch's heroics are again highlighted, in this case by her daughter. Unbeknownst to each other, Aram and Maritsa wrote down these accounts many years later while living an ocean apart. In both accounts we see that the violence came as close as the next-door neighbor's house. Both memoirs paint a surreal picture: a chain across a plaza, a friendly police officer eating his paklava while he guards their home, yet across the city Armenians are being hunted down and killed.

Over the course of the next five days, the ferocity of the massacres diminished but their devastating consequences were to last for years. In a dispatch to the State Department dated November 16, 1895, American Consul Milo Jewett detailed the events that transpired outside the consulate walls during those days:

The massacre we feared at Sivas but hoped might be averted has taken place ... The massacre was anticipated and some Armenians were warned beforehand by Turkish friends that it would occur on Tuesday the 12th instant, as it did occur. On that morning on the demand of the government the Armenian priests directed the Armenian shopkeepers to be in their shops in the market as usual.

About 11 o'clock a.m. the massacre began suddenly in the market, streets devoted to shops and stores. The Mohamedans rushed upon the Armenians and began killing them and plundering shops. The rioters were mostly of the younger rough class of Mohamedans of the city, Kars emigrants and the military force of the city. At first the rioters used their clubs chiefly, but as the soldiers and gendarmes rushed into the market and began to shoot the Armenians, the bashibazooks used their swords, daggers and firearms with terrible effect.

The number killed up to date seems to be between 800 and 1000 Armenians and about ten Turks. The number wounded is much below the usual proportion to the number killed because the wounded were as a rule finished before they found a place of refuge. From personal observation and a very large amount of corroborative testimony there is not a shadow of doubt in my mind that the soldiers, gendarmes and police were about as actively engaged in killing and looting as the Mohamedans and that the Government made no serious attempt to stop the affair until about 9 o'clock the next morning.[3]

The death toll in the city ultimately rose to over 1,500 Armenians, while the total numbers in the countryside were significantly higher. I will not attempt to cover the extent of the death and destruction of Armenian life in the vilayet of Sivas nor in the five other Armenian vilayets and the coastal vilayet of Trebizond. Suffice it to say, the damage had been done. Armenians were to suffer the consequences for years to come.

The Aftermath of the Massacres

Reading through the American diplomatic correspondence in this period of the Hamidian Massacres, I was struck by how narrowly focused was the American concern for life. Yes, diplomats are posted overseas to look after their nation's interests. In the case of the Ottoman Empire, American interest primarily focused on their missionaries and schools scattered across the interior provinces of the empire. At this point in time there were approximately 150 American missionaries in various cities in the Armenian vilayets. Alexander Watkins Terrell, United States Minister Plenipotentiary to the Sublime Porte, the equivalent of an ambassador in today's terminology, sent the following telegram to his Secretary of State, Richard Olney, back in Washington, D.C.:

> Mr. Terrell to Mr. Olney
>
> Constantinople, November 15, 1895
>
> By telegram from Jewett it is reported that 800 Armenians and 10 Turks have been killed in the last few days in Sivas. The approach of Koords on the city is reported by an officer. Killing Malacia [Malatya] Jesuits is not confirmed. Consul of France telegraphs 4,000 killed at Kurun [Gürün]. Barnum telegraphs eight of our missionary houses burned at Harpoot, rest plundered; missionaries safe. Will you authorize me to demand instant payment for burned buildings. Kaimakam of Hadjin threatens to burn town and sow it with barley. Three American ladies are there; I have notified the Sublime Porte that if one of them is hurt, I will demand the head of that governor. No longer an Armenian question, but one of humanity …
>
> –Terrell

Granted that telegrams sometimes convey messages that lack in subtlety, the juxtaposition of the idea that three American ladies are in danger with the striking phrase, "No longer an Armenian question, but one of humanity" is mind-boggling to say the least. Had it not been a question of humanity when the aforementioned 4,000 were slaughtered in Gürün? Some people's lives are worth more than others, especially if they are American. This is true today as it was back in 1895. Secretary Olney sent back to Terrell two very brief telegrams that very same day. The first read: "Demand payment for burned buildings." The second: "It would allay anxiety of missionaries' friends here to know whether Russian ships in Black Sea would not protect American missions at Trebizond, Sassoun [sic], and other points on coast. Answer." The obsession with compensation for the destroyed missionary property in Harpoot and Marash continued into the next century, with even President William McKinley bringing up the issue of Harpoot in his State of the Union address in 1900. Eventually the Porte came up with some compensation for the Americans – the Armenians were not so fortunate.

Compensation was never given but humanitarian aid soon arrived. The Hamidian Massacres gave rise to the first international American humanitarian relief mission spearheaded by Clara Barton, founder of the American Red Cross. Aided by the network of missionaries in the Anatolian interior, relief work began on an unprecedented scale, continuing well into the next century. Much has been written about this period and these efforts, but I will only focus upon the devastating consequences for the Dildilian family. These humanitarian efforts brought members of the Dildilian family into closer cooperation with the American missionaries and their social and educational institutions. While members of the family would struggle on in their ancestral home of Sivas, my grandfather and most of his siblings would soon rebuild their lives and fortunes in Marsovan. Their lives were increasingly intertwined with those of the American missionaries and teachers.

Can I indirectly attribute the fact that I am sitting here in America more than a century later to these horrific events in the autumn of 1895? The massacres would eventually lead to the relocation of much of the family to Marsovan, a city with a significant American presence. Twenty years later, that presence made a difference as to who was able to survive. No member of the extended Dildilian family remaining in Sivas survived the deportations in the summer of 1915.

Aram describes the effects of the massacres on the family. His uncle Haroutioun was now the sole support of the extended family: "All ten of us were looking to my dear uncle who had no job or means to make money. It was not safe for him to go around to search for work, besides there was no work … We did not have enough to eat for several months. Finally my dear brother was able to send us financial help … It is hard to explain the want and sufferings that we went through."

The commercial and agricultural economy was in ruins. Given the autumn timing of the destruction, preparations for the winter could not be completed. Because of the elevation of Sivas, winters can be severe, and the winter of 1895–96 proved to be no exception. As Aram had already mentioned, feeding a family of ten had become a challenge. Maritsa describes scarcities:

As to the farmers, they were themselves impoverished. With only a few dozen cows left in the country districts, there is not even an *okka* [1.2829 kilograms] of butter to be found in town, whereas before, butter double-salted or not used to be delivered to town markets in wooden boxes all year long. Not a drop of honey is available, whereas before, we used to buy two pails in spring and autumn. The cattle market is empty, whereas before, livestock used to be by the hundreds.

The wheat harvest had been compromised, the flour mills and bakeries destroyed. Even putting bread on the table became a challenge:

During that period of destitution, Haroutioun was often told to buy sesame-flour bread – that is low-quality bread – which he had always refused, saying: "As long as I live, I shall never let my nephews eat sesame-flour bread." And, truly, his orphan nephews never ate sesame-flour bread, but Haroutioun bought it for him and his son. At that time, we had to content ourselves with whatever we could find. Haroutioun did not entrust his nephews and nieces to the orphanage newly founded by the Americans and kept them as his own children. And his wife, who was as generous as him, took care of them with all her soul and heart.

Reviving the shoe business was not going to be easy for Haroutioun. With little or no equipment, no credit and most importantly, no customers, alternatives had to be found. Maritsa describes how her mother Haïganouch tried to help the family with home textile work: "At home, we started to spin wool and knit thick woolen stockings for horse-cart and mule drivers, but this did not bring in much money. Haïganouch was doing her best to help her aunt who was not always in good health. She knew that her uncle and aunt made sacrifices for her and her brothers and sisters. At night, with the moonlight to help, she knitted at least one pair of stockings." Though much of the family continued to struggle on in Sivas, the massacres marked the beginning of their dispersal to other cities in Anatolia.

5

The Dildilians Begin their Separate Paths

Marsovan and Samsun in the Life of the Dildilian Family

The years following the Hamidian Massacres were momentous in the communal life of the Armenians of the empire. While there had always been periods of dispersal and migration during the nearly 3,000-year history of our people, immigration increased markedly after 1896. Immigration to the United States was still a relatively easy proposition then; that is, if one was healthy, not Chinese, and had sufficient funds to pay for a long and arduous journey. Often male members of a family, those who were young and fit, would emigrate to establish themselves before bringing the rest of the family over. The first Armenian churches, both Apostolic and Protestant, were founded in New England and California during the last decade of the nineteenth century. Despite the incredible hardships of the years following the Hamidian Massacres, the Dildilians did not emigrate from their historic homeland.

After the death of his parents in 1894, Tsolag increasingly turned his attention to his photography work in Marsovan. His studio had a steady stream of customers as a result of the presence of Anatolia College and the associated Girls' Boarding School. Krikor had died in late August and within a few days President Tracy had sent an invitation to Tsolag to return and take up work for the college with the start of the new academic year. Given the increasing demands of the business, Tsolag brought his talented cousin, Sumpad, with him from Sivas. Sumpad was the only child of his uncle Haroutioun. With the death of his brother Krikor, Haroutioun was now the sole proprietor of the shoe business. Sumpad was 16 years old and among the boys of the household the closest in age to Tsolag. The closeness was more than a matter of age, for Tsolag often refers to Sumpad in fraternally affectionate terms such as "my dear brother Sumpad."

Marsovan, though significantly west of the historic Armenian Highlands, had a substantial Armenian population and as such was susceptible to the troubles that were brewing as a result of Abdul Hamid's increasing repression of his Armenian subjects and their increasing demands for reform. The Hunchakian Revolutionary Party was becoming very active in the region with matters having reached a crisis in January and February of 1893. The American missionaries of Anatolia College struggled to maintain neutrality in this politicized atmosphere, but they became implicated with the so-called revolutionaries when placards denouncing the sultan appeared on the college gates in early January 1893. Two Armenian professors of the college were arrested and tortured, but escaped execution, and were eventually deported after pressure was brought to bear on the Porte by England and Russia. With the start of the next school year, the political atmosphere deteriorated significantly in Marsovan and the surrounding region. Violent incidents and arrests were becoming common. All throughout this period, Tsolag dutifully continued to take photographs in Marsovan but chose not to comment on the turmoil surrounding him. His close association with the college would prove fortuitous when the massacres reached Marsovan on November 15, 1895. There are multiple missionary and consular accounts of the events of November but Tsolag only briefly touches upon them 30 years later in his speech:

> The same year [1895], the governments of [Great Britain, France and Russia] forced the sultan to accept changes to the constitution, the result of which were massacres and looting in the six [Armenian] provinces. At the time, I was in Marsovan College's safety and my brothers [and sisters were] in Sivas where all our possessions were looted. We were naked. My uncle and his wife with love were taking care of my brothers' and sisters' needs.

Though the destruction of the commercial life of the Armenians in Marsovan was as extensive as that in Sivas, the loss of life was significantly less. It appears from some accounts that the government made a greater effort to limit the violence in Marsovan than it did in most cities and villages across the Armenian provinces. Reverend George E. White, who was an eyewitness, described what happened:

> In Marsovan the storm broke on Friday, November 15th, at the hour of the noon call to Moslem prayer. For four hours the city was turned over to the Turkish mob for the massacre of Armenians, and the looting of their property. About 125 men were killed, and most of the Armenian shops were picked as clean as a bone. The first rush of the mob was for the American premises. But we were mercifully spared such invasion. Crowds of frightened refugees flocked into our houses, and some bullets struck the Girls' School. About four o'clock the government, which as it were had been hibernating, resumed activity, and the governor visited our compound with a guard of some forty swarthy soldiers which he left to protect us … It was a black winter that followed that black Friday.[1]

This black winter must have been psychologically difficult for my grandfather. As the eldest of the seven orphaned siblings, he was thrust into a position of responsibility though he was only 22 years old. His brother Aram was only 11, while his four unmarried sisters' welfare called for attention. The primary responsibility for the siblings had fallen upon his uncle Haroutioun back in Sivas, but Tsolag continued to provide financial support as best he could. As reported earlier by Aram, Tsolag sent money and a sewing machine, enabling Haroutioun to reopen the shoemaking business. Yet this despair must have been weighing heavily on him, for thoughts of leaving Anatolia had entered his mind. He admits so many years later: "Financially, I did what I could but fear and fright was so widespread that my brother [cousin] Sumpad and I decided to go to Russia. As it is now like going to America: at that time Russia was rich and had plentiful opportunities." It appears that he and Sumpad traveled to Samsun in order to sail across the Black Sea to Russia. Fortunately for the rest of the family, my grandfather had a change of heart while in Samsun: "Well-positioned compatriots prevailed on us to remain in Samsun where there was a great demand for a photographer. We settled there for a while." I say that this was a fortunate change of heart because 20 years later his profession of photography would be crucial for saving his life and the life of most of his siblings. Unfortunately this would not be the case for Sumpad who perished in those early summer months of 1915.

With the opening of a studio in Samsun in 1895 and his continuing appointment as official photographer for Anatolia College, Tsolag began the expansion of the family photography business that would eventually see studios in a number of cities in Anatolia. While no longer having a permanent presence in Sivas, the Dildilians now had studios in Marsovan and Samsun. At some point around the turn of the century, Tsolag began to adopt the title "Dildilian Brothers" as the studio's name. I was always puzzled when I encountered photos from this period identified as taken by the Dildilian Brothers. Tsolag's brother Aram, who would later join him as a partner in the studio, was too young at the time to be considered the "Brother" in the studio title. But Tsolag's frequent identification of Sumpad as his brother now sheds light on the title of the studio. Sumpad and Tsolag would grow the business into one of the most important sources of photography in the region.

School and Church: Life Continues for Aram and his Siblings back in Sivas

The last decade of the nineteenth century witnessed the emergence into adulthood of the Dildilian siblings who remained in Sivas. Much of what we know of their lives in Sivas comes to us from Aram's and Maritsa's memoirs. Tsolag was increasingly absent from Sivas, having established himself in Marsovan. Aram gives us a rich account of his schoolboy years and describes an important turning point in his life. He explicitly chooses to identify his adoption of the Protestant faith as this "turning point." In many respects this was for Aram his "born again" experience. He admits at times to being a "bad boy" before his adoption of faith. Interestingly enough it was his brother Tsolag who played a role in steering him toward Protestantism by enrolling him in the Protestant school. Why Tsolag chose to send him to this school is not clear, but we do know that at some point Tsolag had himself adopted the Protestant faith. Of course there could have been a much more practical reason to send Aram to the Protestant school. At this time, Aram, as we know, was lame and the national school was much further away from their home than the Protestant school. The latter was just across the plaza from the Dildilian home. Aram writes:

> During all those upheavals, that is, first, my mother's death, then father's death, the massacres, and the following hard years, I had a sore leg but never complained, though most of the time I was in bed and was not able to go to school. Though weak and lame, I was able to get around. So my brother made arrangements, through Nazaret Frangulian, for me to attend the Protestant school, which I used to hate, for no special reason. I used to throw stones at the door and say hateful sayings, and Sivas people had plenty of such hateful sayings for Protestants. Many of our neighbors and friends were Protestant, like Prot Manoog, Prot Avedis, Prot Kaspar, Terzi Bedig, Cham Ovag. "Prot" means "leper," an insulting name.

Aram has identified a tension among the Armenians that is reflected in the memoirs and other writings about this period. Some Armenians of the Apostolic denomination resented the growing success of the Protestant community. Once Aram began attending the Protestant school his hateful behavior toward the Protestants changed. He came to love his teachers and describes the change of heart he was undergoing:

> The first day in school was very pleasant. I did like the schoolroom, the children, and my teacher, Nazaret Frangulian, very much. The school was not coeducational, but we were in the same compound with the girls. Movses Nahabedian, the teacher, was a good, alert, good-hearted man. He used to start the school day with a song or two. He would read from the Bible and utter a short prayer, or we would say the Lord's Prayer in unison ...
>
> Gradually I became a leader. I was not a bad boy, but not so good either! Our house was on the main street, Balık Sokak ... our district was famous for its fighting boys ... I started to play with those fighting boys and to use their swear words and do things that were not so good ... We had fights with the Turkish boys. As I said before, right in front of our house there was a big field, a plaza. The Turks were on the southeast side and we were on the northwest corner of that plaza, but the Turkish boys had the upper hand always. Either they did not go to school or, if they had school must have come out early as every day when we made the turn of Kel Tahir's corner, the Turks would be there and start stoning us. We would either

run off or try to hide and go home with some walker-by. One day, I told the boys to leave all our books in school and fill our bookcases and coat pockets with stones from the nearby river banks. When we came to the famous corner, Kel Tahir, the Turks were there ready to attack us. The fight started. This time we were able to make our corner safely. Then the other boys of our district who were famous fighters, joined us and with plenty of stones on our person, we chased the Turks to their corner … So, for the first time, we gave them a good licking and that was the last time they ever attacked us.

After that, I became a leader. My nickname was "Topal Konsol" after the French consul who had an artificial leg and was a very active man.

Despite his handicap, Aram was a keen observer of events around the city of Sivas. One of these observations relates to an important, yet dark moment in the history of the city:

I used to watch the men who were digging the foundation of the Armenian School on [the] "Sourp Kevork" grounds that is called "Sev-Hogher" (black dirt). While they were digging the foundation, there came out thousands of human skulls and bones piled up in big heaps and also they found a good many gold pieces called "Tukhshoon Hegna." The foreman wanted to keep it for the church treasury and the diggers wanted them for themselves. They had arguments with each other (all Armenians). Finally, the government found out and took all in its possession. It is said that when Genghis Khan came over and captured Sivas, he gave an order to "massacre the people." Then he sent messengers to find out what "the survivors are doing." They brought the report to his camp that "everyone is crying" so he ordered more massacre the next day, and the report back was that "the people are in mourning and crying," so he ordered the same for the third day and sent messengers to report. This time they reported that "everyone who has survived is singing and dancing." Then he let the people go as a vanquished people … The saying is that they piled all the dead or half-dead in that same spot of "Sev-Hogher" and had javelin play on horseback over the bodies. That is why it is called "Sev-Hogher."

This gruesome story has a kernel of historical truth within it. While no record exists of Genghis Khan himself ever having invaded central Anatolia, the thirteenth century was marked by a period of Mongol invasion and domination by the successors of Genghis Khan. Sivas at this time was under the rule of the Seljuks who had brought their Persian-influenced art, architecture, and learning to the city. Their rule came to a rather abrupt end in 1243 with the decisive defeat of the Seljuk sultan of Rum at the hands of the Mongol general Baiju-noyin at Köse Dağ, a halfway point between Sivas and Erzincan. Armenians fought on both sides in this battle, with the Caucasian or Eastern Armenian

83

princes having survived the earlier Mongol invasions as vassals to the Khan. Kayseri was sacked but the historical record merely notes the seizure of Sivas with no wholesale violence against its inhabitants. Aram may well be conflating a later invasion by the successor of the Mongols, the Khan Timur, historically known as Tamarlane. By 1400, the Ottomans had replaced the Seljuks as the dominant force in the Sivas region. Timur invaded Anatolia and marched on Sivas in 1401. The city was sacked and its Armenian population decimated. Soon after Timur defeated Bayezid I, the Ottoman sultan, in the Battle of Ankara on July 20, 1402. The Armenians who had fought with the Ottomans were severely punished by Tamarlane. Accounts vary but all are equally horrific: "Children sent out with garlands of flowers to placate Timur were trampled beneath the hooves of warriors' horses, and some 4,000 Armenian troops organized to defend the city were captured and buried alive."[2] Another account replaces the garlands with copies of the Qur'an but unfortunately the outcome was the same.[3] Sources identify the place where these children were slaughtered as the "Sev-Hogher" referred to in Aram's account.[4] The soil of Anatolia and the Armenian Highlands saw many invasions over the centuries. The Armenian inhabitants, whose long history on these lands dates back at least to the early sixth century BC, often fell victim to invading armies. Foretelling many future invasions, the first recorded reference to the people who would henceforth be known as the Armenians is found in the Persian King Darius I's identification of them as one of his conquered peoples. Yet these stubborn Armenians did not go down without a fight, for the same cuneiform inscription that pronounces their conquest also chronicles five ultimately unsuccessful attempts to rebel from Darius' rule.[5] Despite multiple overlords over the course of nearly three millennia, the Armenians clung to these lands until the catastrophic events of 1915.

Aram's memoir is rich in such historical asides as that of "Sev-Hogher." But central to his account of his school days is his conversion or "born again" experience. He places this in the context of his "bad boy" behavior:

> One day in the afternoon, the teacher was not at his desk to take the children in and start school, so, naturally, the boys started to play. We did not have benches and desks but we used to carry small pillows and put them in rows on straw carpets. Soon the pillows were flying all around, the big room was full of thick dust and we could hardly see each other. Then a bright idea came to my mind – the floor was covered with straw carpets so we put a boy in one of the rugs and rolled the rug over him kicking with our foot and rolling the whole from one wall to the other – we were imitating the felt makers. Just then, the teacher came in and like a mad man started to slap us right and left in every direction. He opened the windows and doors and made us put things in order but he did not give us a special punishment. I guess maybe he blamed himself more than the children because he was away from his duty.

27. Central Evangelical Union, Sivas, July 13, 1903. Rev. George E. White, future President of Anatolia College, 1913–33 (second row, second from left) and Professor Kevork H. Gulian (bottom row, fourth from left). Gulian was a famous teacher of the Armenian language and author of *Elementary Modern Armenian Grammar*.

At 4 p.m. when we were out of school, one of the big boys, Vahaken Ardzerooni, came to me and said, "Aram, you know you were a very bad boy. You know today you did crucify Jesus again." I said, "What? I? I crucified Jesus? Why? and How?" and I started to cry. He tried to explain to me how and why and said, "Would you like to be a good boy? Jesus will make you pure and white as snow." Then he said, "Would you like to come with me downstairs to Room No. 2?" I said, "Yes." When we went down there, some boys were praying on their knees. It was so sweet to see little boys praying and reading the New Testament like that. I went the next day to pray with these five boys. None of them was over 11 years of age, and finally, I, too, surrendered my heart to Jesus and He cleansed my heart and wiped my mouth and made me as pure as snow. When I say "my mouth" I mean to say that going around with street boys and playing with those bad boys, I had started to use swear words and use profane language. But, thanks to God, from that day on, not a dirty word came out of my mouth. Our number grew from five to twelve. Mr. Hubbard heard about us and came to our meetings several times to encourage us.

Aram's spiritual awakening was not an isolated event. The late 1890s were marked by a great spiritual revival, not unlike the great revivals (awakenings) that had taken place in the United States in the first half of the nineteenth century. Known as the Second Great Awakening, these religious revivals served as the impetus for the missionary movement that eventually brought such figures as Albert Hubbard and his wife Emma to Sivas. The Protestant presence in Sivas grew stronger as the century was coming to an end and the lives of the Dildilians were increasingly tied to this community.

Aram's uncle Haroutioun, now the head of the Dildilian clan, was also part of this great spiritual awakening in Sivas. Aram praises him as a man who "never smoked tobacco, never drank any intoxicating liqueurs" and made it his business to reform "the habitual drunkards" of Sivas – an early Armenian manifestation of the Temperance Movement that was gaining adherents in the West.

The spiritual rebirth of Aram was soon to be followed by a physical rebirth as our story shifts back and forth between Sivas and Marsovan.

A Sister's Wedding and the Travails of Marriage

The years 1896 and 1897 mark a significant moment in the diverging paths of the Dildilian siblings. Aram's older sister Haïganouch, a chief source of the family story, married in the early summer of 1896 despite the hardships created by the massacres of the previous autumn. By March of the following year, Aram made his life-changing journey to join his much-admired brother Tsolag in Marsovan.

Aram reports that by the summer of 1896 the family's fortunes were beginning to improve but everyone needed to contribute: "My sisters were kept busy in rug making to help the family's needs. My sister, Haïganouch, was engaged to Vosgian Der Haroutiounian before mother and father died, and before the massacre, but the wedding was postponed on account of those upheavals. My uncle tried to do everything in his power to make a good wedding for her so that she would not feel herself an orphan and neglected."

Vosgian Der Haroutiounian was a talented cabinetmaker and woodcarver. Unfortunately, like the Dildilians, his business was ruined during the 1895 massacres. Maritsa describes how her father escaped: "When the 1895 massacres started, my father managed to get back home. His shop had a small window high on a wall wherefrom air and some light came through, and that window opened onto the dwelling of a Turk. He managed to crawl through that opening and escape. Later, when he came back to his shop, he wondered how he had been able to go through such a narrow opening. Vosgian's shop had been gutted." He had to give up his shop and go to work for another craftsman, Moscofian.

Despite the hardships of both families, Vosgian was determined to marry Haïganouch. His industriousness and the goodwill of the *vali* again play a role in the family story:

86

One day, the new *vali*, who appreciates woodwork, notices my father's work and calls him to his house for some works. Vosgian works there for several months with a good pay. The *vali* in turn recommends him to someone else. That man, when he learns how Vosgian lives at home, advises him to marry. "I will lend you 5 gold pounds. You will refund the money in small installments."

After a two-year engagement, Vosgian made his proposal to the Dildilians. However, the Dildilians were in a difficult stretch and a marriage is always a costly affair, all the more so in those troubled days. And in addition, they wanted Haïganouch, although an orphan, to marry with pride.

Maritsa provides much detail regarding the marriage of her mother Haïganouch to her father Vosgian Der Haroutiounian. Armenian wedding customs play a big part in the description that follows. Haïganouch's orphaned status created difficulties in following the expected customs of the community. But given the hard economic times, these rigid customs were forced to bend. Maritsa continues her account:

Malicious gossip has already started, people sing:

"*Talani hars,*	[Eloped bride,
Tartalay hars,	Grieved bride,
Keloukhe pats,	Without headgear,
Vodkove kenats."	Goes on foot.]

This means that, contrary to tradition, she [the bride] does not wear heavy headgear and is not taken to church in a carriage or on horseback.

My mamig Elbiz [Uncle Haroutioun's wife] managed to get the necessary things by taking off from her own trousseau, so that everything could be in accordance with tradition, and she offered in addition what was left of her jewels, a few rings. The rule demands that the bride wears ten different rings on her fingers and that the ring on the right hand's middle finger be a seal ring. The one for my mother was in the form of a heart and the name "Haïganouch" was engraved in a delicate and tasteful pattern that set off the cleverly intertwined letters of her name when she put her seal on wax.

Some weeks before the wedding, the traditional *yérés déss* [face viewing] visit takes place. On that day, the bridegroom's side is invited to lunch at the bride's house and gold coins are placed around the bride's neck. My mother, who had not had her say previously, strongly opposed that ceremony and, surprisingly enough, won her case. This is how my mother explained it: "My poor uncle Haroutioun is going to organize a meal that will be so costly that he will endure more hardship. And the others, what gold have they to give? And it will anyway go back to them. So why?" Haïganouch was right. The boy's side had not enough money to eat suitably; zucchini soup was often served.

Maritsa goes on to detail the customary activities of the wedding week.

> Custom has it that, late on the Sunday, the bride and bridegroom's garments are taken in procession to the church. Surrounded by relatives, a young man proudly carries on his head a plate containing the bride's gown, headgear, tiara and shoes, and the bridegroom's shirt and necklace, all covered by a veil. The garments are blessed during vespers.
>
> On the Monday, the bride is dressed with the help of the sponsor and then taken to church to receive the wedding sacrament. On this occasion, the bride has to look sad but there are however songs, dances, music and much rejoicing. Even when she tries to smile, the bride feels tears in her eyes for it is now that she fully realizes the situation: she is going to be separated from her folks, find an unknown life, and this is a solemn realization, something sad, in fact.
>
> The bride must pretend she knows nobody. She is accompanied by a young woman whom she knows and who acts as an interpreter and intermediary because the bride must not speak to men. But, within one or two days, that woman will go back to her own home.
>
> The Wednesday is the day of the *arakast* [the nuptial sheet]. When my mother was left alone with my father, he started to talk to her and asked her to tell him about her brothers and sisters, especially about Tsolag who had remained in Marsovan. My mother answered with her naturally loud voice. The following morning, her mother-in-law told her that she spoke with too loud a voice. Haïganouch slowly realized what her situation was going to be.
>
> From the Sunday to the Wednesday, the bride must keep her veil on. And it was in this apparel that Haïganouch was handed the bedpan of her crippled mother-in-law and asked to empty it. To someone who had deplored that it was a pity to impose such a task to a bride still wearing her veil, it was answered that the sooner she got used to it the better.
>
> Such was Haïganouch's wedding who, at 18, was a princess in her home. Her life as a Der Haroutiounian started under these sad conditions.

Being a young bride in a traditional Armenian household in those days was not an easy burden to bear. My grandparents on my father's side of the family from the Palu region had married at a very early age. He was 14 and she was 16 years old. When I asked my parents why marry so early, my mother quickly snapped back something to the effect that my grandfather's mother must have been desperate for more household help. Young brides were servants often under the harsh dictates of their mothers-in-law. This was certainly the case for Haïganouch, especially so since her mother-in-law was a bedridden invalid. Vosgidzarig, Haïganouch's mother-in-law, did break one custom in her household. Maritsa identifies this exception: "My grandmother did only one thing right. In that first week, she lifted the prohibition against speaking which was traditionally imposed on the daughters-in-law. She put a ring on my mother's finger and said: 'I have been left on my own so long that, now I have a daughter-in-law, we are not going to keep silent.'"

A Brother's New Beginning: Aram's Journey to Marsovan

Haïganouch was the second of the Dildilian siblings to leave the family home after Tsolag, the eldest, who had returned to Marsovan to pursue his successful photography career. His success and the success of the ever-growing Anatolia College led to the departure from Sivas of the third sibling, Aram. It had been five years since he had first sustained the leg injury. Aram had continuing problems with infections from the wound that never fully healed. Medical care in Sivas was limited and rudimentary. With the arrival in Marsovan of an American-trained doctor, the opportunity for better medical treatment arose. Aram identifies the opportunity that opened for him:

> About that time in March of 1897, my brother, being quite successful in Marsovan, had established himself as official photographer of the Anatolia College. Anatolia College was one of the American colleges in Asia Minor …
>
> It was in 1897 that, for the first time, the Marsovan Mission had an American missionary physician in the person of Dr. T. S. Carrington. As soon as he organized a hospital, brother went to see him to inquire some information about me. He told him what had happened to me, how it did happen, what has been done so far, and if there was any hope of doing anything as it is over four years that I have been suffering! He said, "I cannot tell you much as one case differs from the other. Let him come over and I will surely do everything that is necessary." So brother wrote for me to come to Marsovan as soon as it is possible.

Aram began his journey to Marsovan with a high degree of hope tinged with the added prospect of joining his most dearly beloved brother:

> Though I had sore feet, I was able to get around and was feeling quite strong. It was in March of 1897 that was the happiest day for me for several reasons. Marsovan and Anatolia College had some kind of enchantment for me, as there I was to see my dear brother who I had not seen for about four years, and my cousin, Sumpad, who was in the college already. I thought I was going to some heavenly place.

The account of the journey from Sivas to Marsovan that Aram provides is fascinating in many respects. Besides giving an account of the villages and towns he passed through, he journeys ahead in time to events that will take place at these locales some 18 years later. For the memoirist this landscape was imbued with the memory of the deportation routes and the tragedies that would mark this land forever. Aram describes his parting: "Uncle arranged with an Armenian driver, a distant relative, to take me over, as he was going to Marsovan with his wife. A day before, I went to see Mr. Hubbard, Mary and Howie (his children), my playmates, to bid goodbye. He gave me a letter of recommendation (which I never had need of). He made me kneel down at the sofa and offered a prayer for me." Little did Aram know at the time but Albert Hubbard's missionary work and that of his family would soon come to an end with the death of Albert in 1899. His wife Emma continued on for a short time but soon brought the family back to the United States.[6]

The six-day journey began inauspiciously. Aram's memoirs often make reference to the wild dogs of Sivas and they appear again here:

> In the morning of my departure, there were tears in all my dear ones' eyes, except mine. I was going places! The wagon horses were beautiful, chestnut brown. They were spirited and ready to go – so was I! I was sitting next to the driver. As soon as we turned the famous corner (fateful for me) of Kel Tahir's Palace, towards my school, the street dogs started barking and ran toward the horses, making them excited and they started running down the hill. The driver was not able to make them slow down at the bridge, "Lan Gamoordge." If he had kept on going to the main road with that speed, it would have been very dangerous as there at the city hall plaza, it was always crowded. To avoid that sure danger, the driver turned the horses towards an empty big lot full of piles of building stones, but the horses instead turned towards a narrow street that leads directly to the river which, at that spot, had a high drop and was very deep. Fortunately, the horses, at that speed, could not negotiate the narrow corner and knocked themselves into a house wall and pierced it. A good thing no one was hurt and not much harm was done. Soon the people came and released the horses, turned the wagon back to the road, repaired the harnesses and we started back and were on the way.

Among the earliest photographs taken by my grandfather was one of a pack of dogs on a riverbank near one of Sivas' stone bridges. Given Aram's references to packs of dogs, they must have been ubiquitous in the urban landscape of the city. This was certainly the case in Constantinople, for in 1910 the newly dominant Young Turk municipality took it upon itself to "sanitize" the city by gathering up the city's dogs and deporting them en masse to the desert island of Sivriada, Oxia in Greek, in the Sea of Marmara where they died from dehydration and starvation, a foreshadowing of events to come.

28. First known outdoor photograph by Tsolag Dildilian around 1888 or 1889.
Stone bridge in Sivas with a pack of wild dogs on the riverbank.

After the mishap with the dogs, the journey resumed and soon Aram's wagon
was in the fertile countryside of Sivas: "The grain fields with spotted wildflowers
of every color and shade and the newly blooming trees here and there were like
fancy decorations. The first night we stayed in Yeni Khan. The innkeeper was an
Armenian and he made us real comfortable."

The description of the second day of the journey is colored in the memoir
by a horrific truth that Aram would only learn years later. They had entered
the village of Artova, which would be one of the primary killing fields of the
massacres of 1915.

Next day we stayed in Artova, an Armenian village which is situated on a plateau
and through it there was a nice serpentine, clear crystal water running and green
willow trees on each bank of the river. It was quite early at night and because it
was an Armenian village, I dared to go around and I saw a small adobe church.
The door was open so I went in to pray. It was very nicely and richly decorated
for a village church. At that time, I could never imagine that in that same village
and at the banks of that crystal clear river would be the slaughtering place of my
dear Uncle Haroutioun, brother Sumpad and Anatolia College professors in 1915.

Hidden behind this dark passage is a knowledge not shared in the rest of the
memoir. I was always puzzled as to what had happened to the Dildilian family

91

members who were not in Marsovan. In the summer of 1915 Aram's uncle Mikael was still residing in Sivas, while his uncle Haroutioun and family were in Samsun. I often stared at that portion of the family tree sketched by Aram in which name after name is identified as having perished in 1915.

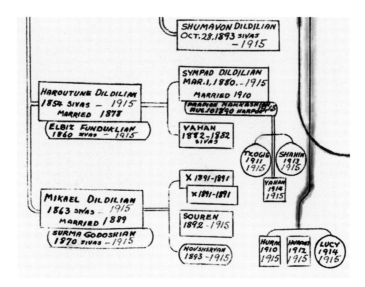

29. Aram's family tree with the dates of death, 1915.

Little is specifically mentioned in the memoir as to their fates aside from this passing reference to the killing field of Artova.

Aram resumes his account of the journey, again moving back and forth in time:

The third day we were in Tokat and we stayed there two days at Maritza Hanums Khan. I had the chance to meet Mr. Kasabashian, a spirit-filled young man, before he became minister of the Gospel. His father was chief of police in Sivas and never approved of his preaching the Gospel. He was persecuted and punished very much and for a long time. Tokat was a picturesque town, situated in a valley on the hillside surrounded with fruit gardens and vineyards. There is an historic Armenian monastery, Ohan Osgiperan, and here was the grave of Henry Martin, one of the first English missionaries to India, a fine monument in the yard of the Armenian Protestant Church. Now, according to Mr. Ernest Riggs, the Turks have torn it down and used it for their school wall, the in-scription on it intact in 1930.

The next stop was Ouch-Khanlar, a Turkish inn and in a very dangerous spot for the travelers. Robbers and highwaymen were aplenty because of the terrain around it. The Iris river (Yeşilırmak) follows the road most of the way from Tokat to Amasia. On the fifth day we arrived in Amasia, an ancient town situated in a rocky

30. Ancient Pontic tomb in Amasia, c.1913.

valley on each side of the river Iris, surrounded by immense granite mountains. On the western side, there were several caves carved in the rocks. It used to be an ancient fort. Each cave is connected to the other with passages and a downgrade passage to a spring of water called "Churanboli." Each cave is cut out of a big block of the main rock and then carved in that huge block, the caves. I guess, to be safe from earthquakes. One of those caves is called "Aynalı Mağara," mirror cave, which is highly polished. This one is not way high up on the top but down near the river … On the ceiling there are pictures of the twelve disciples of Jesus painted in oil colors, still quite fresh looking, and there is a carved baptismal basin … must have been used as a chapel. Later I had a chance to visit that cave and managed to climb up there, inside. There were many inscribed names all over the polished walls, in ink, pencil, and steel point. When I saw the name of my beloved teacher, Professor J. J. Manissadjian, I dared to put my name under his name.

When we arrived in Amasia, I asked people for the home of my Aunt Helline, whose husband, Arakel Potookian, was the lieutenant governor. After the big Armenian massacre in 1895, the big powers forced Turkey, as the supposed Armenian state's reformers, to appoint either an Armenian or a Greek as lieutenant governor for each city. So my Aunt Helline's husband was appointed lieutenant governor of Amasia. When I asked for their home a man obligingly guided me to their house by the river. All were surely surprised to see me and glad, especially Aunt Helline. She was very fond of me and used to take me as her own child (she was my Aunt Elbiz's sister). I had really a very fine time that night with them. Especially there were plenty of good things to eat and my provisions were all gone. Next morning my cousin, Dikran Potookian, took me to the inn where my driver was. Dr. Potookian was a fine and sweet young man, well educated in Beirut, Syria, and was an Army doctor. Later, he was killed [while serving] in the Army with many others by the Turks in 1915.

It was the last day of my long journey, so we started quite early in the morning. We crossed the old Roman-built bridge with three big arches and then we traveled two hours in the very deep valley, the famed Amasia gorge, through vineyards and fruit gardens. Some of the finest grapes, cherries, plums, apricots, and pears are grown there, especially the famed musk apples that grow only in that section of Amasia (they used to send them to the Sultan Hamid, several boxes each year). Then we traveled through a broad valley called "Sulu Ova" (watery valley). It could be irrigated, but was left barren. Soon we arrived at the Armenian monastery, Sourp Asdvadzadzin. My dear brother had come there to meet me. I was so glad and happy to see him, yet, I can't say why, but some kind of gloom overtook me.

Aram does not clarify the source of the gloom that overtook him at the monastery. We know from the memoirs that the monastery grounds were to serve as an important gathering place in the deportations of 1915. The Armenians of Marsovan, including many of Aram's friends and teachers, would be marched out of the city to this location where the men were usually separated off from their families, bound, and taken off toward a remote location for execution. It was also from this location that some of Aram's college friends would take the bold step of escaping and returning to Marsovan where they were hidden for years in the Dildilian households.

Aram's journey was close to an end. As they rested in preparation for the short journey into town, Dr. George White, who would later become the president of Anatolia College, arrived and welcomed Aram to his new home:

During the journey, for five or six days, I did not change my leg bandages though I had my dressing kit with me. So I thought I would change the bandages and wash my wounds at the fountain … After I cleaned my leg and put ointment on it, I felt somewhat comfortable and good. Brother had some food with him so we ate it and felt good and rested and started for our last one-hour journey. Just then, Dr. White came from a missionary trip with the college horse and buggy and stopped at the fountain in the "Koompet," an ancient monument at the road junction, to water the horses and so did we. Dr. White asked brother, "Is this the big brother you were waiting for?" and greeted me with his regular sweet smile. Finally we arrived at the home of Alexanderian where my brother was staying and had his studio.

In the summer of 2011, I visited Marsovan – now only idenitifed as Merzifon – for the first time. I was in search of the family home that I knew still existed. I also recalled the significance of the monastery of Sourp Asdvadzadzin in the family story. Despite being told by many locals that the monastery no longer existed, my traveling companion, Ferda Keskin, and I set off to the location where the monastery would have been. Taking clues from the memoir and some advice from a local farmer in the area, we stumbled upon the fountain that Aram describes above, the fountain at which he washed his wounded leg. Aram's journey had now come to an end.

31. Fountain at the site of the destroyed monastery of Sourp Asdvadzadzin in the present-day village of Yolüstü, formerly the Armenian village of Körköy.

Aram's New Home in Marsovan

Aram did not know it at the time, but Marsovan was to play a much larger role in his life in the years to come. The initial impetus for the trip was medical treatment, followed by a period of recovery. His plan to return to Sivas did not occur, as over the next few years most of his siblings would join him in Marsovan. Their lives were to become increasingly involved with Anatolia College and the opportunities it afforded. Tsolag now lived in the Alexanderian house where he had relocated the photography studio.

Aram describes the city of Marsovan and its environs:

> Marsovan is situated at the foothills of the great chain of Pontos mountains, [near] Tavshan Dagh, rabbit mountain. The town is surrounded by vineyards and is built on sloping ground near a small brook. The college buildings are on higher ground in the north, notable for their red tile roofs and white plastered buildings. Marsovan looks beautiful from the east across the brook (chay) at the center of the town. On the highest hill called "Arevortick" (the sons of the Sun) – which have some historic past and connection with ancient Zoroastrian followers – is built one of the finest and [most] beautiful Armenian cathedrals and the schools. Next to it is the Protestant Church and the Catholic French Jesuit buildings.

32. Arevortik Hill with city clock tower behind on left, Apostolic Church in the center and the Sourp Sahagian School for Boys on the right, *c.*1890. Armenian neighborhood in the foreground.

33. Anatolia College clock tower on the Main Building. The Armenian Apostolic Church on the left, Sourp Sahagian School in the center and Sourp Hripsimé School for Girls on the right, *c.*1910.

On the east is the majestic and picturesque snow-covered Ack Dagh (white mountain). In the south, a vast stretch of wheat fields in Sulu Ova, watery valley, and beyond them, the barren lands, Yedi Kurr (seven wilderness), which could be turned into paradise if it was left to the Armenians.

Marsovan is on the outskirts of Minor Armenia and was used as a training post of Armenian soldiers – "Marz-Avan" means training town. Marsovan has an excellent climate, the winters are not so severe, the summer's heat is tempered by a soft breeze from the north every afternoon that never misses. It has two sources of water, the one from the north is "Bendig" from the mill valley where there are about 12 modern flour mills, all Armenian properties, the other is called "Pasha" and this one is not a big body of water but comes in 12-inch terra cotta pipes; therefore, it was considered the best drinking water, but let me add that the "Bendig" water was much sweeter.

Marsovan was surrounded by fine vineyards and fruit trees. When I came to Marsovan, there were in the north many vineyards and huge walnut trees. When I left for the last time, there was not a single tree or vineyard left, all was dry, barren land … There were thousands of vineyards in the south and on the eastern side and most of them were Armenian properties. I wonder who is enjoying those fruitful vineyards now, or are they all dried up and barren lands.

Aram's nostalgic description of the beauty of Marsovan and its environs was often repeated by my mother and her siblings. During the summer months the family often spent weeks at a time in the countryside. Idyllic summer holidays are captured in the family photo albums.

34. Dildilian children and friends on a summer outing in the countryside. My mother Alice (aged three years) to the center left with her hand on the ball, c. summer 1914.

Aram had traveled to Marsovan in 1897 not for a holiday but for the hoped-for cure of Western medicine. Marsovan had the good fortune of having the highly-trained American physician, Dr. T. S. Carrington, who had established a small hospital near the college campus. This hospital was soon to expand, eventually becoming a state-of-the-art facility just prior to the start of the First World War. Aram describes his experience in this hospital: "The so-called hospital was a private home of six rooms and a basement, with a yard shed used for a kitchen. One upper room was used for operating, one small room for an office for the head nurse, Miss Baldwin, and the rest of the four rooms as bedrooms, altogether 12 beds. The assistant nurse or translator was Miss Rebecca Azhderian. She was so kind and sweet to me."

In the months ahead, Aram would undergo three operations on his leg. Operations in those days were performed using the anesthetic, chloroform. Chloroform is toxic and needs to be administered carefully and for limited durations. The infection in Aram's leg had spread to above the knee and amputation was the only alternative. Aram describes his ordeal:

Dr. Carrington operated on me. The first day when I came through the effects of the chloroform, Dr. White was sitting by me. I was suspicious about my leg, surely the doctor would cut it off, so at once, I tried to feel with my left leg if they had cut it off. No, he did not. Then I felt hungry, so I asked for some bread and tried to sit up in bed, then I threw up and fainted …

Two weeks later, Dr. Carrington operated on my leg again. This time during the operation he found out that the knee bone was infected and decided that it should be amputated. He did not dare to do it then because I was under chloroform too long and decided to do it some other time. Besides, he had to have the consent of my dear brother.

Eight or ten days later, my condition went from bad to worse. I was running a high fever and was unconscious most of the time. All the college circle was praying for me … Later [Tsolag] said, "The doctor wants to do another operation on you, what do you say?" I said, "I do not care," although I was half-unconscious right along. But in the morning, before 6 a.m., they had taken me up and amputated my leg above the knee. As soon as he operated, a half hour later, they say my flesh color came back. That way, my mortal life was saved!

As soon as I was somewhat over the influence of the chloroform and felt able to think and move, I started to feel with my left leg and noted that my leg was gone! So in a childish way, I started to cry saying, "I want my leg! I want my leg!" While I was crying and sobbing, Dr. Tracy came into my room to quiet me down. With his sweet way he told me that it is better to go to heaven with one leg than to be lost with two legs. Next day, his daughter, Mary Tracy, came with nice American toys and played with me and tried to make me forget about my leg.

Aram's recuperation was long and difficult. His 13-year-old life had been saved, but he struggled for the rest of his life to overcome the difficulties created by the loss of his leg.

A New Place to Call Home: The Dildilians Settle in Marsovan

During the period of Aram's recovery, many changes had been taking place within the Dildilian family back in Sivas. The centuries-long roots in the family's ancestral hometown were coming to an end. Life in Sivas had become increasingly difficult for Aram's siblings and his uncle Haroutioun. The family would now be reunited in Marsovan:

One sunny and bright morning, my dear brother came in and said, "I have a surprise for you," and who did I see but my dearest Uncle Haroutioun, Aunt Elbiz, and sisters Markarid, Parantzem, Nevart, and baby brother Shamavon, who came into my room in procession with tears in their eyes. I, on the contrary, cheered them up …

My father had mortgaged our house to Mugurdich Gulbenkian, who was demanding either the money or the house … Well, according to Turkish law, we could stay in our house 15 or 16 more years up to the time my youngest brother, Shamavon comes of age. But my uncle, with his passive, sweet way, surrendered the house to Gulbenkian and brought the family to Marsovan saying, "The cruel grabbed, I gave, the cruel is gone, I am still alive."

Only Aram's married older sister, Haïganouch, remained behind in Sivas. With the arrival of his family from Sivas, Tsolag rented a bigger house near the campus. His photography work kept him very busy, often requiring him to travel to other cities in Anatolia.

While Aram's health was improving, his older sister Markarid's was declining. Tuberculosis was common in much of the world in this period. Malnutrition and the difficult living conditions in the wake of the Hamidian Massacres contributed to its rise. The Dildilians were not immune to this scourge. Markarid probably contracted the bacterium while in Sivas and gradually grew weaker as the year 1898 progressed. Aram describes the passing of his beloved sister in August of 1898:

About that time, my sister Markarid passed away. She died of consumption. The disease must have been far advanced before she came to Marsovan. She suffered by herself in silence. I was with her most of the time and used to sleep in the same room. In the mornings I used to watch her in her sleep. Her forehead and face were covered in a cold sweat and her breathing was short and uneasy. She was so sweet – she never complained, she knew what was what, she was a believer. In her last hour, I was at her bedside. She asked to lie down on her back and then she asked to straighten her again. When she saw the excitement on my sister's face she said, "Do not cry for me, I am going to my Savior." She was smart, bright, very sensible, considerate and her beauty was unsurpassed …

Brother was away in Amasia for picture taking so at once we wired for him to come. Her funeral service was very impressive. Dr. Tracy took care of the service in the same big room where she used to sleep. A big group of sympathetic men and women were there … We buried her remains in the Protestants' old cemetery.

Tuberculosis affected the lives of the next generation of Dildilians. Two of my uncles succumbed to this disease. My mother used to say that the hardships of the First World War and the family's expulsion from their home in Marsovan contributed to her brothers' deaths. Mixed in with my uncle Humayag's papers and boxes of photographs that I inherited were two X-rays taken of his lungs many years ago. I once showed them to a friend with medical training.

He told me that they showed signs of tuberculosis scarring, probably from my uncle's youth.

Haïganouch and her husband had remained behind in Sivas after the rest of the family had moved. Her daughter describes her loneliness and the upsetting manner by which she learned of her sister's passing:

> Haïganouch felt strongly about that separation, but then, what to do? One day, while she was coming back from the *hammam*, she walked past her ancestral home. She felt lightheaded and was sick for several days.
>
> Some time later, again at the *hammam*, a woman approached her sadly: "So your sister Markarid is dead. What a pity!" The *hammam* looked dim to my mother who did not know the bad news.

Vosgian, Haïganouch's husband, decided that the separation from her siblings was too much to bear. Maritsa describes her father's decision to move to Marsovan in 1899:

> He said: "Look, I have neither brothers nor sisters, whereas you have. Why live away from them? I am a craftsman and in any place, I can make a living. If you wish it so, let's go to Marsovan."
>
> Of course, she wanted to! So they set off to Marsovan. It was a long journey in a wagon, with their cow and donkey in tow.

Besides the cow and the donkey, they had their two-year-old son, Haïgouni, with them. As the year 1899 drew to a close, all the siblings were once again reunited, this time in their new home of Marsovan.

6

The End of a Century and New Beginnings

The Marriage of Tsolag and the Growth of the Dildilians in Marsovan

The year 1899 marks an important moment in my relationship to the family story. All of the people I have described and the stories I have told have been based upon the memories of others. I began the family story by recounting my personal childhood memory of my grandmother. I have now come to the moment when she enters our story. For it was in 1899 that my grandfather Tsolag met and married my grandmother. The circumstances of their marriage are recounted by all three of our memoirists, Aram, Tsolag and Maritsa. While the outlines of how they met are the same in all three accounts, there is a mysterious woman who appears in two of the accounts. This mystery woman is not mentioned at all by my grandfather. All three stories begin in Kharpert (Harpoot) during the massacres of 1895, so I will begin there.

Mariam Nakkashian, my grandmother, had been born and raised in Kharpert. She was the daughter of a highly regarded Protestant minister, Rev. Sarkis Nakkashian, who had trained at Euphrates College, known to Armenians as Yeprad College. On November 10, 1895 the massacres had begun in Kharpert and the surrounding towns. Rev. Nakkashian was the minister of the Protestant church in Chunkoosh, an Armenian town south of Kharpert. Aram describes what happened to the Nakkashian family during the massacres:

> Turk and Kurdish mobs surrounded his house and asked him to change his faith and he refused to do so. Before that time, a Turkish friend had come and taken away his wife and younger daughter, Prapion, and was to come back for him and his daughter Mariam for safe keeping in his own home, but by the time their Turkish friend came back, the mob had put fire to the house. [The day before the mobs arrived, Rev. Nakkashian] wrote a masterpiece of a letter to his son, Vahan, who was in Harpoot College [Euphrates College], advising him for the future and [urging] him to take his sister and go to America. About the time [the Turkish friend returned], their floor was in flames so they had to go to the roof of their neighbor but my sister-in-law [Mariam] was caught in the

103

flames and was burnt on the right side from her ankle up to her chest. When they came down to the street, the Turks shot [Rev. Nakkashian], who passed to his rest singing, "My Faith Looks Up to Thee." The friend was too late to save him so he took my sister-in-law and kept the family until they were able to get permission to go to America.

The "masterpiece of a letter" referred to by Aram has survived. The faded original and a handwritten copy by my grandmother Mariam are found in the family papers. Whether Aram had access to the letter when he wrote his memoir is unclear, especially given the inaccuracy of some of the details mentioned. The documentation my grandmother provides with the letter states that it was written by both Rev. Nakkashian and his wife Badaskhan though clearly the voice in the letter is primarily that of Badaskhan. What makes it unique is the fact that it was written the day before the massacres began in Chunkoosh. Vahan was studying for the ministry in Kharpert at the time. He is advised to leave the country for a safer home. This was advice he did not heed because he perished in the 1915 genocide. Both father and son had a similar tragic fate. I quote translated portions of the letter:

> Chunkoosh, Turkey
> November 4, 1895
> Rev. Vahan S. Nakkashian

My sweet child,

Thanks to the Lord's mercy, we passed yesterday's blessed day without danger, thus our hearts were not troubled.

We were hardly awake when Rev. B. Keosayan brought the news that 500 Kurds are coming and they are very close by. This news proved to be certain. It is now 3:30 p.m. and the Kurds are already near Chimjek, on the other side of the bridge at the head of Yenijek. We are in great danger and our lives are hanging by a thread. My beloved son, probably this will be my last letter to you.

I am not afraid of death, however. I want to see "The Son of God who came to us in great glory" and then I can say, "Free your servant with peace because my eyes saw your salvation."

What frightens me is that we might be forced to commit acts which are against modesty and honor, in which case, it is better to die than to be in such a situation. May God protect us. No matter what, we have always prayed, we are still praying and are waiting for our destiny from the Lord. Our greatest consolation is that after death we will all have everlasting life in the person of Christ. Thank God, that if our martyrdom was decreed for the glory of His name, let Him glorify the earth and especially visit our nation.

If this be our last message, accept our last love, parental greetings and affection ...

As an intelligent person, you already know my maternal wishes and inclinations. Trust in God and live accordingly. In memory of your father, carry the first letter of his name.

If none of the ones present here survive, then you will have no responsibility to look after us. You can go where you will consider safe and comfortable, instead of living in this country …

Although I started early to arrange for an inheritance which now might be plundered and disappear within a minute, if you find it, fine. We will try to keep it safe …

May God be with you with his grace and peace. Do not be sad with hopelessness because the life of the Lord is our best inheritance.

Your affectionate mother,

B. Nakkashian

Also in the letter Vahan is given some motherly advice as to the sort of woman he should marry. He does marry and raises a large family in Trebizond but does not heed his mother's advice about leaving the country. When I look at many of the photos of my grandmother, I am often drawn to her eyes. These are strong but sorrowful eyes. Eyes that have experienced much pain and loss. Burned and narrowly escaping with her life, she was an eyewitness to the murder of her father. She would live to see her mother and three siblings, Vahan, Haïganouch, and Prapion, and their families perish in 1915. We will revisit the Nakkashian story when we chronicle the events of 1915.

Earlier in my story I described how my grandfather and his cousin Sumpad had traveled to Samsun after the 1894–96 massacres with the intention of leaving the country, possibly emigrating to Russia. They had been persuaded to stay in Samsun because of the great demand for their services as photographers. It was at this point that Mariam and Tsolag's paths crossed. Mariam and her brother Vahan had fled to Samsun with the intention of emigrating to America. They had been granted permission to go to America and were traveling with a third person whom Aram describes as the daughter of a wealthy Armenian man. Maritsa describes this "mystery woman" as a cousin. Aram remarks that this woman "was running away from a very influential Turkish suitor." In contrast, Maritsa claims that it was my grandmother who was being pursued by a wealthy bey from Kharpert who had fallen in love with her. Aram describes what happened next:

By the time that Turk finds out her [the unnamed companion's] flight and wired the Samsun authorities not to let her out of the country but to send her back with Nakkashian, she was already on a French boat and Vahan and Mariam were about to take the same boat. The Turkish officers arrested Vahan and Mariam. They had a hard time to prove that they are not the party the authorities are looking for but with the help of the Lieutenant Governor, who was a Greek, they were prevented from going back to Harpoot [Kharpert], but were not allowed to go to America either.

Maritsa adds a further embellishment to the story:

> Vahan managed to have the cousin get on board but he and his sister remained in the hands of the police, awaiting the arrival of the bey. A clever Armenian lawyer managed to have the brother and sister declared residents of the town of Djanik to prevent their return to Kharpert. He had added that if Mariam could get married, it would be even surer. This is how Tsolag married Mariam and took her to Marsovan.

Was it my grandmother who was being pursued by this bey? Or was it this mysterious unnamed woman? My mother had told me that her mother's beauty made her the object of the unwanted attention of a wealthy Turk in Kharpert. This had forced her to flee her hometown. If we turn to my grandfather's speech of January 1928, we find no mention of this other unnamed woman. After 30 years of a strong and committed marriage, my grandfather probably saw no need to protect the virtue of his wife by creating this fiction of the other woman. Though not directly stated, my grandfather implies that my grandmother may well have been the object of this unwanted attention. Tsolag writes: "One day we heard from somebody, that a young man and his sister from Harpoot on their way to America had their passage stopped because of the pressure by a Kurdish bey on the Harpoot government." Was the mystery woman in Aram's account simply a fiction created to somehow protect the honor of my grandmother? Who was this cousin who managed to flee? Even though there is no evidence that my grandmother encouraged this unwanted attention, the morality of the time required that she not find herself in situations that sparked inappropriate male desire. The fiction of the "other woman" may find its origins here.

Tsolag in his speech describes how he made the acquaintance of his future wife:

> A few days afterwards, at the church, we met that young man who was released by the Mutasarrif Hamdi Pasha because of a petition by the renowned Ipranosian House. That vigorous young man was the son of Rev. Sarkis Nakkashian, who during the 1895 massacre of Chunkoosh was murdered [and] ... burned. The son, Vahan S. Nakkashian is a graduate of Euphrates College and so was his sister, Mariam S. Nakkashian. Mr. Vahan with his beautiful voice became very valuable in the Young People's Association [Y.M.C.A.] of Samsun. I was the head of the choir and I was always in contact with him. But his sister, what a crime, I barely knew her, so listless and sorrowful, you would not dare to look at her face.

35. Engagement photo of Mariam Nakkashian, 1899.

Mariam soon obtained a teaching position in the Protestant school in Samsun while her brother was hired by the Ipranosian Brothers, an Armenian chain of dry goods merchants.

After Tsolag's sojourn in Samsun, he made the decision to return and pursue the opportunities available to him in Marsovan. For many years he had worked for Anatolia College but now its president wanted to make their relationship permanent. Tsolag writes: "The president of the college, Dr. Tracy, had already with a special letter pledged to guarantee 60 gold [liras] per year from the college if I would somehow settle in Marsovan. I accepted the invitation and permanently settled in Marsovan, bringing my siblings from Sepastia." His uncle Haroutioun had attempted to establish the shoe business in Marsovan but soon returned to his ancestral hometown of Sivas. He was considered an outsider and found it difficult to establish himself within the fabric of this new community. Tsolag remarks that his uncle felt that he had one "last obligation" as head of the family, an obligation to marry off Tsolag thus conferring upon him the responsibility of heading the family.

36. Mariam and Tsolag's wedding photograph, 1899.

In 1899 Tsolag asked for Mariam's hand in marriage through an intermediary, the Rev. Simeon Babasinian. Tsolag claims that her response "did not come very easily." Intriguingly he comments that "if his wife permits," he will tell a "small anecdote" about her response but unhappily for me, none is recorded in the written transcript of the speech. Tsolag does state that Mariam's decision could not have been easy because marrying him entailed taking on a ready-made family, that is, all his orphaned younger siblings who were now under his charge. Tsolag describes this added burden: "Taking into account my burdensome situation, my orphans who will accompany me from the first day, puts one under heavy responsibility. Having the family inheritance plundered, though not poor, surrounded by seven orphans, and then to take a young man with an additional handicap of a beard." This claim that beards are a serious "turnoff" to women seems to be a recurring theme in the memoirs. I would love to have been there when my grandfather gave this speech. I suspect there may well have been a wry smile on his face and a few chuckles from his children when he added the handicap of his beard to the list of Mariam's burdens.

Tsolag, having received a positive response from my grandmother, traveled to Samsun and was married in the local Protestant church. Most of the family in Marsovan were unable to attend but traveled en masse to greet the bride and groom as they approached the vineyards on the outskirts of Marsovan. Aram describes the happy couple: "Brother was looking so nice and happy, and the bride! Oh! She was in her glory. She was a beauty, brown eyes, brown hair, fair skinned. She was kind and tenderhearted and took a motherly attitude towards all of us."

Tragedies Strike the New Families

The year 1899 marked the beginning of the growth of both Tsolag's and his younger sister Haïganouch's families in their new hometown of Marsovan. For the Der Haroutiounians the transition was not an easy one. Unlike Tsolag's better-established and growing photography business – he was the only photographer in the town – Vosgian had to compete with other cabinetmakers and carpenters. The Der Haroutiounians were tenants in the house of an Armenian priest, Der Zénop. Maritsa attributes some of their initial difficulties to the fact that they were viewed as outsiders by many of the locals. Whether correct or not, the insularity of the Marsovantsis is highlighted in her description of the town:

> Newcomers are not liked, whatever the country, but this trait was stronger in Marsovan. When the Marsovantsis say "*tersétsis*" (people from outside), this is a disparaging term in their mouths. They say: "He who has a house and a vineyard does not emigrate, the newcomer will eat our bread." The Marsovantsi is hard-working but somewhat unsympathetic and coarse. This is because the soil is arid and trade and industry are not much developed. Of course, there are rich people, but their way of living is not very different. They are not used to having servants, and some of them even do not wish it. Even the well-to-do women work at the loom at home in order to earn gold coins that they wear around their necks. Weaving is the Marsovantsis' only industry.
>
> Regarding this stinginess, there is a saying. But let me tell first that vineyards are aplenty in the country around Marsovan. The *Mar Garmir* [red] wine is

well-known. These vineyards are also gardens as most of them are enclosed by fruit trees. Here is the saying:

"I bet you are from Marsovan."

"You can bet on that."

"I bet it is wine you have with you."

"You can bet on that."

"I bet you are going to offer me a drink of it."

"You can bet on whatever you wish, but don't bet on that."

Haïganouch's desire to make new friends in this unwelcoming environment unfortunately may have led to the first tragedy to befall the Der Haroutiounians in Marsovan. The year of Tsolag and Mariam's wedding was also the year that Haïganouch and Vosgian were blessed with their second child, Barsam. A red-headed, blue-eyed boy, he had the misfortune of being born in the year of a smallpox epidemic in the town. Maritsa describes the circumstances:

> There were two neighboring women, two sisters, who used to visit us. At the time of the epidemic, they came one day holding in their arms their still-contagious children. My mother, although annoyed at their heedlessness, did not dare dismiss them because they were the only persons with whom she was on good terms. And these foolish women kept visiting her with their children still covered with pustules.
>
> So, one day, little Barsam contracted smallpox in a terrible manner. My mother said that the child's lips had burst into rose-like ulcerations, so the baby could no longer suck. Also he could not urinate due to the ulcerations. She kept him at her bedside day and night.

Despite the fact that vaccines against smallpox had been developed in the eighteenth century and were in use in Anatolia, little Barsam had not been vaccinated. One morning Haïganouch awoke to find her child had quietly passed away in the cradle next to her: "My mother lifts the veil covering the cradle but her view becomes blurred, she feels as if she were in a haze, tears and blood come to her eyes (this caused a chronic watering of her eyes; and this is why she always carried with her a handkerchief in a very soft fabric which she used only for her eyes)."

A similar tragedy was soon to strike Tsolag and Mariam. The new century brought the birth of their first child, Loucia, born on January 10, 1900. Tsolag does not mention this happy event in his speech, for within a month his young daughter was to die. The only account given of this loss is found in Maritsa's notebooks. A *hammam* once again appears and is associated with death:

> Tsolag had his first child, a girl he named Loucia in remembrance of his mother whom he had loved very deeply. He had his mother's sister come from Yozgat to

I had another amusement which was to watch the bear cubs brought from the Sivas mountains. Soon they grew to be unruly and dangerous so Chester Tracy, with the help of the big boys, dug the ground for a new and bigger house with a climbing pole and water pool and a nice cave for them to sleep. When the moving [in] day came [for the bears], we had a housewarming ceremony. All the college, girls school, and orphanages were off. Professor Manissadjian officially named them Oursoos and Oursoola. Then we all sang the Manu of the Bears:

> *Mer archere inch gooden den den den*
> *Yergou shap tee Mar gi meg meg meg*
> *Yerek shap tee Purasa sa sa sa*
> *Chorek shap tee Loupia ya ya ya*
> *Hink shap tee orher Havla la la la*
> *Ourpat orher Mazoon zoon zoon zoon*
> *Shapat orher Pilaf laf laf laf*
> *Giragi orher Kash geg geg geg.*

I cannot help but relate a humorous incident that happened to me when I first read aloud the above account in a public lecture I gave at Anatolia College in the spring of 2009. I had been invited by the president of the college, Richard Jackson, to tell the story of my family's connection to Anatolia and share with them the many photographs I had in my possession. The auditorium contained about a hundred people, including many from the Armenian community in Thessaloniki, the college's home after its expulsion from Turkey. As I came to the point in my story where I was to read the "Manu to the Bears," I paused and made an aside that I would read the song rather than sing it since I did not know the tune. In any case they would not want to hear me sing since I was notorious for singing out of tune. As I read the "Manu" in my somewhat stilted Armenian, I noticed a group of elderly ladies in the front row whose faces broke out into wide smiles. Their lips were moving in unison with my words. When my lecture was over they sprang up to the podium and informed me that they knew the song I had recited. What a pleasant and unexpected surprise! As children growing up in the Armenian diaspora of Greece, they had often heard it sung to them by their parents and grandparents. They never knew of its origins back a hundred years ago in that remote corner of Ottoman Turkey. They offered to sing it for me. This was an opportunity not to be missed. As they broke into song, my thoughts were transported back to that earlier moment in time when a joyous throng of young and old celebrated the new home of two bear cubs, a moment not in my personal memory but in the collective memory of my people, a collective memory that vividly came to life for me in that auditorium.

Public community lectures had a long tradition at Anatolia College. Just as I had lectured to the college and the community at large on that day in 2009,

Aram describes similar events at the turn of the twentieth century: "In the winter months, every Friday night we used to have special lectures by our professors. We used to have a full house, thousands would attend, city folk as well as college people." "Thousands" – now surely this must be an exaggeration. Aram, thinking back to his teenage years, must have taken things out of perspective. I drew a crowd of a hundred or so people to my talk at the college in Thessaloniki but a crowd of thousands, back then, in Marsovan: surely not. My skepticism was unwarranted. In my recent research about my family's connections to the college, I stumbled upon the following passage in *The Report and Catalogue of Anatolia College and the Girls' Boarding School, Marsovan, Turkey*, published in 1901:

> The weekly Friday lectures are a matter of ever-increasing interest. The audience is invariably large and attentive, frequently six or seven hundred people being present – occasionally near a thousand. The lectures, during the last college year, with their subjects, are here-with presented, in their order: –

> Charles C. Tracy, "Music."
> C. K. Tracy, "Silver Chords."
> Prof. J. J. Manissadjian, "Nothing New under the Sun."
> Rev. G. E. White, "The Council of Nicea."
> Mr. A. Gulbenkian, "The Mystic Numbers."
> Prof. F. Margot, "Pestalozzi."
> Dr. T. S. Carrington, "The Brain."
> Prof. A. Sivaslian, "The Heat of the Sun."
> Prof. H. Hagopian, "Bezjian Amira."
> Mr. D. K. Getchel, "Ephesus."
> Prof. D. Theocharides, "Archaeology."
> Rev. Y. Xenides, "Memory."[1]

Well, maybe there was a slight exaggeration on Aram's part but these numbers reflect a genuine thirst for knowledge among the Armenians and Greeks of Marsovan. My research indicates that most of the above-mentioned speakers were fluent in Armenian but I suspect that many of these lectures were probably given in English. If so, these figures are even more impressive.

Aram's disability limited the sorts of physical activities he could engage in at the college. He remarks, "So I tried to spend all my leisure time helping brother in his photographic studio." Aram was no longer the subject of his brother's photography but rapidly becoming a photographer in his own right, a passion he pursued for the rest of his life. Not participating in college sports also afforded him the time and opportunity to act on his religiously based altruism, especially for the less fortunate: "On Sundays I used to go to the orphanage to sing together, read and discuss things in general with the orphan boys" – orphans of the Hamidian

Massacres of 1894–96. Little did Aram realize at the time that almost 20 years later he would be asked to take charge of the orphans of the genocide of 1915 and run an orphanage for Near East Relief in Samsun.

Aram made the most of his days at Anatolia. One adventure highlights the knowledge and creativity of the students of the college: "Once in 1900, Armen Tashjian, who was the translator for Dr. Carrington while I was in the hospital, was trying to transmit wireless signals from one tower [on campus] to [an]other. Hurant Sivaslian and I were helping him – that was a great achievement, we thought."

Aram describes himself as an average student but the talents he displayed would serve him well in his chosen career of photography: "At the college, I was not a bright and first-class student. I was just an average student but I was good in drawing and painting and was awarded first prize among all first, second, and third forms." Aram was clearly talented with his hands and could design and craft useful objects. He writes: "I enjoyed work in the carpenter shop and book-binding shop as a hobby. Later, brother conceived the idea to help me make about 24 photo albums of college and other scenery so that I would have enough money to buy an artificial leg which Prof. Manissadjian ordered from Germany. It was an all-leather leg, not a good leg but it was better than one [I had]." Little did he realize at the time that his multiple talents would be vitally useful in saving the lives of family and friends during the dark days of 1915 to 1918.

Aram's studies at the college soon came to an end. He graduated having completed the third form but did not have the desire to pursue higher-level study. He was now a restless 20-year-old and knew where his passion would take him – a career in photography. He concludes this section of his memoir with the following: "My life was dull, uninteresting and limited. I wanted to get out of my narrow confine. I had a great desire to go to America and try to perfect my knowledge of photography though I knew enough, but I wanted to learn more." A new chapter in Aram's life would now open.

The Joys and Disillusions of Aram's Sojourn in America

As the Dildilian siblings reached adulthood, the burden of caring for two families began to diminish for Tsolag. He and Mariam started a family of their own with the birth of a boy, Hratchia in 1901, followed by another boy, Humayag in 1903. With his two sisters and younger brother still under his roof in 1904, the addition of two young children must have made household management a challenge for my grandparents as the house they were renting also included their photography studio and darkroom. Three siblings, two young children, and clients arriving in order to have their portraits taken, all contributed to the controlled chaos of the Dildilian household. But this soon began to change with the simultaneous departure of both Parantzem and Aram.

Travel within and emigration from the Ottoman Empire was strictly regulated. Internal travel necessitated a travel permit (*mürur tezkeresi*) and to get one required a compelling reason, usually related to your occupation. Aram was determined to study photography in the United States. He had secured admission into the Illinois College of Photography by corresponding with its president, L. H. Bissell. The problem was how to get there. Aram had a plan: "Just about then my dear sister, Parantzem, was invited to teach in the Ordou Protestant Church school as a kindergarten teacher in September 1904, so I thought that was a great chance for me to utilize that circumstance." Ordou was on the Black Sea, allowing for an escape by steamer to ports beyond: "So, we tried to get a passport for sister Parantzem as a teacher for Ordou, and a passport for me to accompany her as a guardian. My plan was to get on board a European steamer and go out of Turkey ... so that I may go to America later."

After a two-day journey they reached the port city of Samsun:

Next day we were in Samsun. There was a Greek steamer in the harbor for Ordou, so at once we took our tickets and went to the custom house. The harbor commission officer insisted that we take the Turkish steamer instead of the Greek steamer. We finally convinced him that we had bought tickets for the Greek steamer and had no time to go back and change it for the Turkish steamer. So he did let us go to the Greek steamer but gave us a fine lecture that it is our patriotic duty to patronize the Turkish companies. He did not know that my intention was to go to Ordou, Kerason, and Trebizond and turn back the same way to Athens.

Next afternoon we were in Ordou. Our friend, the minister's son came and took sister Parantzem to shore and I hid myself in the cabin. Yes, though the police came to the steamer, they had no right to enter the cabins. Next morning we were in Kerason and towards evening we were in Trebizond and Batum, then back again stopping over at Trebizond, Kerason, Ordou, Samsun. I did not go out from my cabin. About 4 p.m. I saw from my cabin porthole a rowboat coming towards our steamer with two ladies and a man. When they came on board, it was Mehlika Bedrossian, who was going to America. I was somewhat glad to have some fellow traveler whom I knew. That night the steamer started towards the west. We stopped in Sinop, Eraghli [Eregli], Constantinople and Smyrna. I did not go out of my cabin in any one of those places that we stopped except in Smyrna. There, I felt somewhat free ... When we started for Athens, I threw my fez into the sea and put on a cap which I bought from a Greek sailor.

Upon arrival in Piraeus, Aram secured passage on a Cunard liner sailing from Trieste to the United States. His dream of studying photography in America had one more significant hurdle to overcome. U.S. Immigration officers often had a dim view of people with handicaps. Despite having an education and the financial means to support himself, Aram could easily be denied admission by being deemed a "cripple." He encountered such a prejudice upon boarding the ship:

Finally the big ship came in and all the passengers started to climb up the big, long steps. I, too, in my turn started to climb with my belongings. I was trying hard to manipulate my German-made artificial leg as well as I could with my heavy load. By the time I got up to the top I was almost exhausted. At the entrance there were three gold-braided officers. One of them gave a passing look at my papers and said, "You can't go to America with this ship because you are lame." I tried to explain that I was going to school and had enough money. After a few muttering conversations with each other, I was told to sit down on a bench next to the entrance. Later, at 6 p.m., they told me it was all right for me to go, so a man led me to my bunk. He told me to put my belongings there and go to the dining room to eat with the rest of the passengers. Later while I was getting ready to go to bed, just then I heard my name being called. There at the entrance, the captain of the ship and other officers told me, "you can't go to America with this liner because you have an artificial leg and if the U.S. Immigration officers refuse your admittance, we will be obligated to bring you back. So we can't take any chance."

Aram was put on a small boat in the middle of the night and sent back dockside.

Stubbornly determined to reach America, Aram sought the advice of the U.S. Consul back in Athens, who did not believe that he would be denied admission and advised him to try again from London. Aram set off to London by way of Marseilles and Paris, stopping on the way to see some sights and receive a welcome from fellow Armenians along the way. He boarded the Allan line S.S. *Corinthian* and sailed from Liverpool to Halifax, Nova Scotia. His disembarkation in Canada was uneventful.

37. S.S. *Corinthian*.

The U.S. Immigration officer in charge of clearing the passengers traveling on to the United States saw no hindrance to his entry; on the contrary he provided Aram helpful advice and assistance. After many hours on trains, his long journey came to an end in Effingham, Illinois.

Aram spent nearly three years in America. These were years marked by a growing maturity both in his personal and professional life. Yet these were also times of hardship and struggle. His memoir chronicles not just the physical or economic struggles of an immigrant in a strange new land but more importantly his moral or what he calls his "spiritual" struggles in America. Ultimately the latter motivated him to return to Marsovan in 1907. Aram's description of his first day in Effingham gives us a hint of the source of the conflict he was to feel:

> I went downtown to acquaint myself with the post office and other stores and things. On the way, a young girl greeted me and said, "How do you do," something that would never happen in Marsovan, especially in our college circle. In the Marsovan College circle we were living a Puritan life … For college boys and girls, things were very strict. We did not have a coeducational school, yet both the boys' and girls' colleges were in the same compound, but we could not see each other or converse with each other even if we were in the same neighborhood. I remember very well a boy of a respectable family was tempted to correspond with a girl and was caught. Poor boy, he was put out of his home and finally his father was persuaded by friends to pay his way to America, and that was his end!

What Aram could mean by "his end" is left to our imagination. Was America his ultimate punishment or his moral downfall?

Aram completed a two-year course of study in only one year and received his diploma on July 1, 1905. He accomplished this while working six days a week doing various odd jobs for the college in order to defray his tuition costs. These were often physically demanding, but Aram did not complain. His memoir describes school life at the college and the cultural adjustments he experienced:

> One night I was awakened by the sound of rifle shooting and factory whistles. I thought there was a fire as in the old country (Turkey) when there was a fire, they tried to wake up the people by gun shots and again, they used to shoot guns when there was a moon eclipse, to scare the devils away. I looked out the window but there was no fire! There was no eclipse of the moon! Then I figured there can't be any massacre or killing because this is America … so I went back to bed and was sound asleep. Next day, I find out that it is customary to meet the New Year with noises and gun shots!

Upon graduating, Aram began to look for work as a photographer. Through a contact at the college he found work in Pittsburgh, but the outcome was not rewarding. Often he was employed by studios that required him to work seven days a week. As a Christian he found working on Sunday, the Sabbath, a violation of his principles. He purchased a branch studio from one of his employers and tried hard to make it viable.

Pittsburgh was a growing industrial city that would soon have over half a million residents in this pre-war period. The city attracted many immigrants, Armenians among them. Aram helped organize these immigrant Armenians into the "Armenian Union," a precursor of the A.G.B.U. (Armenian General Benevolent Union) that had not yet been founded in America. Wealth was being created and the need for photography was growing. The Empire Photo Studio, which Aram had opened in East Pittsburgh, was facing increasing competition. Within a short period of time the number of studios in the area grew from three to twelve. All the competitors were open on Sundays, a compromise he refused to make. Aram gave up on the business and went to work for others who did not require Sunday work. But even here he faced conflicts with his religiously based moral principles. In a rather cryptic remark he states: "Well, I found a real good-paying job and I did not have to work on Sunday, either. But soon I found out that that special place is not a place for me to work as a Christian. I could not stay in such an environment, so I quit. God and I only know why!" What was he called upon to do that compelled him to leave this job? The cause has remained a secret between Aram and his Maker, though he does provide a hint:

> That reminds me of an instance that happened years ago in Sivas. Our family priest, Der Yeghishe Khorigian came to our house to bless the water and the bread (an old custom). At that time, my brother's picture was hanging from the wall. He asked my uncle, "Who is that handsome young man and what does he do?" Uncle said, "He is my nephew and he is a photographer." He exclaimed, "What? A photographer? Please write to him to get out of that profession because photographers are immoral people." I do not subscribe to the idea of that priest but I had seen many that really were so ... during my working life I have been confronted with many cases and things that do justify his opinion. The fight to uphold my ideals and principles was too great a fight for me.

One can only speculate as to the immorality of the photography business. Was he called upon to take, develop or print photographs whose content he found objectionable? Risqué subject matter was not uncommon for photography at the beginning of the twentieth century. One can find many examples from studios in Western Europe and the United States, even some from Constantinople, but one would be hard pressed to find any from the Ottoman photographers who practiced their art in the Anatolian interior.

Aram decided to return home to Marsovan. His moral discomfort in America, his homesickness, the desire of his brother Tsolag for Aram to return and help in the business, all played a role in his decision. But returning home would not be easy.

Wood and Wool: The Der Haroutiounians
Build their Home in Marsovan

While Aram was in America and his brother Tsolag was growing the photography business in Anatolia, Vosgian and Haïganouch were growing their own family and woodworking (joinery) business in Marsovan. Vosgian was a talented craftsman, an artist in wood. Maritsa comments: "He also makes cradles, tables with feet in the form of lion paws which he finely carves with a saw or a gouge. Customers are not many. His productions are expensive for modest people, and the rich are content with ordinary objects." Unlike the photography business, there was competition in the woodworking crafts. Often his work would be copied in an inferior version, which would undercut his prices. In order to make a living he could not limit himself to making high-quality finely crafted objects. Marsovan had a significant home textile business at the time. Often the women in the household worked at home on hand looms. The city had a long-established trading relationship with Manchester, England, the era's textile capital of the world, where Armenian textile merchants had settled decades earlier. Vosgian made many of the looms and much of the associated equipment in his shop.

Despite the competition, Vosgian's excellent reputation sometimes resulted in special commissions that could be profitable. His business had grown sufficiently, such that he could employ six workers and apprentices: "At that time, he worked for the French [Jesuit] High School. He built the big clock tower and many other things. The Europeans noted the quality of his work and asked him to make the altar of the Catholic church based upon a drawing. The two pillars represented winged angels, the size of a child, with arched backs. Every part was to be carved, including the pillar bases." Vosgian used to tease his youngest daughter, Haïgouhi, that if she didn't kiss him, he would "get a kiss from 'his daughter in the shop'," referring to the angels he was carving. Supported by her older sister's collusion, Haïgouhi's naiveté led her to believe in the reality of this imaginary angelic sibling.

In the summer 2012, I visited Marsovan for the second time. I had by then become more familiar with Vosgian's story. I knew that the Catholic church had long since been converted into a wedding hall, stripped of any of its ornamentation, but many Ottoman-era houses still remained. As I wandered the streets of the older neighborhoods of the town, I wondered if any of Vosgian's handiwork still remained, possibly hidden somewhere in these homes. Could this angelic daughter be found hiding in one of these remnants from this time long past?

Vosgian's wife, Haïganouch, began weaving carpets at home to supplement the family income. Aram had been given a few of his sister's carpets to take with him to America. The hope was that they would fetch enough money to help defray the costs of his education. There was no market for oriental carpets in Effingham, so Aram was forced to conduct a lottery for one of them, raising $50 to pay for his room and board. As with my great-uncle's angelic handiwork,

I also wonder if my great-aunt's carpet is still tucked away in a house somewhere in Effingham today.

Vosgian had a number of setbacks during the first decade of the century, the most serious of which was the fire that devastated a large portion of Marsovan in 1904. The fire burned many of the shops in the marketplace and threatened the college campus. Fortunately the college had its own firefighting equipment that was manned by the older students, including Sumpad Dildilian, Haïganouch's cousin. Vosgian attempted to rescue his tools from his burning shop and might have died in the process if not for Sumpad: "My uncle Sumpad and his friends, who were on the spot with the Americans' fire engine, had much difficulty restraining him. Fortunately, Sumpad was commanding the fire engine and, with the help of some companions, he managed to save a few things but these did not amount to much."

Vosgian's setbacks may have aggravated his ulcer, which had earlier been diagnosed in the American hospital on the campus. Maritsa comments that while in the hospital they told him that they were going to "mirror" him. She guesses that this may be a reference to X-raying. Most likely she is correct because my mother had told me that early in the century the first X-ray machine had arrived at the American hospital. Radiology at the time was viewed as "interior photography." My grandfather Tsolag was thus put in charge of running the hospital's X-ray machine. While this was a boon to the diagnosis of a variety of illnesses, little was known at the time of the harmful effects of radiation. My grandfather would work with no protection, often placing his face close to the X-ray machine. While we do not know for certain, the jaw cancer that took my grandfather's life in 1935 was likely the result of his many years of work with the X-ray machine in Marsovan. The hospital that had earlier saved the life of his younger brother Aram eventually took Tsolag's life.

Yet despite these setbacks, Vosgian's business prospered enough to provide him with the means to begin the process of building a house of his own. The Der Haroutiounians had been living in various rental arrangements since arriving in Marsovan, but building a house in this period was not an easy proposition, especially for Armenians. He began by purchasing the land as described by Maritsa:

> My father then wanted to buy a piece of land in the borough called Akkach ["the White Eyebrow"]. It was an open site, one of the plots belonging to Sahatdjian Hagop Effendi. The neighbors were not very friendly to newcomers, as was often the case. Akkach was on a slope. On the higher part of this hillside were Greek dwellings, rather poor, I would say. At the lower end ran a brook, and further on there was the Turkish quarter of Kötü Köy, "the Bad Village," an apt name … The building license has been delivered and work immediately started. The occasion is celebrated by a preliminary gathering of the workers and craftsmen, and a sheep is roasted as it is traditional. I still remember how it was brought from

the baking house complete with its head. Pieces of meat were rolled into warm *pidé* pancakes, and everybody went to sit in the shadow of the neighbor's wall and we had a nice meal.

Building the Der Haroutiounian house began with great hope but, as I hinted earlier, soon ran into difficulties. Maritsa provides a long account of the problems her father faced and also gives us a good idea of how Ottoman-era houses were constructed in this part of Anatolia:

> The construction of our future house is going along. Sturdy foundations have been built. The walls, 20 inches thick, are coming up, especially at the corners where they are reaching the second floor. Suddenly, a municipal decision orders a stop to the works. Inspectors come and ask my father what type of building he is constructing. My father tries to convince them that it is a private house, but it is in vain, the inspectors do not believe him, they insist he is building a church or a *hammam* and has not the authorization required.
>
> I must say that such a house, with thick stone walls coated with lime plaster, was rather unusual in Marsovan, and no wonder, then, that the inspectors would not believe it was a private house. In Marsovan, houses were built with a wood frame and the empty spaces were filled with clay bricks. Then a coat of clay mud was applied outside and inside. Their walls were usually some 8 inches thick and, although in the richer houses walls were covered with lime plaster, plaster coating on the outside was very rare.
>
> Now, construction is suspended. Large quantities of wood, stones and lime are stored in a place located at the end of the town, unwatched, in a poor borough. Each day, materials disappear. Stones and lime vanish. Nearly all the timber beams ready to be installed have disappeared. And the authorization to resume work is still to come.
>
> Construction was suspended in 1906 and resumed only in 1908, when the Constitution was proclaimed. After the Constitution came into force, the situation somewhat improved, and it was then that my father imagined digging a well and using the excavated earth to keep putting up the walls ...
>
> So, using the remaining stones and lime, my father elevated the wall 7 to 10 feet higher. He finished the frame so he could make a roof to protect the carcass against rain and quietly complete the walls. Each evening, he went to the site with one or two apprentices to prepare the adobe. To this end, earth is compacted in a box, or more exactly in a wood form, and the day after the form is removed and the same operation is repeated. Now the walls were completed, and my father had installed a door that opened on the side street. To reach that door, you had to go through the backyard that was at a lower level than the house. He blocked up the front door opening on the high side of the house with clay bricks and installed two main beams to support the roof.

124

Unfortunately, my father had taken as watchman of the site a man who came from the same town as him and who was his friend. And that man had cut 7 feet off the length of the frame timbers … When he saw that, my father was driven mad. These beams had been brought in from a faraway place and were very costly. No immediate substitutes could be found.

This broke his heart; the site remained as it was. The posts were installed but he could do nothing with them. He decided to leave things as they were. He made a sort of temporary roofing with tiles since that roofing was to be destroyed anyway and the house rebuilt.

Just about the time the house construction stalled, the family increased by another birth. In September 1906, Haïganouch gave birth to a second baby boy, Aram, followed two years later by another boy whom they christened Haïgazoun. The family was growing yet they had no house to call their own.

No Place Like Home: Aram Dildilian Returns to Marsovan

Aram had left Turkey illegally, so the return home would not be simple. His internal travel documents had been only for transit to Ordou, the Black Sea port city from which he illegally emigrated. He would need a visa, and reentry was not guaranteed. Homesick and missing his family dearly, he was determined to return. His brother Tsolag also hoped that he would come home and join him in the photography business. As Aram relates, his first attempt to return was not successful. He had friends back in Ordou who had a plan. They had instructed him to first obtain a visa for Ordou in Egypt, which at the time was autonomous but still technically a part of the Ottoman Empire. Ordou's harbor commissioner was a close friend and had promised to ease his entry into the country. Unfortunately when the Greek steamer arrived in Ordou, it was the harbor commissioner's day off, so Aram was greeted by the chief of police. This turned out to be an unpleasant experience: "He looked at my papers, asked me a few questions and with some dirty cursing words said to me, 'You infidel's son, you went to London and Paris, educated yourself and now you are trying to come back to teach your people to revolt against us.' So he ordered me back to the steamer."

Yet the pull of his hometown and family was too strong. Encouraged by his friends, he developed a more refined plan. This time they made sure the friendly harbor commissioner was on duty. Aram was instructed to wire his friends when the steamer left Piraeus for its journey to the Black Sea ports, including Ordou. A code would be used in order not to tip off the police. Aram wired his friends, "three barrels of olives are on board the Zaphos," and departed for Ordou again. He relates that this time the scheme worked:

When the Greek steamer came back to Ordou, I waited on the deck. An hour later our friend, Shafky Bey, the harbor commissioner, came on board and passed by me whispering, "go and sit on your belongings for a few minutes and then go to your cabin and wait till it is dark." A little later, a boatman came and carried my trunk and other belongings, and when it was real dark, the same boatman came and asked me to follow him down to a rowboat where our friend Shafky Bey was waiting in the boat ... We started towards the city. There was bright moonlight so he asked me to take my white collar off. Then when he saw a patrol boat coming towards us, he made me lie down flat. He exchanged a few words with the men and asked his man to row towards the west; we may have passed the town limit, and beached the boat ... His man took us on his back and carried us to safe ground and we started to climb up the hill. It is a beautiful hillside town, white houses spotted among evergreen and fruit trees. Soon we were up on top of [the] Armenian quarter where our friend's house was.

38. Proof of photo of Ordou harbor taken by Tsolag to be used for a postcard, c.1900.

When we entered the house, everybody was waiting for us. When my dear brother in tears of joy embraced me, our Turkish friend sighed in grief, blaming his heartless government which does not let two dear hearts unite with each other.

The plan to return to Marsovan required great caution since Aram did not have an internal passport. A long, back-country mountain route had to be followed in order to avoid encountering gendarmes. Aram provides a fascinating account of the journey home. They were to pass through Armenian, Greek and Turkish villages, whose hospitality varied considerably:

126

We hired three pack horses and started real early. The first day was the longest, it was an Armenian village where we were the guest of an old friend and spent the night in safety. The second day we were in a Turkish village on a rocky plateau. The third day, we were to make a stop in a Greek village but we were bluntly refused to stop there. They were very suspicious and made us keep on going. So we kept on going as we knew there was another Greek village about a few miles away. We faced the same treatment there, too. It was dark and was about to rain. After much persuasion and by promising money, we were allowed to stay outside a big barn wall. We pleaded at least to give some protection for the horses but they refused ... We stretched a canvas over us and the horses to protect us from rain. We pleaded to provide some firewood with money. We were happy that they did that much of a favor. We kept the fire going all night long. We did not sleep that night but we were kept warm and dry. It is hard to understand what goes on in the minds and hearts of those mountain folks – fear, jealousy, hate, or poverty, God knows what!

The next day, we were the guest of a Turkish village. Before we were led to the village guest room, the dinner table was set, there was a big pan full of pilaf, parash (bread) and plenty of diluted matzoon (yogurt). We were provided with woolen beds for all three of us and the horses were well taken care of. What a great difference between those two neighboring village people. The first ones supposed to be Christian yet they acted wild, heartless and inhospitable. On the other hand, the Turkish village people, being Mohammedans, had hearts of gold ...

The fifth day we had to bypass Niksar, an ancient Roman city. We stayed in a Turkish village. On the sixth day, we had to bypass Hereck too, though we had some fine friends there. On the way we saw some ancient Roman fire signal towers and sections of Roman highways paved with heavy, thick slabs of stone. Finally, we came to the spot where the Iris river (Yeshil) and Kelkit rivers join together at the mouth of a narrow and deep gulley (on the south was supposed to be the ancient city Utopia). The bridge we had to cross was an ancient arch bridge but the arch was all gone. They had put big and long logs side by side and put planks on them. Some were fastened and some were loose. There was not any other way to cross the river. We had to pass over that wobbly and shaky bridge. The river was deep, turbulent and swift at that point. We came down off our horses and crossed it safely but fearfully.

Finally, we reached the foothills of Ackdagh, a snow-covered white mountain, a majestic mountain on the east of Marsovan which used to be the symbol, the trademark of Anatolia College, "The Morning Cometh." We had to pass the northeast side of it ... On the way we had to pass by the historic town, Ladik – a mixed population of Armenians and Turks. We did not go through the city to avoid curious police or jandarmas but passed the outskirts of Ladik and came to Hurlaz, a mineral spring bath resort. The owner was a Georgian and had an Armenian wife. At that place, for the first time we felt safe and comfortable. Being early spring, there were no vacationers yet. We were in a civilized place with fine clean rooms and clean comfortable beds. We needed a good clean bath so we went

127

to take baths in those lukewarm waters. We enjoyed the refreshing relief and the restful effect of the baths.

At this point in the narrative Aram describes an encounter that gives us a hint of the political currents of the time. The repressive old regime of Sultan Abdul Hamid II was under increasing pressure for change, a change that was soon to come.

> We came back to our rooms to eat something. Just then, someone knocked at our door and there entered in a tall, refined looking gentleman. Without hesitation he said in Turkish, "Be calm as I am a fellow fugitive friend like you folks, from the Turkish officials ... so don't be afraid of me. I am the editor of *Aksi Seda*, a Turkish weekly, Mr. Jemal of Samsun," and told us that it is not only the Armenians who are persecuted and pursued by Sultan Hamid and hordes of his satellites whenever we say or do things progressive. But soon things will be changed and everything will be fine for everyone ... We did not say where we are coming from. Only brother introduced himself – that he is the official photographer of the American college and that he is interested in fine scenery and nature. He pretended to believe him and bade us goodnight and good luck.

The choice of words here, "pursued by Sultan Hamid and hordes of his satellites," is interesting. The sultan was notorious for the network of spies and informers that he had placed around the empire. You had to be very careful what you said and who you said it to. Curious, then, that this progressive newspaper editor felt comfortable enough with these two Armenian "fugitives" to say what he said. I have always had the perception that my grandfather was a wise and cautious man, for otherwise how would he have survived all the life-threatening events he faced in his lifetime? While it is true that my grandfather took many pictures of "fine scenery and nature," borne out by the hundreds of such photographs that I now possess, the true nature of their journey was not to be revealed to this progressive Turk – a progressive Turk who may well have been an informer himself.

> Next morning, we purposely tried to start as late as possible so that we would arrive home after dark. On the contrary, the horseman (muleteer) was in a hurry ... He never suspected what we were or why we avoided going to any towns and tried to stay in the villages. He was surprised that we took our time and did not hurry, being the last day. He was puzzled and asked over and over why we do not start. We did not mind him and took one more mineral bath and drank some more tea. Finally we started the last lap of our long and tiresome journey. On the way, at the bridge near Havza, we wanted to have our picture taken (as a souvenir, and it was a real good picture but sorry to say, because of the upheavals I do not have a copy of that). We did not stop over in Havza at a restaurant and have a decent meal, but we stopped for lunch in an Armenian flour mill. There, we met some

THE END OF A CENTURY AND NEW BEGINNINGS

people that knew us very well but they were not suspicious about our unusual way of travel. Finally we arrived home safely. It was dark. We paid the horseman in full and sent him downtown with a guard to find a *khan* (inn).

Aram and Tsolag's journey from Ordou provides an intriguing account of the political climate of the time. We also learn that Tsolag's profession of photographer provided him with a fairly unprecedented ability to travel across vast expanses of the Ottoman Empire. My mother told me that he would often be away for weeks at a time. I encounter Dildilian photographs taken as far east as Trebizond, south as Konia and Adana, and west as Inebolu. I even own one solitary yet amazing photograph taken during prayers inside the Agia Sophia mosque in Istanbul. As a result of these travels, Tsolag had many useful contacts and friends across the country. These would become very helpful in the years ahead as the family faced greater dangers and tragedy.

Aram had been gone for three years and much had changed for the family in Marsovan. This was a period of unprecedented expansion for Anatolia College. The physical plant of the campus had grown considerably. Tsolag had completed the construction of the family house and studio on College Street across from the Professors Gate of the campus. Aram describes what he found upon his return:

> Though I knew that my brother had built a studio home and knew the location too and had sent him plans and studio arrangements, it was a great revelation when I went around and saw that it was a fine studio and home … It was a 4-story high building, a comfortable place to be in, and something singularly fine and unusual was the family bath with hot and cold water heated automatically.
>
> Besides our house, there were built other beautiful houses.
>
> I saw that very many changes had taken place, especially with my dear ones. When I left for America, Hratchia (Franco) was 4 years old. (I used to have nicknames for each one of them). Now he was grown and was in grammar school. Humayag (Greko) was only a year old and now he is in kindergarten. Jiraïr (Ducho) was not even born and now he is a chubby, red cheeked, lovely child. Ara (Dungelo) was just born. Darling Alice was not yet born. Sister Haïganouch and brother-in-law, Vosgian, were doing just as well. They had built a home of their own at the outskirts of the city, the last house on the corner. When I left for America, Haigouni and Maritza were babies. Now Aram and Haigouhi were added and Haigaz had just been born … Sister Parantzem had gone from Ordou to Vezirköprü to teach and was engaged to Yervant Shirinian. Sister Nevart was graduated from college and was away in Talas teaching … Cousin Sumpad was graduated from college, was helping brother, and was engaged to Prapion (brother's sister-in-law) … Uncles were in Sivas with their families and brother Shamavon was in school.

39. Dildilian family home and photo studio. First house
in Marsovan with hot and cold running water, *c.*1912.

40. Professors' houses on College Street. The house on the left belonged to A. T. Daghlian, professor of
music. The house behind it belonged to J. J. Manissadjian, professor of natural science. The Djizmejian
house is in center front. Behind is the house of V. H. Hagopian, professor of Turkish. The Dildilian
house and studio are on the right, *c.*1906.

Aram was now back home. He was a talented 24-year-old photographer and artist who was determined to create an independent life for himself.

The Dildilian Siblings Pursue their Separate Paths

The memoirists of our family story have done a remarkable job chronicling the events in the lives of their extended family. Maritsa has provided a wealth of information about her aunts and uncles, some from the stories told by her mother Haïganouch, while other facts come from her first-hand experience. The latter will become much more pronounced as we move into the second decade of the twentieth century. Both Aram and Maritsa also have much to say about Sumpad, Haroutioun Dildilian's only son. As I had mentioned before, the Dildilian siblings often treated him as a brother, calling him as such in many places in the memoir. Aram remarks that the "Brothers" of the Dildilian Brothers studios are three individuals, Aram himself, his older brother Tsolag and his cousin Sumpad. Maritsa was especially fond of him and devotes a whole section of her memoir to him:

My uncle Sumpad:
I think that artistic gift was innate in the Dildilians, especially in the fields of music and drawing. One day, Sumpad had a disagreement with his art teacher. He had two years to go to complete his schooling. The teacher complained to the headmaster and requested that Sumpad be excluded from school. Sumpad, when called in, courageously defended his position and thereupon was asked to make a drawing he would imagine himself. He worked all night and the next morning submitted his drawing ... The headmaster did not dismiss him and moreover asked him to give art lessons in the school, which he did until he graduated.

After graduating brilliantly, Sumpad settled as a photographer in Samsun, in the borough of Sou Bache. He had his parents join him from Sivas and forbade his father to work.

When Sumpad was still studying in Marsovan, Prapion, my aunt Mariam's sister, was also attending the College. I must say that Prapion was a girl who knew how to get her way, and her sister even more. She set out, with her sister Mariam's help – I pass over the details of their efforts – to seduce the boy. At the beginning, he had complained to my mother about the girl's attempts. But with the passing of time, he confessed to my mother that he could not resist any longer and had fallen in love. Although Sumpad's father and mother were absolutely against this choice, the marriage took place, and in addition in the Protestant rite. Sumpad used to say: "My faith is solid" ("Djérmag's khas é," that is "My white is pure"). However, gradually, he began to accompany his wife to the temple, then he stopped going to the Apostolic church, and he ended up as a Protestant.

41. Sumpad (holding the palette) and classmates
at Anatolia College, c.1905.

That situation was painful for my mamig. I do not know how things were with
Haroutioun and Elbiz, but one day when they had come to Marsovan and we were
having a picnic, Elbiz had sighed from the bottom of her heart: "Oh! My only son
acting in this way! May he at least make one of his four children an Apostolic!" I
do not know why that remark made quite a strong impression on me even though
I was very young.

I saw their first child, little Tsorig, a very alert little girl, when she was two. It
was at the celebration of the 1500th anniversary of the invention of the Armenian
alphabet and of something else relating to the College creation.[2] All the former
pupils had been invited and Sumpad was present with his wife and child. Thus
I got acquainted with my cousin Tsorig whom I liked very much because of her
great alertness.

Uncle Sumpad was fonder of us, the Der Haroutiounian children, and showed
more concern to us than to my mother's brothers and sisters, although these were
closer kin to him. When he came to Marsovan, be it for a one-day visit, he stopped
at our place ...

One day, a nation-wide contest was organized in Turkey in order to recruit
a railroad engineer. Sumpad came first. With two other engineers, a Swiss and

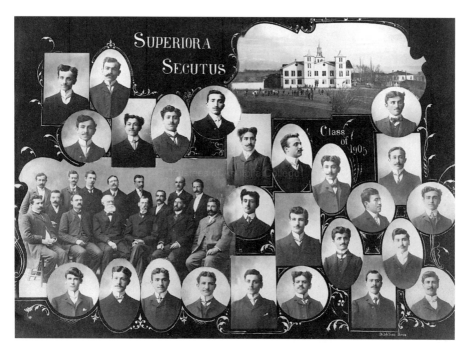

42. Sumpad's Anatolia College class graduation photo.
Sumpad is pictured just below the words "Class of 1905."

43. Sumpad and Prapion's wedding in 1910 in Marsovan.

Belgian, he was involved in the contract for the building of the Samsun–Sivas line. His duty was to make drawings of some special sites, such as for the construction of bridges, tunnels, ramps, etc. He made drawings on scale for the preliminary design studies, and works were then commenced under the supervision of the two other engineers.

The starting point of the line at Samsun was located near Maranian's flour mill, a bit beyond the Yéshilermak River ...

Samsun had not at that time harbor basins, and a metallic-frame wharf carrying a railway track extended far into the sea so as to connect ships and trains.

The line had reached Kavak when Sumpad came to see us for the last time, and the line was already three hours farther than Kavak. Sumpad had been provided with a horse and a tent to go around as required for his job. The two European engineers had a separate tent.

On this occasion, Sumpad said to my father: "Pésah [brother-in-law], if I want, I can have the line routed next to your house and continued up to Çorum." And he added: "Over there, in Samsun, you'll have opportunities; your work will be appreciated. Although, for the moment, I don't advise the move because the air you breathe there is unhealthy and the hot season is bad. But in a few years, the swamps will be drained, we are working on that. When this is done, I'll take you there absolutely."

And in truth, when we went to Samsun, I saw when arriving there that, on the road to Bafra, they were digging the mountains and moving earth to fill in the swamps. Sumpad had been actively involved in these works.

44. A map of the Middle East in Armenian prepared by Sumpad Dildilian.

I must also add that the geographical maps in the book written by Professor Manissadjian had been drawn up by Sumpad, and the professor had mentioned it in his book. I have one of those maps that I have kept as a souvenir.

Maritsa writes about both her aunts, Parantzem and Nevart, in similarly endearing terms. Parantzem and Nevart benefited from the educational opportunities afforded them by the presence of Anatolia College. Parantzem had trained to be a nursery school teacher, while her younger sister, Nevart, had graduated from the Anatolia Girls' School and qualified to teach at high-school level. Maritsa writes:

Nevart Dildilian:
    She could enter the American Girls' College thanks to a special intervention. Nevart was bright and was doing fine, especially in English and music – and in particular regarding singing.

45. Nevart playing the mandolin with her nephew
Hratchia, the eldest son of her brother Tsolag, *c.*1910.

Three months before her graduation, she was, as proposed by the headmistress, Miss [Charlotte] Willard, appointed as schoolteacher in the American College at Talas [near Kayseri].

As an end-of-course present, my father had made for her two batons to beat time: one was white and cut from a horn, the other was tapered in a succession of white and black rings. He had also made a nice leather case to put them in.

Nevart worked four years in Talas, then one year in Bolis and two years in Bafra.

Each time she changed place, she came to visit us in Marsovan, just as my aunt Parantzem did. This was a great pleasure for my mother who was very fond of her brothers and sisters and longed for them when they were away.

My great-aunt Nevart's travels would eventually bring her to the United States. Though she lived in California for part of my adult life, I only have a vague memory of seeing her once on a trip she made to New York when I was a very young child. Given the central role of photography in our family's life, there is probably a photograph of that visit stuffed away in some box that I possess. I have met two of her daughters, Lucy and Alice, both extremely talented artists. Alice possesses the musical talents of her mother. Lucy, who currently lives in Las Vegas, also sings but is a noted painter and like her mother a teacher, but in her case a teacher of art.

Nevart's older sister, Parantzem, who had served as the excuse for Aram's "escape" from Turkey in 1904, had been teaching nursery school first in Ordou and then in Vezirköprü, a town close to Marsovan. Maritsa describes her aunt's wedding from the joyful perspective of a seven-year-old who attended and could years later give us this first-hand account:

Parantzem had spent four years in Ordou and two years in Vezirköprü as a nursery school teacher. A Protestant family, the Shirinians, asks for her hand for their elder son, Yérvant, and an engagement is agreed. The wedding will take place in August, after the end of school year, so that Parantzem may prepare her trousseau.[3] My other aunt, Nevart, has returned from Talas and is spending her vacations in Marsovan. My father hires a carriage and, with Nevart, we go to Vezirköprü. And there, the three sisters busily prepare the trousseau.

I will never forget the welcome, kind hospitality and care of the bridegroom's family. Each evening, Mr. Samuel took his horse to drink at the temple [church] fountain. In fact, he was coming to play with us, the four brats. He took us on horseback around the yard … One of his games was to take my sister from the window, lower her to the ground and then put her up again after she had said "manavant" (this word means "especially, in particular," but such was the game).

They also offered me a pair of white-leather ankle boots, which they had made themselves. The day before the wedding, my aunt Mariam arrived from Marsovan, and on the same day, mule drivers delivered my father's present, a bed split in several packages, sent to the bridegroom's parents.

They asked us to stay over after the ceremony, which was not the custom. We lived there as if we were actual members of the family, and each day was a festive day. My mother could, at last, have some rest: they would not let her work. Each day, we went to visit relatives or friends, the Shirinians, the Samuélians, the Semsarians and others I have forgotten …

We went to a *tekke* [shrine of a Sufi saint], which contained the tomb of a Muslim religious [figure]. On one side, a green turban had been placed on the stele. My uncle Yérvant put it around his neck and came out so attired and all the women chuckled. He was a very playful man although he always looked serious. So he let us laugh at length and suddenly he asked: "Now, what's all this about? Why do you laugh?" with such a stern look that we all stood totally bewildered.

They had brought with them hammocks and ropes to suspend them and we had much fun swinging in the hammocks. My uncle threw me so high that I went on a complete turn. I was very excited but my mother had been so afraid that my uncle stopped the game. All the men and big boys went swimming in the river but we, the small ones, were not allowed to enter in the water. My mother gathered us around her so that we would not be tempted …

Suddenly, my aunt Nevart rushes to us out of breath. She had been afraid: "Sister, sister," she cries, "he looks exactly like an ape." She was speaking of the bridegroom's father who was very hairy.

We were still in Vezirköprü when a sort of fear came hovering upon the town. We did not leave the house for a few days, and suddenly joy burst out. "Hourouvét" [brotherhood] was shouted in the streets. The Constitution had just been proclaimed. Official festivities were organized … but finally [the constitution turned out to be] an empty shell!

On our way back, we stopped in Havza where we all went to bathe in the hot springs of the little *hammam*, which are very famous in our region. My aunt walked in, the place was hot and misty with steam, and in this dimmed atmosphere she did not see the edge of the pool and tumbled over. And, as the pool had not much water, she twisted her ankle.

Odd, the things that stand out in the mind of a seven-year-old: the hairy in-law, the Young Turk victory forcing the sultan to restore the constitution, and her aunt's twisted ankle.

On my second visit to Istanbul, my friend Ferda decided to take me to one of the truly Armenian restaurants in town, "Jash." The word "*jash*" is the common word for meal in Armenian. The owner, Dayk Miricanyan, was there to give us a very warm welcome. On every subsequent visit to the city, I have made it a point to have a "*jash*" at Jash. The walls of the restaurant are decorated with many fine pictures and old photographs. Dayk had heard of my exhibition of the Dildilian photography collection, so on a recent visit, he was anxious to show me a photo of his distant relatives taken more than a hundred years ago. The photo captured an outdoor *"jash,"* or what we more commonly call a picnic. He told me that these folks were the Shirinian side of his family. Shirinian is a rather common Armenian surname, one I have often encountered before, but as most Armenians typically do, I asked about the family's hometown. His response, "Vezirköprü," gave me a start. I told him that my great-aunt Parantzem had married into the Shirinian family from Vezirköprü. After showing him photos on my iPhone of my Shirinian relatives from a hundred years ago, we both agreed that we were related, albeit by marriage. This must be true because the hospitality shown to my family a hundred years ago at Parantzem's wedding is replicated every time I walk through the doors of Dayk's restaurant.

Yet as a child growing up, I had never heard mention of the Shirinians. Many, many years later as I was sorting through some of the old family photographs that had been left to me by my uncle Humayag, I came across a large family portrait with faint Armenian writing penciled on the back.

46. The Shirinian family including Parantzem and husband Yervant, top left, *c.*1908.

I could make out a word or two but needed the help of my mother to decipher the rest. She diligently copied out a translation of her father's writing that turned out to identify members of the Shirinian family pictured in the portrait. This was the family that my mother's aunt Parantzem had married into back in the summer of 1908. My mother could not recall whether she had ever met this aunt though she kept saying that the face in the portrait was very familiar. My mother, who was born in 1911, could not have been much older than four when her aunt perished. As a very young child she had seen many photos of her aunt and her name was often on the lips of her parents and older siblings. The photographic image and the reality of the person had merged in her memory. As she struggled with the translation, a few of the names began to appear: Parantzem Dildilian, the Shirinian bride; Yervant Shirinian, Parantzem's husband. The others in the portrait were identified solely by their relation to the groom, that is, the brother, the sister, the mother, the father, another younger brother, an aunt (the father's sister). But soon my mother's face became sullen as if a dark shadow had descended upon her. Her eyes were glistening from the tears that slowly began to appear. The sentences she jotted down were fragmentary since some words would not reveal their meaning to her. She wrote: "Afterwards there came two nephews, Hurant and Hratchia ... 10 people all, full of life ... all family was deported ... were lost 1915." These were her cousins who were born in 1910 and 1912 respectively. Not mentioned was the baby girl, Lucy, born in 1914 and named after Parantzem's beloved mother. My mother was the youngest of the Dildilian siblings and the only girl. Her cousins were all older than her during those early years in Marsovan. She could not tell me if she recalled ever seeing these young cousins, these young playmates she was never to know.

Great Expectations and Disappointment: Restoration of the 1876 Constitution

The joy and celebration of Parantzem and Yervant's wedding had been further heightened by the news that the 1876 Ottoman Constitution had been restored by Sultan Abdul Hamid II. The restoration was not a voluntary act. Ottoman armies under the leadership of reform-minded Young Turk officers revolted in the Balkans and Macedonia, culminating with a march on Constantinople in July 1908. The constitution was restored on July 24, 1908 and preparations soon began to convene the parliament. Both Aram and Maritsa explain how these events are perceived by the Armenian minority. Since the establishment of Ottoman hegemony over them, Armenians had held a second-class status that deprived them of many legal rights. They now for the first time would have equal status, at least in principle, with all other citizens of the empire regardless of ethnicity or religion.

Aram titled the chapter chronicling the Young Turk revolution, "Turkish Constitution and Freedom!" The hoped-for end of the 40 years of repressive rule by Abdul Hamid seemed near:

> One day, Dr. Riggs came to visit us and among other things, brother asked him, "Dr. Riggs, what do you think about all those persecutions. Is there an end to it?

What do you know about them within your own circle?" He said, "These are really the darkest days I ever remember. Let us not be despondent, the night is most dark before the dawn. Things can't keep on this way. I do not know what, but something surely will pop up, something good or something worse will take place." Sure enough, a few months later, July 24, 1908, the Constitutional Government was proclaimed.

47. President Tracy's announcement from the balcony of the Main College
of the restoration of the 1876 Ottoman Constitution, July 1908.

140

*Procession in Celebration of the Opening of the Parlament.
Merzifoun (Marsovan), 17. Dec. 1908.*

48. Photo card, "Procession in Celebration of the Opening of the Parlament [sic],
Merzifoun (Marsovan), 17 Dec. 1908." The procession filling College Street (now
Kolordu Sokak), Anatolia College on the left, the Djezmijian residence in the center and
the gate to the Dildilian home behind.

Yes, we were free and we were given equal rights with Turks ... That is the land we were born in, is our land now. The country where our fathers and forefathers have lived many centuries, have fought for it, have created a Christian civilization for which they sacrificed everything until the Turks took it over and subjugated them to the Ottoman tyranny, was ours. It was unbelievable but they assured us that it was true, that the country was ours, we were equals, no more subjects. We will have free action to do or go places that we wish, which gave us new vision for the future. Yes, we were free from the fear of persecution or death at will ... we were equals, brothers with one another, that is, Turks, Greeks, and Armenians, and other nationalities ... After many days of real joyous celebrations, parades and speeches were over, everybody had a bright outlook for the future and started all sorts of new plans and endeavors.

Soon, all kinds of new enterprises were undertaken, [such] as electric generating, coal mining, machine shops, and many other ventures. We, too, three brothers (Tsolag, Sumpad, and Aram) organized a company, Dildilian Bros. We planned to start branch studios in Samsun and other towns. Soon Sumpad went to Samsun after getting married. Soon my dear uncle, Haroutioun, Aunt Elbiz, and my younger brother, Shamavon, went to Samsun from Sivas to be together, and Shamavon started to attend the French Jesuits College for higher education.

At this point Aram must have felt that he had made the right decision in returning to his homeland.

Maritsa, in commenting on this new constitutional era, gives us an account of why Armenians have fared so poorly over the many years of Ottoman rule:

As a minority, they had not their say and it can even be said that they had no rights at all. In the cities, it was possible to live but in the villages, life was unbearable.

Even if we could come to a modus vivendi with the Turks, how were we going to get along with the Kurds, Laz, Cherkess, Kezelbachs, Arnavouts [Arvanites] and others who, as Muslims, benefited from the help and protection of the government? ... But all those peoples were [considered] Turks since they were Muslims.[4] Among the minorities were also the Jews, not numerous and not appreciated. Besides, no Jew in any country confesses he is a Jew, at least in those days. He is more Turk than a Turk, more Christian than a Christian. He is not discernible.

The Greeks also form a minority. But they have a protector, Greece, which even though distant, is a European country, and the Turks do not like to have political disputes with Europe.

Only the Armenian was a designated victim. Indeed, who is going to care about a race shedding blood and tears within the depths of Turkey? Yet we were a nation, we were human beings, we did not have the scent of game ...

At the cost of innumerable sacrifices, Armenians took part in the movement, thinking that if the Red Sultan quitted, life would be bearable, at least it would come back to what it was before his accession to the throne.

"We are brothers, we are compatriots," we had chanted with the Turks. We acquired the right to give soldiers to the country and bear arms ...

Great festivities were organized in many parts of Marsovan.

The son of our neighbors, the Tourchiyans, was to join the army. For days, his mates came on the evenings to visit him and there were songs and music. A very courteous Turk, who was passing by, probably guessing that it was not a wedding, asked what the occasion was. "He is going soldier!" "Hey, my boy, you don't know what it is, yet," said the Turk, and he resumed his walk.

Given what lay ahead, first in the Balkan Wars and then in the First World War, an Armenian aspiring to be an Ottoman soldier would prove to be an unwise aspiration.

As is well documented, this period of optimism was soon dashed by new persecutions and massacres the following year. Historians have established that the massacres in Cilicia were perpetrated both by the old guard and the new guard; that is, the conservative forces of Abdul Hamid and elements from within the Young Turk movement. Aram writes extensively about these events. He is especially concerned about the impact the massacres had upon his Protestant co-religionists:

We two were doing fine in Marsovan and were planning bigger things for the future. But our joy and gladness of our newly acquired freedom was soon gone. Soon that freedom and equality became a bitter experience on account of the Cilician massacres in April 1909. Imagine, not even quite a year of that so-called freedom. Thousands were killed, robbed, homes were pillaged and ransacked all over Cilician towns, Adana and other towns. That was a great tragedy. They killed more than 35,000. There was a regular organized group of fanatic Turks who carried out their ferocious and sinister slaughter from town to town. Only two towns were spared, Duert Yol [Chork-Marzban] and Hadjin. In Hadjin they had been informed beforehand and were organized to resist and they were able to do that because of the town's unique geographical position, so the Turks were not able to break the resistance. It is nice to know that four American lady missionaries helped them to resist.

That Cilician massacre hit very hard the Cilician Protestant churches ... The Cilician Church's Union Convention was to convene in Adana in April 20, 1909. On the way to Adana, one group of ministers and delegates (10 ministers and one professor) were congregated in Osmanieh [Osmaniye] Church for prayer meeting, when they were surrounded by Turks who put the church on fire on all sides and burnt them to death. Those who tried to escape, were shot down on the spot. About two years later when I went there, there was a nice white church building built on the spot. Another group of five were shot on the way. Near Osmanieh, another group of 15 ministers and 4 ladies were killed in Dagh Getchid. I stopped there at the bridge in quiet reverence where many others were killed and thrown into the river. Many other ministers and delegates were killed … in their homes. Only 15 ministers survived out of that Church Union. It was really a great deadly blow to those Protestant churches, but two years later when I visited some of those churches, every one of them were as strong as ever.

When the bad news came to every city, town, or village and people heard the details, they were shocked … They open their pocketbooks and sent financial help … for the needy, orphans, and widows … I remember very well that special mass meeting in Marsovan when many gave till it hurt, many gave all they had.

Unlike the massacres of 1895 and 1896, these atrocities did not spread across the length and breadth of the Armenian highland. Isolated violence took place but nothing was reported in the memoirs about violence in Marsovan.

Much was written about the Cilician events at the time. Whether it was the official military or parliamentary investigations, the gripping and heartbreaking account of the massacre's aftermath in Zabel Yesayan's *Among the Ruins*, or the horrifying and gut-wrenching poetic rendering found in Siamanto's *Bloody News from My Friend*, the Cilician massacres had a profound effect on a younger generation of Armenians who believed that if there were massacres in the future, as inevitably there would be, they would be prepared to defend their community. Aram tells a story in which during a summer holiday he comes face to face with such a reality:

After awhile when things went back to normal … we rented an idle flour mill in the valley for the summer so that the children would have fresh air and enjoy swimming and hiking in the hills for the vacation. In the meantime, we used to have some guest girls from the girls school who could not go home for the vacation, as my sister-in-law had a tender place for such lonely girls. We had wonderful times playing, singing, reading and telling stories.

Every other week, I used to take turns with my brother to attend the business and stay home … [One] week it was my turn to go to the mill. Towards evening, I took care of everything, looked to see that all doors and window shutters were closed tight and after, as usual, some singing and story telling, we all went to bed. My sister-in-law was in town with my brother so I was the only responsible one in the house … About midnight, I was awakened by some footsteps. I knew for sure that no one would go about the mill during the night as that mill was the last one and there was no road up the valley. I was somewhat scared and at once I put on my leg and silently listened (a good thing the children were not awake). Finally I heard a soft knock at the back door, so I went over there and tried to hear their conversation. I heard some Armenian words so I took heart and said "Who is it?" One soft voice said, "Aram, open the door, open the door!" When I opened the door, there was our neighbor, Hovhannes Sivaslian. I did not know that he was a group master training boys for the hard life out in the mountains. He told me that he took his group out for training for the week and on the way back home Sunday night, they saw a lonely mounted jandarma going towards a Turkish village. At once everyone hit the ground but against his strict orders, a trigger-happy boy fires at the jandarma and misses, so at once the jandarma turns back. Soon many jandarmas go out hunting for the boys, so they had to go into the hills to be out of sight and hide themselves. They were very hungry. He knew that I was at this certain mill so he dares to try to come over and ask me to give them some bread. I gave him three big loaves of bread and cheese and asked him not to linger around. So they had to hide their guns in the rock holes and walk about 30 miles through the mountains to Kavza. Then, as individual travelers, took the ride in flour wagons and came back home one by one.

That was the first time I was aware that there was such a movement of training young boys like that, and I did not like it as I was sure it does more damage than good overall.

As we will see later in our story, learning how to survive in the hills and mountains around Marsovan became a life or death necessity for young Armenian men who had escaped the death sentence of the deportations in the summer of 1915. Aram would once again be called upon to provide assistance that made a difference in this life and death struggle.

7

The Prosperity and Premonitions of the Pre-War Years

Growing Restless in Marsovan: Aram Expands the Photography Business

Aram's return from America had much pleased his older brother Tsolag. He had plans to expand the business, and Aram was to play a significant role in this expansion. The newly gained legal rights in the restored constitution may have also motivated Tsolag to think big now that his brother and Sumpad were actively involved in the business. Tsolag writes the following in 1928:

> New equipment, new home, and the latest American skills mastered, the only thing left was to organize the work, making Marsovan the headquarters, to make a big circuit. I leave my brothers in Marsovan. I go to Sepastia and cities nearby, then occurs the new constitution and "Ittihat's" [Committee of Union and Progress, İttihat ve Terakki Cemiyeti] new massacre in Cilicia. We retract from our objective and establish two branches, one in Konia and the other in Samsun. There again there was difficulty and a year afterwards, we close Konia and consolidate in Marsovan, barring political surprises.

I do not know what to make of this cryptic remark about "political surprises." The rest of my grandfather's remarks condense a lot of pre-war family history. Much of the details of this history are provided by Aram and supplemented by Maritsa. The Samsun branch continued to operate under Sumpad's supervision but the Konia expansion fell on the shoulders of Aram:

> Our business was good and I was kept busy always. I did not have … any time to do any kind of recreational activities. As it was before I went to America, I did not go downtown much and did not care to go to market unless there was some urgent demand for me to go. I had very few friends and did not have a chance to make friends downtown. The only places I

would go were my brother-in-law's carpenter shop or to Mr. Nerso's printing shop, which was a book shop too. On Sundays I would very seldom go to the downtown church services but used to go to College Hall services ... and song services in the evening. Each Sunday one of the college professors used to preach. Among those, my idols were Dr. Tracy and Professors Manissadjian and Xenides ... Although I was one of the ones who organized the Y.M.C.A. in town next to our church, we had readings, assembly, and playroom, I did not go often unless I had to, because every time I go downtown, the street children and some grown Turks would ridicule me on account of my artificial leg and unusual walking ...

Later, I was in the group of boys [who] held Bible classes every Sunday afternoon in the Armenian Gypsy quarter (in snow, rain and wind). We were very eager and happy to do so. (As far as I know, in all Asia Minor, only in Marsovan and Kastemony were there Armenian Gypsy communities. What their origin is and where they have come from, no one knows.)

49. Armenian Gypsy quarter in Marsovan, c.1908.

But I was fortunate to have a few intimate friends ... My only rendezvous was the college carpenter shop to talk with the boys and make toys and other things for the studio and for home.

Sometimes I used to go to the fields and vineyards for a walk and fresh air if it was a real nice day. I had free access, or I felt I had, at the home of Nerso, because with Haïg, often we used to experiment with carbon printing, color photography or collography.

50. Anatolia College Workshop. "Wickes' Industrial Self-Help Department." Students in the high school and college could pay for their tuition and board by learning a craft, such as furniture-making, *c.*1905.

From the last remark about "carbon printing, color photography or collography," it is clear that Aram was not limiting himself to simple portrait photography. Employing printing processes including collography is a sure sign of Aram's artistic inclinations. Various forms of collography were used by visual artists since the late seventeenth century.

Aram's remark about the Nerso home foreshadows the story he tells about his first romantic interest, Armene Nerso. Again, it is his handicap that causes him pain, in this instance the pain of the loss felt by a forbidden love. I find it hard to even use the word "handicap" in reference to my great-uncle. He was a man of many talents who never let the loss of his leg prevent him from accomplishing amazing things. I also admire the frankness with which he discusses his frustrations with the discrimination he experienced. He bares his soul as follows:

> My next interest was Armene Nerso, the first neighbor girl I met the first day when I came back from America. She came along with her parents to welcome me. We were friends with the family before but I was not even aware of her existence. I used to go to visit her often and she used to come to my workroom almost every day with her baby brother. Soon we became intimate friends but our friendship did not go any farther than mutual respect … I was sure she loved me and I assured

her that I loved her, but I did not propose to her. In fact, I did not dare propose as I was not fixed financially. Yes, our business was good and I was working always, but I did not have some special amount of money that I could call my own. About that time, her cousins came for a visit from Russia. I noticed her attitude was suddenly changed towards me. A few weeks later, they took her along to Russia for a few months. Before she left she had to act that way because all her folks and cousins did not consent to her seeing me ... Next day, she left with her cousins for Russia. She did not send me even a post card but I had my hopes that when she came back she would feel differently. Finally, when she came back she was altogether indifferent towards me and told me that she loves me but she had to forget all about me because all her folks were against the idea except her brother, and their only objection was my leg ... Well, it was a hard blow to me. I was hurt and hurt very much. It pierced my heart ... I had been hurt very many times on account of my leg, but this was the hardest ... I pondered in my mind and asked myself how many more times will I be subjected to humiliation. Often I have been hurt, refused, deprived and neglected because my leg is amputated ... once more I was downhearted and lonely ... had nothing to live for. I felt there was no future for me, no prospect to stay in the same position any longer, so I decided to go away to some other place where I could paddle my boat and try to establish a business of my own.

51. Mr. N. L. Nerso, Master of the Self-Help Department, and his family. Deported with the faculty and staff of the college on August 10, 1915. Nerso was murdered along with all the men from the college on August 12, 1915 near Zile, south of Amasia. His family pictured here also perished. Armene is not identified but is one of the two standing girls, c.1908.

A strange turn of phrase, "paddle my boat," but this humiliation convinces him that he "must paddle his boat" independently and away from Marsovan. Aram writes to contacts he knows at the Jenanian College, officially known as the Jenanian Apostolic Institute, in Konia, and receives an invitation to come to the campus as a teacher. Given his skills in the visual and mechanical arts, he will eventually secure work as a drawing teacher. He will also teach geography, not a surprising choice given all the world traveling he has done. He will take this opportunity to open a photography studio of the Dildilian Brothers in Konia.

As Aram gathered his supplies and equipment for the move to Konia, another large fire broke out in Marsovan. As was the case with the fire that consumed Vosgian's shop in 1904, this fire spread rapidly and threatened major portions of the city. Aram describes the events and the false accusation that almost led to the imprisonment of his brother Tsolag:

> Just before I was to start for Konia, there was a great fire in Marsovan and about 1/5th of the city was burned. Our church and school building were in the path of the fire so all the Protestants and college boys fought hard to stop the fire. Otherwise, if our church and school were burned, the fire would have spread and burned the mother church and schools too and the Armenian quarter on the highest peak called "Arevortick." At night, my brother volunteered with a few others to keep watch so that the fire would not start again. Sure enough, at midnight the fire broke out again in some other section. Brother and the others that were on the watch did everything possible to quench it at once. Later, a fanatic Turk told the police that he did see Dildilian Tsolag re-stir the fire, but good thing a very respectable Turkish gentleman did testify that Mr. Dildilian and himself were the first ones to reach the spot and put the fire out.

Despite the constitutional reforms, the implication from the above is that the old rules still applied. The testimony of a non-Muslim had no validity in court unless supported by a Muslim. Luckily for my grandfather there was "a very respectable Turkish gentleman" to save the day, for otherwise he may have faced the fate of his father Krikor who had spent two years in jail back in Sivas for the lack of a Turkish witness.

Aram was now free to set off for Konia. He chronicles this trip in a similar fashion to that of the other trips. I find the details he records quite impressive. When he sat down to write his memoir some 40 years later he must have had either a diary to work from or an incredible facility for recall. His trip from Sivas to Marsovan was his first, followed by his long journeys back and forth to America by way of Ordou. I condense his account for our purposes.

Aram hired a Turkish driver to take him first to Ankara by way of Çorum, Sungurlu and Kalecik and then on to Konia. He comments that, "The trip was uneventful, dull and hard. There were no roads or bridges." Staying either in one-room inns (*hans*) or with Protestant acquaintances, they eventually reached Ankara. Like his earlier account of his childhood trip from Sivas to Marsovan, future dark events will intrude into his description:

> Finally we arrived at Ankara, the ancient Galatia, the future capital of Turkey. I stayed there several days as I had to visit and see some old friends. While I was there, I could never imagine that this place will be the butchering place of my people and some of our college teachers and our minister, Rev. Demirjian, who were going to Constantinople as U.S. citizens. In 1915, Ankara was one of the designated stations to eliminate the Armenians. Finally I took the train for Esgishehir [Eskişehir]. What a train – a wood burning toy. It could hardly make 12–15 [miles per] hour. We had to wait till next day to take the train for Affion Karahisar.
>
> It was too early to go to bed. I did not care to stay in the coffee house in the smoke-filled room so I took a walk around. The Germans had built some nice uniform houses for the railroad workers ... Next day I arrived at Affion Karahisar, an old picturesque city situated in a rocky valley. My friend, Mr. Samuel Alexanian, was the head teacher of the Protestant schools. I was the guest of Rev. and Mrs. Yeranian, the minister. I took some group pictures of the school children and some other people and started for Konia.

During this period the Germans were busily expanding the Ottoman railway system. The Anatolian Railway that connected Constantinople, Ankara and Konia had been built by the Germans in the 1890s and expanded almost to Adana by the early years of the twentieth century. Great efforts were being made to complete the hoped-for Berlin to Baghdad railway in the years preceding the First World War. Many Armenians were hired by German companies to work in the construction. Aram's cousin Sumpad, one of the partners in the Dildilian Brothers studio, was soon hired as an engineer for the Samsun to Sivas line whose construction had begun just prior to the war.

Aram arrived in Konia and took up his teaching duties at the Jenanian College:

> In Konia I stayed at the Rev. Kantamour's and boarded with the family and soon started teaching drawing and geography. Prof. Haigazian was the president of the Jenanian College. He was a real Christian believer, an all-around scientific man, one of our greatest men. He was a victim, with others of our great men, in 1915 ... He was very kind and sweet with me. He permitted me to build my studio in the Jenanian College grounds because I was not able to find a suitable place for my studio outside in the city. So I started doing business and was quite satisfied with everything.

Thus began the Konia studio of the Dildilian Brothers. Though many of the photographs that I possess from this pre-war period have three cities' names,

"Merzifoun, Samsoun, Konia," identified below the name of the studio, none of these are images or people from Konia. There is one solitary photo of Rev. Kantamour and his wife but little else from Aram's sojourn in Konia. All three studios adopted the logo that contained the name of the city of Konia.

Dr. Armenag Haigazian (1870–1921), who invited Aram to open his studio on the campus of Jenanian Apostolic Institute, was one of the great Armenian intellectuals of the early twentieth century. Born in Hadjin, a graduate of Columbia University and the Union Theological Seminary, he went on to earn his Ph.D. from Yale University in Semitic Languages and Biblical Literature. Returning home to pursue the ministry and an educational mission, he became president of Jenanian Apostolic Institute. He was versed in at least 12 languages and the author of textbooks on biology, logic, psychology, an Armenian–English dictionary, and a voluminous encyclopedia. He also was an ordained minister and an accomplished musician.[1] It also should be noted that Dr. Haigazian was a photographer, most likely accounting for the invitation to open Aram's studio on the campus.[2] He was able to send his wife and five daughters to safety in the United States early in 1915. He continued working in his community but was eventually deported. Having survived the massacres, he returned to do relief work at the end of the war. In 1921 he died in Kharpert after being arrested and maltreated by Kemalist forces. His daughter and son-in-law helped found a college in his memory in Beirut. Haigazian University is one of the leading institutions of higher learning in Lebanon.

Aram was relatively successful in Konia but success did not last long. This time it was not a fire but a severe winter snowstorm that brought an end to the studio:

> While I was building my studio in Konia, I did not have enough money to spend freely to build a firm and strong one. I tried to suffice by using cheaper materials that did not serve the purpose. But that year in Konia we had an unusually cold year for that part of the country. One morning as I started to go [up] to work in my studio, there was about 15 inches of snow on the ground. The college boys had already opened a path to walk. There was a real cold misty wind blowing hard at my face, wetting my eyes and face. When I went to the spot where my studio was supposed to be, there was no studio standing and everything was covered with snow. The cold wind watered my eyes and became more wet … I did not know what to think or to do. All my new-acquired courage was gone and I felt really downhearted and weak. I could fix up everything over again and keep on going but I can't tell why … At once I let go everything and decided to go to Adana, Cilicia, for a new venture.

Aram informed his brother back in Marsovan and sister Nevart who was teaching in Talas of his plans. Why Aram decided to move on remains a mystery, for as he writes 40 years later in his memoir, he is unable to give an explanation.

Aram's journey to Adana inspired some of his most religiously moralistic writing. The beautiful Taurus Mountains separated the fertile plains of Adana from the interior of Anatolia. The railroad from Konia to Adana was still under construction in the mountains, requiring an interruption in his journey:

I took the train down to Oulou Kushla [Ulukişla]. At that point the Constantinople-Baghdad Railroad ended … I had to stay there for a few days to be able to hire a wagon and driver for Adana …

The horse and wagon journey from Oulou Kushla to Adana was very interesting. The scenery was breathtaking, especially the Cilician Pass through the Taurus Mountains where Armenians fought, reigned, and died, where the Armenians gave a helping hand and showed hospitality to the Crusaders, and where our last Lousinian Kingdom of Cilicia was lost … Right and left you could see the remains of those old crumbled Armenian fortifications … The road goes through a valley called "Turnic Bogazy" almost parallel to a swift and turbulent-running river, which passes by a white clayish land. All the way it was milky and muddy but every few hundred yards, a pure, crystal clear water runs down the hillside and mixes into the muddy water. Some bigger body of water would keep its cleanness for awhile but soon it, too, intermingles with the muddy waters and becomes part of the main body. At one special spot I noticed a higher brook came down the hillside and made a path of its own parallel to the river, creating a lovely contrast for awhile but finally it too went into the dirty waters. This time it took quite awhile to mix itself with the dirty waters, almost a fight for life or death. That reminded me of our young in Christian homes, pure upright, clean, innocent, who have come in contact with the dirty world … sure enough, for awhile they do struggle to keep their pure and rightful principles and good Christian virtues but finally they give up the fight and intermingle with the rest of the crowd. While I was deep in those thoughts, we came to a spot on higher ground where we saw the blue Mediterranean Sea in the distance and in a bird's eye view, the great Cilician fertile valley. I could see that dirty, muddy Devleg river and the Seghan and Ceyhan rivers pouring down into the big bosom of the sea. For a few miles, those big dirty rivers seem to strive to change even the blue color of the sea into tan, but eventually it became the beautiful blue Mediterranean, which brought to mind this bright thought, that all of us in the rush of life, in dirty, sinful lives, finally will go to the bosom of the Infinite to be purified.

Aram then introduces a new extended metaphor in comparing the Cilician forests to the plight of the oppressed Armenians: "Some huge trees had fallen down by the cruel hands of the hatchet man and, for some reason, left to rot there … How thorough an example and a picture is this story of the trees to my peoples who are neglected … and the rivers to this suffering humanity." Thus begins Aram's sermon-like Adana travelogue, with its extended, religiously grounded metaphor of the Armenian nation's struggle between good and evil.

Aram finally arrives in Adana, a city that still shows the scars of the massacres from the spring of 1909. He immediately establishes a photography studio. Sadly for us there are again no definitively identified photographs from this period that survive in the family collection:

> I arrived in Adana, a half-ruined, burnt, dusty, dirty, but thriving city. Soon I was able to secure two rooms and a big north-exposed balcony, an ideal place for operating room and a big basement, which I used as my dark room. Adana did not have city drinking water or running fountains though the big river Ceyhan was next to it. The water boys bring the water with donkeys and each house has big earthenware jars to store the water.

52. Delivering water by donkey. Location of photo uncertain
but could be Adana or Samsun, *c.*1910.

> After it is settled down, it is ready to drink. It is sweet water to drink but not safe. Adana, though a big city, did not have [a] sewer system either. Each home had its own septic dugout or tank system but not modern style, for all the well water was not safe for drinking and was acidic. There were all kinds of disease germs in the water and in the air, especially there were plenty of malaria-carrying mosquitoes and though I had mosquito netting over my bed, yet they bit during the day. It was not a healthy place to be in but it was an agricultural and financial center. There was plenty of money for the party who had business ability and who knew how to make money, but not me, I was not a businessman. I was fortunate to meet and make some friends like Dr. Nakkashian, a fine Christian doctor ... His Highness the Catholicos of Cilicia, [from] Sis, Sahag Khabayan [Sahag II, 1849–1939]. It was very sweet of him to take me by his side and we discussed things

pertaining to our nation … Twice I tried to kiss his hand but he refused me with a sweet expression that "you are a Protestant" and shook my hand. He was a fine Christian, a great and goodhearted clergyman.

While in Adana, Aram received what he thought would be a lucrative commission from an important client. Near Adana in Mercimek was the Imperial Stud Farm. Ottoman sultans were noted for their love of horses and horse breeding was an imperial pastime. Mercimek was one of the most important stud farms of the sultan. In the imperial photography collection of Abdul Hamid II there are numerous photos of these horses. A famous collection of 1,819 photos taken in the late 1880s and early 1890s was given as a gift to both the United States and England. These photos were primarily taken by three famous Armenian photography studios located in Constantinople: Abdullah Frères, Sébah & Joaillier, and Phébus. I assume their commissions were more lucrative than the one Aram received more than a decade later:

> While I was in Adana, the manager of the Royal Farm of Sultan Hamid, took me over to that Royal Farm. There was no regular road. Most of the time we drove on a dry riverbed. The farm area was a vast area of land, maybe several thousands of acres of fertile wheat fields. There were plenty of well-built stone stables for the beautiful Arabian horses. I took pictures of the horses in groups and separately and of some of the farm buildings. He ordered three copies of each, and I was not paid a cent. No matter what I did, he would not pay me. Not only was I not paid, while I was at the farm more than six hours, I was not given any food, which is customary. I was served only one small cup of Turkish coffee.

I wonder if these photos ever made it into the imperial photo collection. Sultan Abdul Hamid II was "retired" by the Young Turks at this point. He had been replaced in April 1909 by his brother, who was to reign as Sultan Mehmed V. I suppose that sending the bill to Yıldız Palace would have been a fruitless gesture on Aram's part. I cannot help but think of the scene in Atom Egoyan's film *Ararat* in which an Armenian photographer asks Jevdet Bey, the military governor of the vilayet of Van, to pay for a portrait he had just taken. The time was April 1915 and the "butcher of Van" is not at all pleased by this request. Fatal consequences result.

Despite this setback, Aram appears to have been very active in pursuing his profession. Using Adana as a base, he traveled to many of the surrounding cities including Mersin, Tarsus, Osmaniah, and Hamideah. On one of these journeys he became very sick:

> On the way to Ceyhan, I did visit the spots where in 1909 about 32 ministers of the Gospel were killed. In Ceyhan I rented two rooms in a hotel and was doing quite

well in spite of the terrible heat. It was hard to develop or make prints without any ice. There I became terribly sick but, thanks to God and Mr. Nishan Nakkashian, I was well again even though I was near death.

It is clear from the memoirs that these were lonely years for Aram. Humankind was often disappointing him. He especially missed his family and friends back in Marsovan and Samsun. Nonetheless another major change was about to take place in Aram's life.

Domestic Life as Seen through the Eyes of Maritsa Der Haroutiounian

While Aram's memoir provides many details of his home life, especially when he was growing up in Sivas, Maritsa describes at length domestic activities within the home. The difference in gender and the highly patriarchal structure of Ottoman Armenian families may account for the heavy emphasis on domesticity on Maritsa's part. As we will see, much of what we call domestic work soon became important for the survival of the family.

Haïganouch and her daughter Maritsa supplemented the family's income with their textile and rug weaving work. Often in her memoir, Maritsa describes the sewing, knitting, weaving, chair caning and textile work that were integral to household activities. She describes knitting stockings and sewing linen underwear. Maritsa provided the muscle power for cranking the sewing machine while her mother guided the stitching. These long days working with her mother were culturally enriching for the young Maritsa: "While she was mending or knitting, she took us around her and told us stories, asked riddles or sang songs. Also, she related stories about her family, and this is why I still remember all these things. She recited poems she had learned at school, which shows what a sure memory she had." Haïganouch used to rely on her daughter to keep track of the daily household chores, often referring to her as "my telegraph daughter."

Haïganouch's skills at sewing and weaving brought in crucial income, for soon her husband Vosgian moved to Trebizond to earn the money needed for construction of the family house. Maritsa describes how her neighbor Marnos taught Haïganouch how to weave beautiful carpet mats. Recycling the thread from old and discarded linen made the process profitable because there was no need to purchase the raw material:

She produced such attractive things that the neighbors were coming to see them. Marnos was very proud of her pupil: "She weaves better than me. Look, it stands upright like a wood board, and aren't the colors well matched? You'd say it is a carpet."

53. Weaving and textile work, staged photo in the Dildilian Marsovan studio, *c.*1910.

54. Alice Dildilian, Athens, *c.*1930.

Khrimian Hayrik (1820–1907) was a much-revered figure in Armenian history. A strong advocate for Armenian social and political rights within the Ottoman Empire, he served as Patriarch of Constantinople from 1869–73 and as Catholicos from 1892–1907. His life-long quest for social justice often put him at odds with Sultan Abdul Hamid II and Tsar Nicholas II.

Maritsa's longing for her father came to an end in the summer of 1911. His return became the occasion for another family holiday, this time at the thermal spa of Havza. Maritsa provides a fascinating account of the town that had been a favorite retreat for Armenian and Greek families from this region of Anatolia:

When the exact date of my father's return was known, my mother said we would go and meet him on his way. We decided to go to Havza. We knew that my great-uncle Haroutioun and my great-aunt Elbiz, babig and mamig as we used to call them, had taken residence there for vacations and spa treatment. Journeys were rare at that time. People were born, lived and died in the same town, often in the same borough, and even in the same abode. So that when the carriage that was to take us stopped in front of the house, the neighbors came around, full of curiosity. The carriage was a *yaylou*. It was a brand new vehicle, very attractive to look at from the outside and even more from the inside. You could see multicolored flowers, pictures of landscapes, little mirrors. And there were curtains decorated with bobbles, held by tiebacks, as may be seen in sitting-rooms … Needless to say I was very happy. We are off.

Finally, we reached Havza's main street, a wide avenue lined with hotels and khans. At a window of the Armenian *millet* khan, we saw three heads. My mother immediately recognized two of them: "Ha, here are my aunt and my uncle!" she cried. "But who is this young man with them?" We walked in and, in the midst of a large turmoil, we met them … and the third one was my father!

We had there a very pleasant stay. Fruit, which is cheap in August, was aplenty … because fruit came from Amasia, Tokat and mostly Turkhal and was shipped to Samsun, by way of Havza. I will never forget that two-foot-wide melon. Even cut, its slices were so big that we did not know how to make a start on them.

Facing our khan, across the street, was the shop of Zorikian, the cobbler, where I often met my babig. Our Haïgazoun, who was hardly three, cried when he saw babig: "Baboug, bring us watermelon!" Every other day, at least, we went to bathe. Mamig entered the hot water pool because she thought this would cure her. When I say hot water, it was really hot water. I could not dip my hand into it. And the poor woman had great difficulties getting in. They gave her cold water to refresh her face but, in that *hammam*, even the cold water was hot.

As to drinking water, it must be taken from the *hammam* the day before and let to cool off overnight. It was said that this drinking water was very palatable and health-promoting.

Once or twice we went to a picnic by the cedar grove called "The Forest." On these occasions, we took all the necessary things. My sister and I carried the drinking water in earthenware jars from Tchanak Kalé [the Pottery Fortress] which my father had brought from Trebizond. We ate kebab.

There was a bazaar called "the women's bazaar" where, in the morning, women from the country bring their products: milk, yoghourt, eggs, poultry, etc. One has to go there early for by 10 a.m. everything has gone.

As everywhere else, the three *hammams* were reserved for men during the evenings. However one was open to men in the daytime. One *hammam* had a circular pool, 11 to 12 feet in diameter, with a ledge – this is where my aunt had sprained her ankle. The great *hammam* had two pools, a rectangular one, 8 feet by 7 feet, and a circular one at least 17 feet in diameter. Hot water flowed from the small pool to the big pool. The latter probably dated back to very ancient times. At one of its corners, there was a stone at least 3 feet by 1 foot in size, convex-shaped with a concave part resembling a stoup, where water gathered. That water was rather cool and could be drunk. The legend says that a young girl of noble birth had embraced the Christian faith and, to escape persecutions, she had taken refuge in the thermal baths, crouching to hide, and when they had wanted to take her, she had petrified into a statue, and water was now pouring from that statue.

As is typical of Maritsa's memoirs, chronological order is often ignored and some dates can be off. In this case, she jumps ahead by six years to describe what seems like another sightseeing trip, though this is hard to comprehend given that it takes place during the war years in 1917. Her uncle Aram was stationed in Amasia as a military photographer late in the war, so this may have been during a family visit.

Amasia, Vezirköprü, Marsovan are very old cities, founded long before Christian times. In Amasia, there are very ancient grottoes, especially Aynale Maghara (the Mirror Grotto) and Kezla Saray (the Girls' Palace). I visited these two grottoes in 1917 … The Mirror Grotto has its name from the fact that, after you have passed the entrance opening, the rock is smooth and shiny like a mirror. Visitors carve their names on it, sometimes so high that one wonders how they managed to do it. There are paintings on the sidewalls. On the left, the drawing of a spear can be seen. The entrance is at a height of at least 10 feet and a ladder is required to reach it. The vault of the grotto is also decorated with very interesting oil paintings. These grottoes are located by the riverside and water flows at their foot.

When my sister and I visited these grottoes, we borrowed a ladder from a peasant. It was a long ladder, at least 10 feet long and we had difficulties putting it in place due to the configuration of the place: the ladder was always standing too steep. I climbed up but was not able to see the drawings and paintings. Night was coming and, at that time, it was not prudent to linger on …

As to the citadel, it was a place where only Turks could go. As I said, we could not risk going to such places at that time.

Amasia seems to have been a favorite holiday destination for the family. There are dozens of photographs of the sights of the city in the family photo album, one of which shows Tsolag's children having successfully climbed a ladder to enter one of these tombs. In the summer of 2011 when my friend Ferda and I traveled to Marsovan in search of the Dildilian home, we took a side trip to Amasia. We spent the night in the city, sleeping in a beautiful Ottoman-era house that was once the home of an Armenian priest. The house was now an inn for tourists like ourselves. I suppose "tourist" is not the right word to describe us given the journey we were on. The sights we were visiting were historical, but in my case, historical in a very personal sense. As Aram told us earlier, Amasia was the home of his dear aunt and uncle Helline and Arakel Potookian. Their fine home graced the river that flowed through the heart of the city. Could they have been neighbors of this priest whose home was also on the riverside? They surely would have visited this house, sat in its beautiful garden, talked about matters both religious and political, as Arakel was vice governor of the sub-province, and may have even broken bread together here. The Potookian family disappeared in the maelstrom of 1915. As I fitfully tried to sleep that night, I could not help but feel that the ghosts of this past were keeping me company – an uneasy company, one I needed to experience. I was not a tourist; I was on a pilgrimage. Later we will return twice more to Amasia.

Maritsa concludes her story of that happy childhood holiday:

> Our holidays also came to an end. Again, a carriage was waiting for us in the khan courtyard. We were sad to leave and at the same time happy to return. Outside of town, beggars were extending their hands while wishing us bon voyage. My father threw one or two 10-para coins to them. Children were offering wheat sheaves for the horses, which is another manner of begging. In the fields alongside the road, women did the same while expressing happy journey wishes. They had sometimes a child tied on their backs while they were reaping with sickles or scythes ...
>
> We reached home before sunset.

The end of the holidays also meant the beginning of the school year for the children of the Dildilian and Der Haroutiounian families. Maritsa provides a lengthy description of the Armenian national schools in Marsovan. The educational curriculum in these schools was quite advanced for its time and place. Graduating from these schools gave one the qualifications to pursue advanced study in Constantinople and Europe. The three school systems in the city, the national schools, the Catholic Jesuit schools and the Protestant schools associated with Anatolia College, graduated many students who would go on to receive advanced degrees in varied professions, including law, medicine and engineering. Greeks and a few Turks also attended these schools. Maritsa provides a detailed description of the curriculum and activities of the national school that she and her siblings attended. I excerpt a small part of this account:

At the Sourp Sahagian High School, courses were given in Armenian. Schooling lasted for eight years and … the institution had received from the Turkish government the *idadiye* [preparatory] qualification which allowed graduates to be directly admitted in the military academy [*Harbiye Mektebi*] in Bolis [Constantinople]. With a two-month additional effort in English, students could be admitted in European or American universities. French was taught as second language. Some Turkish pupils attended the Sourp Sahagian High School.

Maritsa attended the Sourp Hripsimé High School for Girls. She describes the subjects that made up the curriculum: "Armenian, arithmetic, etc., were taught in the mornings. In the afternoons, we had writing, drawing, civics, religion, gymnastics, singing or sewing. Our needlework articles were sold on Speech Day. Some of these were sometimes very pretty pieces." The schools published a bi-monthly newsletter to which the boys and girls of the schools contributed. Maritsa notes that "Each high school had a library lavishly provided with books." While cultivating the mind, the body was not neglected. Hygiene classes were given and an abundance of athletic opportunities were available for the students.

Much has been written about the advanced levels of education brought to Anatolia by the American missionary system. While it might have been the case that the local national schools were in a rather primitive state when the missionaries first arrived, by the pre-war period they had more than caught up with their Protestant rivals.

The Home That Was to be Forever Out of Reach

Upon the family's return to Marsovan, Vosgian resumed his ambition of building the ill-fated family home. As Maritsa explains, the whole purpose of the sojourn in Trebizond was to earn enough money to complete the construction:

> Regarding the future house, my father thought that, if he himself supervised closely the construction, he would fend off any future mishaps. Inside the thick walls of the room which was to be the wash house and fireplace, he made two rooms by erecting – following in that the building pattern of most houses in Marsovan – thinner partitions of dried-clay bricks between the timber posts which were now shorter than initially intended as the posts had been sawed off by the person in charge of keeping the site. The materials stored had disappeared or were no longer usable. He built the floors with boards from dismantled crates, usually disposed of as firewood. Only the doors and windows could be reused, in his opinion.
>
> "Another winter," my father used to say, "and the house will be finished."
>
> My father found a shop located across the street in front of the town hall. A new shop means little business. So he took advantage of this slack period to make

our doors and windows. In the evenings, he came back sooner and continued work on the future house.

Finally, we could move in at the end of October [1912] …

The house had two rooms on the ground floor. An empty space for a future stairway was used as kitchen. It was at a slightly lower level and was fitted with a chest of drawers and an oven. There was a small window through which water was thrown outside.

The house was cramped for the eight of us, including the aunt from Sivas. However, the place could be conveniently heated.

I referred to the house as ill-fated because the construction was never to be completed. Vosgian's progress over the next two years was slowed by financial difficulties. Illness in the family also would sap their financial resources. In close succession, first Maritsa's sister Haïgouhi, then mother Haïganouch, brother Haïgouni, and the "great-aunt from Sivas," all became severely ill. All recovered after lengthy periods of recuperation. But medical care was not free, even the care provided by the American missionary doctor. Maritsa writes, "The doctor came twice a day. Oh, what an expense was that Dr. Marden, an American! Each visit cost 20 ghourouchs, whereas the daily wage for a worker was 2½ ghourouchs. Drugs also were expensive. And, should the illness last for a number of weeks, it would have meant ruin for us." Maritsa does point out that Dr. Marden's Armenian assistant, Dr. Puzant Donikian, was a lot less expensive.

During these years before the war, the Der Haroutiounian children worked together to accomplish their father's dream of completing his house. Vosgian built a workspace in the house, enabling him to bring work home from the shop, which allowed the children to help with some of the carpentry work. One example was a commission he received from the French Jesuit High School in Samsun. It was an intricate and difficult unit to construct. None of the other joiners in town were willing to take on this task. Maritsa relates their concern: "The other joiners from Marsovan came to see my father and told him: 'Vosgian, if you manage to build this unit, we will cut off our moustaches.'" Vosgian recruited his whole family in the work, especially the varnishing, of which Maritsa provides a detailed account. She concludes this episode, "Finally, the unit was completed and carried to Samsun securely braced on a cart … and no joiner in Marsovan cut off his moustache!"

Finally some progress was made on the house, actually the stable, which was going to serve as a summer bedroom:

After a hard winter, my father, helped by Haïgouni, built the stable and, in the upper part, he arranged a barn with four little windows, one of which looked upon the access stairway. My brother and I prepared the sun-dried clay bricks used to fill in the spaces in-between the framing system. Boards from crates were again used for flooring. And then, once the walls had been plastered with clay mud, a big room was available above the stable. Thus we had, like any other Marsovantsis, a stable and a barn.

Although my brother eagerly wanted it, no cow or donkey was put into the stable. The stable became my father's workshop and the barn a summer bedroom offering a very pleasant view onto the Catholic and Protestant cemeteries, the village of Herka, the entry to the Pacha Deresi valley with the road leading to the watermills and to the vineyards of the Kiremidjians, Avedigians and Peynirians. These were gardens surrounded by walls, with a house and a stream flowing though the garden. The Kiremidjians' vineyard in particular had a nice one-story house, with a fountain in front of the house. The water from the fountain was conveyed by means of stone-made channels to the fruit trees and the vegetable garden. My father had lived for two years in that house and he enjoyed a right on a blackberry tree he had rented in the vineyard. We went there every Sunday, and the children played and gorged themselves with blackberries. We spent these days in the country in a healthy and peaceful environment.

The families that Maritsa identifies here were the wealthy notable families of Marsovan. The Kiremidjians were especially important in the city. Besides business interests in the textile trade, they owned the hotel in town. Their large family home still exists in the city, though when I last visited, it was nearly in ruins despite the fact that a family still occupied the ground floor. At a crucial point in 1915 Kiremidjian was to play a pivotal role in the survival of the Dildilian and Der Haroutiounian families.

Aram Returns to be with Family and Friends

Aram's endeavor to establish himself in Cilicia had not achieved his hoped-for success. He had set up a studio in Adana for his base and traveled to other towns in the custom of Ottoman photographers in decades past. The rigors of travel were taking a toll on his health. When an opportunity to return home arose, he immediately jumped at it: "When I came back to Adana, I found a letter from my cousin Sumpad, saying he has a fine job with the Samsun-Sivas Railroad Company so he would gladly transfer his studio to me if I care to go back to Samsun. That was a God-sent message. At once I packed my things and started back to Samsun as I was tired, sick, and lonely."

While Samsun was not his hometown of Marsovan, it was close enough to feel like home. Samsun was an overnight journey from Marsovan and with its port served as its primary outlet to the rest of the world. Many family friends lived in Samsun along with a thriving Armenian and Greek community. All of Tsolag's photographic supplies would come through Samsun, and he often made the journey to this commercial center on the Black Sea.

With many accounts of my family's journeys back and forth between Samsun and Marsovan in the back of my mind, I arrived in Samsun in the summer of 2011. Ferda and I flew in and soon rented a car for the journey to Marsovan, now only referred to by the name "Merzifon." We drove through some very scenic countryside, passing through hilly terrain with a small, rapidly flowing river as our companion. We even stopped for tea somewhere near the halfway point in our journey. A hundred years ago, this typically two-day journey required an overnight stop and a fresh set of horses. A faded photograph in our family album captures my grandmother standing with my mother and uncles at a *khan* (highway inn) somewhere between Marsovan and Samsun.

55. Highway inn with my grandmother Mariam and her children,
including my mother Alice standing by her side, *c.*1914.

The highway Ferda and I took was for long stretches a four-lane motorway. Road construction was rapidly converting the remaining winding, two-lane, yet nostalgically scenic road, into a motorway. In little over two hours we found ourselves in Marsovan. I must admit having a slight letdown at journey's end. Was I expecting a more demanding trek? Progress does make it difficult to relive the past.

Aram's arrival in Samsun was a joyous occasion. Family was there to greet him: "When I arrived in Samsun, Sumpad and Prapion had moved to [the nearby] Kavak Station of the R.R. Company. My dear Uncle Haroutioun and Aunt Elbiz, were home to greet me in warm love. Soon my young brother, Shamavon, came donned in French school uniform, a nice and good-looking young lad. I had not seen him for the last 12 years." It is interesting to note that

Aram's uncle and aunt were at this time living in Samsun near their son Sumpad. Since the chief protagonists in our memoirs are no longer in Sivas, information is scarce as to the family back in the ancestral hometown. It is unclear at this point whether Haroutioun is still running the family shoe business. We know that at some point after the Hamidian Massacres the ancestral home had been forfeited to pay off the family debt. Haroutioun is approaching 60 years of age and may be near retirement. His son, Sumpad, had been highly successful with the photography business in Samsun. At the time of Aram's return, Haroutioun and Elbiz appear to be living in Sumpad's house. Maritsa's memoir has them spending their summers taking the spa waters in nearby Havza.

Aram soon became involved in the activities of the local church and the Armenian General Benevolent Union (A.G.B.U.):

At once I started working and gradually my business started to grow better and better. I was happy, very happy, because I was among loved ones and among friends and not among cold and indifferent strangers. Soon I was active in the church and in young people's work. They all loved me and respected me and that was more incentive for me to do more. Soon I was elected an officer in the church council and was teaching Sunday school. I did not have much time to engage in other national and social activities, except A.G.B.U. membership, which was organized just then. We had a night party to acquaint the people with the A.G.B.U. and its work. That night, I took a flashlight picture in the Armenian theater, something new then in Samsun ... I was never interested in joining other organizations. The only mass meeting that I ever went to in the Armenian quarter was on Sunday, 1912 in May. The speaker was the well-known writer, Varoujan.

When I first read this section of Aram's memoir a dozen years ago I did not realize the added meaning it would have for me years later. Aram describes a "mass meeting" in which the speaker was Daniel Varoujan (1884–1915). Varoujan was a leading Armenian poet and public intellectual in the pre-war period. He was one of the founders of the *Mehian* (Temple), a journal at the heart of a literary movement that advocated for an Armenian cultural renaissance based upon a modernist and pre-Christian aesthetic. Varoujan was arrested on orders of Interior Minister Talaat Pasha on April 24, 1915 in Constantinople. He, along with hundreds of the Armenian cultural, religious and political elite, was imprisoned in the Anatolian town of Chankiri. Varoujan was murdered on the orders of Yunuz, the responsible secretary of the Chankiri İttihat ve Terakki Cemiyeti (Committee of Union and Progress) committee, on August 26, 1915 as he and five other Armenians, including the poet Dr. Rupen (Sevag) Chilingirian, were being transferred to Ayash.[3] Aram describes Varoujan's talk that day as "almost a prophetic pronouncement on what was to come." Aram continues: "He did not say what will come or really that it will be a world war.

He did not say either that he himself, will be one of the first victims with the Armenian intelligentsia before the terrible upheavals that wiped out his and our dear people, but he said that some big things are to come through big upheavals such that the world has never experienced!" Though Aram does not explicitly state that Varoujan recited any of his poetry at this gathering, undoubtedly he did so. Poetry was a typical component of Armenian oratory, especially at times of social and political change. Among the family papers I inherited from my uncle Humayag was Varoujan's last volume of poetry, *The Song of Bread* (*Hatsin Yerge*) published posthumously in Constantinople in 1921. These were the poems he was writing at the time of his murder. The volume was never completed but the manuscript was rescued through the use of a bribe.

Little did I know 20 years ago when Varoujan's book came into my possession that I would be teaching his poetry in my classes at Columbia University and Southern Connecticut State University. The theme of my course is literary and artistic responses to the persecutions and massacres of Armenians in the late Ottoman period. Poems from *The Song of Bread* engender much discussion in my seminar. I became curious as to why Varoujan's poetry and in particular this set of pastoral poems came to find a place among the few books my grandfather chose to keep with him when he was forced to flee Turkey in 1922, leaving behind most of his possessions and the house he had built. Could it be that these poems brought back strong memories of his childhood in Sivas and its environs? With my mother's passing, there is no one alive now who might help me answer this question, so I can only speculate. *The Song of Bread* celebrates the joys and honest virtues of the rural life. One could even say that it makes sacred man's interaction with the cycles of nature. In an essay about these poems, Eddie Arnavoudian writes:

> So *The Song of Bread* sets out to chart the process that produces "Sacred Bread," from the ploughing of the land, the sowing of the grain and all subsequent stages to its consumption at the family table. The adventure alas came to a halt after the threshing and milling, with the remaining journey being indicated only by titles Varoujean [Varoujan] left us – "The Flour," "The Cattle Shed," "The Kneading," "The Oven," "The Family Table" and the final celebration "The Song of Bread."[4]

Varoujan's poems with such titles as, "The Tillers," "The Carts," "The Oxen," and "The Haylofts," stood out in my mind as I was sorting through hundreds of my grandfather's photos, trying to determine which would be suitable for an exhibition I was planning. I suddenly realized that my grandfather's photos captured the images Varoujan had created in his poems. I was seeing with my eyes what Varoujan had painted with his words. I needed to know more and soon traced both men, Varoujan and my grandfather Tsolag, to the same soil of the countryside around Sivas.

56. Harvest time in the province of Sivas, *c.*1910.

"The Carts"

The carts move on the village road
At sunset, loaded with crops,
Looking like pyramids in motion
Clad in fading rays.
Boys with deep tans, piled on top,
Spur now and then
The quivering, shimmering flanks
Of the giant oxen.[5]

Varoujan was born in the agricultural village of Perkinik, just north of the city of Sivas in 1884. The village, now known by the name Çayboyu, was an Armenian village at the time, almost exclusively made up of Armenian Catholics. In 1909, after studying in Europe, he had returned to his native village and taught school there until 1912. There is no way to know the exact location of the scenes captured in my grandfather's photos but it is safe to say they are from the countryside in the province of Sivas. This same soil inspired Varoujan. I often show these photos to my students when we discuss *The Song of Bread* poems.

In the summer of 2012 when I made my second pilgrimage to my ancestral homeland, I needed to go back further in time than my family's days in Marsovan. With the help of my friend Osman Koker, I explored my ancestral home in Sivas. With Daniel Varoujan in mind, I asked if we could visit Pirkinik. Despite its proximity to Sivas, the village is still fairly rural and seems to retain some of its agricultural connections. Our walk through the village was interrupted by a herd of cattle slowly meandering down the main street. Aside from one lintel with Armenian letters and the date 1909 etched into the stone, there was very little that would have told you that this was an Armenian village. The ruins of the *hammam* where Varoujan's family would have bathed was still there and scattered among the dilapidated shacks were a few more stately structures that could have been inhabited by wealthier Armenians in the Ottoman era.

57. Keystone with Armenian letters and the date 1909 in the village of Pirkinik.

But we must now return from this ghostly present back to the story of Aram in Samsun 100 years ago.

Aram's initial months in Samsun appear to be much happier than any of his years since leaving Marsovan. He writes:

> In Samsun, because of my profession, I made lots of friends, especially the Armenian Bishop [Sahag] Odabashian Vartabed, who was killed by the Turks on the way to his new office in Erzirum. We were very friendly with the Armenian Catholic Bishop Kuzirian and made friends with a Franciscan brother, many Greek, American, and European businessmen. My business was getting better and better. I tried to

173

introduce one price policy that went fine with everybody except Turks. Bargaining had become so natural, it was hard for them to pay the price no matter how low a price was asked, they should surely bargain. I made some enemies for that.

Vartabed Odabashian was originally from Sivas, so Aram had much to talk about with him. The incident he reports about the murder of his newly made friend took place on January 1, 1915. Patriarch Zaven I (1868–1947) had appointed Odabashian to the vacant post of primate of Sivas and Erzincan. Much against the advice of friends in Constantinople, he accepted the position. He arrived safely in Sivas but was murdered on the road to Erzincan on the basis of secret orders from the Interior Ministry.[6]

Despite the constitutional changes of 1908 and the promises of the Young Turk government, Christians were still in many respects second-class citizens. Aram describes the difficulties faced by Christians, especially strict Protestants, in their dealings with the law. He himself angered the sub-governor (Mutasarrıf) by refusing to work on a Sunday. After turning down three requests conveyed by the police, Aram suggested that a Greek photographer could take the photos: "When the governor was told what I had said, he was surprised, saying, 'What kind of a man is he and what kind of religion is it that he is following?'"

Despite these difficulties, Aram had ambitious plans for the business: "My business was growing more and more. My fame was all around. I was making plenty of money so I was planning to buy an automobile and have a driver bring my customers and wedding groups from the Armenian quarter to have more business, and the rest of the time to use it as a taxi to take people places – and I had a good many other plans for the future."

Aram's success turned out to be short-lived. For it must have been sometime in 1912 that his health started to deteriorate again. He ends this chapter in his memoir with these words, "I was working hard and did not have much chance to rest. I did not have much appetite, but I was never aware that I was sick."

The seriousness of Aram's illness became apparent when he began to cough up blood. The diagnosis was an infection in one of his lungs. The memoir does not specify if this was tuberculosis, but the symptoms seem to indicate so. In short order my grandfather Tsolag came to Samsun to bring his brother back to Marsovan. The journey home was marked by an overnight rest stop in Kavak and a poignant last visit with his dear cousin Sumpad and Prapion, Sumpad's wife. Aram's long convalescence, Sumpad's work for the railroad and the travel restrictions imposed at the outbreak of the war, would prevent them from ever meeting again. Sumpad and his whole family vanished in those dark days in the summer of 1915.

Tsolag knew that Dr. Jesse Krekore Marden at the American Hospital could provide the best care in the region for Aram. Dr. Marden's arrival in Marsovan to take charge of the hospital marked the beginning of a major expansion in

59. My great-aunt, Nevart Dildilian, *c.*1912.

1913: A Year of Great Contrasts

The year 1913 stands out in the family saga for the stark contrasts in the well-being of the Dildilian and Der Haroutiounian families. The Dildilians were prospering while the Der Haroutiounians continued to struggle with economic and health problems. Anatolia College and its associated Girls' School had reached their zenith by the end of the year. The success of the college contributed to the fortunes of the Dildilian Brothers photography studio, yet the political climate worsened as the year progressed. A year later the fortunes of both the family and the college would be drastically reversed.

179

Aram's long recovery kept him in Marsovan during the pre-war years. His illness indirectly saved his life, for if he had remained in Samsun in 1915, his brother Tsolag would not have been able to protect him as he was able to do for family members in Marsovan. Tragically all the Dildilians and their relations in Sivas, Amasia, Samsun and Vezirköprü were to perish in the deportations and massacres that ensued in 1915. Aram would eventually return to Samsun after the armistice in 1918 but it was a return to a city vastly altered by the ethnic cleansing of its Armenian population.

Despite the fact that for the first time Armenians had fought and died in significant numbers for the Ottoman army in the Balkan Wars, the "loyal millet" was increasingly seen as a danger to the integrity of the empire. General Antranik had led a highly effective force of 273 disciplined Armenian volunteers who fought on the winning Bulgarian side. As a result the loyal millet's loyalty was being questioned. Maritsa comments on these events: "The Turkish–Bulgarian war is over. Bulgarians are independent. The mobilized Armenian boys who survived combats and diseases are back … But the end of the war did not improve our situation. The Turks felt anger against Christians and openly showed it. They shouted: 'Everywhere, villainous Bulgarians put their flags over the mosques.' And yet, how many times had they converted churches to mosques in the countries they had conquered." The Armenians were lumped together with the Christian victors of this war, the Bulgarians, Greeks, and Serbians.

The year 1913 brought the misfortune of a miscarriage to Haïganouch and a subsequent decline in her health. A period of convalescence was called for at the nearby Armenian monastery in Körköy, a village known today as Yolüstü. It was not uncommon for Armenians to stay as guests of the monks at the monastery. The sojourn to the monastery must have taken place in March 1913 for Maritsa remarks that Easter was approaching, which fell that year on March 23. One would hope that such a rest cure would free one from many of the family chores entailed by a family of five children and a husband. Yet as we see in the memoir, Haïganouch took her five children with her, leaving behind her husband who had to run the family carpentry business. Maritsa writes that they were given one room for the entire family. Communal meals were served by the monks since individual kitchens were not provided. Yet, with five children and herself in one room, how did Haïganouch get any rest? Maritsa describes this brief "holiday":

> The carriage came and we put into it freshly baked bread loaves, food supplies and the traditional *tcheuréks*. *Tcheuréks* in Marsovan country were round and sprinkled with poppy seeds called *khachkhach*. Baking *tcheuréks* for Christmas, Easter, Ascension, Assumption and Exaltation of the Cross was a tradition in each family. We also loaded all the necessary bedclothes and pillows. And we are off.

It was decided that, once school resumed after holidays, the children would remain at the monastery and do the daily walk to and from school, same as the children from the village next to the monastery.

At the monastery, we were given a room, and my mother cleaned it from top to bottom. As it was Holy Saturday, we happily broke fast after vespers. The monastery had 40 guest rooms, which were nearly all occupied. We met some people we knew. During three days, my mother was very relaxed. Then, on the fourth day came little Alice, my cousin, whose mother was sick.

My mother imagined to hang a hammock from rings embedded in the walls. The child received all our love and attention but my mother's work was made somewhat heavier. Alice cried every night, everything was new to her; she was not used to that setting and that bed. Anyway, days went by, the child had grown more or less accustomed to us.

Then, we had to resume school. Joyfully, we walked the full way down, which took us approximately three quarters of an hour.

Haïganouch's so-called "vacation" was cut short by the illness of her husband. The family had to return to town before the month was up. The "little Alice" referred to here is Tsolag's youngest, less than two-year-old child, who would grow up to become my mother. With five children of her own, the youngest a five-year-old, what were they thinking when they sent my dear great-aunt Haïganouch off for a rest cure at that monastery!

Today much of this monastery has disappeared. As I wrote earlier, I first visited the ruins in the summer of 2011. Besides the fountain, there are the partial remains of three small chapels incorporated into a barn. In one you could see the faint outlines of the 12 apostles carved and painted high up on the rounded walls. In April of 2013 I again visited this site. This time I brought with me some of my cousins. I was accompanied by local Turks who were cognizant of the evil that befell the Armenians of their city in 1915. One of these locals, Suat Ayan, I had met on my first trip to Merzifon. We became friends. Upon opening the barn door and seeing the appalling condition of the chapels, I glanced over at Suat. I could see in his eyes the sadness and shame he felt at that moment. As a believer, he could not but feel strong revulsion at seeing a holy place used as a barn for animals. Having more time to explore the grounds on this visit, I opened an adjacent door and discovered what had been one of the monastery rooms. Had this room at one time been occupied by monks or possibly some of the guests? Could this have been the room in which my fearful mother, little Alice, had cried all night long? What I do know is that the room is now a chicken coop. With chickens flying over my head, I quickly took a photograph and departed, for I had clearly disturbed the most recent "guests" of the monastery.

Maritsa's father's illness referenced in the monastery episode was the chronic ulcer that would often trouble him. As was common in the day, Vosgian was sent

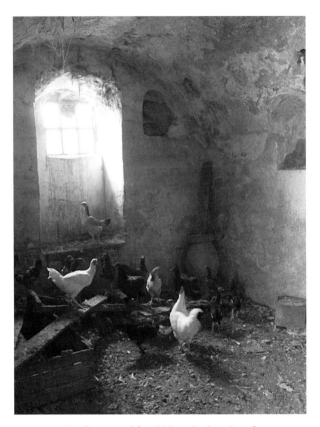

60. Room used for chickens in the ruins of
the monastery of Sourp Asdvadzadzin.

61. Chapel now used as a barn in the ruins of the monastery of Sourp Asdvadzadzin.

for a thermal cure at the Hurlaz "mineral spring resort" near the town of Ladik. His absence and the lack of income it represented further contributed to the family's hardships. Tsolag soon sent his family to the self-same resort but this meant that Vosgian would have to remain an extra month, as he was the only adult male present in this group of women and children. Maritsa intimates that the wealthier Tsolag was oblivious to his brother-in-law and sister's financial difficulties, not foreseeing that the prolonged absence would further deprive them of needed income. Vosgian's family back at home continued to find new ways of making extra money, including "folding paper sheets for the printing shop or preparing hanks for weaving."

Vosgian's fortunes soon appeared to have taken a turn for the better when he was offered the position of head of the joinery shop in the Wickes Industrial Department at Anatolia College. He closed his shop near the *konak* and assumed his new position but soon discovered that he was being asked to do much more than teach and assist students who were learning joinery skills in the college's self-help program. Maritsa attributes the extra demands put upon him to the prejudice displayed by his Protestant boss, Ghazaros Effendi. In a telling turn of phrase she writes: "And above all, he was a Protestant, which helps understand many things." The hoped-for relief with his new job was illusory:

[Ghazaros] gave my father other assignments where his competence would go unnoticed, he sent him to perform repairs. My father's wages fell to 3 pounds, which was really inadequate for a family of seven people …

The Armenian Protestants are building a new temple (church). It is not yet completed and, in the meantime, the Americans have made available to the congregation an old building in the College to be used as school and temple. One Saturday, my father prepares to go home, but Ghazaros Effendi asks him to go and repair the roofing of that building because it is raining heavily and the roof must be sealed before the congregation comes on Sunday. My poor father accepts; he cannot refuse because he cannot quit.

Indeed, that Ghazaros had given him many jobs to perform beyond my father's remit. He had asked him to fit all the window panes of a huge building housing the museum and library, and I remember seeing my father preparing putty on the evenings at home. And many other jobs of such sort were imposed on him.

The museum and library referred to in this passage was soon to be completed and would house the richest collections of natural specimens and the largest selection of books outside of Constantinople. On my most recent visit to Merzifon, I was granted permission to enter this building that now serves as a branch of a vocational school. From the perspective of one accustomed to college buildings today, this building is modest in size. Yet I was struck by the fact that this substantial building had not been altered. Some of the original woodwork in the building was still in

62. Anatolia College Alumni Museum-Library, c.1913.

place. As I touched the window frames I wondered if these were the handiwork of that skilled ancestor of mine from so many years ago.

I began this section by highlighting Anatolia College's growth. A veritable building boom was taking place on campus. North College, a large building that housed classrooms and offices, had opened in 1911, the Alumni Museum-Library described above would open by the beginning of term in 1913, and the state-of-the-art hospital would be fully functional by the beginning of 1914. Architectural plans had been drawn, monies had been collected and the ground prepared for Union Hall, a building that was never to be built due to the outbreak of the war. The collections of the museum were primarily the work of Professor J. J. Manissadjian and his students. For decades prior to the museum's opening, he and his protégés, including the gifted Sumpad Dildilian, had been exploring central Anatolia and collecting specimens of its minerals, flora and fauna. A summary description of the museum's contents included more than 7,000 plant and animal species, 40 mammals and other larger animals, 70 birds, 50 mollusks, 2,500 different kinds of insects, 1,200 plants, 100 tree samples, 1,100 fossils, and 900 minerals and rocks. Two hundred visitors came through the museum's doors every week.[8] Just as impressive was the library of the college. By 1915 the collection had reached 10,000 volumes with an average yearly circulation of 5,000 volumes. The academic year 1913–14 saw 400 students admitted into the college-level program. This was to rise to 425 by the following academic year. The breakdown of nationalities of the college population in January of 1913 is interesting to note. While the college was predominantly Armenian in its first decade, drawing upon the local population of the region, by 1913 the population was increasingly diverse, attracting students from regions and countries far from Marsovan. Only 140 students were from the province of Sivas, with 79 coming locally from Marsovan. The college bulletin of 1912–13 cites the following numbers: 197 Greeks, 148 Armenians, 8 Russians, 15 Turks, 2 Poles, 1 Persian, 2 Jews, and 1 Hungarian.[9] President Tracy had for years tried to attract more Turkish students and instructors from the region, but the authorities threw up many roadblocks to his efforts, sometimes forcibly removing students who had enrolled. But by 1913 things were changing and one Turkish professor had joined the faculty. The enrollment figures cited above do not include the even larger preparatory school, the kindergarten, the Girls' School, and the King School for the Deaf. The library and museum were open to the general population of the city, which numbered roughly 30,000 in this period. With 5,000 books being borrowed, an astonishing amount of reading was taking place in this supposed "backwater" of the Ottoman Empire.

One can imagine that with the growth of the campus, both in numbers of students and buildings, the Dildilian Brothers cameras were kept very busy during these years. Tsolag documented all the construction taking place on campus. Many of these photographs were made into postcards that students mailed home to family and friends. The sheer number of students and staff wanting to have their portraits taken resulted in a steady stream of customers. Around this time Tsolag's eldest son, Hratchia, started assisting his father in the studio while still pursuing his studies across the street at the college's preparatory school. His name would soon appear on the studio's stationery, to be followed by the name of his younger brother, Humayag. The academic year 1913–14 also marked the jubilee year of the founding of the Girls' School, an institution predating the founding of the college. Tsolag began a major undertaking to photograph all the buildings, activities and students of the school. The intent must have been a major publication to mark this important anniversary, but with the outbreak of the war the following year, no such publication would see the light of day.

Despite the growing political and social turmoil in Europe and the Empire, the Dildilians began the new year of 1914 with a sense of optimism for the future. This optimism would soon prove to be misplaced. Fourteen years later Tsolag would write: "It had appeared that we had reached the zenith of our success. Then came the deportation, massacre and suffering. Deportation and war were the last things on our minds."

8

The Clouds of War and Catastrophe

The Calm before the Storm: The Family Faces a World at War

The year 1914 began as optimistically as 1913 had concluded. The Dildilian and Der Haroutiounian families were busy with their jobs connected to the college. The Dildilian siblings' families were growing. Tsolag's sister Parantzem in Vezirköprü had just given birth to her third child. Nevart in California had also given birth to her first child. After many years of separation from his siblings, Shamavon Dildilian joined his older brothers Tsolag and Aram in Marsovan in order to attend Anatolia College. Aram was busy with the photography studio and actively assisted his brother with photographing the campus and its life.

Besides being a talented photographer, Aram was an accomplished painter. Some of his paintings survive to this day. He even contributed to Manissadjian's museum, for he writes: "I tried to keep myself busy with painting and I did some beautiful things, especially two big paintings of stone-age mammoths and dinosaurs for the college museum." Aram had also immersed himself in the life of the Marsovan Protestant community.

> Our church building was real old and was small so they wanted to build a new one, but there was no permit to build one for many years. Just about that time, we had the permit so we tore down the old one and started to build the new. There was a big mass meeting to raise money. To start the ball rolling, Dr. Charles Tracy, in the spirit of an Armenian, got up and with his usual sweet gestures and said, "I have not much money but I have been with you dear folks about 40 years, so I will give 40 Turkish liras." They had figured each pillar and each window at 40 liras each. Soon others followed him and there was enough money pledged. I did not have money, so I promised some paintings, which sold for about five Turkish liras. They did build a real beautiful and modern building and we had the chance to have the dedication service, but before we were ready to move in, the Armenian people were ordered to move, were deported, killed.

In the spring of 1914, Dr. Tracy was in the last year of his presidency of Anatolia College. He was to leave his beloved Marsovan after commencement ceremonies that year, returning to the United States after 47 years of service in Turkey. The new Protestant church was completed late the following spring, but no church services were to be conducted under its roof because of the worsening conditions for the Armenians. The church still stands today though it has been radically altered into a cultural arts center for the municipality. It survived for many years as the city's cinema. I visit it each time I return to Merzifon. Standing in front of it I have often wondered what my grandfather, who was a deacon of the church, would have thought of its transformation into a house of entertainment and not of worship. Sadly no plaque indicates that the building was once an Armenian church.

Shamavon, the youngest of the Dildilian siblings, had enrolled as a third form student in the preparatory program of Anatolia College in the autumn of 1913. He was 20 years old and desired to improve his English language skills. His second language had been French since much of his education had been at the Saint Bernard French High School in Samsun. Shamavon had been raised by his uncle Haroutioun and aunt Elbiz, first in Sivas and then in Samsun. After retiring from the shoe business, Haroutioun and Elbiz had moved to Samsun to be near their son, Sumpad. Because he was raised in separation from the three memoirists of our story, we do not know as much about this talented and handsome young man. Unlike the often mentioned aunts and uncles of my mother, I cannot recall my mother having talked about her uncle Shamavon. This is understandable enough given that she was four years old when he was killed and was only three the one year he lived in Marsovan. Since he had grown up apart from his older brothers and sisters, including my grandfather Tsolag, there was little in the way of collective memories passed down to the next generation. Maritsa seems to have the most to say about her uncle Shamavon:

> From morning on, he was humming, especially French songs. He had pinned a picture of Joan of Arc in his room. And this in the Protestant house where he lived! He was nicknamed "the Catholic" for he definitely refused to turn Protestant.
>
> The French High School had wanted to send him to Paris where his studies would have been paid for. Shamavon too was very eager to go, it was his fixed idea. But his family flatly refused, especially his elder brother who said they would have turned him into a Catholic. What a fatal mistake that was!
>
> He was fond of music and played in the school band. Music for him was as easy as eating bread and cheese. He was virtuous, patriotic, intelligent, and he always found ingenious solutions to one thing or another. "Dildil's grandson has invented something," he then used to cry gaily. He was such a wise, sensitive, unresentful boy. Maybe he thought the sort of life he was living would not last long and he would soon become an independent man. When the school year ended, he told my mother he could no longer stay here and intended to go back to Samsun.

When school ended, he and a friend packed up some of their belongings and headed north on foot to Samsun. This was a rather dangerous step given the worsening political climate. In addition, he was now subject to conscription in the Ottoman army, having turned 21 in May of 1914. Conscription became compulsory for all Ottoman citizens, Christians included, in July 1909, though there still were ways of avoiding the draft if one had the financial means. A payment, called *bedel-i nakdî* (cash payment-in-lieu) would do the trick.[1]

Maritsa comments on the problems Shamavon faced with conscription: "In Turkey, boys were called for military service at the age of 19. The police had first looked for Shamavon in Sivas, where his uncle Mikael, instead of saying he did not know, had given his address in Samsun. When they looked for him there, Sumpad immediately sent Shamavon to Marsovan, in care of Tsolag." The conscription age was actually 20 but would be lowered to 18 in May of 1914. Having turned 20 on May 27, 1913, Shamavon was thus eligible for the draft, which may account for his enrolling in Anatolia College in September of 1913. College students could more easily avoid the draft. But his decision to return to Samsun in the summer of 1914 put him in imminent danger of conscription. According to Maritsa, it appears that he soon found employment as an interpreter for the "French railroad company." The reference to a French company was at first confusing to me since I knew that the Germans were backing the construction of a railroad line that was intended to eventually reach Sivas by way of Amasia. Sumpad was busily engaged in surveying work for a German company of engineers. The confusion may have been caused by the common use of French to identify companies and business enterprises. French was the international language of commerce. The railroad company that was starting to build the line from Samsun to Sivas may well have been the Deutsche Bank-financed Chemins de Fer Ottomans d'Anatolie. This would explain my grandfather's remark ten years later that his "two brothers had obtained wonderful positions with the Samsun-Sivas Railroad company." Tsolag always referred to his cousin Sumpad as his brother.

Matters turned significantly worse for the "two brothers" in the summer. When the general mobilization in anticipation of the war was announced on August 2, 1914, it became doubly difficult to avoid conscription. We do not know where or when it happened, but by the autumn of 1914 Shamavon was in the army stationed in Adana. In the bulletin of Anatolia College published in March 1915, Shamavon's name is listed as a third form preparatory student for 1913–14 who was summoned for military service. The bulletin states: "On the ground of their education, about half have been assigned to training courses provided for preparation of officers."[2] His prior high level of education and the fact that he was sent to Adana and not the front, probably indicates that Shamavon was training to be an officer.

Maritsa commented on the year Shamavon spent with his family in Marsovan before returning to Samsun: "He stayed there one year, a hard year for such a restless boy." There was something mysterious about this young man, for I knew so little about him until a few years ago. Maritsa calls him "restless." The mysteriousness and the restlessness became combined for me when I received an e-mail from a stranger in Turkey in the winter of 2012. Out of the blue this e-mail arrived written in broken English along with an attached photograph of a rock, yes, a rock. Scratched on the rock were the following words: "Je vien ici. 24 Avril 1914. Chemavon Dildilian." The name "Chemavon" was hard to read but given the fact that the writing was in French, it could not have been another Dildilian because he was the only one fluent in French at that time. (Shamavon preferred the more uncommon spelling of his name with the letter "C.") I began a correspondence with the author of the e-mail, Bünyamin Kıvrak, who lives in Vezirköprü. He is a teacher and an accomplished photographer who has been curious about the Dildilians since first encountering the graffiti on the side of a rocky mountainside near his hometown. During his childhood, his family owned property in this rocky valley through which a river swiftly runs. Decades ago he had discovered a rocky slope covered with graffiti, some in French but mostly in Armenian. As he grew older, he came to know that the Dildilian name was associated with photography in the area. Upon encountering my name on the Internet associated with an upcoming Istanbul exhibition of historic Dildilian photography, he sent me the e-mail. He wanted to know who this "Chemavon" was and what had happened to him. I filled him in as best as I could. The last known whereabouts of Shamavon were in Vezirköprü in the spring of 1915. Let me relate what little we know about the last year of Shamavon's life as pieced together mostly from Maritsa's account.

As I stated earlier, at some point after the general mobilization in August 1914, Shamavon was conscripted and sent to Adana for training. The situation for the Armenians deteriorated rapidly over the course of the winter of 1914–15. War Minister Enver Pasha's ill-fated campaign in the Caucasus during the height of winter and against the advice of many of his experienced commanders resulted in the devastating losses in the battle of Sarikamish. Despite the fact that Armenian soldiers saved Enver from being taken as war prisoner at the front, he returned to Constantinople and blamed his defeat on the Armenian volunteer forces who had assisted the Russians. The pretext of Armenian treachery was used as the basis of an increasing campaign of persecution of Armenians across the empire. On February 12, 1915 an order was given by Enver to disarm all the Armenian soldiers in the Ottoman army. These soldiers were formed into labor and transport battalions who in the course of the following months were either worked and starved to death or executed outright. Desertion had been endemic in the Ottoman army in the past and was so again in World War I. The scholar Erik-Jan Zürcher estimates that by the end of the war the number of deserters was four times the number of soldiers on the frontlines.[3] Desertions were not restricted to Armenians; Greek and Muslim soldiers also deserted in high numbers. Throughout the spring of 1915, deserters returned to Marsovan and its countryside seeking help from family and friends. This was the case with Shamavon. Maritsa describes Shamavon's situation and paints my grandfather in a very negative light:

One month before my father's departure, uncle Tsolag, who was the president of the Armenian Protestants, and the Protestant minister had gone to Vezirköprü because Tsolag had learned that his brother Shamavon had taken refuge in their sister Parantzem's house after he had escaped from the Adana barracks. Parantzem was living in cramped conditions with a husband, three children, a father-in-law and a brother-in-law. Now, in addition, she had to hide her brother.

While there, Shamavon had begun to learn Russian and German but he could not get the appropriate dictionaries in Vezirköprü as it was a small town where the range of available products was limited. So he asked his brother Tsolag, during that visit, to send him two dictionaries from Marsovan when he gets back there, which Tsolag refused in spite of Shamavon's urging. Shamavon, then, asked to come to Marsovan, which was also rejected. He made a last attempt: "Brother, I will travel hidden underneath your carriage. Is that possible?" Again, this was rejected. Tsolag could have shown some pity to his sister, if not to his brother! This had much grieved my parents.

I have always found this portrayal of my grandfather troubling but also very puzzling. I know from Aram's memoir and my mother's accounts that Tsolag took great risks in hiding and assisting young Armenian men, many of whom were deserters. His actions in the summer of 1915 saved the lives of Haïganouch and her family, including this self-same Maritsa. Yet it is clear from the above that Maritsa and her parents blame my grandfather for the death of Shamavon. I may never know the reasoning behind my grandfather's decision not to bring Shamavon back home with him. Did he believe that the risk to his family was too great to have a known relative who was a deserter in his house? Recall that this was well before the deportations had begun and the killings had escalated. Had he guessed at the severity of what was yet to happen, would he have acted differently? I will never know the answers to these questions.

These questions were on my mind when I visited Vezirköprü in the summer of 2012. I was traveling with my American friend Carel Bertram and her Turkish colleague, Ayçin. They were both very much interested in my project and had volunteered to help me in my endeavors. Bünyamin had agreed to meet and take us to the head of the valley where Shamavon's graffiti was scrawled on the rocky hillside. The site is an active quarry and to reach the remote location of the graffiti we had to cross a swiftly moving river. I had not come prepared, for I wore casual shoes not Wellingtons. One of the quarry workers, who was to accompany us, rolled some boulders into the river to allow us to cross; so off we went. My academic colleagues wisely demurred and stayed behind. I was shocked as to how rugged and steep the trek was. As we climbed higher and higher up the side of the valley my hand often grasped the soft soil in order to keep my balance. I suddenly found myself holding a handful of soil with a broken piece of bone. I was not certain at the time whether this was a human or an animal bone. Looking over at my companion, I asked, "human?" and he nodded yes. This was a piece of human femur bone. After we returned, I inquired further but could get no explanation as to why human bones would be scattered along this cliffside. Given the history of Anatolia and the civilizations that lived, fought and died on these lands, it is no surprise that bones would dot the landscape.

We reached the site of the graffiti high up on the cliffside. In order to reach this spot, one had to stand on a rather precarious ledge. There were dozens of Armenian and French writings in different handwriting, with some signed by Shamavon. A few seemed to be dated later in time than the April 24, 1914 date that was in the original photo that Bünyamin had sent to me. The April date roughly coincides with the Easter holidays of 1914. Shamavon must have taken a break from his studies at Anatolia College to visit his sister and take a hike in the countryside. The cliff was also dotted with nearly inaccessible caves. As we made our return journey to join my friends, more and more questions kept filling my head. But soon a practical consideration interrupted my thoughts. The river had risen considerably, so the kind and muscularly built quarry worker had to carefully carry me on his back through the swiftly flowing waters. This was a momentarily hilarious diversion from the questions that kept troubling me. Had Shamavon come to this remote spot to hide from his pursuers? If so, how long was he there? When was he caught? Where was he caught? Only later I was to learn the truth, but at the time all that I could be certain of was that this elusive ancestor of mine had disappeared into the maelstrom that was 1915.

But now we must return to the summer of 1914 and the start of the First World War. While by the end of August much of Europe was at war, the Ottoman Empire was not yet an official participant; that was to come in November. The country was on a war footing as the general mobilization continued. Elements within the Committee of Union and Progress (C.U.P.) strongly favored the German side, especially now that Russians, the long-time enemy of the Ottomans, were at war with Germany. Maritsa describes the growing hardships faced by her family as the summer was coming to a close with the prospect of a difficult autumn and winter ahead:

> In August, Turkey sided with Germany, and it was war again. My parents bought candles, matches, soap, edible oil, cheese and flour in as large quantities as they could afford. They asked us to eat less …
>
> We dreaded a blockade that would have cut off food supplies. My mother cooked *péksimits* and kept them in storage.
>
> Hovhannes Yeghpayr was again called up as a soldier …
>
> Mobilization extends now to all married men with children. For most of them,

the Marsovantsis were not wealthy people. There were not many traders among them. In general, they had manual professions. For instance, many people worked in copperware making. And hammer-wrought copperwares from Marsovan were highly appreciated.

Weaving also was a widespread activity in Marsovan. Wide-sized fabrics were often manufactured by men. With the war, that activity too decayed because orders decreased. As to the threads and yarns, they used to come from Europe, and their prices suddenly soared, especially for wool yarn, which was in strong demand for Army uniforms.

The cost of living was rising and incomes were decreasing. An unusual poverty was prevailing … Progressively, Armenian deserters are coming back to hide.

As the Ottoman armies returned from the Russian front defeated and demoralized, tangible signs of the war were to be seen everywhere. Military tents filled the fields around the college, and the American Hospital began to fill up with war casualties. The year 1914 had come to an end on a note of extreme pessimism for the Dildilian and Der Haroutiounian families and all the Armenians of Marsovan. The year ahead would soon be marked as the most cataclysmic in the history of the Armenian people.

Into the Heart of Darkness: The Cataclysm Begins

The winter of 1914–15 was especially long and bitter. After the defeat of the Ottoman Third Army in Sarikamish in January and the disarming of the Armenian soldiers in February, the sorry remnants of these events began arriving in Marsovan. These casualties of the war, many of them suffering from typhus, filled the wards of the newly opened American Hospital, while deserters returned to their homes seeking refuge from the cruelties perpetrated against them by their one-time comrades in arms. Soon Marsovan saw the arrival of 80 gendarmes from outside the city, ostensibly to search for deserters and the hidden guns and bombs of the Armenian revolutionaries. As we will see, they were to play a much more sinister role in the events ahead.

If you ask any Armenian what they know about the genocide, you will most likely hear, aside from the claim that more than one million perished, some remark to the effect that the genocide began on April 24, 1915. This date marks the symbolic start of the Armenian Genocide, for it was on April 24 and 25 in 1915 that upwards of 250 Armenian poets, writers, journalists, doctors, lawyers, merchants, architects, teachers, musicians, political leaders, philosophers (such as myself) and clergy were arrested in Constantinople and transported to prisons in Ayash and Cankiri in the Anatolian interior. Most of these intellectual, political and religious leaders soon perished under the most horrific conditions.

All Armenians are aware of this date because it is the date on which Armenians worldwide commemorate the genocide.

I cannot recall when I first became aware of this date, but by 1965 I was certainly cognizant of its significance. For it was in that year that Armenians took their often internalized personal grief and turned it outward for the rest of the world to see. My brother Gary and I had joined the local junior chapter of the Armenian Youth Federation (A.Y.F.) years earlier. In my universe at that time the A.Y.F. Juniors primarily served a social function. Boys and girls in their early teens had much more on their minds than politics and what now has come to be called genocide recognition. The A.Y.F. is the youth division of the Armenian Revolutionary Federation, known in Armenian as the Dashnaktsutyun. The Dashnaks were one of the leading political parties formed in the waning years of the Ottoman Empire and were initially allies of the C.U.P. They had played a role in the politics of Marsovan, but less so than the more dominant Social Democratic Hunchakian party. On a sunny Saturday morning of April 24, 1965, dressed in black slacks and a white shirt with a black armband, I joined my A.Y.F. friends in an honor guard at a ceremony to mark the Armenian Genocide in Madison Square Park in lower Manhattan. This was one of the first public commemorations to mark the genocide. After 50 years of mostly silent mourning, Armenians were starting to publicly speak out for justice and recognition of the crime.

Fifty years earlier in April 1915, the Armenians in Marsovan were not aware of what was transpiring back in Constantinople. They were ignorant about the arrest of the nation's leadership. Wartime censorship prevented news from easily reaching the interior. Even if the arrests were known, past experience and the incremental ratcheting up of the violence may have conditioned people into thinking that the violence would be limited in extent and duration. The arrested leadership could not have guessed as to what lay ahead for them and their people and neither could my family and the Armenians of Marsovan. Yet the pattern had been set in Constantinople, for between midnight and four o'clock on the morning of Thursday, April 29, the arrests began in Marsovan. The residents of the city woke up that morning to a heavy snowfall and the news that 25 Armenian men, including the entire leadership of the Hunchakian party and other community leaders, had been arrested. They were first sent off to Amasia, with some sent further on to Sivas. All were tortured and within a month executed or died after being exposed to typhus.

Even in these early days some thoughts were given to resisting the actions of the gendarmes. Aram reports and multiple sources confirm that leaders such as Mr. Kakig Ozanian, Mr. K. Atamian and Mr. Barsoumian were among those dispatched to their deaths:

> Word came that the leaders were to be sent to Amasia or Sivas for trial, K. Ozanian,
> K. Atamian, and other prominent men. The boys outside had decided to cut the

road and release them and go to the hills and fight for their lives ... But they, the leaders, refused and pleaded not to do anything foolish like that because such an action will put the people in danger and the consequences will be worse. They said, "We do not care for ourselves. We have not done anything wrong. We are sure God in some way will save us." Next morning, they were taken away, no one knows where and what happened to them.

God did not find a way to save them nor the many others who would follow in the weeks ahead.

Even before the arrests of the leadership, the gendarmes terrorized the community in searches for deserters and weapons. Many accounts describe desperate Armenians buying old weapons in order to turn them in so as to avoid having their houses torn apart in these searches. Aram describes these tactics of terror:

The town crier announced that everyone without exemption should surrender at once to the jandarma headquarters all their guns, swords, and all kinds of war weapons. Those people who had any, at once surrendered them in fear of reprisal, and those who did not have any ... bought any old thing from Turks and surrendered it as their own so that they would not be subjected to suspicion. In the meantime, the police and the jandarmas made sudden searches of homes for guns and revolutionary books and papers, and each time they took the man of the house to jail ... and that was his end.

Maritsa describes similar events:

The police began night searches. On the pretext that they were looking for deserters, they enter into houses and beat up the occupants. Finally, the police said that all the houses would be searched. In case a deserter was found, the occupants would be hanged and the deserter shot. Some deserters, realizing that they were endangering the lives of their folks, went to surrender.

Then, another decree was issued, saying that all those who could walk, even with a stick, would have to report to the authorities in order to register. Unfit people would be exempted after medical examination.

Then, children aged 12 were called up. "We will check their age and send them back to their homes." Boys are taken to the barracks, their hands are tied in their backs, at night, four by four, and they are taken to unknown destinations. Many are unsparingly beaten up and tortured to make them reveal where deserters or arms are concealed or who has weapons in his house.

Maritsa comments that by March 1915 the police had searched most every house in town. A rifle that the family had hung on their wall as a deterrent to robbers was turned in out of fear of denunciation.

By May 10 travel between cities was restricted, effectively cutting off the family from all contact with their relatives in Samsun, Vezirköprü, Amasia and Sivas.[4] More and more Armenians were arrested and imprisoned in the city's military barracks. They were deprived of food and often tortured. The arrests now hit a member of the extended family:

> Zénginian's sister [the daughter of Haïganouch's aunt] came weeping and told us her brother Hovhannes had been arrested and she wanted to take some food to him. My mother went with her as many Armenian women had done, going to the barracks with hope but coming back in tears because they had not seen – or had seen – their beloved ones.
>
> Through a window, they had seen Hovhannes lying on the ground with his feet and hands nailed to the floor, motionless and with his face so beaten up that it looked like a *tepsi* [a mezze platter] ... Screams were coming up from below; there were heart rendering weeps and moans. One on top of the other or in each other's arms, children cry and implore amidst smells and fumes impossible to describe ... you can hardly conceive or imagine such things.

Soon the tragedy would strike closer to home.

Haïganouch's husband, Vosgian, was 44 years old and in poor health. Given the latest decrees there was no way he could avoid reporting for military conscription. By this time it was clear that any new recruits would be placed into the labor battalions that were being brutalized across the face of Anatolia. The hope was that he would be granted a medical exemption. Maritsa describes what happened:

> After this new decree, my father reported to the authorities. The physician who treated him, Doctor Marden, gave him a medical certificate, saying that, with that paper, he will be released within an hour. So my father and another Armenian – a man who was partially paralyzed from a stroke and had been lying in bed for years – rented a carriage and went to Amasia where the Army chief doctor was to examine them. A tin bracelet held by a string with a wax seal had been put on his wrist. The day before – it was a Sunday afternoon – my father and my brother had carried up to the upper story the good-quality timber we had purchased to complete the house, so that it would not be robbed. Monday morning, he went, saying he would be back within one day.
>
> We are still waiting for him.

By late spring of 1915 the plan for the extermination of the Armenians was being implemented. The pretense of conscription was a mechanism for the removal and destruction of the able-bodied male population. The Der Haroutiounians did not know this at the time or if they suspected so, they did not want to believe it. This was soon to change.

By early June it was becoming increasingly clear to Haïganouch that the persecutions were taking a new direction. Maritsa states that her mother heard some very troubling news:

> There were two villages [Alkhad and Ladig] where many Armenians lived. They were incorporated to the diocese of Marsovan.
>
> One day, my mother heard that the Armenians from Alkhad were being transported. She rushed to bring the news to her brother Tsolag who did not really believe her.
>
> The Papelians who lived next door had a daughter who was married and lived in Ladig. We heard it said that this daughter had met a woman on the road and told her that the Armenians from Ladig were being deported ...
>
> My uncle found an explanation for that also, saying that people from villages were being gathered in larger towns. My mother thought differently and maintained that it was deportation and that we too could be in it.

More gendarmes had been brought into the city, this in addition to the 100 *çetes* (gang members) who had been recruited earlier from the surrounding villages in order to do some of the dirty work of torturing and killing.[5] After witnessing the arrest of her neighbor's son, Haïganouch decided to take some action of her own:

> My mother's fears increased. "This is no longer the occasional slaughters we are used to, this is something else," she said.
>
> She thought that the small hideout [in the house] was no longer adequate and she asked my brother and Haroutioun Tchavouchian to enlarge it. Access to that hideout was concealed by a cupboard in the wash house ... One end of the hideout looked over the garden by a height of one half-story, and that part was closed by a stone wall. But two stones could be removed from the wall to provide breathing air and an observation post over the garden. All this was designed so that, in case the house took fire, one part of the hideout would not be buried under rubble.

As we will see, this would be the first of many more elaborate hiding places constructed by the family.

As the troubles increased, Tsolag's photography work diminished considerably. Despite all the hardships taking place in the city, the college and the hospital tried to carry on with some semblance of normalcy. Tsolag had managed to prepare the class photographs for many of the remaining graduating students. Graduation at the college took place on June 17, just about five days before the first deportation orders were made public. The graduation of the nurses from the training program at the new hospital had taken place on June 1, and Tsolag prepared a very attractive group tableau that incorporated a photograph of Dr. Marden and his new hospital.

63. June 1915 graduating class of Anatolia College Hospital, *c.*1915.

Bertha Morley, an American teacher at the Girls' School, in her diary entry for June 2 describes the celebration following this graduation. Given the horrors taking place around them, this mundane description takes on a surreal aspect:

> Last evening was Hospital Commencement. First one in new hospital. Very pleasant occasion. This evening we had our Seniors and 4 Hospital graduates for supper ... Enid and her actors repeated "Perseverance Rewarded" [a morality play] for them. For supper, first course, Chicken with biscuit and gravy, bread and butter; second, rice pilav with nuts, jelly, bread; third, cherry salad, bread; fourth, American coffee and doughnuts.[6]

For some of these young Armenian women much perseverance would be required in the days and months ahead if they were to survive. There would no longer be four-course suppers served with plenty of bread and topped off with a doughnut. They would be lucky to get one scrap of inedible bread on the deportation caravans.

On Sunday, June 13, there was an unusual event at Tsolag's church. He was the head of the Protestant community in Marsovan and had often advocated moderation and cooperation with the authorities. Bertha Morley reports the following: "Last Sunday in Protestant Church, Messrs. Hagopian, Demirdjian, and Gulian urged people to be loyal to government, to give up arms and deserters. Some did so. There was much fear of a massacre."[7] Before the summer was out, Professor Hagopian and Pastor Demirdjian would be dead and Professor Gulian would be a convert to Islam.

On Friday, June 18, the Dildilians were busy taking a different kind of photograph. Aram describes what transpired:

> One day in the morning, we saw a big crowd of soldiers in the Armenian cemetery across the valley, supposedly digging out a coffin full of guns, rifles, hand grenades, powder, and knives. They held a parade in the streets, each soldier carrying a gun or something high above his head so that the people would see … Later they called us to take the picture of the display [of weapons] in city hall (all fake). They must have buried the coffin full of guns themselves because both the coffin and the guns or swords had no trace of rust, rot, or tarnish.

While the family decided not to keep a copy of this photo, I managed to find it in a book written by Talaat Pasha, published in 1916.[8] Talaat is widely considered one of the prime architects of the genocide. This was one of the earliest examples of denialist propaganda that attempted to provide evidence for an Armenian rebellion, thus justifying the harsh measures taken against the Ottoman Armenian population. Unfortunately this propaganda is still being produced almost a hundred years later.

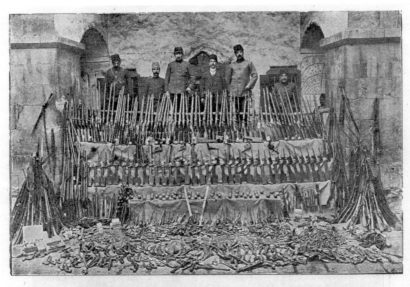

سیواس ولایته تابع مرزیفون قضاسنده ارمنیلردن مصادره اولنان اسلحه وبومبالر

In Mersifun (Vilayet Siwas) von den Armeniern beschlagnahmte Waffen und Bomben.
Armes et bombes saisies chez les arméniens à Merzifoun (Vilayet de Sivas).
Arms and bombs confiscated from the armenians at the Caza of Merzifon (Marsovan) in the Vilayet of Sivas.

64. Guns confiscated from so-called "Armenian Revolutionaries." Kaimakam Fayk Bey in center, accompanied by Commandant Mahir Bey of the Gendarmerie and Chief of Police Salih Effendi. June 15, 1915.

On Wednesday, June 23 a deportation order is given for all non-Marsovan inhabitants to leave for their home towns.[9] By some reports the decree applied to those who settled in Marsovan in the last 30 years. If true, this meant that both the Dildilians and Der Haroutiounians would have to move back to Sivas, a rather fatal prospect. Decisions needed to be made.

Despite the construction of the hidden shelter, Haïganouch was growing steadily uncomfortable in her home near the outskirts of town. She and her five children felt increasingly isolated as many of their neighbors disappeared:

> However ingenious that improved hideout was, my mother did not think it fully reliable. "They are not preparing a two- or three-day-long massacre," she said, and one morning she asked us to pack our bedclothes and she took us to Tsolag's. We had the key to their lower door. We go in, we climb up to their house, and they are surprised to see us. My mother, then, very staunchly said: "With my five children, we cannot live by ourselves in that isolated borough. Even if you ask me to leave, brother, I shall not go." So we stayed.
>
> We had brought with us all we had as food, which did not amount to much anyway. This was in June 1915. In Marsovan, it is in June that people start to prepare foodstuffs for the year, and particularly for the cold season. Not many people were left in town. A sort of funerary veil was hanging in the air. We eagerly waited for each piece of information.

Yet despite this move the family was still threatened by new edicts issued by the local authorities.

The mass arrests of Armenian men began on June 26. Depending on what report you read, between 500 and 1,213 men were arrested and confined to the barracks.[10] Small groups of men are tied together and marched out of the barracks at night toward Amasia but reports came back indicating that they are axed to death and buried in trenches outside of town. Garabed Kiremidjian, one of the wealthiest men in town, who had close personal and financial connections to the Turkish notables and municipal authorities, was also arrested at this time, a sign that no Armenian was immune from the tragedy befalling their nation.

Up until late June, Anatolia College had not been directly affected by the arrests and searches. Given the fact that the United States was not at war with Turkey and had not yet entered the war against Germany, a sense of immunity continued to prevail on the campus. Many of the Armenian professors and staff either lived behind the walls of the campus or in close proximity. On June 28 this sense of immunity was shattered. Aram conveys what happened: "News came that Professors Manissadjian and Hagopian were taken to jail with several other leading Armenian intellectuals. Next day a few were sent back home after being severely beaten ... Then the two professors were released and were ordered to get ready to go to Bagdad." Aram reports that the professors had received a temporary

THE CLOUDS OF WAR AND CATASTROPHE

reprieve. What he did not know at the time was the fact that President White had paid a large sum of money in gold liras to free the professors.

Aram also fails to convey how close the danger had come to the Dildilian household. Professor Hagopian was the next-door neighbor of my grandfather. The two houses still stand today a few meters apart, though on my most recent visit, I sadly noted the increasingly rapid deterioration of the Hagopian house. Though no one was there to rescue Professor Hagopian back in 1915, I have a dream that someone today will help me rescue his beautiful historic home. Professor Manissadjian's even more magnificent house was across the street within the walls of the campus but no longer exists.

Morley describes what happened next door to the Dildilian residence that evening in June. The gendarmes, in their search for Professor Hagopian, also invaded the Sivaslian home. The Sivaslians happened to live next door, but on the opposite side of grandfather's house from the Hagopians.

> Next was a knocking, loud and repeated, at the Hagopian gate. Professor Hagopian had stayed at Dr. White's. Prof. Hagopian's maid ran away, frightened, and Mrs. Hagopian told them that there was no one there. Not believing it, they angrily knocked more; she tried to get some one from the neighbors to come before she opened the gate. They broke the latch, forcing it open, searched the house, then came to the college and sent a messenger to Dr. White. Then Prof. Hagopian came [and gave himself up]. They knocked at Sivaslian's gate by mistake searching for Prof. Manissadjian. Prof. Sivaslian and Manissadjian got over the wall, and Prof. Manissadjian went to the Pye house. Mrs. Sivaslian received the gendarme courteously; when asked for Ohannes, she assured them that there was no one there … Mrs. Sivaslian offered refreshments … Prof. Hagopian and Manissadjian were taken and put into the basement of the barracks. Afterwards they were given a place upstairs. A day of great distress.[11]

Mrs. Hagopian had tried to get help from one of her neighbors, perhaps my grandfather next door, but the gendarmes had quickly broken the gate. President White comments about the horror of that night: "Those who heard the screams of a professor's wife [Mrs. Hagopian], as her husband was sought at his house, can never forget what a degree of human agony that signified."[12] That evening must have been equally as frightening for the Dildilians as it was for the Hagopians and Sivaslians. Could Tsolag Dildilian have been next? Was my dear grandmother thinking of that night back in 1895 when her home was attacked, set on fire, her father killed, and her body burned as she tried to flee? What went through the minds of my family as they heard those screams on that frightful night?

Negotiations immediately began for the release of the professors. But this was to be a two-track process. While the men negotiated dollars and cents, or should I say gold liras and paras, the women tried their hand at a more subtle form of diplomacy. A photograph of the kaimakam taken by my grandfather provided a cover for this second track of the negotiation. Morley describes what happened next and the role her sister Lucy played in the process: "The lawyer and our men made plans to offer ransom money for release. Lucy, with the lawyer's wife, went to see the kaimakam Bey Hanum, ostensibly to carry flowers and the kaimakam's photo. But Ahmed's [the lawyer] wife communicated a message to the kaimakam's wife. Turkish methods."[13] I suspect that it was not through the intervention of the kaimakam's wife but the 275 gold Turkish liras given by President White to the kaimakam that facilitated the release of the professors the next day.

President White provides us a hint of the horrible conditions the professors and the rest of the captives had faced in what he calls the "Black Hole" of the barracks:

> The great dark cellar was packed with a mass of helpless, hopeless, suffering men. Professor Hagopian stood among them as a tower of strength and offered a prayer that calmed and strengthened them all. Our two professors were later released for a time, and returned to their homes, but Professor Manissadjian showed a nervous strain equal to the ordinary results of half a lifetime.[14]

Aram gives a chilling account of what transpired next in the "Black Hole" of the barracks. Though he does not acknowledge it at the time, the events in the barracks would eventually convince some of the Armenians of Marsovan that the only alternatives available to them were either death or conversion to Islam. This was to be the choice the family was soon to face:

> A few days later they had gathered together all the men folks at night from 17 up to 65 and jailed them in the big stone barracks and soon started to send them in groups of 50 bound together arm-to-arm in secret without any travel bag or any food or provisions. This unusual movement of those prisoners attracts the attention of a jandarma who was in his civilian life a household servant of a wealthy Armenian, Aram Payniryemezian. So he, being off duty, just follows one of the groups to satisfy his curiosity. A few miles away in the hills, he sees two big tents. There they undressed them bound arm-to-arm, make them kneel down at the edge of a big trench, one knock to each on the neck with a sharp ax, they tumble down … He, being a Turk, is shocked by what he saw. At once he comes to his former boss, Aram Payniryemezian, in the barracks and pleads with him to do anything within his power to get out of that barracks, as it is sure death for everyone. Aram Payniryemezian talks to Garabed Kiremidjian, a very influential Armenian and the two talk with a few others and decide to get out by changing their faith and get out of that horrible place and sure death. They send word to the commander in chief of jandarmas, and finally managed to get out of that jail with their sons and brothers. Naturally, some of the fellow prisoners in that room heard all about what

was going on and were scared and in panic ... The place was a frightful place to be in anyhow, windows were boarded, no light, no food, no water, no sanitary section (water closet). That night, one of the frightened men became temporarily insane and bit the arm of the man next to him while he was asleep. Naturally, he cries in fear and starts running around. Everybody else was in turmoil and in uproar ... At once, the commander in charge orders them out of the room and down to the stairway and then to the basement. On the other hand, an army captain orders the jandarma to shoot them down. Poor men in fear, they ran down and jumped down through an opening to the basement on top of each other, fearing to be shot down ... I wonder if any one could ever imagine their fearful situation when in the dark they hear a fearful order shouting, "Shoot them! Shoot them!" Good thing folks in the other floors and in the other wings of the barracks did not hear or know anything and were not aware of what was happening!

The only survivors of the "Black Hole" were the converts, some of whom provide accounts that confirm the horrific conditions described by Aram.

What Aram does not note in his account was the cost incurred by each Armenian who agreed to convert. In fact the commandant of the gendarmes and the kaimakam were engaged in a vast extortion scheme in which they reaped an enormous fortune. Garabed Kiremidjian, who was one of the wealthiest and most influential men in town, gives his own account of what transpired in the barracks. He writes that upon becoming suspicious of the nightly departure of "200 persons, bound in groups of 8 or 10," he inquires of the commandant and is told they are being sent to Aleppo and will be unbound once they are a safe distance from the city. Kiremidjian offers to collect 50 liras from each group of six so that they may be transported to Aleppo by carriage. He continues:

[The commandant] agreed, and directed a list be drawn up of those who wished to go by carriage. We wrote the names and gave them to the commandant, and those who did not want to pay were transported the following night, bound as usual. Afterwards they told us that those who agree may [each] pay 50 liras to us, be converted, and remain in the town. We agreed, and everyone who personally paid the bribe to the commandant, were then released from the jail and made application for conversion. We thus became Mohammedans with all our families.[15]

It sounds as if the original scheme of accepting bribes for carriage transportation had quickly changed into bribes for conversion. Maybe the pretense of securing enough carriages was too difficult to manage, while accepting a bribe to let someone fill out some paperwork was a lot simpler and cleaner. The sum of 50 liras seems inexpensive given the fact that President White had to pay 275 liras for Professors Hagopian and Manissadjian. Maybe the commandant had a sliding scale, charging more for those who could afford it and less for those who could not. One report notes a sum of 2,200 liras (2,000 pounds sterling) for one conversion application.[16] Genocidal killers practicing a form of welfare socialism! I suspect not.

Aram goes on to note that once the news got out about the nightly killings, conditions in the barracks temporarily improved:

> Because the secret of wholesale killing was out and the place was somewhat known, they stopped sending any more groups to be killed. At once they were provided drinking water, sanitary means, etc., and allowed them to have food from their homes. One of my best friends, Mihran Iynejian, an artist, our church choir leader, wrote me a note asking for some stockings, a flannel shirt, pants, paper and pencil. Poor boy, he did not know what was to happen to him … He added, "These last two days we went through so much tortures that even Christ did not suffer in the garden of Gethsemane or on the way to Calvary … Oh, God! forgive me. Mihran Iynejian." Three days later, not a single one was left in those barracks. No one knew where they were taken or what happened to them.

Someone did know, for Kiremidjian does acknowledge that for those in the barracks who did not pay the conversion bribe their fate was to be bound together and transported to the Turkish village of Türnik, "killed with axes" and "thrown into a ditch."[17] Mihran Iynejian's Calvary was to be an unmarked ditch in the Marsovan countryside.

The Erasure of Armenian Life in Marsovan

By the end of June most of the able-bodied Armenian men of Marsovan were gone, except the converts and those Armenians associated with Anatolia College. The latter included the faculty, staff and boarding students on the campus. The teachers and staff who lived in the city had moved onto the campus for more protection. The Dildilians and Der Haroutiounians were still huddled together across the street from the campus. Women, girls, boys generally under the age of 15 and elderly men still remained in the Armenian quarters of the city. This was soon to change, as Maritsa explains:

> On the Sunday [July 4], following the day of our arrival at Tsolag's, my mother went back to our predominantly Armenian borough to obtain some information. She came back in the evening with a dire confirmation … My mother heard a town crier shouting in the street, so she went out to see what was going on. The town crier, accompanied by policemen and the Armenian borough warden whom we used to call One-Eyed Melkon, was announcing in front of the Kavak Fountain that the Arévortis borough, a mostly Armenian borough, would be transported within three

days. She asked Melkon: "Melkon, where will they take us?" "You'll follow your husbands." My poor mother came back with her blood running cold in her veins.

The Armenians at that time did not fathom a grim irony: the order that would eventually lead to their destruction was being announced on the 4th of July. The Americans, now fully aware of the horrors engulfing them, did not have their normal 4th of July Independence Day campus celebrations. Bertha Morley notes: "The only celebration of the day was singing of patriotic songs at Children's singing and having the dinner table decorated with red, white and blue."[18] After commenting on the announcement of the deportation order and the frantic efforts to exempt the college from the order, she concludes that day's diary entry with these simple words: "So the day ends, darker than any yet."[19]

The Der Haroutiounians busy themselves in preparation for the deportation. Maritsa describes their preparations:

> There is no room for doubt now. My mother cut into our clothing *shalwars* for her and us, the two sisters. We also sewed bags made out of a sturdy fabric to carry our linen, stockings and other essential belongings. We also took candle wax which we could nibble to stave off hunger.
>
> It is clear that we are going to be taken away one borough after the other. The town is stirring feverishly. Armenians carry their belongings to Greek homes to be kept there until they come back: the chests wherein the delicate Armenian women put their dowries, carpets, and valuables. Those who knew Americans entrusted to them their belongings, even their gold and jewels, fearing they could be robbed on the way, but keeping one part however. Others buried or safely concealed their valuables.

Both Aram and Maritsa describe the arrival of the oxen carts that had been requisitioned from the surrounding villages. Maritsa notes that the promised three-day notice in order to prepare for the departure was not always kept:

> The first caravan was formed with people from the Armenian Arévortis borough.
>
> And our "fellow-countrymen" (as the Turks liked to call themselves when it suited them) had the "nice touch" of bringing in oxen carts from the surrounding villages, assigning one cart per home. As the carts were in greater number than required, it was decided to also transport other boroughs that were normally to be moved two days later. Forced to leave immediately, people wept, begged, implored, but to no avail.

As to information about their destination, Aram notes that the families were told the following: "'Your men folk are in Sivas waiting for you. Soon you will join them over there.'" Of course this was not to be the case, for the men had already been killed by this time.

The sudden departure of certain households led to surreal scenes in which household life and activities were cut short in mid-stream. Maritsa chronicles some examples:

> Thus, when my mother went to visit our former landlords, who were due to leave only three days later, she was told by the tenant who had succeeded us that they had already been taken away, with only two hours notice to get ready. They had taken with them bread, food and had prepared *tcheuréks* – *tcheuréks* in Marsovan are somewhat special, they are *paghartchs* made of spiced pastry, round- or oblong-shaped, oiled with a brush and sprinkled with crushed poppy seeds or cloves. However, they had insufficient time to bake them although their oven was hot. A boiler still full of linen to be washed was left on the fire, in an empty house.
>
> Things followed the same course in the other houses. The wife of Der Mampré Tépigian, the main Kahana [secular married priest] of our town, had forgotten her shoes. She realized it when she was about to climb onto the cart. She had wanted to go back to the house and fetch them, but was not allowed to do so and was pushed onto the cart with her slippers on.
>
> Thus we waited for days in that state of uncertainty. Meanwhile, here and there, news began to spread …
>
> You should have seen the numbers of stray animals: hens, cows, donkeys, dogs and cats, miserably roaming in the streets. Turks were busy with more profitable tasks and they concerned themselves with animals only later.

On my second visit to Marsovan, I decided to venture to the neighboring city of Amasia. Amasia was on the deportation route of the Marsovan Armenians. As I waited to board the bus, my eyes scanned the local vendors selling their wares in the bus station. One was selling *tcheuréks*. As I paid him the one Turkish lira price and held that warm local delicacy in my hands, my thoughts returned to the above passage and the unbaked *tcheuréks* that were left behind by this Armenian family. The *tcheuréks* have remained but the Armenians are now all gone. The Dildilians had become the eyewitnesses to the disappearance of their community.

Both Maritsa and Aram comment on the fact that empty oxen carts began returning after only a few days. It was clear that the deportees were either now walking on foot or were no longer alive. Aram states, "Almost all those oxcarts came back empty in a few days. What did happen to those thousands of women, children and old men? No one knows. Surely they were killed within a short distance." Maritsa comments that empty carts meant a change in what they should pack: "The oxen carts came back after a few days for another caravan, which meant that the transported people had been left in open country, forced to continue on foot. It was therefore futile to take too many things with us, only what we could carry ourselves. We had better forget about cushions and blankets." Though now living with her brother near the college campus, Haïganouch believed that they were in imminent danger of being deported along with neighbors back to her neighborhood. Maritsa states, "And finally our borough was transported." Rumors were rife as to when the remaining Armenians associated with the college would be transported.

Yet there appears to have been a temporary reprieve. The Der Haroutiounians were still living in Tsolag's house and it is clear that by this time my grandfather was in the army working as a military photographer. In the Morley diaries there are a few references to the fact that my grandfather was allowed to travel to Amasia. He is often depicted as bringing news back to the Americans at the college. Travel was highly restricted, especially for the Armenians, so these trips must have been for official business. While in the memoirs there is no explicit reference to his conscription or to having volunteered for the military, my mother had a clear memory of seeing him in an army uniform. She often stated that he would leave the house in his uniform carrying his camera. He was usually gone for days and would return home grim-faced and downhearted. My mother remarked that Tsolag would tell her mother that many dead bodies littered the sides of the roads he traveled. The accompanying officers told Tsolag that these were Turks killed by the nation's enemies, but he knew very well that these were Armenians. Whether or not he was instructed to photograph these victims is unclear. I had not seen any such photos in the family collection and assumed that my grandfather had no desire to preserve such horrible images. Yet one day as I was sorting through a box of glass negatives I encountered a rather strange image. This was not the typical landscape or portrait image. I was not certain what was captured on this piece of glass, so I had it developed and was shocked to see the image below.

65. Unidentified victims, foreground and background, of the Armenian Genocide, c.1915.

I do not know much about this photo aside from the fact that it was taken sometime during the war years. One cannot be certain as to whether the person stretched out in the foreground is dead or alive. I suppose this is fitting, since in the summer of 1915 Anatolia was a landscape of the dead and the dying.

Working for the killers must have been difficult for my grandfather, yet this seems to be what was keeping the family alive. Bertha Morley in her diary comments on one photograph my grandfather was required to take at the height of the deportations, killings, and torture that were taking place all around them. Two sentences in her entry for July 16 capture this moment: "The lieutenant of the Commandant who had charge of the work of torture got Mr. Dildilian and came to the College garden on his fine horse with son and pony, and had picture taken. Then he began picking flowers; all without even asking permission."[20] Picking flowers without permission was probably the least of the crimes he had committed that summer.

As the deportations continued day by day through July, the family felt increasingly isolated. The professors who lived in houses surrounding them, including Professors Hagopian and Sivaslian, had moved onto the college campus. The kaimakam continued to insist that all Armenians would have to go, though he conceded that the college Armenians would probably be the last. The Dildilian household appears to have been momentarily spared from the deportations either because Tsolag worked for the military or had a close connection to the college. Aram expresses his worries:

> Our house and studio was in the professors' quarter. All our neighborhood was sent away. One afternoon, we heard all the professors and their families had gone to the college compound for safekeeping. That was shocking news for us because in that block, we were the only family left to our fate. It was a terrible feeling. We were segregated ... were not among the condemned who were taken and were killed. Blessed be their memory ... and we were not in the preferred group in the college compound under American flag ... We came together and started to pray ... While we were praying, Professor Xenides and Theocharides came to comfort us, as the Greeks were safe then and free to go around. (It was Mr. Elmer and Prof. Xenides who went out from the country to take the news of butchery to the outside world.) That afternoon, brother went to see the commander to ask his guidance. He assured brother that the family is safe and will be left alone "as we need you (we were the only photographer in the district) so go home and do not worry." Then brother asked about sister who had moved to our house because her house was the last house at the city limits, and about keeping Yester Hanum, our next-door neighbor, as his housekeeper. So he gave him three stickers for each house so that no one would bother us ... It is time to state here that Yester Hanum Der Kasparian is the mother of my darling wife, Christine. Both mother and daughter used to live next door of her grandmother,

Marinos Khubeserian (Anoush Mayrig) [Sweet Mother] whose house Dr. Tracy
had built for her.

As we will see, this initial assurance given by the commander, Mahir Bey, was not
enough to fully guarantee the family's safety.

Maritsa also reports that Tsolag and family had been granted permission to
stay by the commander of the gendarmerie, Mahir Bey. Mahir Bey is a very
controversial figure. He was a central figure in the deportations and massacres that
happened in Marsovan. He and the kaimakam Fayk Bey profited immensely as
a result of the bribes they received from both the Armenians and the Americans.
The kaimakam and Mahir Bey sometimes disagreed about the extent of each
other's respective authority. At other times they clashed over how to divide up
the spoils and the monies they extorted. From the writings of the missionaries
and others, the kaimakam comes across as the more fanatical and rapacious of
the two. He was an individual who was completely untrustworthy. Mahir Bey
was more trustworthy but not wholly so. He was later arrested by the Turkish
authorities for his illegal activities during the war and then was taken into custody
by the British and exiled to Malta with other war criminals and nationalists.
Maritsa writes:

At that time, the police commissioner was Mahir Bey, who granted exceptions
quite generously. He had the notice "remain here" written on doors. His assistant,
Saléh Bey, got worried about those exceptions and he toured the houses, ordering
the occupants to go. "But Mahir Bey allowed us to stay. Look, it's written on the
door." And Saléh answered: "A permission given by a giaour to another giaour is
not valid." It was said that Mahir Bey was an Armenian. But this is hard to believe.

Some time after that, Saléh Bey was appointed chief commissioner and Mahir
Bey became his assistant.

I also find it hard to believe that Mahir Bey was an Armenian. The reference
is probably to the fact that one of his ancestors may have been a converted
Armenian. Still Maritsa does cite another incident in which Mahir Bey showed
some sympathy to the family and may have saved the life of Maritsa's older
brother. By this time it was clear that any male of draft age who was found in
a household would be arrested and most likely killed. Maritsa reports Tsolag's
decision to turn her brother in to the military authorities:

Tsolag took Haïgouni to the authorities. All the members of the military commission
were sitting in the courtyard, waiting for the cannon shot (announcing the end
of the Ramadan for the day) so that they could at last drink something. The
police commissioner sees my uncle, he rushes to him: "I brought my nephew," says
Tsolag. "Take him back, take him back! He is still a child," says the commissioner,

Mahir Bey, and he then rushes back to the others so that they do not notice his move. Assuredly, my uncle Tsolag had a respect-inspiring appearance, but he had nonetheless a streak of luck that day because Mahir Bey has sympathy for Armenians. This is how my brother was spared.

How far Mahir Bey's "sympathy for Armenians" extended is an open question. It certainly did not extend to the thousands of Armenians who were killed that summer in Marsovan and its environs.

Haïganouch was certainly not convinced by the assurances that Tsolag received from Mahir Bey. She continued her family's preparations for the deportations.

My mother cut my younger brother Haïgazoun's hair; his beautiful golden locks falling down to his shoulders on each side of his fine and proud face, which had aroused astonishment and admiration from Armenians and Turks ... Why did my mother cut his nice curls? She had said to herself that, "If they believe he is a girl, they will take him." As to our hair, us the girls, she planned to cut it at the time of our departure. She used to say: "They'll take you away by twisting your hair around their hand."

As I said, we had prepared carrying bags with straps in order to wear them on shoulders. And my uncle Aram made a special bag for my elder brother. That bag was designed to carry a large rug, which pitched on poles would be used as a tent, and the appropriate tools (adze, hatchet, saw, etc.) to make poles. "You'll see, he had added jokingly, watermelons from Dikranakert are so big that they must be cut with an axe, and a man can sit in their rind." He had not sized up the danger or had wanted to evade the question.

We had more than 40 hens. We started to kill six or seven each day in order to prepare meat for the road.

In Maritsa's account, Aram seems either to be making light of the dangers ahead or possibly trying to keep the family's morale up. This stands in contrast to his own retrospective account of those hellish days at the end of July and early August:

We were comparatively safe in those dark and bloody days as we had the blood mark on our door like the people of Israel, Ezechial 12:13 ... We were about 16 of us living together in those fearful days, sometimes 20 and one time up to 23 of us were living together in those terrible months. We were feeling somewhat safe for awhile but it was a terrible state of mind and life to be in. All the Armenians were sent to sure death! Our dear ones are gone! We were left alone to live so, and for what? We were in constant fear. The whole city was in dead quiet, no one is seen in the streets or in the fields, no one in the marketplaces. Strange, not even Turks for awhile, no shops or stores were open, no school, no little children around playing, no one goes out or in from the doorways, no lights in the windows, still deadness, not even the deadly sound of the oxen carts' wheels. Their nauseating noise is stopped, their cruel work is finished … Somehow we were glad for the college professors, teachers and workers to whom was given refuge in the college compound – about 200 persons in all. Somehow Dr. White was assured from the U.S. Ambassador, Mr. H. Morgenthau and Dr. W. W. Peter [William Peter, U.S. Consul in Samsun, 1906–17] that the college people will be left alone … In the meantime, Mr. Zimmerman [Zimmer], a German farmer in Ata Bay who had a big farm near Amasia somehow gets a permit from the Mutassarif of Amasia to take Professors Manissadjian and Daghlian and their families to his farm as German descendants. That was a real comfort and joy to all of us.

When I first read the words that began this passage, "the blood mark on our door like the people of Israel," I recalled from my childhood Sunday school days the story in Exodus of the blood mark that protected the first-born children of the Israelites from God's wrath against Pharaoh. But not being a student of the Old Testament, I passed over the reference to Ezekiel 12:13. As I write this today, I thought it wise to check this passage in the Bible. I was surprised to find the following: "My net also will I spread on him, and he shall be taken in my snare: and I will bring him to Babylon to the land of the Chaldeans; yet shall he not see it, though he shall die there" (American King James Version). Clearly Aram had intended to convey the sense of fear they were feeling – fear of being snared in the net of the death marches.

Aram's memoir is rife with passages that alternate between the false hope that the American presence was conveying and the gut fear that no matter what was said the reality was certain destruction. This is captured in the following passages:

The college hospital was occupied by the Army, yet, Dr. J. K. Marden was the head of the hospital so he was able to secure the safe stay of Mihran Daderian and his family as druggist and 10 or 12 more others as nurses and other helpers. We were glad for that … The Sivas State Governor Mouammer, the organizer of those perfect and systematic killings, had ordered the local officers to deport all the college professors and others in the college compound by force, if it is necessary!

Though the news from Constantinople was that the professors will not be sent as [they were] Protestants, at least Talaat Pasha has assured the U.S.A. Ambassador and Dr. Peter. But the local government officials acted as if there is no such order.

These last remarks are borne out in the diplomatic correspondence and in the accounts given by the missionaries. When told of the assurances and the cables that Talaat and Enver Pasha had supposedly sent, the kaimakam repeatedly states that he has not received such instructions.[21] Historical research in recent decades reveals that a similar pattern was followed across the Armenian provinces. Talaat Pasha would send cables ostensibly limiting the scope or mitigating the harshness of the deportation orders. This would serve as a cover for the true orders that were secretly conveyed by the responsible secretaries of the C.U.P. in the various cities. Often the "official" cables arrived too late because the dirty work had already been done. Unfortunately the Turkish government's genocide denial narrative continues to rely on these supposed mitigating cables to support their contention that there was no "intent" to exterminate all the Armenians of the empire. Reputable historical research has proven this argument false.[22]

Aram was not fooled as to the ultimate intentions of the Young Turk government: "Whomsoever I came in contact with or I had the occasion [to meet], I advised to do anything and everything and avoid deportation as that meant sure death ... I was convinced that Turks had decided to wipe out the Armenians of Turkey so we must try to save as much [of the] remnant as we were able as those days were very critical days." This realization that the fate of the Armenian nation was at stake gave Aram and the whole Dildilian family the resolve to survive and resist in the days, months and years ahead.

A Bid for Survival: The Forced Islamization of the Dildilian and Der Haroutiounian Families

Keeping family secrets can be motivated by a variety of reasons. Secrets hidden by one generation from the next are often the result of shame or fear: the shame that comes from believing – often falsely – that one could have behaved differently in a morally challenging situation or the fear of causing harm if a trauma is passed on to the younger generation. For many Armenians the personal trauma of 1915 was often buried but would not stay buried forever. To a large extent both my mother and father were very open about what they and their families experienced in 1915 and its aftermath. Yet the Dildilian survival story was not complete. The most crucial life and death decision was kept hidden from my generation. Unspoken when I was growing up was the fact that, despite the importance of my grandfather to the government, he and his family ultimately had to convert to Islam and adopt Turkish identities in order to avoid the deportations. Once I began to study the genocide as an adult, I realized that many such conversions had taken place. What I had not realized was that our family was one such example of actions taken in a desperate attempt at survival. Was this a family secret kept from our ears? I must assume that to some extent it was. No relatives of my generation were aware of this conversion. The full description of what had transpired was not revealed to me until the spring of 2009.

In April 2009 I was staying on the campus of Anatolia College in Thessaloniki, the city that had welcomed the college after the Turkish authorities closed the school in 1921. The American College of Thessaloniki, the university division of Anatolia College, had invited me to give a series of lectures as a Michael S. Dukakis Visiting Fellow. The president of the college, Dr. Richard Jackson, had extended an invitation when he heard that I was the grandson of Tsolag Dildilian, the college photographer during its days in Marsovan. He knew that I had a collection of photographs from that period and he wanted me to share them with the college and talk about my family's experiences in that period. As was my custom then as it is today, I never seem able to prepare my talks except at the last minute. Before leaving for Greece, I had a rough idea of what I wanted to say, so I packed all the relevant sources that I would need to write the talk into my suitcase. This included a translation of Maritsa Médaksian's memoir notebooks that had recently arrived in the mail from my cousin in Paris. I was aware of this manuscript and had seen a French copy of it once during a visit to Paris. Haïk Der Haroutiounian and his brother Edouard had been editing and preparing translations of this document. Late one evening I sat down to read through relevant portions of this lengthy manuscript. I was especially interested in the sections dealing with the events of 1915. I was familiar with what Aram had written about this period, but I wanted to get an alternate perspective on these important years in the family story. As I read the chilling account captured in these pages, my heart starting pounding. The anxiety I was feeling as I read these pages was palpable but in no way could it match what my family may have been experiencing. When I reached the section describing the decision to convert, the arguments among the family members about this decision, and the actual description of the conversion ceremony, I was shocked and then emotionally drained. There in those pages were my uncles, two of whom I knew well, along with my four-year-old mother, sitting in a room in Marsovan's town hall, as the adults in the family recited the words of the conversion ceremony. My mother was a fairly open individual. As far as I knew, she generally had not kept secrets from me. I suspect she was too young to have any memory of these events. Her older brothers certainly did but may have kept her in the dark about them. I so wish that I could talk to her about what happened, maybe jar her memory about what was said and done in the days and months after this episode, but alas I was nine years too late for such memory work.

Maritsa was 14 years old at the time of the conversion. She describes in detail what happened between August 6 and 12 of 1915. She chooses to preface her account with a conversation she had with a family acquaintance who was returning to Marsovan as a convert. I suspect the choice of placing this before the section on the family conversion was deliberate. She wanted to highlight the consequences faced by those who did not agree to convert:

A woman whom my aunt had known back in Trebizond came back with her single daughter. She had a white veil on her head. It is true that, we too, were thinking of wearing on the road white veils as worn by Muslim women. I went to hear what news she had.

She related that the caravan driver, an Albanian, had come to her and said: "If you give me your daughter to marry, you too will be free." If she had said no, the Turks would have taken her daughter some time later. "There is no other road to salvation for you, the man had added. Supposing you get through the Turks and stay alive, the Kurds further down the road are even more bloodthirsty and ferocious." The woman had been convinced and this was why she had been back two days later. "You are our property, they had told her, we bought you ... for 60 paras each. You belong to us."

Multiple historical accounts, including missionary diaries, record that Marsovan had one of the largest number of forced conversions during this period.

The deportations had been continuing for almost a month now. Remnants of the Armenian population were still being kept at the monastery as the kaimakam and others continued their schemes for extorting the remaining wealth from the community. Maritsa captures the mood of the remaining Armenians: "A sense of void and uncertainty has spread over Marsovan. We do not know what may happen within the next hour." On Friday, August 6, the commandant, Mahir Bey, rang the doorbell of my grandfather's house. Maritsa describes what happened next:

The Turks are still in the Ramadan period.

That Friday afternoon, around 5 p.m., the doorbell rang at Tsolag's. I went to open the door. A high-ranking officer was there. By the time he walked down the 70- to 100-foot distance from the gate to the house door, we had warned my uncle and, as it was forbidden for girls to appear before Turks, I walked away.

The officer stayed with my uncle one hour or more. My mother brought them coffee, hoping to learn something. The officer was Mahir Bey. After he had left, my uncle gathered every one of us in the dining room to let us know what Mahir Bey had said: "I'm back from the Friday meeting," Mahir Bey had warned. "I have not yet eaten but I have immediately come to inform you. It was said at that meeting, 'That poor Dildilian has put himself in the hands of the College. It will be a pity for such a large family.' Dildilian Effendi," he had added, "Don't wait. First thing tomorrow, apply for a conversion to Islam. This is the only way out." Upon these convincing words, Mahir Bey had gone.

We knew that applications for conversion had been made, some accepted, others rejected. But it was said that the applications backed by lawyer Saléh were always accepted.

66. View of the path from the house to the front gate. The gate
through which Mahir Bey entered to inform the family of the
fate that awaited them if they did not convert, c.1914.

The subsequent paragraphs describe an argument between Tsolag and his wife
and sister as to what they should do. The women were strongly opposed to such
a conversion:

> My mother and my aunt protested. "I shall never turn Turk, it would be my
> death," my mother kept saying. "It's impossible, I cannot accept. I would rather be
> transported," repeated my aunt. Then my uncle, seeing no other argument to put
> forth, cried: "Very well, if you don't want to, I cannot do anything about that. But
> I warn you, you will go, both of you, but I shall not give you your children, neither
> to one nor to the other. You will go on your own."

More persuasion seemed necessary though being parted from one's children was
a big incentive to convert. The next day Tsolag sought the advice of one of the

notables of the city, Hadji Garabed Kiremidjian, who had played a major role in the conversion of Armenians earlier in the summer. Maritsa describes the meeting:

> Saturday morning, my uncle went to see Kiremidjian Hadji Effendi. We had heard it said that he and some other prominent people had escaped deportation up to now by a certain means (by giving money). However, money was no longer an escape. You had to turn Muslim in order to stay.
>
> Kiremidjian had a beautiful house built in white stones, the only one of that sort in Marsovan. It even had louvered shutters. Two armed policemen were on guard at the door and they did not allow Tsolag to enter. My uncle insists and finally a shutter is opened on the upper floor. Hadji Effendi tells the policemen to allow Tsolag in. Kiremidjian's personal bodyguard is waiting on top of the stairs and waves Tsolag to come up. He was a Cherkess, always clad in his traditional costume and armed, who always walked two steps behind Kiremidjian wherever he went, alone or with his family.
>
> Tsolag enters in a room plunged into darkness, with closed shutters and drawn curtains. Hadji Effendi is sitting there, with a downcast look on him, without shirt, without necktie.
>
> When my uncle finished talking, Hadji Effendi told him: "Go along, Dildilian, go along! Should they ask us to become dogs, we would have to do it. There is no other way, no other escape from this situation. Go along! Put your preacher in front of you and go to turn Muslim. You, Protestants, are not many. Us, we are many but my people do not listen to me, and a lot of them are suspicious of me. Go quickly and be saved."

The remarks of Kiremidjian regarding the Protestants are interesting. There appears to have been some difference in the treatment of the Protestants and Catholics from that meted out to their Apostolic brethren. Whether true or not, Garabed Kiremidjian in his unpublished memoir claims to have facilitated the conversion of upwards of 3,000 Armenians to Islam.[23] This was reduced to 1,200 because of a further decree that limited the percentage of Armenians who could remain to 5 percent of the town's population. The result was the deportation of a large number of converted Armenians after the July deportations had ended. Morley's diary documents converts being deported as late as September 1915. The selection of who stayed and who went was probably made on the basis of economic necessity, that is, what occupations were necessary for the essential functioning of the city. Morley also reports that the kaimakam was "incensed that Catholics and Protestants should be exempt when turned Armenians must be sent." He appears to have undermined the decree exempting the Protestants. Morley continues: "It is said that he has tried not to send the latter class [converted Protestants], and will leave as many as possible. He is reported also to have said that he felt he had played his cards pretty well to simply say always he had no orders till nearly all Protestants had been sent."[24] The implication here is that the kaimakam protected his paying customers, the converted Protestant Armenians, while turning a blind eye to any decree exempting the general Protestant population, that is, all those who refused to convert and pay him a suitable bribe.

Garabed Kiremidjian's words seemed to carry much weight with my great-aunt and grandmother.

My uncle then made his application and came back home. When Tsolag reported Kiremidjian's words, my mother was assuaged and convinced. "If such a man has advised conversion, a man who goes to church every Sunday with his wife and four children, and everyone of them receiving Holy Communion at the Tabernacle Feasts, and who has no personal interest at stake in our converting or not, then I too I accept and I will stay."

So my uncle went to see the authorities and he was told we were to report at the town hall on Tuesday afternoon to be renamed with Turkish names.

On the morning of Tuesday, August 10, the deportation of the Armenians from the college campus began. Ramadan had ended that day, so the increased religious obligations of charity and prayer of the preceding month were now diminished for the devout. Maritsa picks up the narrative:

We are in mid-summer, nights are clear, but anyway, who would be able to sleep soundly. Around 5:30 a.m., we heard the creaking sounds of oxen carts in the street. We ran to the upper bedrooms to see what was going on: carts were entering the American College. Alas, Mahir Bey had been right when he had said: "On Tuesday, the Armenians of the College will be transported."

As you recall, my grandfather's house was across the street from the college, separated by a street and the high walls of the campus.

I now pick up the narrative from the college side of the wall. These are the words of Carl C. Compton from his book *The Morning Cometh*:

The second morning after my return from Constantinople, we awoke to find the campus surrounded by armed soldiers. One group broke through the main gate and began driving the Armenians from the buildings. Ox carts were lined up in the road just outside the gate. The women and little children were loaded onto the carts, clutching the few bundles of food and clothing they were allowed to carry with them. The few men and older children trudged along beside them as they started on the pathetic journey. Word seeped back that on the second day the men were separated from the group and were taken a short distance into the hills, where they were shot, stripped of their possessions, and buried in a mass grave.[25]

67. Dildilian family home, far right, c.1912. Most houses in this neighborhood belonged to Anatolia College faculty. The Dildilians observed the deportation from the top floor of their home. On August 10, 1915 the oxen carts were lined up in the street near the wall of the college.

A very similar account is also given in President George E. White's book *Adventuring with Anatolia College*. In Aram's memoir these same events are described from a slightly different perspective. Aram happened to be on the grounds of the college early that morning attending to some work. He is warned when the gendarmes entered the campus and quickly headed home across the street. He too views the tragedy from the top floor of my grandfather's house. Aram provides this moving description of the expulsion of his teachers and friends from the campus:

> Brother had the concession of the college stationery store so that my cousin Ardash Kurkjian could help pay his school expenses (he went home to Yozgat to be with his family and was killed on the way). That same day, brother asked me to go and take the inventory. While I was busy counting the goods, Mr. Getchell, the dean of the college, a fine Christian and lovable teacher of mine, said, "Aram, you better go home as the jandarmas and soldiers have come to deport professors and their families." So at once, I locked the place and went home through the teachers' private gate. I told my folks that the professors are to go, so we all went upstairs and through the western window overlooking the main gate we watched them go. It was a tragic scene for us to watch but we wanted to have a last look at them. One by one all the oxen carts loaded with their most valuable possessions came out of the main gate where soldiers with bayonets were stationed … watching them closely, all our dear and able professors, teachers with their wives and children and all the

218

college students and other workers … With tearful eyes, we watched them go one by one, our last hope of the survival of our nation's cream, followed by 10 or 12 mounted jandarmas.

Picking up the narrative in Maritsa's memoir, the following transpires for the Dildilians who had watched the deportation from across the street earlier that day:

On Tuesday afternoon, we all went to the town hall, the konak, as we used to call it, where all the administrative departments were housed. We climbed up to the first story where the mufti's office was. It is a big room. The mufti, a small man wearing a white turban, is sitting behind a desk with a clerk beside him.

He asks the men to sit on a wooden bench placed along a wall and the women to sit on the floor. Then he orders the men to repeat after him:

"God is One.

Wherever you are, you may call on Him, He is present and ready.

Muhammad is his prophet and Hésa (Jesus) his disciple."

If I am not mistaken, this was all he said. After the religious ceremony, we were taken to an adjacent room for the administrative ceremony, where our new Turkish names were registered. Professor Gulian [Anatolia's professor of Armenian, Krikor H. Gulian], a very knowledgeable man in Turkish, had chosen nice names for us.

Professor Gulian had converted earlier in the summer. Maritsa goes on to list the names of the 14 members of the family and most of the Turkish names they were given. This is where I learned that my mother, Alice, was given the name "Leman," meaning "beautiful, shining," and my grandfather, Tsolag, was called "Pertev," meaning "ray, glint."

From the eldest to the youngest, these were the names:

Dildilian

Tsolag	was now Pertev, i.e., ray, glint	
Mariam	Meryem, i.e., Mary	
Hratchia	Zeki (I think), i.e., intelligent, clever	
Humayag	(I have forgotten)	
Jiraïr	Fatih, i.e., conqueror, competent	
Alice	Leman, i.e., beautiful, shining, glittering	
Aram	Zeki, i.e., intelligent, clever	
Ara	Fehmi, i.e., the one who understands	

Der Haroutiounian

Haïganouch	Nadire, i.e., rare, unique	
Haïgouni	Ziya, i.e., glow	
Maritsa	Bediye, i.e., marvel, beauty	

Haïgouhi	Münir, i.e., the one who gives light
Aram	Fahim, i.e., the one who understands
Haïgazoun	Mahir, i.e., adroit, skillful, talented

Let me tell you an amusing incident. Tsolag was enumerating the names of his children to the employee who at the same time had in his hand the list of the Turkish names. So Tsolag goes: Hratchia, Humayag, Jiraïr, and he comes to "Ara." Now "aramak" in Turkish means "look up, look for something." "That I look for?" cries the employee, "but where?" Maybe he had not understood, maybe he was joking. Anyway, he wrote down the name.

Tsolag's servant, Yester Hanum, had come with us, together with her daughter Christine, Yester's aunt, Anoush, and still other ones whom I will not mention for fear of giving wrong names.

The families were now to survive as "Turkified Muslims."

On a recent visit to Merzifon, the former cultural affairs director of the municipality gave me a history book about the city. In it was an article about the Armenians who had remained in the city in 1915. The list of names included their occupations and the new Turkish names they were assigned. The list only included 307 names; clearly this was an incomplete list for the numbers of converts were far greater. A lot must have been lost in translation between Ottoman Turkish forms of the Armenian names and their translation into modern Turkish. Tsolag Dildilian is listed as Ulak Viladisyan. Ulak was certainly my grandfather because he is the only "*fotoğrafçı*" listed. Aram is also listed and in the notes it states that he is "*topal*," lame. There are some differences in the given names but this is where I learned that my grandfather was given the Turkish name "Ahmed Nuri," residing in the Hacı Balı neighborhood of Marsovan.

Maritsa notes the feeling of relief she and her mother felt once the conversion had taken place: "Hardly had we come out that my mother gave a sigh of relief: 'So, that was it?' As for me, I felt as if a heavy burden had gone away from my heart."

Resistance and Rescue in Marsovan: The Story behind a Photograph

I begin this section with a photograph, one I had first seen years ago when I was casually browsing through a rather old, leather-bound photograph album at my uncle Humayag's house during one of my visits to his home in Newington, Connecticut. It was a strange photograph of people I did not recognize. Years later this photograph and the glass negative from which it derives, along with hundreds of others, are now in my possession. When I first saw this photo, I only knew the rough outlines of the family story in the "old country." I knew that

68. The Dildilian and Der Haroutiounian families secretly celebrating Christmas in January 1916. Aram Dildilian stands behind his sister Haïganouch in the right of the photo. In the center of the photo are four college friends of Aram who are being hidden in the Der Haroutiounian house. January 6, 1916.

the family had survived because my grandfather was a photographer, but I did not know the particular details of their survival story during the darkest years for the Armenian nation. What did they do during those years? Thanks to our memoirists, I now know much more about these years of struggle and survival. Unlike most memoirs of those who survived, the stories recorded by my family are unique for they chronicle what happened to those who remained behind once the deportations had cleansed the Anatolia landscape of most of its Armenian population. This is the story I will tell in this section.

This unique photograph is a guide to understanding what the Dildilian and Der Haroutiounian families were doing once they had assumed their new Turkish identities. While they struggled to survive during a time of hardship brought on by the deprivations of the war and the loss of their livelihoods, they also applied their intelligence, resourcefulness and courage to rescue and hide the surviving remnants of the Armenian population of Marsovan. These were young men and women who had managed to somehow avoid the deportations or had escaped from the caravans and returned to Marsovan.

Some simple questions about this photograph arise: When was the photograph taken? Where was it taken? Who is in the photograph? What are these people doing in the photograph? There is a more complex question that I would also like to ask: What are these individuals trying to convey to us in this photograph? Is there a message here? The final question and the most important for our story: How did these individuals come to be in this particular place at this particular time for this photograph to be taken?

The answer to the first question – When was it taken? – is rather easy to establish. The banner hanging behind them on the wall reads in Armenian, "Յիսուս ծնաւ, 1916" transliterated as "*Hisous Dzenav*, 1916," which translates into "Jesus was born, 1916." The individuals in the photograph are celebrating Christmas, in this particular case, Armenian Apostolic Christmas, which is traditionally celebrated on January 6. We know from accounts in Maritsa's memoirs that her mother Haïganouch, who is pictured in the photograph leaning her head on her left arm, and their children secretly celebrated their first Apostolic Christmas after their conversion to Islam in the Der Haroutiounian household. This would answer our second question as to where this photograph was taken. The only known photograph of the Der Haroutiounian house, where the photo was taken, is cropped from a large panoramic photograph of Marsovan taken by Tsolag sometime in 1914. Having scanned this high-resolution print, I was able to enlarge a portion of it that matched a hand-drawn sketch by Aram, Maritsa's brother, that was found in the family papers of the Der Haroutiounians.

69. The Der Haroutiounian house in Marsovan at the edge of the city, *c*.1914.

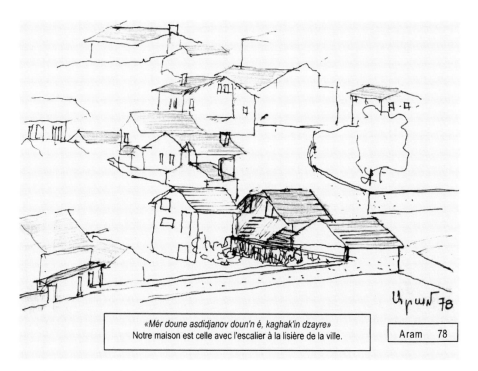

«Mér doune asdidjanov doun'n é, kaghak'in dzayre»
Notre maison est celle avec l'escalier à la lisière de la ville.

Aram   78

70. ["Our house is the one with the staircase near the edge of the city."][26] A sketch of the
Der Haroutiounian house drawn by Maritsa's brother Aram in 1978.

Der Haroutiounian House

Dildilian House

71. Tsolag's home and photo studio on the right with indentation in the roof for the glass of the
studio. Haïganouch's house on the bottom left. Anatolia College behind, c.1914.

Answering the third question – Who is in the photograph? – takes us directly to the topic of the individuals who were rescued by my family. It should be evident from a cursory glance at the photograph that the five males pictured are all relatively young men who would have been of draft age in 1915. Young males were called up for service prior to the deportations unless they had an exemption for a serious medical condition or managed to bribe their way out of service. Conversion to Islam and the adoption of Turkish names enabled one to avoid the deportations but did not exempt one from the draft. There were a number of young men and women on the campus of Anatolia College in the summer of 1915 who had been hoping to avoid the deportations. Their association with the Americans was to be their protection, but as we saw, all this changed on August 10 when almost all the remaining Armenians on the campus were deported. Aram Dildilian, pictured in the photograph in the back row on the right (clean-shaven but with a moustache), was exempt from military service because of his prosthetic leg. The four other young men pictured would be considered deserters at this point and subject to arrest and immediate execution.[27]

By matching earlier photos of the individuals pictured in this Christmas photo, we have been able to identify the four: Khatchadour Gorgodian (back row, second from left with the cap of a priest); Haïg Felisian (back row to the left of Aram with his hands on the shoulders of the man in front); Garabed Médaksian (the bearded man in front of Felisian); Lemuel Shirinian (seated below Médaksian, playing the musical instrument).[28] Khatchadour, Haïg, and Lemuel had all been students at the college, while Garabed had worked as an instructor in its carpentry shop. Here is a picture of Lemuel in his happier days at the college.

72. Lemuel Shirinian, a music teacher and Aram's friend at Anatolia College, *c.*1914.

The four other younger individuals in the photograph are four of Haïganouch's five children: Haïgouhi (holding the Bible, far left, back row); Maritsa (seated below Haïgouhi); Haïgazoun (seated next to his mother Haïganouch); and Aram (far bottom right of the photo). The fifth child, Haïgouni, is missing from the photograph because he probably took the photo that had been set up by his cousin Aram, the photographer. A second photograph with Aram and Haïgouni switching places also exists.

The last of our four simple questions – What are these people doing in the photograph? – has already been partially answered: They are celebrating Christmas mass. In addition to the Bible and the cross that Khatchadour is holding, there are a number of objects that would be used in the mass (*badarak*) including a wafer and a glass of what appears to be holy water (*muron*), a candlestick with the candle missing, and an incense holder. Could the missing candle and possibly incense reflect both the reality of their deprivations yet still be symbolic of their faith in carrying on?

73. Close-up of proto-Armenian flag, crucifix, candlestick holder, incense holder, wafer, and holy water used in the Christmas celebration.

The much more complex question of the photograph's message is a matter of speculation. They are certainly documenting this Christmas celebration for posterity. But one could also say that they are affirming their true inner faith despite the fact that they have outwardly adopted the faith of their oppressors. In addition to the spiritual message, there may be a political message here. Notice the flag on the table that has three horizontal stripes and two oblique bands with three stars in each. This resembles the flag of the Society of Armenian Students of Geneva.[29]

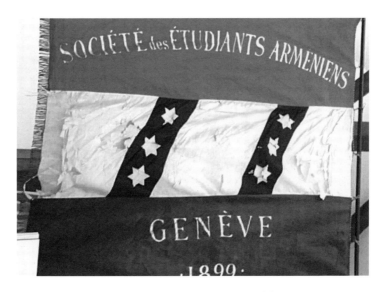

74. Flag of the Society of Armenian Students of Geneva, 1899.

Geneva was the center of diasporan Armenian nationalist activity in the 1890s. Both the Social Democrat Hunchakian Party (S.D.H.P.) or *"Hunchaks"* and the Armenian Revolutionary Federation or *"Dashnaktsutiun"* were active in Geneva, with the former being founded by Armenian university students. The photograph is thus a statement of resistance – resistance spiritually and in the name of the nascent Armenian nation.

We now come to the final but most important question regarding this old photograph and the topic of the rescue of Armenians in Marsovan: How did these individuals come to be in this particular place at this particular time for their photograph to be taken?

As the deportations continued into July and August, there was a growing awareness among the Armenian students of the college that the walls of the campus would no longer protect them. Three of them, Hovhannes Sivaslian, Hagop Kayayian and Garabed Médaksian, close friends of Aram, agreed that when their time came for deportation, they would attempt to escape to the mountainous countryside of the Greek village of Gelinsini. A Greek classmate of theirs, Andrias, had agreed to help them once they reached their destination. They had asked Aram to assist them with their plan: "All they want is to take them in our house for a night or so and bring their guns from college grounds. They showed me where they have kept them, I promised to do so. I used to sleep out in the garden next to the wall … At night, they were supposed to drop pebbles on my bed so that I would wake up and take them in in secret and hide them." Their plan was to "rough it" through the autumn and winter hoping that by spring the Ottoman armies on the collapsing Russian front would be defeated.

Earlier they had buried rifles, ammunition and hatchets in hiding places on the campus. They would use these rifles to live off the land by hunting but they soon realized that their access to these weapons would be cut off once the deportation began. They obtained a promise from Aram that once the campus had been cleared that he would go back and smuggle the weapons across the street to his brother's house. They would attempt to break off from the deportation caravan and return at night to collect the weapons and other supplies.

These endeavors of rescue and refuge began almost immediately after the deportation of the Armenians from the campus. The promise that Aram had made to his friends, Hovhannes, Hagop, and Garabed (Garo) had to be kept. The three friends would make an attempt to escape from the deportation caravan, return to Tsolag Dildilian's house in the cover of darkness, be provisioned with supplies, including the rifles recovered from their hiding places on the campus, and make their way to the mountainous countryside around the Greek village of Gelinsini. Late on the night of August 10, the following transpires in the Dildilian household:

> About 12 midnight, we heard a knock at the back yard door. But brother stopped me saying, "you stay away, this is my house, I am the responsible one and I must know first who it is." I tried to explain but he did not give me a chance, he went to the window to look, finally he opened the door, there come Hovhanness, Hagop and Garo. Brother was very much surprised and scared yet glad at least that a few had tried to escape. He was somewhat calmed when I explained what was what. At once I put them next door in the neighbor's oven house, they [the Djizmedjians] were sent to Osmanjouk and there was no one there in the house.

Both Aram and Maritsa's memoirs describe the circumstances that led to the escape of the three friends. In Aram's memoir, on the night of his arrival, Hovhannes explains to Aram and Tsolag how the group managed to escape from the caravan earlier that day. In Maritsa's notebooks the story is conveyed to Maritsa by Garabed, but sometime after the events. (It should be noted that Garabed marries Maritsa eight years later once they have emigrated to France.) Aram writes of the account given to him by Hovhannes:

> Hovhanness, who was a born machinist, said when we came to the Armenian monastery (Vank) Sourp Asdvadzadzin, they make the group take a rest under the shade of huge walnut trees. The farm manager came and asked for a college machinist to come out of the group and help fix the harvesting machine which was out of order. The monastery had several thousands of acres of wheat fields. It was harvesting time, Turks had already deported all the farm hands and monks … Later they had to look for skillful men to handle farming equipment. A smart Armenian (a forced apostate) [Aram Peynirian] volunteered to operate

those harvesting machines but there was something wrong that he could not fix so when he sees the professors' group passing by, he asked the manager to call the college machinist to come over and help fix the engine. So Hovhanness and his two companions come out of the group to fix the threshing machine. Of course, they took their time … When the group starts moving, the boss man said, "Hey, your group is moving on, you better go to join them." At once they pretend to anxiously join the group and start running towards the group but instead hide themselves in the wheat fields. About nightfall they start back towards the college compound.

Maritsa's account is emotionally more upsetting but contains a surprising, yet morally courageous act of assistance on the part of a Turkish policeman. Recall that this account was conveyed to Maritsa by Garabed, an eyewitness. The caravan that Garabed was on also included his mother and sister. For practical reasons the plan of escape and refuge in the mountains could not include his mother and sister. Garabed would be forced to leave them to their fates. Maritsa writes:

> Garo's mother tells him to take her own coat (motherhood) and his sister unhooks her christening medal from her neck, saying that they, mother and daughter, were going to die and the medal would be useful to him to get some money by selling it. Garo and his companions then go and hide amidst the wheat stalks. Some moments later, the transportation caravan sets out and, when his mother and sister, walk past him, Garo wants to rush forward, but his companions hold him back because their hiding place would have been revealed. And anyway, of what help would he have been to his mother and sister? He would have been executed before the caravan reached the Field of Irises. This was a vast spread of land covered with blue, white and yellow irises.

This was the last time that Garabed saw his family. No one knows when or where they perished. One can only wonder if it took place in a field of blue, white and yellow irises.

Earlier in her account Maritsa gives a much more detailed account of the "smart Armenian (a forced apostate)," Aram Peynirian, whom the friends had met outside the monastery. It is in the context of this encounter that we learn of the assistance provided by the Turkish policeman, Ipek Agha:

> When the group arrives at the monastery, Garo and Hovhannes, who are able mechanics, start to talk with Aram Effendi. Next to them, there was Ipek Agha, a Turkish policeman who was born and still lived in an Armenian borough. He comes to them and cries: "Dzo, why did you come here? Get the hell out of here! Go! They would cut your throats, run." "Run? But where to, Ipek Agha? How?" "Hell, beat it, they kill! Look at those policemen who are quarreling. A few moments ago, they have brought in Professor Hagopian and some others, and

now they are haggling over the reward. Are you chickens? Go away and wait until it is dark. I'll put you on the way to town and then you'll have to manage on yourselves." This shows how difficult it was to get in or out of the town.

Once the young men had returned to Marsovan and were welcomed by Tsolag and Aram, they were temporarily hidden next door at the Djizmedjians. In Maritsa's account, she was disturbed by the midnight events taking place in the house but was ordered to go to bed. She continues:

> The next morning, we saw that a board had been placed which ran from the wall of my uncle's house to a high-up window of the Djizmedjian's wash house which was no more than a small opening. It was an arrangement to bring food to the deserters who had been put in hiding there. They stayed for a few days, and uncle Aram even brought back to them the weapons he had gone and picked up at the College. Boghos *dayı* [uncle or swaggerer] later joined the group.

By this time in August, the four houses surrounding my grandfather's house were all empty. Professors Hagopian and Sivaslian along with Mr. Nerso, the director of Anatolia's Self-Help Department had been deported on August 10. The Djizmedjians had left on their own accord with a group of Protestants to the village of Osmanjouk because of the initial exemption of Protestants from the deportation orders.[30] Tsolag was worried that some of these vacant houses would be occupied by *mohadjirs* (refugees) or worse still, by the greedy authorities of the city. There is an entry in Morley's diary to the effect that "the Kaimakam is to move into the Manissadjian house and the Commandant of Gendarmes into the Djizmedjian house."[31] Fortunately this did not come to pass.

As Tsolag and Aram were providing refuge for the three young men, matters across the street at the campus took a turn for the worse. The young women of the Girls' School, along with its Armenian staff and nurses from the hospital, had for some reason not been deported on August 10. Suddenly the gendarmes appeared early on August 12 to deport them. Much has been written about the heroism of the missionaries, Miss Charlotte Willard and Miss Frances Gage, who followed the deported women and girls to Sivas and succeeded in bringing them back to Marsovan. Aram had to delay his plans to assist his friends' escape until matters quieted down on campus. Aram's memoir then describes the lengths to which he went in order to secretly bring the weapons from the college back to his friends hiding next door. This was one instance in which his artificial leg would serve a double function and be a help and not a hindrance:

> After the girls were gone, at noon I went to Dr. White, the college president and told him that we are not sure what will confront us but we must be ready for any emergency …

You know that I can't carry any load or burden on my back on account of the suspenders of my artificial leg. I want to build a push and pull cart so that I could put my belongings and little Alice on and go that way in case we be deported too ... So, "May I go to the carpenter shop and make a cart?" He said, "Why, sure," and he gave me a bunch of keys. I was really surprised of my success in my first white lie, which was not the last either ... I am sure God had forgiven me as my intention was not selfish but to save lives ...

I had free access to the college premises though there were some extra guards and jandarmas but they never suspected me, so many times I went back and forth carrying revolvers, ammunition and two army rifles. I put the rifle in my pants, point down and tied it to my artificial leg and the butt under my arm and put my heavy overcoat on, passed by the main gate coughing and heavily leaning on my cane ... When Hovhanness went over everything that I brought over he said he has some rifle ammunition and powder and his little hatchet that is hidden some other place ... I had to dig [them] out at the entrance of the machine shop. So I had to go back again and start digging at a certain spot, but to be on the safe side, I did find a big crate box and put it by me so that in case someone would come in, I could cover the dirt by turning the box over the hole and put some iron piece on the vise to pretend I am building something on the work bench. It took quite a long time to find the buried tin can. While I was scratching out the loose dirt, a sharp corner of the can cut my finger very badly. The pain was terrible, I did not know what to do.

After bandaging himself, he figured out a way of disguising the small sharp hatchet inside a painted box he had made. This allowed him to hide the hatchet in his coat sleeve and slip out the side door across the street from my grandfather's house.

Well, by nightfall they were all well supplied with carrying bags, blankets for each one and plenty foodstuffs. My sister-in-law had prepared a good meal for them, brother offered a prayer for their safety and we let them go on their way at midnight. I was quite sure that they will be safe and quite comfortable in the mountains as Hovhanness knew very well every rock, cave and ravine around and about that Greek village "Gelinsini."

By happenstance during my third visit to Marsovan, my hosts took us to a mountaintop north of the city. The panoramic view of the Marsovan plain was spectacular. As I gazed out upon this landscape I asked my host if he had heard of a Greek village called Gelinsini. He pointed to a cluster of houses down the mountainside a few kilometers off in the distance. Could these young men so many years ago have been standing on this spot gazing off toward the Marsovan plain below them – a plain dotted with the tiny specks that may have been the ox carts that were carrying off their friends and family to their uncertain fates? This painful thought was hard to dispel from my mind.

Aram kept in touch with his friends through a go-between, even providing them medicine when one of them fell ill. In Maritsa's account we have a much more detailed description of what transpired in the mountainous countryside. Her account was told to her by Garabed, her future husband:

> They set off for Gelinsini … village, through detours to avoid roads and settlements. Traveling by night is all right, but you can imagine the hazards they went through. Each tree looks like a standing man, each rock seems a seated man, you can stumble on an obstacle, fall into a hole. Once, the others shouted to Garo to stop: he was on the verge of a drop, one step more and he would have tumbled down a canyon. This happened on the mountain called Kel Tepe [the Bald Mountain] that has a top devoid of vegetation. From a distance, it appears as a rounded shape but, on the spot, it has gravel soil, and for each three steps forward, you go two steps backward because you slip back.

The young men slept in a damp cave, where "water oozes from the walls and rain wets everything. Food has to be shared with ants and other insects." Unlike the Greek deserters in the area, they cannot seek shelter in the village but must remain on the mountainsides struggling with the cold and the occasional bandit. It is August but the 6,000-foot altitude makes it feel like early winter. "Patches of snow still remain in the crevices" on the mountainside.

Though provided with some food by their Greek friend, and the game they were able to shoot, life became unbearable for Garabed and Boghos, who had joined the group later. They decided to slip back into town and hide on the college grounds. Once they slipped over the wall onto the campus they parted company. Boghos had been a gatekeeper for the college so both he and Garabed knew the premises well. Garabed discovered that the house of Professor J. P. Xenides was vacant and a Greek friend, Youvan, from his days working in the joinery shop was caretaking it.[32] His friend hid him there for a period of time, even arranging to turn on the water for him to have a bath. Eventually Garabed's anxiety at being detected led him to abandon the campus and to hide in a nearby unused mill. Youvan brought him food until the college cook began to suspect that something was up. Aram, Haïganouch and her children then proceeded to bring him food at the mill.

As the autumn slowly turned into winter, the active deportations came to an end. Aram reported that Tsolag has been assured by the commandant that they would remain in Marsovan:

> By that time, we were made sure that we were to stay permanently. The commander in chief asked us to go to his office and informed us that we will stay but we can't use our Armenian names. So brother is called Enver, my name is Shavkey, sister-in-law's was Mariam, they said Maryam … Christine's was Zakihe, and so on. Up to that time, my widowed sister Haïganouch with her five orphans, was with my brother's

family, that is ten children in the same house. It was fun for a few days but to extend that situation for several months was too much for all concerned.

It is interesting to note that Aram gives a different Turkish name for his brother than Maritsa provides in her memoir. The two versions of Aram's name, Zeki and Shavkey, are close enough that they may be the same. By this time Haïganouch and her children were feeling safe enough to consider moving out of Tsolag's home and back into their own. With all but the converted Armenians gone, the city had returned to a semblance of normalcy – a normalcy punctuated by the silent reminders of the empty and ransacked Armenian dwellings.

Life had become unbearable for Garabed at the mill, and Aram asked his sister to take him in. With the winter arriving early in the mountains, Hovhannes and Hagop were finding it increasingly difficult to survive. Aram had a plan. He would build a safe hiding place at his sister's house for his friends. Aram describes his request and his sister's response:

> So I told my sister if she would be willing to take care of three young men in her own home if I made some safe hiding place for them. I told her they will be willing to pay for their board ... She at once said, "Oh, my brother, sure, why not. My life's expectation is all wiped out and I have nothing to live for, if I can't serve the broken pieces of my people in some small way, if not, what am I to live for!" Before I sent word to Hovhanness, with the help of my nephew Haïgouni, we built a temporary hiding place out in the yard and then I sent for them to come and arranging it so they would arrive at a certain time to avoid the street patrols. Sister's house was the outermost northern end house in the corner. It was a cold and rainy night. I kept watch at the wall, finally they came, at once we opened the door. We were expecting three, there came four of them. Well, we had to take them all in anyhow. They were Hovhanness, Hagop, Garo and Bogos.

These young men remained in Haïganouch's house for upwards of two years. This is how Garabed Médaksian came to find himself in the Christmas celebration captured in that old photograph.

Upon the arrival of the four young men, Aram began the process of building a secure hiding place. There was construction material on the premises because Haïganouch's husband had been in the midst of building the house when he reported for military service. Aram describes his efforts:

> We built a very safe and comfortable underground hiding place in two sections so that in case one section is found, the back section will be safe, and the entrance was inside the room, altogether misleading. I made a fresh-air ventilation [system] and there was room enough for 8 persons ... I put up a watchtower with mirrors to look and see in every direction so that the watchman (one of the boys in succession)

would signal the boys to go down in case of suspicious people out by the house and he would come down too.

A similar description is given in Maritsa's notebooks. More easily detectable hiding places were made in other places on the property. This was done so that if the police searched the house and found these "fake" hiding places empty they would then be content that no one was hidden in the house. Secretly at night they raised the height of the outer walls with the addition of sun-baked bricks that originally had been prepared for the home addition.

All seemed secure but the family's worries did not end. Fortunately their neighbors' houses were empty but this created the additional worry that someone unwelcome could move in. Aram describes what occurred on one occasion:

> The house and the yard were safe from onlookers as we had high walls around and we did not have any windows exposed to the outside streets. So we were comparatively safe ... But one day my nephew, Haïgouni, told me that in the house next door he saw a man. That did not sound good to me so I decided to investigate. I went to the house and sure enough I find a very scared young lad. He told me that his mother was afraid for him to be kept at her home and had told him to get out and take care of himself the best he could. So he did find that house empty, got in and was trying to get along. I told him that this is not a safe place. Sooner or later he will be caught. I will take you to a better and safer place ... the only condition is that once you enter, you will not get out till we all are free. You will not go out or see your mother or anyone else. Later he told me his brother is out in a precarious condition, if we could get him in too? So we got in to the house those Gorgodian brothers.

This is how Khatchadour Gorgodian came to be hidden in Haïganouch's house, the second of the four young men pictured in that old Christmas photograph. Now there were six young men hiding in the house but the story doesn't end here, for more were yet to come. Aram continues:

> Later I heard that Lemuel, who was hiding by himself in the college grounds, was caught by Dr. White and was ordered out. Well, quite naturally I would do anything for Lemuel as he was related to my dear sister Parantzem's family, so I had to bring him over too. Besides he was the only living brother left of my dearest friend, Edward Shirinian, one of the most talented of the musical family of four brothers ... Later, we got in Haroutioun [Tchavouchian], who was hiding by himself at Marderos's silk factory and then Mihran [Mihran Gharabed Hovagimian] trying to hide himself here and there, and Haïg Felisian who managed to hide himself in the college attic room and got along by himself more than six months. He somehow managed to get into the college kitchen and get hold of can goods, but he was so

lazy to dump away the empty cans and throws them around there where he was hiding. One day, Dr. White in his regular search sees those empty cans around so he gets suspicious and waits there for someone to come around. When Haïg came up, both were surprised to see each other. Dr. White orders him out, but Haïg instead moves to another spot and stays there a few more weeks. Finally, we had to take him in too. Now we had 10 men, too many to keep in one place and too dangerous for safe keeping.

With the addition of Haïg, we have solved the mystery of how these four young men, Garabed, Khatchadour, Lemuel, and now Haïg came to be in that Christmas celebration photograph of 1916.

But the saga continued. We now had ten young men hiding in Haïganouch's house. Aram soon realized that the hiding place he created would not be big enough to hold ten individuals comfortably and with the prospect of the addition of more escapees, plans soon began for a much more expansive hiding place that could hold upwards of 20 individuals. The decision is made to make use of three of the abandoned Armenian properties that border the Haroutiounian property.

The decision to expand was prescient because soon Hovhannes and Hagop returned from the mountains to join their classmates. But the numbers were to grow again, for these 12 men were soon joined by eight women and girls. With Haïganouch and her five children, we now had 25 individuals living in the Haroutiounian compound.

The growing numbers called for immediate action to implement the expansion plan. As already mentioned, this would require utilizing the abandoned properties next door, especially the Varjabedian's house. Aram describes the steps they took:

We had to have a bigger and safer hiding place. There was an Armenian house next to us, so far, no Turk took possession of it yet … After the Armenians were deported, most of the household goods were looted by Turks and the rest were moved by the government into the churches and other warehouses with the merchandise and other properties under a new law, so-called "Envali Matrookeh" (neglected goods committee). There was an apostate former Armenian police chief of Sivas. His name was Aram. I went to see him and asked if we can have possession of the next door house so that my sister who is a widow with five orphans … would have a bigger room for her weaving business. He said, "Why sure, go ahead and do anything with it. No one will say a thing and in case someone objects to it, you let me know." So at once we tore down the partitioning wall and Haïgouni made his bedroom. That house was 5–6 foot lower than sister's house, so we bore a hole in the foundation wall and started digging towards sister's house a zig-zag tunnel. The dirt was clayish so we were safe of any cave in. We dug about [a] 30 yards long tunnel up to the foundation of my sister's house to the highway. In that new hiding place we had water from the well, plenty fresh air, enough room for more than 15–20 people. We used to hold prayer meetings on Sundays, we could sing to the top of our voices yet no one could hear us from outside. We used to do target practicing too, and the entrance I made it so that no one could even suspect its existence. To eliminate the dirt that we dug out, as I said before, we had plenty sun-dried bricks and with them we raised the walls of the yard about two feet higher so that neighbors would not be able to see what is going on in the yard. We filled the yard with that fresh dug-out dirt in garden beds so that if someone accidentally walks into the yard they would think we are digging a new garden bed to plant ... Soon after we finished digging, we closed the hole in the foundation, we plastered the whole wall of that basement room so that no one would suspect anything.

Aram and Maritsa's memoirs provide a fascinating account of their efforts to keep these hiding places and their human contents a secret. Back at Tsolag's house, according to recorded oral testimony by my mother and my uncle Ara, an effort was made to hide additional young men during this period. My mother often told me that when she was very young she believed that there were ghosts lurking around her home because suddenly she would see figures appear from odd places in the house. Given what is stated in the memoirs, Tsolag and Haïganouch were for a long time unaware of each other's efforts to hide young men and women. Aram, who ostensibly lived in Tsolag's house but spent much time at his sister's home, was certainly aware of the activities in both households. Tsolag eventually visited his sister's house toward the end of the war. Only at that time did he make the joyful discovery that many young men and women had survived the destruction that had been visited upon his people. Though neither of them explicitly says so, I suspect that by keeping each other in the dark about their "illegal" activities, my grandfather and great-aunt were protecting each other in case one of them had been discovered. If tortured, neither would be able to implicate the other.

The risks that Tsolag, Aram, and Haïganouch took were enormous. Aram acknowledges that if they were caught hiding an Armenian, they, along with their escapee, would be publically executed by hanging in front of their front door. The record shows that during this period a number of Armenians and a few Turks were thus executed for attempting to hide their friends and neighbors.

The War Years: The Day-to-Day Struggle for Survival

The deportation of the Armenians of Marsovan meant that life for the Dildilian and Der Haroutiounian families was forever changed. A year of war had already created shortages and economic hardship for the families, but now that nearly half the city's roughly 30,000 inhabitants were gone, there was an economic collapse. Armenians constituted a disproportionate percentage of the skilled and professional classes. Scores of young men of Turkish and Greek ethnicity were also gone, serving in the army and perishing in high numbers, more from disease than from combat. Many among the better off Greek community who witnessed the deportations of their Armenian neighbors foresaw the dangers that loomed for non-Muslim minorities and emigrated to Constantinople and Greece.

The local authorities, realizing the self-destructive economic consequences of their policy of deportation, had earlier encouraged a limited number of skilled Armenian workers and professionals to convert and stay in Marsovan. Maritsa notes this policy: "Thus, my uncle Tsolag, as photographer, and my mother, as carpet weaver, were kept. Cobblers, joiners, blacksmiths, tailors, and bakers thus escaped from transportation. Mute watermills came to life again. And Armenians, progressively, resumed their businesses in the bazaar. Of course, all these people had, as us, turned Muslims." Yet with few customers, most skilled workers were barely able to make a living. A city that had at one time needed many joiners, metal and stone workers, now had barely enough work for the few remaining craftsmen. The building boom that was taking place at Anatolia College came to an abrupt end at the outset of the war. The college had reopened in September 1915 with a greatly diminished teaching staff and student body, mostly made up of Greeks and a few Russians and Turks. Even this activity came to an end when the military closed the campus and took over most of the buildings in May 1916. All the Americans were forced to leave at that time, with only Mr. and Mrs. Dana Getchell returning a few months later to safeguard some of the school's property.

With the summer having ended and still no word regarding their father, the Der Haroutiounian children clung to the hope that their beloved father would return. Maritsa tells a story that reflects this ever-diminishing hope:

> In the garden of the Papelians' house, one of the houses we had rented, there was a quince tree that had given seven fruits. What a nice surprise for our father if we could keep these fruits until the time he returns! So beautiful, so big quinces! I had never seen the likes before and have not seen the likes since. Oblong-shaped, they had the size of a half-sheet of paper and weighed two pounds. My sister suspended two of them from the ceiling of our room and every evening, before going to bed, she looked at them tenderly, dreaming that one day she would see them in my father's hands. But they did not last to springtime. One was rotting so we brought it down. As to the other, we found it on the floor one evening. It was wholly rotten inside although still of a nice yellow aspect outside.
>
> Both my sister and I felt this little fact was a bad omen.

With no husband and little income coming in, Haïganouch was able to find work for two of her eldest children. Maritsa was sent to work in the household of Hohvannes Effendian while her older brother, Haïgouni, got a job working in the Kiremidjian store:

236

Upon a request by my mother, Kiremidjian Hadji Effendi took on my brother Haïgouni as shop boy in his store. Haïgouni was a handsome boy ... with something of a kind and gracious manner about him ...

I said Kiremidjian's shop, but in fact it was a commercial undertaking housed in a vast store located at a street corner. The store presented large windows closed at night with metallic shutters. Inside, there were wax dummies used to exhibit women and children's garments, cloth rolls and all the articles that feminine elegance and finery demanded. In his office, Kiremidjian dealt with import and export matters. With time, that office had become a meeting place for prominent figures and officials. On the upper story, there were guest rooms and a tea and coffee saloon, very neat and modern, not open to the public at large.

The Turkification process that was central to the C.U.P.'s ideology was being practiced in subtle ways with the "officially" converted Armenian population. The young were more malleable than their elders whose conversions were naturally suspect. This is evident in the description of Haïgouni's treatment by the Turkish notables in the Kiremidjian store:

With time, my brother became the son of the house. As I said, the Armenian and Turkish big shots, the mayor, police commissioner, judge, etc. used to meet at Kiremidjian's store. Thus, they became acquainted with my brother who brought them water, tea and the different things that may be served on such occasions. They called him "son," giving him his Turkish name of Ziya. And even, when one of them called him "*oğlum*" (my son), the others protested: "No, Ziya is *my* son," and they discussed the matter without coming to an agreement ... and small rivalries were arising from that.

The mayor and the military commander entrusted him with errands ... The mayor asked him one day to bring his two brothers to his home so that they [might] play with his own children. But they did not go. He often had open conversations with Haïgouni. One day, he told him: "Ziya, we know perfectly well that neither your mother nor your uncle will become Turks. Our hope is with you, the young ones."

This process of cleansing the remaining Armenians of their ethnic identity would continue for decades after the killing had stopped. Haïganouch went to great lengths to ensure that the Armenian identity of her children would remain strong despite the fact that they were forced to live as Turks.

With the winter close at hand and little in the way of prepared foods for the cold, dark days ahead, many remaining families were forced to slaughter their oxen. In normal times such beasts of burden would be used for transport or rented for use in the fields and vineyards. The family ox now had to go, so Haïgouni slaughtered his first ox. He soon got a reputation for his handiwork and was hired by other families: "Hearing this, our Armenian neighbors, the Meryemkulis, asked my brother to also slaughter their ox, which he kindly did." Haïgouni's skills not only helped satisfy the material needs of the family, but soon also their spiritual needs. The neighbors could not afford to pay Haïgouni for his labor but their daughter Haïgouhi, who was a gifted music teacher, offered to give music lessons in return. Maritsa was able to rent a harmonium "and Miss Haïgouhi came twice a week to give us lessons free of charge. 'You helped us without asking anything from us, and in turn I want to do you a service which I consider a debt,' she said." I was moved when I first read this passage. For in the midst of all the hardships and violence, the family appreciated that survival was not merely a matter of food on the table but also music to nourish the soul.

As should be clear by now, my great-uncle Aram was a highly creative and technically skilled individual. His talents would come in handy during these difficult times. It was clear that photography was not going to support the family:

> There was no photographic business because Turks never had a personal or family picture taking custom as it was against the Mohammedan religion. There were no more Armenians to be photographed and the Anatolia College circle had no more students or professors and most of the American missionary personnel have been sent out of the country, so no more picture taking except official orders for which we were not paid and if paid was not enough ... I was thinking and thinking hard but I did not know what to do. Though my brother never did himself express any anxiety. I knew he was worried very much.

By a happy circumstance, a partial solution was found for the sudden drop in income faced by the Dildilians. An old friend of the family, Mr. Hovhanness Demirjian, who had survived because he was an expert flour mill worker in Amasia, was visiting the family. Aram relates what happened next:

> [Mr. Demirjian] realized our hard situation and he suggested starting a poppy seed oil business because there was no olive oil on the market. On the other hand, there was plenty poppy seed on the market and quite cheap. The poppy seed oil was something new for us but it was good for cooking, as salad oil, and for other purposes. He said he will send us couple of roller cylinders, brass gears, bearings, press screws and all the other essentials. He explained to me what to do and how to put them together and make it work. It was so easy to build the press and the iron basket for the press though I had no idea about roller presses at all. It took quite a long time and experiments ... to put the grinding mill in working condition, but I did it ... Finally, we were quite successful not only producing in quantity more than others but we were able to produce salad oil almost equal to olive oil. Soon we were quite fixed and started to make more

than our living. The whole family was slaving ourselves and were soaked in oil. My sweet little nephews used to grind, my mother-in-law used to fry, and all the rest of us used to press and do other kinds of chores pertaining to it. I was informed that poppy seed oil could be burned in regular kerosene oil lamps if the oil is about the level of the burner, so I built a special vacuum tank next to the burner so that it would supply oil as much as is burned to the level of the wick end. I built a good many of them in several styles and shapes and sold [them] to others.

Maritsa notes that kerosene for lamps had gotten scarce because most of it came from Russia and supplies were cut off as a result of the war. She describes in detail Aram's invention and oil lamp manufacturing business. Maritsa had nothing but words of praise for her uncle, "What an ingenious man my uncle was! He was really a Dildilian! They were all talented."

Not wanting to waste any byproducts of the process, Aram soon developed a way of making soap from the leftover old and dirty oil. This was not an easy process but he taught himself how to do it using a procedure he found in an old Armenian book. He was quite successful in all these endeavors. As is clear from all the family sources, he shared the fruits of his talents with all his neighbors. Unlike others during these war years, he did not profit from other people's hardships: "I gave all my life to others during those war days, I gave my all, while others made money and lots of money."

Despite the efforts of Aram, Tsolag, and Haïganouch, the financial strains of maintaining two large households were becoming evident. Between the two households there were well over 40 mouths to feed and many of these individuals could not emerge from their hiding places in order to earn a living. The escapees had made it through the first winter with no major incidents. But with the prospects for the family limited, the Dildilians had to turn to outside help. Anatolia College had closed on May 10, 1916 and all the Americans were sent to Constantinople. Mr. Dana K. Getchell, the principal of the preparatory school and treasurer of the college and his wife had returned to their house on the campus in late June in order to safeguard the American properties. Up until the closure of the college, President White had been vigilant in assuring the authorities that no Armenians were present on the grounds. Both the missionary and family memoirs cite incidents of President White discovering young men hiding on the campus and ordering them out. In his orally recorded memories of the war years, my uncle Ara has testified to the fact that White was a stickler for adhering to the rules unlike some of the other Americans associated with the college. I can only assume that he feared the authorities would shut down the college and mission if he was caught violating the law. But now the college was closed and he was gone. Aram turns to his dearly loved former teacher, Mr. Getchell:

We had 15 or 16 mouths to feed. We had no other source left, so I went to Mr. Getchell and asked for some help for the boys ... Mr. Getchell at once gave me 60 dollars, but soon that was gone as foodstuffs were in very short supply and became scarce with prices high ... So, soon I went to him again. This time he gave me 30 dollars and said, "Aram, you know I am willing to do more but I have no way of marking this in my books. I do not want to endanger our work." He added, "I understand the surviving Armenians have organized a relief fund to help hard cases like those boys and needy widows, so you better go to them."

The Getchells seem to have had a special relationship with one of the escapees, Lemuel Shirinian. Lemuel's siblings had attended the school and his deceased father had been a Protestant preacher. Maritsa relates that Lemuel was taken in for a period of time by the Getchells, temporarily relieving them of one of their hidden guests. He would also spend time hidden at my grandfather's house but eventually returned to Haïganouch's.

The relief fund referred to by Getchell had been organized by Kiremidjian. Aram is hesitant to turn to Kiremidjian since he believes that the request should come from someone with higher standing in the community, that is, his brother Tsolag. Up to this point it appears that Tsolag was unaware of his brother and sister's efforts to hide the young Armenian men. But now they needed Tsolag to secure funds to help support these hidden Armenians. In a touching scene, Aram relates how they broke the news to him:

During those long years, brother had never come to sister's house and he was never aware of what had happened to those boys. We were really surprised to hear him consent to come over. At noon when he came over and entered into the sitting room, he was surprised to see a big table set and so many plates and forks and spoons on it, so he said to "Haïgouni, what a big table, I did not know you have that many friends!" Haïgouni said, "Yes, uncle, we have a good many friends. Soon you will see them all." When he sat down in his place and I next to him, sister opened the door and Hovhanness walked in! When brother saw him, he was shockingly surprised and exclaimed, "Hovhanness, you are alive and here?" Then Lemuel walked in. "You, Lemuel? You? You? Are you alive too?" When I saw him so much excited, I told him not to be so excited, there are others yet inside, they are all well. "Be calm! Soon others will come in. We just wanted to surprise you. Be calm!" When everyone walked in and greeted him, he said to me, "How did it happen? Why are they all here? Where did you hide them? How did you gather them together? Why did you not inform me so that I could build a better place to hide?" and many other excited questions without waiting for an answer. Then the boys calmed him down, assuring him there was nothing to worry about. We have the best hiding place, and they challenged him to find it. (To confuse suspicious people ... we had built some make-shift hiding places so that when they search and find no one hiding, they will give up the search). He looked around and took my cane and moved a board and said, "Oh! Aram, is this all you could do? Why you did not consult with me so that we would build some better and safer hiding place?" Finally, when we showed the real one, he was quite satisfied, and calmed down. Then we explained to him all about what we had done so far. "We did not want to bother you, but now all our financial means are exhausted. So now you do whatever you can do to get some help from that Armenian Relief Organization."

From the memoirs it is unclear on what date Tsolag approached the relief organization set up by Garabed Kiremidjian and the other rich converted notables. This could not have been before late 1916 and may have been later. We know that sometime in 1918 Kiremidjian left Marsovan for Constantinople. Aram relates Tsolag's failed attempt to secure aid:

> So brother went to the head man, Kiremidjian Hadji Effendi, who in turn very thoughtlessly tells to the fellow members that "there are some boys in hiding, send some aid to those boys." But the treasurer and others do not dare to do anything because in the group there was a traitor (Mugadich Yeprem). So they told brother that they can't very well do anything about those boys. In that Armenian Relief group, there were three leading Protestant young men ... who were "new rich." Sure enough they were afraid of that traitor, Yeprem, but they personally could help in secret, but they did not. During those terrible four years of war, I did learn a whole lot about human nature ... I could very well become one of those new rich myself as I was not less in brain and ability but I did not choose to.

Armenian traitors, this was something not talked about when I was growing up. In my youth, especially during my years in the Armenian Youth Federation, everything related to the genocide was always set out in black and white terms, there were no gray areas. All Armenians were good and Turks bad, it was as simple as that. I now know and certainly my grandparents knew then, that this was not the case. An Armenian traitor, Harouotiun Mugerditchian, helped compile the list of Armenian leaders whom Talaat Pasha had arrested on April 24, 1915, so it was not surprising that there was an informer among the converted Armenians of Marsovan.

We do know that at some point, probably during the difficult winter of 1916–17, Haïganouch appealed directly to Kiremidjian for aid: "With no means left to us, we applied to Kiremidjian Hadji Effendi, confessing we were hiding deserters and had neither food nor clothes left. Kiremidjian first sent Boghossian ... to see what was really on. Boghossian came, looked and went back. Kiremidjian had then a bag of 50 *kashs* of flour delivered to us, and cloth in which we cut clothes for Haroutioun and Garabed." But we will soon see that the clever Garabed Kiremidjian found other ways to help the Armenians in need.

Both Aram and Maritsa's memoirs often discuss the activities of Garabed Kiremidjian. Kiremidjian's work on behalf of Marsovan's Armenians was described in his own memoir and is verified by my family's account. I do not want to exaggerate the parallels but there is a striking resemblance between Oskar Schindler's activities saving the lives of Jews during the Holocaust and what Kiremidjian did during the Armenian Genocide. Of course, Schindler was not a Jew, while Kiremidjian was saving his own people, albeit under the guise of being a Turkified Armenian. Maritsa writes the following about him:

> The war however, was going on at that time, and they started to enlist older men. To escape call-up, that inventive man [Garabed Kiremidjian] imagined a way out. He had already founded a charity society where women in need could receive flour. Given the new situation, he had the idea of supplying cloth for Army uniforms. He founded a company with a board of directors that included Armenians and the three Turkish representatives as required by law. The company purchased wool that was washed and cleaned by Turks, combed and spun by Greeks and woven by Armenians. The cloth produced was crude and lacked quality. So Kiremidjian found a Turkish specialist in Rumania and had him come to Marsovan to take charge of the dyeing process and the folding process of this thick cloth at the output end of the line.
>
> That specialist worked in Leblebidjian's large watermill factory which processed the raw cloth received from town, dyed and folded it prior to its delivery to the Army. Two young Armenians worked there in order to evade service in the regular army. My brother Haïgouni knew them …
>
> One day, Hadji Effendi said that, as he looked older than his age, Haïgouni could be drafted. It was therefore better for him to enlist before call-up so that he would not be posted to a combat unit. It was better to lose two years of one's life rather than risk one's life.
>
> In this way, my brother entered the factory with the two other boys.[33]

Haïgouni was not the only draft-age Armenian who was to be saved by this method. Eventually a number of the young men hiding in Haïganouch's house would also be enlisted in the army and put to work in Kiremidjian's factory. A strange irony how army deserters became valued enlisted soldiers who provided a vital service for the Ottoman army. Kiremidjian must have been kept busy bribing and providing lists of deserters' names to the army recruitment officers. I do not suppose that a famous Hollywood director would ever make a film entitled "Kiremidjian's List."

Two Years in Hiding: Waiting to See the Light of Day

The more than two years of hiding, feeding and entertaining the young deserters had taken its toll on both families. For the young men themselves, their physical well-being was taken care of, but the psychological costs of the isolation must have been severe. The pain of their isolation is compounded by the fact that these young men were dealing with the loss of their deported families and friends. Most of them simply did not know what happened to their brothers, sisters, parents, grandparents and friends. They heard rumors, rumors they hoped were not true. Both Aram and Maritsa remark that they had expected the war to quickly end and that the remaining Armenians would be rescued by advancing Russian forces.

The summer of 1916 had seen the Russian forces advance their furthest into Ottoman territory. Maritsa comments: "During winter, they had taken Mamakhatoun [west of Erzurum] and were now heading toward Erzincan and Sivas. If they had taken these two big cities, nothing, I think, would have then prevented a collapse of the country." The family believed that as a result their ordeal would soon come to an end, but with the start of the Russian Revolution in February 1917, the Russian advances into Anatolia came to an end and the Imperial armies melted away.

At first the deserters had busied themselves making preparations to defend themselves. This gave them a shared sense of purpose and must have eased the strains of their new communal life. They had a few guns but no cartridges or knives. Putting their skills together they set to work, though not always successfully. Maritsa reports:

> Haroutioun, who had apparently worked with a blacksmith, took some files from my father's tools, heated them red-hot and hammered them to make flat blades. He then cut grooves into them, intended to make blood flow more easily. And he heated again the blades to blue (which is a delicate operation) and dipped them in water or oil to re-harden them …
>
> Once everybody was provided with a dagger, we turned to cartridges. But, here, it was a more arduous matter. After some trial and error, Haroutioun obtained gunpowder in three colors: black, red, white. My brother Haïgouni, who had taught me how to shoot with his rifle, came one day with a small gun he gave me, saying: "You must always keep the last cartridge for yourself. There are nine of them, eight for the others and the last you must absolutely keep for you so as not to fall alive in the hands of the Turks." Haroutioun filled up empty cartridge cases with his powder and securely fitted lead bullets on their ends. And happy as larks, we went down into the shelter to perform tests with my gun.
>
> With the first shot, the bullet ricocheted off the target and came back whizzing past me. At the second attempt, the bullet did not come off the barrel, the whole thing blasted and melted. My beautiful gun had become useless.

243

As I had mentioned earlier, life became much more complicated as the number of guests increased. Maritsa describes the growing difficulties:

> When they were only four, my mother could keep her balance of mind. In winter, we gathered around the fire in the small room. We told stories, quoted proverbs or played riddles. Lemuel would read a book aloud or play something on one of his two small zithers, and we sang in choir, in particular *sharagans* [hymns]. From that time, I have been very fond of these hymns ... We sang them with love and faith, putting in them all our hearts and expectations, in the hope that our lives would cease to be an inferno and we may feel at last as human beings and free Armenians.

With the arrival of three more deserters, "Hovhannes Sivaslian, his brother-in-law Hagop, a huge-bodied boy, and Boghos *dayı* the College gatekeeper" the family's difficulties had multiplied. Maritsa hints that behavioral issues began to arise: "Another sort of life was introduced with them." This was soon to be compounded with the arrival of eight Armenian women, three of whom were school teachers from the college. Through the heroic efforts of Miss Charlotte R. Willard, the principal of the Girls' School, and her dedicated teacher, Miss Frances Gage, 48 girls had been rescued from the last deportation caravan from the college and returned to the campus. With the college closed in the spring of 1916 pressure was put on the Armenian girls and teachers still on the campus. Numerous attempts were made to marry them off to the children of Turkish notable families or government officials. Many of them left the campus and sought shelter in the homes of some of the Armenian converts. Maritsa describes her mother's efforts in this regard:

> My mother had hidden the girls in Varjabedian's house as she did not want them to be in touch with men. These girls had come for the following reason: the Turks, at one time, had wanted to convert the College to barracks and, with that in view, had initiated a new "sieving out" of the Armenian people still remaining in the College. So these Armenian remnants had fled, scattering here and there. The girls had come to our place. However, they did not stay for very long. When the evil wind decreased, they left our house, together with Gorgodian's brother.
>
> We breathed out a sigh of relief and enjoyed some rest. Imagine that at one time, during these weeks of turmoil, we were more than 23 people. We had no soap for the washing-up. And cooking meals in large pans, without attracting attention on us! My mother was of course overloaded with work and was running all day. My sister and I were in charge of dish washing and housekeeping. We always had a broom in hand. With the departure of the others, we had some relief.

As long as the young men had a project to keep them busy, tranquility was maintained in the household. They kept busy preparing weapons, including grenades, to protect themselves if that time ever came. Fortunately for all, these measures were not needed because the elaborate precautions the family had taken to protect the hiding places worked to perfection.

Yet the Dildilians and Der Haroutiounians were forever fearful that their deserters would be discovered. The deserters themselves were not as cautious. A system had been worked out in Haïganouch's house that would alert the young men to run to their underground hiding place if a stranger was knocking at the door. Aram "had a particular manner of knocking" that let them know it was not necessary to hide. But Maritsa laments: "I must declare that the boys we were hiding and whose necks we had just saved, behaved without any caution. They paced openly through the gardens of the three [surrounding] houses [the family had rented]. Even more, Khatchadour used to bask in the sun heedlessly."

Aram and Haïganouch had established strict rules as to what was allowed and what was not allowed during this long period of hiding. Permission was required for the boys to leave the house. But this rule was sometimes violated, risking the lives of all concerned. One life was indeed lost but thankfully not in Marsovan and not at the hands of the gendarmes:

> Though I had strict orders for the boys not to go out of the house, before discussing with me, as they would be endangering all the rest of us. But Backji Boghos, the former college night watchman, one night takes all his belongings to join Greek guerrillas, supposedly to cross the frontier with them and go to Russia. Sorry to say, Greeks killed him for his money and for his excellent German-made rapid firing gun.

An even worse incident soon occurs that truly endangered the lives of all concerned:

> Hovhanness and Hagop ... the two boys whom I used to trust more than anyone else for having sense and used to rely on them for the safety of others, insist to go to the hills for a change, for fresh air and try to find out what is what for themselves. Sister opposed them vigorously but no use, they went out anyhow. Two weeks later, they come back at night. When they are near the home, they see a jandarma patrol. At once they turn back and run down the street. As soon as they turn the corner, they open fire on the jandarmas, and then gradually disappear to the river bottom and then back to the hills. At home we heard lots of shooting at night for a long time. Next day the police force searched almost every house in that neighborhood except my sister's house. God was surely protecting us, especially my sweet nieces and nephews ... three or four days later, they came back home promising never, never to go out again.

After this long period in which they were housebound the boys began experiencing "cabin-fever." "Now, the deserters wanted to have visits, but this time my mother put her foot down. Her concern was to keep the number of people knowing about us as low as possible ... and to tell the actual truth, they wanted women. One day, they started another row." Aram describes his intervention to break up the fight: "They had a terrible fight with each other for almost no special cause. Sister was not able to quiet them down so she sent for me. I at once rushed there as soon as I could. When I entered, all of them were sitting down side by side like scared rats ... I was very angry ... I said, 'What kind of creatures are you, are you men or not.'" Aram severely admonished the boys but it was becoming increasingly clear that changes had to be made.

While no specific dates are provided by Aram, we must be well into 1917 at this point in our story. It is often mentioned that the deserters had been hidden for two years starting in the summer of 1915. Maritsa is more explicit when she writes of the departure of the first of the boys: "In the spring of 1917, when the war was ebbing away, these undesirable boys left." It is well known that by this time the dangers to the remaining Armenian population had diminished, though the level of violence varied from locale to locale. Kiremidjian plays an important role in finally unburdening the family:

> To relieve us from the burden they represented, the deserters had to come out in the open and earn a living. This was now easier because the war was practically finished and the situation was less tense. So Kiremidjian made the necessary arrangements to have the boys enrolled in the army, with Garo appointed as mechanic in the mill where my brother Haïgouni was already working, and Haroutioun as supervisor of the weaving shop. To Mihran, who was a short boy, he said: "Go get your name changed to Mihri, and if they ask for your papers, tell them I am your reference."

Aram comments on the departure of his good friend Lemuel: "By that time, Turks were not persecuting much of the surviving Armenians, so first Lemuel got out in the open and started teaching piano playing. I ventured to go to Samsun and bought a piano, crated it myself and brought it myself in an open wagon." Aram soon arranged for the departure of the remaining young men: "While I was there I helped [arrange] for the safety of Gorgodians ... Hovhanness Sivaslian and Hagop were able to go to Ata Bay to Mr. Zimmerman's German farm. Garo and Mihran were able to get some jobs in the College and Haroutioun started to work in one of the flour mills ... Thanks to God we were relieved of obligations and dangers."

With the departure of this last group of young men, the saga of the hidden Armenians ended.

The Calm after the Storm: The Family Waits Out the End of the War

As 1917 drew to a close, a calm started to settle in upon Marsovan. The Russian advances in the east had come to a halt in the summer and the security of Constantinople had been assured by the withdrawal of the Allies from Gallipoli the previous year. For the most part the "Turkified" Armenians who remained in Marsovan were left in peace. Kiremidjian had managed to place the young Armenian men in the enterprises he had created to support the war effort. The great irony, of course, is that these men who had initially armed themselves for protection against the state authorities were now in uniform and ostensibly supporting the war effort in defense of the state.

It must have been toward the end of 1917 that Haïganouch invited Kiremidjian to dinner in order to thank him for all he had done for the Armenian community.

> So, in 1917, before he left for Bolis, we invited him for dinner to express our gratitude. At that dinner, we, the children, were not allowed to sit at the table; there were only my mother, Garo, Haroutioun and Mihran. Kiremidjian told about his efforts to help Armenians. In the face of the question of life or death for our millet, he had invited the kaimakam, offering him the best he had in food and drinks, and had made a last attempt to convince him: "Save us. Through one means or another, but save us," had insisted Hadji Effendi. The kaimakam had answered he had not a free hand; he had orders to transport everybody and not leave a single soul in the district." "Now listen, you mulehead!, save us and you'll receive money for it." "But I'll be dismissed!" "You'll receive [50 TL] for each head saved. If you keep to your post, you'll get only your salary: that is, 'the tail of a donkey' [a colorful Armenian expression is used here]. In contrast, with the money received, what do you care if you are dismissed? You'll be rich for the rest of your days. So, take the money and enjoy it. Whereas, if we are transported, what profit will you get from it?" After Kiremidjian argued and insisted for three hours, the kaimakam accepted not to sign the transportation order provided the Armenians turned Muslims, which is what happened. In this way, some Armenian families were spared in Marsovan.[34]

Kiremidjian himself had managed to use his influence and wealth to move his wife, sons and daughter to Constantinople during the early stages of the deportations. He himself would move to Constantinople sometime in 1918. He had been granted permission to travel "to Germany in order to buy mechanical looms and other necessary machinery" in order to improve the quality of the cloth he was producing. He notes that permission was granted by Omar Nadji Bey, the Circassian *vali* of Sivas. He considered this new *vali* his friend.[35]

My research revealed that Nadji Bey had replaced the previous *vali* by 1917. The previous *vali*, who is often mentioned in the memoirs, was notoriously vicious and rabidly Armenian-hating. Ahmed Muammer Bey had served as *vali* of Sivas from 1913 to 1916 and was then transferred to Konia. After the Armistice he was arrested by the British as a war criminal and exiled to Malta for a period of time. This change in *vali* may in part account for the changed atmosphere in Marsovan in the latter years of the war.

With the young men out of hiding, Aram and Haïganouch's burden had been lessened. It also appears that Tsolag was no longer giving assistance to his hidden guests. Photography customers were nearly non-existent but he continued to work for the army, leaving home on "official business." Aram's skills as a photographer were not needed in this atmosphere. He writes: "Thanks to God we were relieved of obligations and dangers ... By that time I rented a small corner store and started fez blocking, umbrella repairing, and selling fruits." He did this for four months and found it all very degrading. But all this was soon to change for the better.

This change for the better happened because of one individual, Pertev Bey, whose love of art and music rescued Aram from blocking fezzes and repairing umbrellas. Pertev Bey was Lieutenant General Pertev Demirhan, a distinguished officer in the Ottoman army who not only displayed aesthetic sensibility but high moral values. He would today be called a Righteous Muslim. Aram knew this at the time:

Just about that time Pertev Bey was appointed division commander in Amasia, so I sent him a gift, one of my oil paintings in miniature as an expression of gratitude. He was a just man and had done lots of good to save the lives of many Armenians ... During the Armenian deportation, he was in Sivas in charge of the workers' brigade. Mouammer Pasha, the *vali* of Sivas gave orders to kill all the unarmed Armenian soldiers, contrary to his promises to Miss Graffam, and had killed several thousand. On the other hand, Pertev Bey tried to protect as many as [were] in his power and better their condition and put them in different industries and in charge of bakeries and in the kitchen at the barracks of Kavak Yagi. One day rumors went all around that the Armenians have poisoned the Turkish soldiers as about 150 soldiers were suffering from pain and were taken to the hospital. At once, the civilian governor, Mouammer Pasha ordered the round-up of all the Armenians and put them in jail to be shot en masse. As soon as Pertev Bey hears about this, he rushes to the barracks and as military commander, he discharged all the jandarmas and abolishes the death order of the *vali* of Sivas and goes to the hospital and asked the doctor in charge if anyone was dead yet. He said none. Did you analyze the food they ate? No, so he orders them to analyze all the food, the pots and everything else. He orders an extensive search everywhere for poison. After a several-hour investigation, a private soldier reveals that they had given poison to the dogs a day before but it did not take effect but that day a minute after those dogs ate the extra soup, they fell dead. So, when those Turks saw the dogs dead, they all had imaginary pains and created all that turmoil. After that, he protected those Armenians like his own. He was an Albanian and a real gentleman. When he got my handiwork, he

248

was so pleased and he wrote me a letter of thanks saying, "You are an artist, an artist among artists, and no one knew of you. What a tragic situation." And added that he would like to see me if it is possible for me to do so. So I went to Amasia to his palace. He was very kind and sweet with me. After some more personal conversations he said he will appoint me as division photographer. At once he gave all the necessary orders to provide me everything that I would be in need of, even a private to help and serve me, and told me to look around at the Armenian houses ("left property") and whichever one I wanted, he will let me have it.

Those stray dogs of Sivas seem to have entered the picture again. Maritsa also comments on Aram's new patron and adds that their good friend Lemuel had also benefited from Pertev Bey's generosity. Pertev Bey was impressed with Lemuel's musical talents and gave him a *vesika* to freely travel. Aram took up Pertev Bey's offer and chose the empty house of a returned deportee, thus allowing the woman to return to her own home as his housekeeper. Repairs were made and a studio opened.

On his return journey home to Marsovan to retrieve his photographic equipment, Aram stopped at Ata Bay to see his friends and former teacher, Professor Manissadjian, who had been sheltering at the Zimmer German farm. There he met Hovhannes who had earlier been hidden in his sister's home. Unfortunately one of the other rescued young men had met a mysterious death: "I stopped over Ata Bay Zimmer's farm to see Hovhanness, whose brother-in-law, Hagop, has been choked to death in his bed at night. It was a terrible thing. Whosoever was the murderer, had cut the screen off the toilet room window of his apartment and choked him to death. We were sure one person could not do the work all alone as Hagop was as strong as a bear."

While Aram was there he visited the nearby "killing fields" where a group of the last deportees had been executed:

[I went to] see the place where the killing took place of the last group of Armenians deported that were ordered by Mouammer Pasha, the governor of Sivas state. After all the Armenians of Marsovan were sent and the college professors and the girls of the boarding school ... Mouammer Pasha ... came to Marsovan for personal inspection of his heroic murder plans. By the given reports, he sees too many Armenians have been allowed to remain, so he ordered at once to deport about 80–100 more persons. We know that they were killed nearby Ata Bay, as Mr. Zimmer and Prof. Manissadjian went to the spot and saw the remains and all the signs of terrible struggles for life ... I, too, after more than three years wanted to go through that spot to give my respects ... My driver was a Turk. I was all alone in my feelings. It was a tragic sight for me to pass through more than a mile on both sides of the road, I saw so many bleached human bones. Finally, I arrived home in a very depressed condition.

The human remains that Aram witnessed belonged to the converted Armenians who were deported on September 11 subsequent to *Vali* Muammer's visit to Marsovan and his insistence that the 5 percent rule be adhered to.[36] Among these bones were the members of the Djizmedjian family, my grandfather's Protestant next-door neighbors who had converted to Islam in the spring of 1915. They were afforded neither a Christian nor a Muslim burial.

Upon returning to Marsovan to prepare for his move to Amasia, Aram proposed marriage to his future wife, Christine Der Kasparian. Christine and her mother lived next door to the Dildilians and were a constant presence in their household:

> I did not know for how long, did not know what the future had in store for me, but anyhow, I wanted to have a heart-to-heart talk with my sweetheart, Christine Der Kasparian, my darling future wife … We were together all during those fearful and terrible days of war and deportation, ruination and annihilation of our fine nation. She became near and dear to me …
>
> So before I left for Amasia, we went to the fields under a huge walnut tree. She had a Turkish bourig on her, specially designed headgear to cover her head, face, and body to feel safe as no Armenian woman would dare to go to the fields, especially in those days … I made everything plain to her as if she did not know! I told her that I have no money. I don't know if in the future I will ever have plenty [of] money. I will try to get along as much as possible now in Amasia but as soon as the war is over, I will try to go to Samsun and start over my photographic business if God will be willing. You know that I love you and I know that you love me too. We have to be separated for the time being. We don't know how long … When the time comes, will I be sure about [you]? Will I be depending on you?
>
> I explained to her how several years ago a sweet girl used to love me but later she turned me down on account of my amputated leg because her folks opposed me. She said, "Yes" – So we came back home with a free mind and a light heart.

Love had blossomed during the worst of times. Christine would remain his true love for the next 45 years.

Aram was now back in the photography business, setting up shop in Amasia. Maritsa also comments about Aram's move to Amasia and the fact that they were able to visit him on a few occasions during this period. She does add an interesting aside about his activities for the army: "Although he dealt with photography, his activity was mostly dedicated to design. Officers' wives wanted him to design for them sleeves, collars or dress fronts." Aram photographed the officers and designed dresses for their wives. In either case he was happy:

> A week later, I was back in Amasia. My house was already cleaned, the windows and every other thing was fixed, and an Army signboard in red and white,

"Division Photographer" in Turkish, was put up on the door. I fixed my dark room and printing room and decorated my reception room as much as I could and was ready for business. I was quite busy, but not enough. Every morning I used to go to the soldiers' disbursement center, which was our Protestant Church near to me, and used to get a private to help me to clean the house, sweep the yard, bring water and do my buying. Each day I tried to get a Christian Armenian or Greek if it was possible …

I had [a] very good time in Amasia. I had some old friends and made some new friends like Mrs. Kasabbashian, Ida Ipekjian, Der Menjians, Frida and Garbis family, and many Armeno-Germans. They were very friendly to me. In and around Amasia, the Germans have tried to colonize several times but each time they have failed by intermarrying with Armenians. In time they had lost their identity. It was fortunate for them because being [of] German descent, they were saved from deportation and sure death.

Aram would spend the closing months of the war in Amasia doing what he loved best, taking photographs.

Back in Marsovan, the Dildilians and Der Haroutiounians did their best to survive the hardships of the final year of the war. Tsolag continued the photography work for the military while Haïganouch and her children benefited from the military garment enterprise that Kiremidjian had established. Haïgouni, who had been placed in the factory to serve out his military duty, took advantage of his newly found freedom to begin a flour milling business for the family. The milling enterprise soon became the family's primary means of support. Maritsa describes how Haïgouni adapted one of the government-confiscated mills that was used to dye and waterproof military uniforms to suit his own purposes: "The motive power for the machinery of that big textile factory was provided by a waterwheel moved by the strong flow of a bypass canal. As part of that flow was lost, Haïgouni imagined using it to actuate a small flour-milling device, built with our own money, which would bring us a small revenue. Haïgouni had been appointed to the factory as a soldier and his soldier's pay was quite meager." His idea was approved by the company running the mill and he enlisted the mechanical skills of Garo to assist him. Maritsa remarks, "Thus, our concern for our daily bread was alleviated." Soon Haïgouni and Garo expanded the business by renting another mill upstream from the first that had been owned by Leblebidjians. It afforded another way out of their difficulties:

Those who wanted to have their wheat milled came and left their wheat at our place in the morning and took their flour back in the evening. In this way, they were no longer obliged to carry their wheat all the way to a mill then go and get it back as flour. Our customers were generally Armenians and mostly widows. My brother purchased a cart and a mule for the transport to and from the mill …

251

Garo and Haïgouni did not come back home every night. When this happened, the transport was performed by my brothers Aram and Haïgazoun. These two courageous boys carried out their task gladly whatever the weather: snow, rain, wind or sizzling heat.

This family enterprise flourished for a period of time, providing a vital service to a town whose everyday routines were crippled by the diminished numbers of able-bodied men. Maritsa comments on the side benefits of running the mill: "In our flour mill, there were always grain and seed leftovers. So we started breeding poultry. As the venture was going on finely we also raised geese. Water and grain were almost free. A great help for us after all these years of restrictions, a welcome revenge on fate."

Banditry was always endemic in the countryside and became more so during the war years. Even in the city itself crime was on the rise. The influx of large numbers of refugees from the eastern provinces and the Caucasus altered the character of neighborhoods. The gutted houses of Armenians often served as makeshift shelters for these people. Maritsa describes the horrible conditions of these "Tartar" refugees and the government neglect of their plight. She notes the robbery of their Greek neighbor's house followed by the theft of "woven products, a pan we used for our cow's milk, and beehives" from their courtyard. Many young Turkish men, in addition to Greeks and the few surviving Armenians, had deserted the military and were living and thieving off the land. Even an enterprise supplying cloth for the army was not immune from robbery. Given these dangers, the young Armenian mill workers were given guns. The bizarre irony of all this is that two years earlier Armenian soldiers had all been disarmed and these young men would have been executed for possessing a gun. This change in policy now allowing for the arming of these Armenians was life-saving for Garo and Haïgazoun, Haïganouch's youngest:

Haïgazoun once asked to spend a night at the mill factory with Garo. Around midnight, the dog starts to bark and keeps barking louder. There are organized gangs of Greeks and Turks who live by plunder ... Garo wakes up and listens ... It is a group of horsemen. They shut off the sluice gate of the bypass in order to entice the warden to come out to see what is wrong; they would then kill or capture him to enter the factory.

The factory had been the property of Armenians, and there was a hiding place that Garo and Haïgouni had found from the first day. So Garo pushes Haïgazoun into the hideout, advising him not to come out before daylight. Then, with his gun in hand, he watches each door. The bandits attack the upper door, which is small and seems easier to break open. Garo shoots. The bandits shoot several times around the door lock. From inside, Garo retaliates. The others now try to break through the wall on the lower level. Garo shoots in that new direction.

Finally, he climbs up to the attic where he can protect himself behind the framework beams. He shoots at each bandit who tries to come near. The thieves now want to break the door locks by aiming their shots at the locks from a distance with rifles. Garo fires back. Finally, at dawn, the thieves retreat.

Unfortunately this was not the only incident of banditry against the family. The upper mill that Haïgouni had rented for the purpose of expanding the flour-milling enterprise was even more vulnerable. One night while Haroutioun was sleeping alone in the upper mill, thieves struck: "They take away everything: Haroutioun's bedclothes, his clothes, the wheat, tools, and even the one 250-pound grain measurement container. On the next morning, my mother happened to be out and she saw, coming from the river valley, a man all clad in white. She stares and recognizes Haroutioun wearing only his shirt and underpants." Surprisingly, justice was rendered in this case but ultimately it proved to have negative consequences for the family. The thieves had chosen to rob the mill at the wrong moment:

> Wheat belonging to police commissioner Saléh was part of the stolen goods. When informed, he immediately guessed who the thieves were. Accompanied by Garo, he went to the village he suspected and found not only his wheat but also many stolen things, [all of which] were seized by the police.
>
> However, this had an unfortunate consequence on us as the Turkish deserters who had committed the theft decided to take vengeance on us. One night, they came in large numbers and Haïgouni, who happened to be sleeping in the mill, escaped danger only by jumping through the window and seeking refuge in the Erzeroumtsis' mill. They followed him for a while, shooting at him, but as dawn was breaking, they retreated. My brother was very angry and wanted to avenge himself but my mother talked him out of this project. And she said he should not go back to the mill but find another occupation.

With the flour-mill enterprise at an end, the family was forced to rely more and more on the home weaving work for their livelihood. Besides small carpets and mats, they expanded their line of products to accommodate the demographic changes in the city: "We started to weave *yazmas* (the head veil of Muslim women)." As the year 1918 came to an end, the Dildilians and Der Haroutiounians had found new ways to survive.

9

The Years after the Great War: Rebuilding their Shattered Lives

The Armistice Arrives and the Family Begins to Pick Up the Pieces

As the summer of 1918 came to a close, the prospects for an end to the war at first looked bleak. The Western Front between Germany and France appeared to be at a stalemate. Russia had exited the war and the Ottoman Third Army was finally achieving some success on the Caucasian front against the outnumbered and ill-equipped Armenian and Georgian forces. The War Minister Enver Pasha was still pursuing his dream of a Turkic Empire stretching into the lands of the Caucasus. Ottoman forces on the Arab front were in retreat as the British moved north with the goal of capturing the oil fields of Mosul. Armenian volunteer units were now fighting with the British and French.

Yet all this suddenly changed with the unexpected defeat of Turkey's ally, Bulgaria, on September 28. Suddenly the Ottomans faced the prospect of being cut off from vital supplies from their German allies. Within a month both Germany and the Porte were seeking peace with Britain and France. Talaat, now the Grand Vizier, and his ministers resigned on October 13. A new cabinet was formed and on October 30 quickly signed what came to be known as the Mudros Armistice agreement with the British. On November 2, the C.U.P. leaders, Talaat, Enver and Djemal, secretly fled Constantinople for Germany. Aram was still working as an army photographer in Amasia when he heard the news of the end of the war: "One fateful day in (November 11) 1918, I was visiting one of those German-Armenian friend's garden. We were cooking jam out of grape juice. Their son came from downtown and gave the good news that there is word of Armistice. Our joy was great. Soon I started preparations to leave for Samsun as soon as possible." Aram is here referencing the Armistice signed between Germany and the Allies, and not the Mudros Armistice that ended the hostilities for the Ottoman Empire. It was years later when he wrote these words and he may have conflated the two dates, quite understandably, since November 11 would long be celebrated as the date that marked the end of the First World War.

The end of the war brought a great sense of relief and a newborn sense of freedom, yet it was also marked by great sorrow, a sorrow for the human and cultural loss of the war years:

> The last three and four years, we were deprived of any kind of religious gathering or church services of any kind. We were confined in our family circles.
>
> The following Sunday for the first time, a group of mixed Protestants, Armenians, Germans, and Greeks decided to take our lunches and climb up to Amasia's famed ancient forts. Before that day, often we wished to climb up to those caves but we did not dare to make this attempt as we had to pass through the Turkish quarter. It was a long and hard hike for all of us but finally we make it. When we arrived at the right spot, we took a deep breath. The scene was profound and breathtaking. The whole of Amasia with its grandeur was spread in front of us. On my right, way out in green vineyards and gardens, the Iris River makes a graceful turn towards the city. Way up on the hillside I could see half-ruined Sourp Garabed ...
>
> Right in front of us we could see the Armenian quarter burned to the ground (Turks burned the Armenian houses as vengeance ...) and on the river banks we could see those dirty, dingy houses of Turkish quarter. Foolish people, they burned the Armenian quarter as some heroic achievement. They burned those nice homes to ashes and yet, four years later, they still live in those shacks and in poverty after robbing the Armenians. Further up on the rocky slopes, the poorest Armenian houses cling to the rock in the deep valley. We could see those small houses still waiting as orphans for their owners to come back, with their individual small rickety bridges ... a heartbreaking scene. On the left we could see the government houses, the bridges, the marketplace and shops, and the Souk Punar valley with resort houses and vineyards up to the peaks. And down on the foothills, the Protestant quarter, which was left intact as most of the houses being nice homes, was occupied by German and Turkish officials. Farther out, many vineyards and vineyard houses and flour mills on both sides of the river, and the ancient Roman bridge with three big arches over which all our loved ones and beloved nation passed to their death ... Way up on high, on the rock, we felt wonderful, joyful, and victorious, and unconsciously started singing songs of victory and praise ... Just about then, the Greek church bells started ringing for the first time, which brought tears out of our eyes, yes, tears of joy. Each one of us was in tears for different reasons ... I was crying for the first time over my lost dear ones who passed over that river bridge and walked through the same highway, which winds a way into the green vineyards. I was crying over my lost people and lost glories that are gone, never to come back again.

Aram decided to return to Samsun in order to reopen the Dildilian Brothers studio that he had taken over from Sumpad some six years earlier. His return would be marked by trepidation for he knew that Armenian life in the city had been forever changed by the events of 1915.

> The next week, I left for Samsun … I was sure I would not find my dear folks, friends, or church people who were near and dear to me. I was sure I would not find my studio or even an article of it six years later. But how fortunate I was to find a fine Christian Greek friend who gave me a cheery welcome and hospitality in his home till I was able to find a suitable house in the Greek quarter for a studio. Soon, I started doing business just by putting up a signboard in Turkish, English, Greek, and Armenian. I was the first Armenian to come back to Samsun and the first Armenian to use the Armenian name (ian). [Armenian surnames end in either "ian" or "yan."]

Aram was no longer Zeki, the Islamized and Turkified army photographer but Aram Dildilian, the proud Armenian Christian photographer. With the famed Dildilian Brothers studio gone, Aram had to start all over again, this time in the Greek quarter of the city. Much of the Armenian quarter was in ruins. As for his family and Armenian friends that he had left behind back in 1913, not one was now to be found.

The Sorrowful Toll of the Genocide

The chapters in Aram's memoir are written in a fairly straightforward chronological order. In contrast, Maritsa's memoir, written in a series of 13 notebooks, jumps around in time often repeating and expanding upon previously described episodes. This made my job of weaving the two narratives together much more challenging. Having read both manuscripts more than once over a long period of time, I was fairly familiar with what they contained, though with each reading I discovered something new, some new tidbit that I had glossed over on an earlier reading. I did not at first always grasp the significance of some detail that on a second reading stood out and required further scrutiny. Aram's memoir had been written in English sometime in the late 1940s and early 1950s, though he had been working on it for many years. At the point in the story when he is about to describe his life in Samsun after the armistice, he interrupts the flow of the chronology in order to speak more generally about the destruction of the Armenians that began in 1915. He titles this chapter, "Our Destruction." As I reread this chapter in order to write my chapter, I made a startling discovery. I will explain.

Aram's memoir had been written in longhand on lined notebook paper. Sometime in the early or mid-1980s my uncle Ara had it typed, probably by his secretary. As I mentioned at the beginning of this book, the project of writing the family history that Ara and his older brother Humayag had commenced in the 1980s came to an abrupt end with the sudden death of Ara in 1986. When I received the manuscript in the late 1980s it consisted of this typed manuscript and a photocopy of the original handwritten pages. I had looked at sections of the 376-page handwritten version and saw that it correlated fairly well with the much easier to read typed version. Editorial changes had been made of a minor nature. On a few occasions I referred to the handwritten copy when something was not clear in the typed version. For the most part, the handwritten copy did not help clear things up, for the versions appeared identical. However, as I consulted the handwritten copy on the most recent occasion, I made the startling discovery of an additional 15 pages from the chapter on "Our Destruction" that had not been typed. Moreover, there were roughly 30 pages of text and notes titled, "The Destruction of Armenians in Asia Minor." The latter is both a history and a reflection upon the plight of Armenians over the course of the Ottoman Turkish rule of their homeland. There are pages of population statistics for the Armenian cities and villages across the length and breadth of the empire – a meticulous attempt to demonstrate the Armenian presence that had been erased.

For our purposes what interests me are the additional 15 unnumbered pages from the chapter on "Our Destruction." The chapter begins with a general overview of the events of the genocide, including the now familiar symbolic start of the destruction on April 24, 1915. Aram describes the horrors experienced on the death marches and the final destination of the few survivors in the deserts of Der El-Zor. This macro-description switches to a micro-description of Marsovan in the missing pages. He describes the cultural and material possessions of the Armenians before the destruction of 1915, that is, the churches, schools and businesses, and so on. Aram explains: "We were taking Marsovan as a miniature example. Yet in the same way each individual had several loved ones lost as I have had. So let me tell about them to have a complete picture." He now shifts to a direct discussion of what happened to his family members. This is where I learned of the fate of those members of my family who were not fortunate enough to be living in Marsovan and were never heard from again after 1915.

Aram begins by first describing what happened to the male members of the family in Marsovan. Adult males were subject to conscription: "Therefore twice they collected indemnity from my brother, over $500.00, the same they demanded from my brother-in-law Vosgian and because he did not have any money they took him away and not a word from him ... I was exempted on account of my artificial leg." The $500 referred to here must have been the *bedel-i nakdî* that at this time would have temporarily exempted one from military service. He then continues by claiming: "All my other relatives, in Vezirköprü, Samsun, Amasia, Sivas and Yozgat, were all killed, we don't know where and how they were killed." This was a refrain I had often heard from my mother. In a videotaped interview for

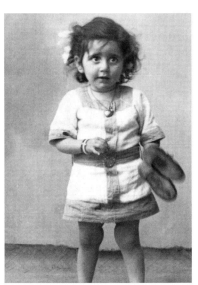 

Clockwise, from top left: 75. Prapion Dildilian (née Nakkashian), 1890–1915, my grandmother Mariam's sister, *c.*1908; 76. Tsorig Dildilian, 1911–15, daughter of Sumpad and Prapion Dildilian, *c.*1914; 77. Vahan Dildilian, 1914–15, son of Sumpad and Prapion, *c.*1914; 78. Chahine (or Tsorig) Dildilian, 1913–15, daughter of Sumpad and Prapion, *c.*1914.

the Zoryan Institute's oral history project, my mother answered the interviewer's question about the deaths of her aunts and uncles. She is asked, "How do you know they were killed?" To which she responds, "Well, they never came back, honey. How do I know when they were killed? We heard some stories." Aram tells one of these stories:

> Brother Sumpad was a railway engineer and was stationed in Kavak. The family
> was in Samsun. They had a neighbor, a telegraph officer Neshan Tahmizian, the
> first Armenian who heard the news of Armenian deportations. Aunt Elbiz really
> believing the Turks that they will surely meet their men folk, tells Prapion [Sumpad's
> wife], "What shall I say to my son when we meet him?" Well they all perished on
> the way, poor Prapion, could not endure constant molestations as she was beautiful,
> she throws herself and her children into a well … We do not know what happened
> to Aunty Elbiz, she was old, weak and tender, could not last much longer.

Aram does not tell us how he heard about their deaths. Prapion was my grandmother's younger sister. Their children and their ages were Tsorig, four, Chahine, two, and Vahan, one.

In her video interview my mother also tells the story of how Sumpad had been taken. This is a story she heard from her parents and was often repeated in the family. She states that her father had many friends among the Turks and this is how he heard about his cousin's fate. Sumpad was light complexioned with blue eyes and spoke fluent German. He was working with German engineers for the railway being built to Sivas. He was initially released from an earlier roundup because they thought he was German. He was arrested a second time and this time he insisted that he was an Armenian. He was taken away and never heard from again.

Aram's sister Parentzem and her family lived in Vezirköprü. Following the same pattern as in most of the deportations and massacres, the men were initially arrested and sent on ahead to a remote site for execution. The remaining women and children would be informed that they needed to gather up some minimal belongings and leave the city in order to join their menfolk. Aram continues to describe the family's losses:

> Now let us go back to sister Parantzem and her family, we were told that all the men
> folk of Köprü were killed in a nearby place: "Köprü bashi" but we were not sure
> about the women folk. Years later a woman survivor told me that she was with my
> sister Parantzem at the Euphrates River bank. My sister was very sick, she asked for
> a cup of tea. She tried to sip a bit and passed away singing or rather muttering, "My
> faith looks up to thee." I don't know if that woman was right or wrong but I know
> that my dear sister Parantzem, she would do just that, Glory to Him.

My curiosity led me to look up the English words to the hymn Parantzem was singing when she died. The words seem very appropriate for the ordeal she was going through:

"My Faith Looks Up to Thee"

My faith looks up to Thee,
Thou, Lamb of Calvary.
Savior divine!
Now hear me while I pray,
Take all my guilt away.
O let me from this day
Be wholly Thine!

May Thy rich grace impart
Strength to my fainting heart,
My zeal inspire;
As Thou hast died for me,
O may my love to Thee
Pure, warm, and changeless be
A living fire!

While life's dark maze I tread,
And griefs around me spread,
Be Thou my guide;
Bid darkness turn to day,
Wipe sorrow's tears away
Nor let me ever stray
From Thee aside.

When ends life's transient dream,
When death's cold, sullen stream
Shall o'er me roll,
Blest Savior, then, in love,
Fear and distrust remove;
O bear me safe above,
A ransomed soul![1]

79. Parantzem Dildilian, c.1910.

Aram does not mention what happened to her two children, Hrant, aged three and Hratchia, aged five. The extended Shirinian family also disappeared, all except Lemuel who had been hidden by Haïganouch back in Marsovan.

This brings me to Shamavon, my grandfather's youngest sibling. I had written much about him earlier in the book. This was the great-uncle that my mother and her brothers rarely talked about but also happened to be a favorite of Maritsa. When I wrote the earlier section on Shamavon I had not as yet discovered the missing pages in the memoir. I knew that he was last with his older sister Parantzem in Vezirköprü in the summer of 1915. I had wondered if he escaped the deportations and hid in those remote caves I had seen in the summer of 2012. I have now learned that he did leave his sister's family and tried to hide but not in those caves. What I now know is more upsetting, not for the way he died but for the way Tsolag and Aram learned of his death:

80. Shamavon Dildilian, c.1914.

Now about my younger brother Shamavon, as soon as he was graduated from the French school, he was drafted and was taken to Gamereck, an Armenian town. He was so sweet a boy, so delicate, tender and sentimental … He was not able to stand the immoral ways of those rough and tough Turkish soldiers in the barracks so he makes up his mind to run away and managed to come up to the river Alice, there he had to cross the famed double bridge, "Kesig Köprü." There were guards on each end of the bridge; it was impossible to cross, even in the dark night. Fortunately soon there came a caravan of oxen-carts loaded with wheat for the army, so he finds a driving stick and follows one of the carts [acting] as one of the drivers and comes to Sivas safely and goes to Uncle Mikael's home but he does not consider [it] very safe to stay there, so he kept on going. On the way he figures to himself if I go to Marsovan to my brother's or to Samsun to uncle's house sooner or later I would be caught, so he decides to go to my sister Parantzem's house in Vezirköprü and surely he was safe there as no one would suspect. But soon it was Köprü's turn to be deported, which took only two hours to wipe out all the Armenians from Vezirköprü. Shamavon tells sister that, "you have to go, so you go. I will not go with you, as no one knows of me here. I will hide myself and try to go to Marsovan if I can." He jumps out of the window to the church yard and hides himself in the basement ... Six months later in Marsovan, during a conversation, one of the police officers tells [Tsolag] about my brother Shamavon. How they went to the Protestant Church to figure or plan how to make some changes to turn it for İttihat ve Terakki club house and then how he found three young men hiding in the basement and sent them away to be killed. But one of them, a blond, blue-eyed nice looking young man pleaded not to send him away as he can be very useful as he knows German, English, French, Greek, Armenian and Turkish.

The governor (kaimakam) [Bekir Bey] becomes excited and at once wires to Köprü Bashi (killing station) to send him back, thinking that he must be an important person. When next day they brought him back, he [the officer] sees that he is just a boy. Shamavon pleads again not to send him away but let him go to his folks in Marsovan but they sent him away. That same officer later came to Marsovan for picture taking. He told all about [it] and apologized, saying if I had known that he [Shamavon] was your brother surely I would have spared his life and sent him to you.

Imagine having to take the photograph of someone who was responsible for sending your brother to his death. Tsolag then had to listen to an apology from one of the killers. When I first read this section I was so upset that I had to put down the pages. I could not read on. What could my grandfather and his brother have been feeling at the time? A controlled rage? A feigned smile and goodbye as the killer left their studio? What would I have done? This is all so very hard to imagine.

Doing More Than Taking Photographs: Aram and Tsolag's New Responsibilities

Aram restarted his photography business soon after his return to Samsun in the winter of 1918–19. As he was building up the business, he was more and more troubled by what he saw on the city's streets. Aram was never the kind of person to put his own interests over those of his family, friends or community. He soon moved into action to help those in greater need:

Here and there I saw some little children in rags and barefooted roaming in the streets, and Armenian women in rags, survivors of those vicious and terrible three years of deportation and wholesale killings. I thought something should be done for those wretched people, so I wrote some special letters of invitation for a meeting to all those Armenians who have survived ... In response, there came more than 20 men and women to that meeting. I expressed my real surprise that so many have survived and are now present there and told them the good news that an Armenian Republican government has been established firmly in Erevan ... But we are far away and most of us have no means to go there ... But right now, we have got some work to do here. No doubt, you and I have seen many Armenian children in rags like this, and showed them some pictures that I had taken before.

263

81. Orphan boy before and after rescue, Samsun, December 1918.

I told them we must do something for them ... So we did elect a committee of five and I was elected secretary. Our first step was to ask the Turkish government to give back the Armenian Apostolic Church building, the parsonage and the Armenian Club and other income properties. At once, we were given back all including some rugs, tables and chairs. Next, we found some kind-hearted woman who volunteered to supervise the women. We put four orphans in the club house and a woman to cook for the children. Soon the number rose to 24 children and then started to grow bigger and bigger. In the meantime, more and more survivors came from the interior and the Armenian population was growing in number. We cleaned the church building and found an Armenian priest from Charshamba to take care of the church services.

Aram had used his camera to record the plight of the remnants of the Armenian nation. From those initial photographs of orphaned street children to recording the establishment of orphanages in Samsun and Marsovan, both Aram and Tsolag documented the relief efforts. Our family photograph collection has dozens of group photographs of these, for the most part, nameless orphans. Posing upwards

82. Boy orphans in front of the Samsun Armenian Apostolic
Church. Aram in jacket and tie, *c.*1919.

of 125 young boys and having them hold still long enough to take their photograph
must have been one of the most difficult shots they had ever taken. Yet these
photographs provide an invaluable visual record of the scale of the Armenian
catastrophe. When Near East Relief finally arrived to aid in the recovery efforts,
many Dildilian orphan photographs would be used in the campaign to help raise
relief funds.

Armenia had declared its independence in May of 1918 but because of
wartime censorship, news had not reached Aram until after the war had
ended. He read about it in the Armenian newspapers that had reemerged in
Constantinople after the armistice and were now available in Samsun. Though
Aram often writes hopefully about the prospects for an independent and
prosperous Armenia, he and his brother were still committed to the rebirth of
Armenian life on Anatolian soil. His hopes for a peaceful rebirth hinged on a
belief that the victorious Allies, especially the United States, would keep the
promises they had made during the war. President Wilson's Fourteen Points
were to serve as a ground map for a brighter future. The United States had
never declared war on the Ottoman Empire and there was the belief that she
could act as a fair and honest broker in sorting out the conflicting interests of
the ethnic forces at play in Turkey. The Porte had initially sent out feelers to

the United States in the hope for fairer treatment under an armistice brokered by the Americans. As it turned out, the vagaries of the armistice negotiated with the British and the machinations of the victorious Allies sowed the seeds of a Turkish backlash in the years ahead. In the early months of 1919, Aram still had confidence that the United States would keep its promises. His initial encounter with an American delegation strengthened what turned out be a misplaced confidence in America's word:

> Admiral Bristol's flagship "NOE" came into the harbor with two U.S. destroyers with Near East [Relief] workers and supplies. At once, we, the National Committee people, hired a motor boat and went to meet him in his flagship but we were told that he went to Mr. King's house, who was the president of American Tobacco Company. So we went to the Greek quarters and went to King's house. When Admiral Bristol was informed about us, he said he would gladly come with us to the Armenian quarter. We had American and Armenian flags with us, so the flag bearers who led the procession started marching from the Greek quarters to [the] Armenian quarters, passing through the Turkish quarters. On the way, the crowd grew bigger as we marched on, singing songs …
>
> We started from the fresh looking brightly painted Greek quarter houses, past dingy looking Turkish houses and then we came to [the] once beautiful Armenian quarter, now all ruined with half-ruined houses and those houses that were standing were neglected with broken glass panes, boarded windows, and along such streets that were left untrodden for many years, the grass was growing by the gutters and around the cobblestones pavement. It was not a pleasant place to bring a high commissioner of the U.S.A., but we had to do so that he would come over and see the people and those ruined houses. We knew quite well the Christian attitude of the Americans (from our childhood days, we had enjoyed the love and sincere fellowship of our American missionaries …). The club house was the only place that we could take him. We tried to furnish it with borrowed rugs and chairs. The only entertainment or refreshment that we could serve him was a whiskey and Turkish delight (candy). I did not go into the room with him as we had three Armenian physicians with the group as hosts and translators. Most of the National Committeemen were Anatolia College students. Finally he showed up at the balcony to cheer the people outside in the yard and said, "You Armenians, we have come to wipe your tears out of your eyes and fear from your hearts … You will never be subjected to destruction as you have experienced. We came for you folks and we will stay here for your safety." Those words are as vivid in my ears as [if] I have heard them yesterday.

There is a bitter irony in these words of comfort and protection. Aram may well be remembering them as much for their hollowness as for their promise of hope.

Admiral Mark L. Bristol would play a pivotal role in shaping the direction of United States policy toward Turkey in the years after the war. Bristol had arrived in Constantinople on January 28, 1919 and probably visited Samsun sometime during the next two months. For Aram, the visit of Admiral Bristol would leave him with the bitter taste of betrayal, for the admiral had not come to display "the Christian attitude of the Americans." Commercial interests were high on Bristol's agenda as could have been guessed by his first stop in the city, the home of the president of the British American Tobacco Company, Mr. King.

83. Admiral Mark L. Bristol, c.1922.

Aram was determined to make the United States understand the extent of the suffering undergone by the Armenians. American diplomats and missionaries had been instrumental in getting the word out to the public about what had happened. A fundraising campaign had already raised millions of dollars for the relief effort but there seems to be a willful ignorance on the part of some to the plight of the Armenians:

A tall, fine looking U.S. Navy officer came to me and asked me a few questions. He was a physician. His name was Dr. Chase, as I remember. Anyhow, he asked me to go a few yards away where we had a better view of the sea and the Armenian quarter. First, he asked me why everybody was so sad and were crying and are they all Armenians. Then he asked why the two Turkish women were there and why they were wiping their eyes too, and I noticed they spoke with you? I said, "They are Armenian girls but they do not feel safe yet to let go their bourigs (Turkish headgear)." Then he asked me about the marked difference between the Armenian quarters and the Greek quarters, about the half-wrecked houses and house foundations yet standing. I told him that after we were deported, Turks occupied those houses and in time they tore down those houses and used them as firewood. They did the same thing all over the country, in every town. I noticed that he was not informed well of what really went on during the war days so I tried to tell in brief what had happened in 1915, how, within a few weeks they, the Turks, killed more than a million and a half Armenians ... I gave him some pictures taken by German soldiers to prove how Armenians were killed and many other things

… and asked him to tell everyone in America. He thanked me and said he would and with a hearty hand grasp, we were separated.

What happened to most of these photographs I do not know. Either they were lost or wound up in some government or personal archive.

While sorting through boxes of unidentified negatives in the family collection I did discover one that is most likely one of these photographs taken by German soldiers. My mother has testified to the fact that German soldiers would often stop in the studio during the war years to have their film developed and printed. Why my grandfather chose to save this one negative, I will never know.

84. Print from negative in the family archive. German soldiers holding the bones of Armenian victims near Hekimkhan, Turkey. November 10, 1918.

I have subsequently been able to identify the location where this photograph was taken. This was confirmed by comparison to an almost identical photo card sent to the family that identified the location and date. The card was sent to Haïgouni Der Haroutiounian by a friend, Hagop, from Amasia on January 1, 1919. The card identifies the killing field as Hekimkhan, a place on the deportation route from Sivas to Malatya where many of the caravans were set upon and thousands killed. The photo card even gives the date when the photograph was taken: November 10, 1918. Were these soldiers in a celebratory mood as they

85. Photo postcard of victims of the Armenian Genocide sent to
Haigouni Der Haroutiounian in Amasia by a friend on January 1, 1919.

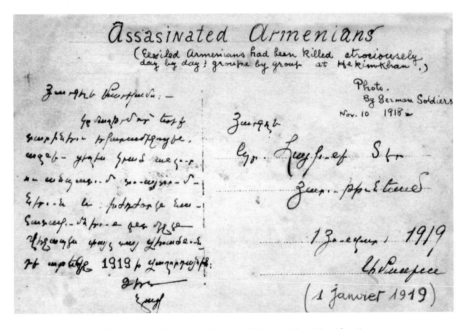

86. Reverse of photo card sent to Haïgouni that identifies the
time and location of the event depicted.

prepared to withdraw from Anatolia now that the war had come to an end? Was the photograph one last macabre souvenir of their experience of the Great War? Why did my grandfather choose to keep this negative? Was it because this may have been the final resting place of the members of his family from Sivas? Can one even call it "a resting place"? I will never know the answers to these questions.

Aram's immediate concern was for the welfare of the orphans who were now under his care. An American flotilla arrived with relief supplies desperately needed for his orphanage. He was in for a pleasant surprise at the harbor:

> I went down to the pier to look around and what do I see? I saw Dr. White in khaki N.E.R. [Near East Relief] uniform. We were so happy and excited to see each other. He was in a hurry to go to Marsovan to start anew the Anatolia College … So he introduced me to Mr. Stephen Peabody and rushed on. I asked Mr. Peabody if they intend to start an orphanage here in Samsun as they are to do in Marsovan. He said, "No, we do not have any place to start one here, only we will have a warehouse here." I told him that we have gathered together quite a few boys and girls out of the streets and are trying to do the best we can. He promised to give us blankets, white muslin and anything else we are in need of. Then he took me to the warehouse and his office and he told me he will be there every afternoon. So at once I called the National Orphanage Committee and gave them the good news. Yes, we need many blankets and lots of muslin for underwear but we decided first to find sewing machines and volunteer women to sew. After we did provide a sewing room and volunteers to sew, then I went to Mr. Peabody for the white muslin and blankets.

All did not go well for Aram upon his return to the warehouse. He learned that all the remaining supplies had been donated to the Greek orphanage. Aram was indignant because he felt that the Greeks had not suffered as much as the Armenians at this point. The Greek orphanage had long been in existence and was supported by the better-off Greek community. Eventually more supplies arrived, which was fortunate because the orphans swelled in numbers: "In the meantime, the orphanage started to grow day by day, so we had to have an efficient person to manage the orphanage. We were fortunate to obtain Dr. Hampartzum Guleserian as director to govern the orphanage, who was a former Army doctor."

Aram's disillusionment with Admiral Bristol's mission grew when he was called upon to take some photographs of Bristol and his party. Bristol's fact-finding was not restricted to reporting on the ravages of the war:

> While Admiral Bristol was in Samsun, there was a horse race. I was called to take some pictures from the top of a specially built platform right across from the grandstand. The seats were filled with a neat looking crowd, young men with white trousers and sport coats in tan and black, low blocked fezzes

a là Enver, and sleek canes in their hands. The Turkish women with their multi-colored bourigs or chershafs and many of them were open face. There came Namly Zade's beautiful red convertible and with him came as his guest, Admiral Bristol and fellow officers and were led [to] where the governor was [seated] on rug covered seats ... Neat and bright looking uniformed policemen were everywhere to take care of order, special refreshments were served right along and, during the recesses, the Army band was playing marches ... It is hard to know what Admiral Bristol and his group think about the great contrast when he was at the Armenian quarter ... They were never given a dinner party or any other kind of entertainment in [their] honor – yet during his stay in Samsun, every day he and his group were invited to dinner and dancing parties by some wealthy Turk.

Aram believed that all this wining and dining swayed Bristol's sympathies to the Turkish side. Given the commercial interests motivating Bristol's mission, I suppose it is understandable that he was swayed by the hospitality he was shown. Unfortunately the Armenians were ill-prepared for the competition.

Back in Marsovan changes were also taking place that would affect the family. The first group of Americans to return to the city arrived on March 14, 1919. Dr. Ernest Pye, formerly of the staff of Anatolia College, headed the first party of relief workers. As was mentioned before, a small group of Americans had been allowed to remain on the campus after the college was closed in 1916. Mr. Dana Getchell and his wife had secretly assisted Aram and members of the family during those long years of hardship. Dr. White describes the Americans' return to the city: "Mr. Getchell, who had held out on the ground, with a group of three, said, 'The Relief workers seemed like angels of the Lord, bringing help and food just at the time that the faithful American garrison had reached the breaking point.'"[2] Along with the relief workers came a small military occupation force. The presence of these troops temporarily lifted the fear of repression and violence that had marked the Armenian remnant in Marsovan. Unfortunately, their presence also engendered resentment that would feed the nationalist backlash against the Allies and their wards, the Armenians. Dr. White quotes from a letter of Dr. Pye regarding the shift in power:

Dr. Pye wrote, "Shortly following military occupation by the British Black Sea Army (the middle of March, 1919), Mr. Getchell was made the official representative of the Allied Powers in the Merzifon area. At the same time a detachment of British troops was stationed at Merzifon; but owing to the shortage of British officers, the direction of these troops was placed in the control of Mr. Pye. Under the police service of these troops, order was restored in the city and surrounding towns, and with the restoration of order, the rights of the oppressed were recognized."

271

Some hundreds of unhappy Armenians who had registered as Moslems on invitation of the Turkish officials to save their lives, or often more truly to save the life and the honor of a wife or daughter, were issued fresh citizenship papers restoring their Christian names and nationality.[3]

Aram also describes what happened in those early days of what many thought would be a new era:

When Admiral Bristol and the British control officer went to Marsovan, it was a glorious day for the Marsovan Armenians as Captain Saulter, Mr. Getchell, and the college crowd put down the Turkish flag and put up the English flag on the City Hall plaza ... and appointed Mr. Getchell as his representative for Marsovan and surrounding towns and Mr. Getchell, in turn, appoints my brother Tsolag so that he would have an office in the City Hall to take care of the interests of Armenians and to see that each Armenian who had changed his name would be given back his original Armenian name certificate.

Tsolag's work for the occupation authorities would come back to haunt him as the political environment worsened.

During the course of the year Aram's activities in Samsun extended far beyond setting up the orphanage. His studio was next door to the United States Consulate, so he was often called upon to assist those Armenians who were seeking emigration from Turkey. His multilingual studio sign attracted those who needed help in negotiating the language barriers facing these would-be emigrants: "Though I was busy at home with my work, I don't remember that I ever refused to help anyone who came to me for some kind of help or other, to send them away with proper papers or help to notarize their papers or arrange with the U.S. Consulate to get a visa to go to America, and the number of such people was not few ... My house was open for people from Marsovan or Amasia who came and sometimes stayed with me for weeks till they were able to arrange their journey." Aram relates many stories of assistance and rescue during those first months in Samsun. In a few instances these were individuals he knew from back home in Marsovan, but sadly these were rather rare because few survived the deportation caravans of the summer of 1915.

Similarly, those early months of 1919 were marked by the recovery efforts of the Dildilians back in Marsovan. For Tsolag, the arrival of the Americans next door on the campus was a welcome relief. The college and the mission plant were restored to the Americans on April 2. George White remarked that the campus "had been changed from a vast hospital with patients up to the number of 4,000 to a vast orphanage with real human children up to the number of 2,500."[4] Dr. Marden, with new equipment and American physicians supplied by Near East

Relief, reopened his hospital that had been appropriated by the army in 1916. Armenian and Turkish doctors had struggled during the war to save the lives of thousands of sick and wounded. Wartime conditions made typhus and other communicable diseases rampant among soldiers and civilians alike. By the winter of 1918–19, the Spanish influenza had reached Marsovan. Tsolag himself came down with it, but fortunately soon recovered.

Tsolag's relief work took on a very personal aspect in the early months of 1919. The painful process of searching for any information about his lost relatives was frustrating and mostly fruitless. He learned that his wife's family in Kharpert had not survived. My grandmother's sister, Prapion, in Samsun and her brother, Vahan Nakkashian, in Trebizond had not survived. But Tsolag's extensive network of friendly connections allowed him to locate Vahan's daughter Adriné in Constantinople. Aram describes how she was found:

> It was about May first that my darling Adriné came from Constantinople. She was the daughter of my brother's brother-in-law, Vahan Nakkashian, who was established in Trebizond and was quite successful in business. During the deportation, he was killed with the intelligentsia. His wife, Agavny, and little boy were killed by the seashore. The oldest daughter, Tzoline, was taken by a wealthy Turk. Later, [the Turk's] son had some indecent relations with her, then in a rage, had killed her with a red hot fire nipper. The second child, Adriné, we were able to trace her in Constantinople with a Turkish merchant. Our friend, Der Aprahamian, was able to free her with the help of British police and managed to forward her to me in Samsun with an Armenian merchant.

I often remembered my mother talking about her cousin Adriné, for she had grown up with her in Greece in the 1920s and 30s. Frequently the name was mentioned in conjunction with her sister, Meliné. As far back as I can remember I recall hearing the rhyming sound of their names, Adriné and Meliné. I did eventually meet my mother's beloved cousin Adriné on one of my first trips to Greece when I was studying classical Greek philosophy and language in London in the winter of 1976–77. I was escaping the cold, damp winter, a winter made more difficult by power outages due to industrial actions and strikes. I received a warm greeting from her and her adult son, Marios. I knew at the time that she was one of the "rescued orphans," as she and her sister were often called in our family. I did not know much more than that. Anxious to leave Athens for one of the warmer islands to the south, I had no thought of probing the past at that moment. Oh, the questions I would ask today.

Over the years I would hear a lot more about these orphaned sisters. The story of Meliné's rescue was often told by my mother and others in the family. Aram provides one version:

The third child, Meliné, was with a Turkish officer who was transferred to Constantinople ... he was traveling by land, the hard way. We were given a hint about his passing by Marsovan at [a] certain time so we invited them for a family dinner. During the dinner, my brother used psychological persuasion. He was able to convince them to let Meliné stay with us. That night, we gave her a hot bath at home. (In Marsovan, my brother had the only Turkish bath running hot and cold water [in the house].) Poor child, she was full of lice in her hair, body, and dress. We cleaned her and put her in [a] clean nice bed. She was much surprised and exclaimed in Turkish as she had forgotten her Armenian, and said, "So this, Oh is this my bed?" Next morning when we were all around the breakfast table and said grace, she kept silent for a while and then said, "Oh! My father used to pray that way too." Two surviving sisters this way were saved and lived with us happily till we came to Greece.

My mother found this reference to the "psychological persuasion" of her father quite humorous. She would laugh as she told me that alcohol was the persuader in this encounter. In keeping with their strong religious conviction against the consumption of alcohol, neither Tsolag nor Aram drank or kept alcohol in the house or so it was believed. Thankfully my grandfather was pragmatic about such matters and had the foresight to "lubricate" the conversation with drink. A bribe also did not hurt matters in this regard. In a slightly different version of this story, the soldier's stay in Marsovan was precipitated by a conveniently "arranged" accident to the carriage transporting the soldier and his family.

Despite devoting much time to relief work and the orphans, Aram's photography business in Samsun prospered in the early months of 1919. Samsun was a large and active port city that saw large numbers of Westerners escorting supplies or passing through to points in the interior. Besides Aram's official Near East Relief work of taking photographs of the

87. Adriné and Meliné Nakkashian in Marsovan, c.1919.

274

orphans and their activities, many Westerners came to the studio wanting souvenirs of their visit to Turkey. Aram's confidence and optimism for the future must have been high because he decided that this was the moment to marry his true love, Christine:

> So when Adriné came to Samsun, I could not send her to Marsovan by herself as she was about 12 years old. Besides, the roads were not safe as Turkish *chetes* used to harass the Christian travelers ... I, myself, was tired of hard work and needed a vacation and rest, so I thought this was the best time to go to Marsovan and get married. So I wrote to my Christine and arranged my work so that I could be away from my work and obligations. I bought lots of the finest fancy French candies, a case of English biscuits, fancy paper candy baskets, and everything else for the ride, and started our journey to Marsovan. My sweetheart was so happy to see me, so [were] all my dear ones, but not so with her near relatives when they understood our intention ... They all opposed our marriage and some others for selfish interest and motives, tried hard to change my mind of the idea of ever getting married but we plainly told everyone that this does not concern them, that we are mature and we know what we are doing.

After receiving a clean bill of health from Dr. Marden, they set a date of May 23, 1919 for the wedding. Given Aram's artistic sensibility and creativity, this was to be a rather unique wedding:

> I made a novel and artistic photographic invitation folder for the wedding party. Our wedding was a unique and ideal one in every respect. We had more than 200 invited guests which had an international tint as we had Armenians, Americans, English, Frenchmen, Greeks, Russians, and Turks. Surely everyone was happy and in jovial mood and very friendly with each other and were very respectful to each other ... Our Protestant new beautiful church was not given back to the Armenians yet so we did not have a church wedding. We [had] to use our big photographic studio. I made enough small flags in even numbers of six different nationalities, all face down so to each guest one flag was fastened on their lapel or chest. We had set up two big tables to sit 25 persons in each serving. We had tea, cookies, donuts, paklava, ice cream, and a beautiful basket full of fancy candies. We had two ministers for the wedding ceremonies, Rev. Sahagian performed the engagement ceremony and Dr. Pye performed the wedding ceremony. My dear nephew, Hratchia, played violin solos. He was a born artist ... Our friends organized a special choir and sang songs, hymns, and choruses. There was continual music of some kind or other during the refreshments. Just for fun, let me mention this [one] instance. In Marsovan we did not have artificial ice, so we ordered some snow pack from the mountain. It was late when they brought the snow and it was too late for them to go back to

their village so we let the men and donkeys stay in the backyard. Upstairs, when the choir leader gave the key note and [we] were just to start singing, the donkeys started braying on the same note, giving a good laugh to everybody present ... Then our neighboring Greek village people came together and said, "Our Aram Effendi is getting married and we are sitting still here?" So they took their big drum and pipe and held a folk dance out in the street. That made everything complete. All in all, it was a fine wedding.

88. Wedding photo of Aram and Christine, May 1919.

The future looked bright for Aram and the Dildilians, but this was not to last. While the family was busily preparing for the wedding, back in Samsun the first steps of a struggle that would lead to the end of Armenian life in Anatolia had begun. On May 19 Mustafa Kemal Pasha, the future Atatürk, had landed in Samsun, a date that is celebrated as the start of the national struggle for Turkish independence. Soon Aram and Atatürk's paths would cross, almost.

The Rise of Nationalism and Growing Fears of the Family

The unity and friendship that was on display at Aram and Christine's wedding belied the festering antagonisms that were evidenced across much of Anatolia. The Allies had authorized Greece to land troops in Smyrna (Izmir) and their arrival on May 15, 1919 caused great resentment among the Turkish population. The countryside around Samsun and Marsovan was already in turmoil with competing bands of Turkish and Greek guerrillas. Mustafa Kemal had arrived in Samsun on May 19 but because of the unease created by the presence of the British occupation forces and Greek irregulars in the countryside, he moved his entourage to Havza on May 25. Havza was less than a day's ride from Marsovan. This is where a chance encounter with Atatürk would have taken place if it had not been for my grandmother's interference:

> A few days later, we were told that a small … convoy of British soldiers are to go to Samsun. So I asked the captain Anderson if our wagon could follow their caravan for safety. He said, "Surely." So we got ready and started on our journey back to Samsun. My sister-in-law came with us to help us arrange things. Although Turkish guerrillas were harassing, raping and killing the Christian caravans, we arrived safely to Samsun. On the way the first day, we stayed in Havza and went to a *han* (inn). There we were told that Mustafa Kemal Pasha (the future Atatürk) was staying in that same place. First we did not mind much, but later my sister-in-law said, "We will not stay here." She went out and 15 minutes later came back and said, "Come on, we will all go to our friend's home nearby." So we spent the night at that friend's house. Next day, we spent the night in Kavak.

So Aram was never to meet Atatürk in person. What a missed opportunity! Aram, of course, always traveled with his camera. I wonder if he would have tried to take a photograph of Atatürk and his staff. This "never-to-be" photograph would have been famous, one for the history books.

Aram and Christine arrived in Samsun and settled into their new home with the belief that this would be their home for years to come. Aram describes their feelings: "Soon my studio was finished completely, so we moved there to make it our home and business place there. Home! Yes, we had a home for our future family. We had made Samsun our permanent home! How badly we were mistaken. We could never imagine that some day we would be driven out of our home, our country that we loved so much." With the birth of their first child, Margaret, Aram and Christine were ready to put down roots in soil of the land they loved: "God blessed us with a precious bundle as a gift, our darling Margaret on April 29, 1920, a really lovely baby, beautiful, blue-eyed, light hair and fair complexion, our pride and joy. We were happy and thankful for we had everything we wanted." While many fearful Armenian survivors were leaving Turkey at this time, Aram and Christine felt comparatively safe, living next door to the U.S. Consulate. Aram had come full circle in this regard. As a young child growing up in Sivas, the family home was also close to the U.S. Consulate, a proximity that afforded them safety during the Hamidian Massacres of 1895. Aram ends this happy chapter in his memoir with his reasons for remaining in the land of his birth:

> There were no restrictions for travel, there was a boat or two each day and we could go to Armenia or Constantinople or anywhere else but we did not care to go away. Why? First, we were blind and did not see the future plainly. Second, I loved my nation and my homeland, right or wrong. It was my contention that once we are away from our homeland, no more Armenian question and all those sacrifices would have been all in vain.

May 1919 had marked the beginning of Aram and Christine's life together but also marked the start of what would later be called the Greco-Turkish War or the Turkish War for Independence, depending on one's perspective. These two interrelated struggles would bring to an end Armenian life on the soil of its homeland.

As spring turned into summer in 1919, tensions began to rise in all the ethnic communities. Rumors of conspiracies and plots to seize power abounded. Aram comments on one such incident though no date is given:

> One Sunday afternoon we all went to the beach for [a] picnic and sunshine. We were told that Mustafa Kemal is planning to hold a national conference in Samsun. Suddenly, there was a commotion in the crowd. News came that one of the delegates of that conference from Trebizond was killed near Charshamba on the way to Samsun. That news of the killing was shocking news for both Christians and Turks as no one knew who the killer was. For a change, Turks were scared more than we were.

Given what we know about Mustafa Kemal's activities in late spring and summer of 1919, it is unlikely that this conference would be planned for Samsun. We know that congresses would be held in Erzurum and Sivas before his nationalist government was established in Ankara the following year.

Aram is clearly worried about the activities of Mustafa Kemal, but since he writes from the perspective of hindsight, his worries would be quite understandable. He even reports that he warned the British as to Kemal's intentions but was assured that there was nothing to worry about:

> I did report to Capt. Saulter, the British Control Officer, that a certain Mustafa Kemal Pasha had come over to establish a separate government in the interior.

He is now in Amasia and we think he is a very dangerous man for the Christians … But he said, "We know all about him, there is nothing to be afraid of. He is a fine man and the allied powers have O.K.'d his coming over." We all could feel some uneasiness all around us, some unexplainable tension. Sure enough, Mustafa Kemal, after Samsun, he tried Sivas, Harpoot, and finally he was able to hold a conference in Ankara and there he established his government with his unpunished cohorts, that is, the İttihat ve Terakki Club.

What the British knew or did not know is a complicated story, one outside the scope of this book. Whatever their knowledge, the troops they had on the ground in Anatolia were insufficient to change the dynamics of what was taking place. The demobilization after the war, and the domestic pressures to bring the troops home, left them with limited military capabilities, as Aram reported in the following incident:

My youngest nephew, Buzdig [little] Ara, was coming over to visit us from Marsovan. There was a big caravan coming to Samsun, about 10 or 12 wagons, and were following the British convoy for safe traveling in charge of Captain Anderson. When they came to one of the dangerous spots at Chakallar, suddenly Turkish guerrillas gave a signal to stop. At once the British soldiers hit the ground to give a fight but Captain Anderson surrendered to them because other travelers were mostly women and children. Naturally, the Turks disarmed the British soldiers and robbed the travelers of all their belongings. Ara had a real fancy handbag. In it he had the finest album collection of postage stamps. So he gave his box to one of the *chetes* and holding his arms up he says, "I surrender, I surrender too." They throw his bag into the mud but Ara did not understand and did not know what they were talking [about], he just kept on saying and following the guerrillas, "I surrender, I surrender too" (in Turkish) … As a consequence of the holdup, poor Capt. Anderson, a fine gentleman was court martialed.

Having only arrived in Marsovan in March, the British troops were ordered to withdraw in June. The college and relief personnel thought this was too precipitous. President White was sent to Constantinople to argue personally against this withdrawal. Like Aram before him, White's convoy had to pass through Havza, the temporary headquarters of Mustafa Kemal. A bridge had washed out near Havza and the trucks could not cross. White and two British officers forded the river and encountered Mustafa Kemal in Havza. After some polite evening conversation, "he offered us the use of his automobile for our trip to Samsoun the next day and my companion Britishers accepted his courtesy."[5] White successfully convinced the British to retain troops in Marsovan, a temporary reprieve since the troops eventually pulled out on September 28, a few days before Anatolia College reopened for the academic year.

Conditions worsened as the summer wore on. Both Greek and Turkish guerrillas contended for control of the countryside. Aram reports dealing with both groups but strictly on a professional basis as a photographer:

> A neighbor Greek came to me and told me to get ready to take several big groups of Greek guerrillas' pictures. He foretold that it would be a dangerous job but he added that he personally would take me over and bring me back. He advised me not to refuse. So next morning early, he came over with two horses. We p[ack] my big folding cameras, 10x12 and glass plate changer and start for the mountains. I did not tell my dear Christine where or why I am going. I only told her I am going for picture taking. About noon we arrive at their hideout. After some password ceremonies, we were in their midst. They were having food. I was anxious to finish my work and go back home but I could not act impolite so they insist [we] sit at the table ... (We had Khazan Kebabi). When everybody was satisfied and was feeling fine, I asked them to group together and took more than 12 different groups and started back home. It was 9 p.m. when we arrived home. Poor girl, Christine was waiting at the window with wet eyes. I tried to excuse myself but ... Next morning I developed them and without losing time, finished the required number of prints, delivered them, was paid promptly. (On the contrary, later when I photographed the Turkish guerrillas, they did not pay me a cent.) It was a daring act for me to go to that Greek village ... If I had been caught, it would have been my last because about that time, Turks became awful suspicious about Greeks in Samsun.

Aram would not discriminate in his role as a professional photographer. In my search for Dildilian Brothers photographs and postcards on the Internet, I have often seen photo postcards of groups of Greek guerrillas or freedom fighters, depending on your point of view. The photographer is rarely identified. I wonder if some of these were the handiwork of Aram. For that matter, there is a puzzling set of photographs in the family album of Topal Osman, the notorious Turkish guerrilla who would come to play a prominent role in the family story. Another commission? Maybe. Was Aram paid? Probably not.

In the summer of 1919, Aram and many Armenians placed their hopes on President Wilson and the prospect of an American mandate for Armenia. The Allies had promised that the Armenians would never again be placed under Turkish rule. Armenians hoped that the six Armenian vilayets and Cilicia, or some portion thereof, would be placed under American protection. The territory would be reunited with the newly independent Armenian republic that had emerged from the collapse of Czarist Russia. The surviving deportees would be brought back to these lands, fostering the rebirth of the nation. President Wilson had authorized a fact-finding mission headed by Major General James G. Harbord to visit the Armenian provinces and report back. The mission included specialists to assess the conditions on the ground and identify the costs, both in material and manpower, to take up this mandate. The mission traveled overland from Constantinople to Adana and then north to Sivas. A smaller contingent split off to visit Marsovan and then Samsun. The main party headed by Harbord went east and visited the capital of the new Republic of Armenia. In late September 1919, the secondary contingent of the mission reached Samsun. Aram reports his encounter with these fact-finders:

> One day my dear teacher, Mr. Getchell, gave me a surprise visit and asked me to be in Samsun Palace Hotel with Christine to be his fellow guest to Colonel Cherkerian at noon ... He was a member of General Harbord's group, who was sent by President W. Wilson to investigate the country and bring back a report ... Everywhere they went, the Armenians in groups or in person tried to inform General Harbord's party that the United States of America's name is enough to keep the Turks in line, and to do that, a few thousand American soldiers are more than enough ... On the contrary, the other group, including our missionary friends, reported that it is necessary to have several hundred thousand U.S. soldiers to take the mandate of the Armenian state. So General Harbord gave his report that there should be more than 200,000 U.S. soldiers to mandate the Armenian state. So we lost our cause because of our friends.

A complex set of factors led to the American abandonment of the mandate, only one of which related to the issue of troop strength. Aram provides an analysis similar to the one he gave earlier regarding the impoverished state of the Armenians encountered by the Americans. Admiral Bristol had been swayed by Turkish hospitality, a hospitality that the few impoverished Armenians scattered across their homeland could not provide. Aram does point out that the wealth that allowed some Turks to "entertain" their American guests was created by the illegal confiscation of Armenian properties. He believes a cynicism pervaded the American attitude: "You can't tell and make them believe that once all those fine buildings and business places used to belong to Armenians who have been killed by the Turks who are [now] running those businesses. They would say, 'So what? What is the use anyhow, there are no more Armenians.'"

Despite the Allies' lack of action on the Armenian question, Aram and his fellow nationals began the gradual process of reconstructing Armenian life in Samsun. The church properties had been restored, and now the survivors' spiritual and educational needs required attention:

> By this time, I was still serving as a member of the National Union to look after the interests of our Nationals. We started a national school for the orphans and outside children, with some capable teachers, and I was appointed as school

trustee. Then we asked the Constantinople Armenian Prelate to send us a bishop as a leader, so they sent the former Bishop Spranosian, who had had some mental disorder at the start of the deportation and was taken back to Constantinople. They should have not sent him back to the same spot. Sorry to say, he was not able to stand the pressing duties and obligations and he broke down again. So the Government sent him back to Constantinople to the Sourp Pergich Armenian National Hospital. I was with him when the Turkish officials bound him on a stepladder and took him off – it was a terrible experience for me. I was very fond of him ... Soon after that, Bishop Injerian came to us from Constantinople. Everything went fine. We started with nothing and God gave us everything. With a few people, we became an Armenian community, more than 2,000. Later, I resigned from the National Committee so that I would be able to serve better on the Orphanage and School committees. The orphanage was growing in number and in problems. Besides the housing problem, we had some new problem and that was about those girls who were taken by Turks as wives. Those girls were coming to the orphanage as orphans and workers. I insisted we should not put them in the orphanage with the orphans as they may be a bad influence. Instead, put them all together some other place, or send them to Marsovan where they have a separate institution just for such unfortunates. But I was voted down. Later, we had trouble with them more than once.

Today the desire to separate girls who had been removed from Turkish homes, as possible "bad influences," can be viewed as a case of "blaming the victim." Given the unique type of sexual trauma they experienced, they probably needed special counseling, not moral disapproval. Aram's reference to sending them to Marsovan refers to the "Home" set up by Mrs. Gannaway in one of the Anatolia missionary houses on the campus for the "more than one hundred young women of Christian families by heritage, birth, and up-bringing and living perforce for the time in Moslem homes ... each with her own sad story."[6]

In Marsovan the missionaries took the lead in running the orphanage and restoring some semblance of education for the returning Armenians. A strict non-discrimination policy meant the students of any ethnic or religious background could attend the reopened primary, preparatory and college level schools. At the upper levels, those students who could not pay were expected to work in exchange for their tuition. Anatolia College reopened on October 1, 1919 with a staff of five Greek teachers, three Armenians, one Russian and one Turk. Given the ravages of war and the massacres of young Armenian men, there were initially no students enrolled at the college levels. George White reports that there were 166 students enrolled in the preparatory department, including 77 Armenians. Included among the 77 were four of Tsolag's children: Hratchia, Humayag, Jiraïr and Ara. All had been home-schooled during the war years by my grandmother, Mariam, who had trained as a teacher in Kharpert before her marriage.

Eight-year-old Alice, my mother, continued to be schooled at home despite the full reopening of the Anatolia Girls' School, where the two rescued nieces, Adriné and Meliné, were soon enrolled. White points out that the school "had not been officially closed" and continued to quietly operate during the war years.

The continuing demobilization of the British Army required the withdrawal of the small British contingent from Marsovan. Their withdrawal seems to have worried Haïganouch most of all. She began contemplating a move to Samsun with the ultimate goal of emigrating to the United States. Her financial condition was increasingly precarious, as her eldest son, Haïgouni, who had played an important role in supporting the family, died in August 1919. Surprisingly, Maritsa does not describe the circumstances of her brother's death, but Aram writes: "my dear nephew, Haïgouni (sister's oldest son) who came to visit me in Samsun, while on his way back home was stricken with Tropical Malaria and died in terrible high fever." Samsun was surrounded by low-lying marshy areas that were a breeding ground for malaria-carrying mosquitoes. Maritsa briefly comments on his passing: "After my brother's death (August 1919), we had a difficult winter. We knitted clothes for the orphans. When spring came, my mother could start weaving, as most of the Marsovantsis did, and life became more bearable for us." She also mentions that Garo, her future husband, "had resumed his employment at the College ... and was now head of the joinery shop."

Initially the relations between the college and the local authorities were cordial. Dr. White reports: "Our city governor was greatly disturbed that so many Armenians had gone from our region, and he urged that whether or not the College could keep up full numbers or keep up to normal standards, it should at least keep going, not only for the sake of the students in attendance, but for the sake of its public influence as a steadying and encouraging factor in the post-war situation."[7] In the same spirit of friendship between ethnic groups in which Aram had organized his May wedding, Dr. White and the college attempted to bridge the divide between the Muslim and Christian communities. Turkish enrollment peaked in these two post-war years. Sports even played a role in the reconciliation process: "Basketball matches were staged and were witnessed by crowds, in which the champion team was made up of one American, one Armenian, one Greek, one Russian, and one Turk."[8]

As the worst decade in Armenian history ended, no one knew what the next decade would bring. The optimism that Aram and his missionary friends clung to would be tested in the years ahead.

A Saddened Reunion of Brothers: Tsolag's Loss and Aram's New Burdens

Though Tsolag did not know it at the time, 1920 marked the beginning of an inevitable process that would see the eventual exile of the Dildilians from their beloved homeland. The nationalist movement that began in the spring of 1919 gained strength and momentum daily. The Military Courts-Martial of the Committee of Union and Progress leadership and their underlings that began in the spring of 1919 would lose momentum and come to an end by January of 1921. During 1920 a power shift took place across Anatolia. The local authorities, whose allegiance was to the Ottoman government in Constantinople, were now replaced by functionaries, who owed allegiance to Kemal and the nationalists in Ankara. This shift boded ill for the Armenians and my family.

Relief work in both Marsovan and Samsun continued throughout the year. Both orphanages continued to grow and more and more children were brought in from remote corners of Anatolia. As mentioned earlier, British troops pulled out of Marsovan in late September 1919 and with them the last vestige of Allied protection for the Armenian minority was gone. Tsolag was viewed by some local nationalist Turks as collaborating with the enemy because of his appointment to a position in city hall by the British occupying-military authority. He issued new identity papers to many of the wartime converts, thereby restoring their Armenian names. His actions stirred hatred among some locals. As reported by my mother, a Turkish friend warned him of a plot to assassinate him and that he should leave town until things cooled down. By early 1920 he had packed up some of his photography equipment and moved to Samsun to join his brother. Aram describes the circumstances of the move:

> Both Turks and surviving Armenians were looking and acting with hatred toward my brother and threatened him with bodily harm. So I wrote my brother to let go everything and come to Samsun because my business was good and plenty enough to support our two families. So he left Humayag, Jiraïr and Ara in the care of sister Haïganoush so that they can keep on in their school in Anatolia College, and brought along Hratchia and the rest of the family, sister-in-law, Alice, Adriné and Meliné.

This would be the final time that Tsolag and many members of my family would see Marsovan. My mother was nine years old at the time. She had very fond memories of the house my grandfather had built across the street from the college. Because of the war and its aftermath, my mother was mostly confined to that house and its walled garden. As I was growing up, I often heard her lovingly describe this house and its beautiful gardens. She recalled those warm summer nights sitting on its balcony eating supper with her family and the cold winter mornings when, clothes in hand, she ran down the stairs to the warmth of the large studio room as her father toasted bread on the cast-iron stove. The smell of her father's toast, the smell of the evening's garden air as it mingled with the aromas of her mother's cooking as she sat on the balcony, these sights and sounds of her childhood home were forever etched in her memory.

89. Alice Marsoobian (née Dildilian) in the family home, c.1915.

By 1920 Hratchia, Tsolag and Mariam's eldest son, had reached the age of 18. He was a talented musician and an artistically creative young man. He had taken on increasing responsibilities in the photography studio, and I suspect that his father was hoping that someday he would take over the family business. Sadly this was not to happen. Aram reports:

Hratchia was sick. Poor Hratchia, was an artist in heart and soul. One unfortunate day after the Armistice, while he was coming home from his violin lesson, two Turks were waiting in the Hagopian's corner to attack him. When he sees them in threatening mood, he tries to run as fast as he could. Before he turns at our house gate, they start shooting at him. Fortunately they miss him and he makes the door. After that, day by day he grew weaker and pale. Finally, Dr. Marden said he had T.B. As soon as he came to Samsun, we put him in our sunny room and did everything humanly possible to make him well and happy. The table was turned, as ten years earlier, I was in the same condition in my brother's home. Now my dear nephew is in my house in the same fix. But alas! All that we did was in vain, it was a losing battle.

No explanation is given here as to why someone would shoot at Hratchia. Certainly there is no medically causal connection between the incident and his exposure to the tubercular bacterium. That being said, medical research has demonstrated in recent years a direct connection between high levels of stress and anxiety and the suppression of the immune system. One's ability to fight off the tubercular bacterium is diminished under such conditions. Aram may well have been correct in linking Hratchia's death to that violent assault on the streets of Marsovan. We do know that with the departure of the British, the security conditions had worsened in Marsovan by the end of 1919:

90. Hratchia Dildilian, c.1919.

> Hratchia was fading fast, just melting away like a burning candle … He was so sensitive and was growing melancholic. He did not play his violin anymore though his violin was at his bedside. He used to read poetry – that was his only enjoyment. One bright morning he called me and brother to his bedside and asked us to sing for him the song, "I am a Stranger" and hardly had we sang one verse when he closed his eyes and went into a sweet and calm slumber. Just then the doctor came up and asked us for some boiling water. At once we provided him with what he asked for. He put a small pill into it and injected it through his chest. Poor child, he opened his eyes in fear. He suffered half an hour more and then went to his loving Jesus and his eternal rest.

On January 24, 1920, Tsolag and Mariam's eldest son passed away. His younger brother Humayag was also learning the art of photography at the time. If Hratchia had lived, there may well have been a second generation of Dildilian Brothers photographers. Years later Humayag would fill his brother's shoes and take over the family business on the death of his father in 1935. My uncle Humayag continued working professionally as a photographer for the next 50 years. In his declining years, he entrusted me with the family's photography collection and one additional precious artifact, Hratchia's violin.

Finally the winter was over. It was Palm Sunday so we put the best clothes and shoes on the orphans and took them to church. Each child had a small bunch of flowers but I was in the wrong again because I was ignorant about church regulation, that is, we should not have carried flowers into the church but have taken the anointed palm leaves out of the church … In the meantime, I had put on my Sunday suit but had forgotten my money which I left at home. They passed around seven times the collection plate and I felt awfully cheap as I was not able to put money in the collection plate. I heard people blaming me because I was "Protestant" and did not care to help the church. The next Sunday it was Easter so we took the children to Church again in their best. This time I was sure to take plenty of money. They, as usual, passed seven times the collection plate and I put one dollar on each time to compensate my wrong of the week before. This time, they who saw me putting in the money muttered to each other, "Sure, he can afford to put that much money, it is easy-earned American money. Why not, he has plenty." I did not mind as I had gotten used to those insults … But surely, it hurts.

This verbal abuse finally came to a head when an anonymous threating letter was directed against Aram. Christine had seen a local Armenian, a Mr. Simonian, put the letter on their gate. It read: "If you want to sit on your Orphanage Throne in safety, then stop persecuting the Armenian St. Apostolic Church (The Mother Church). The first warning was sent to you by a Protestant friend. Evidently you ignored it. Do not wait for a third warning that will come in action." The letter was signed, "The ones who know how to punish." Aram asked the chair of the National Committee to call a meeting. Aram relates what happened next:

They all were so polite and sweet to me and wanted to know what it is all about. Well, I made it plain to them that someone had put this letter at my house gate, and I read it to them. All of them in accord said, "We have nothing to do with that letter. It is the work of street people. Please do not pay any attention to it." (The man who put the letter on the gate was in the room). I said, "Yes, maybe you all do not have anything to do with this letter but I know for sure it was you who are the responsible ones as you spoke those things in this room and let the street people know and act against me and you did not make any effort to put an end to it. On the contrary, you accentuated that unfriendly attitude … This is your orphanage, the children are your own flesh and blood. I did all I could to better their condition and you, instead of helping me to perform my duties better and in a sweeter way, you put all the opposition you could … All I want is that you let me alone with my orphans." I enumerated one by one all the troubles they have raised against us. "On the other hand, with a little effort and good will, you could lighten my burden and make those children happier, but you did not. About church or religion for which you are accusing me, you know that I and my family are the only Armenian Protestants. None of our teachers are Protestant. Yes, I did not take the orphans to church for good reasons, but you should be glad and happy that we are bringing them up to be Armenians and Christians."

After this meeting the threats from the Armenian community lessened but new threats soon arose.

The Nationalist Threat against the Armenians of Samsun and Marsovan

As the spring turned into summer in 1920, the security conditions for the Armenians and Greeks of Samsun and Marsovan seriously deteriorated. Those who could afford to leave had been fleeing the country for months. With the departure of the British, the flow of refugees increased considerably. The long-established merchants in the Samsun area, the Ipranosian Brothers were the next to go:

> The British soldiers were gone out of the country, the British control officer and with him the British flag, which was not supposed to come down…! Naturally, everybody was in panic. There came the last steamer of the Ipranosian Brothers to carry their own merchandise and passengers who were fortunate enough to have a permit for travel. The merchandise was piled high up to the Captain's bridge and the passengers had only standing room. All were Armenians. That was our last hope.

Back in Marsovan the Armenians, Greeks, and the Americans of Anatolia College were also being put under increasing pressure by the nationalists. Maritsa gives no specific explanation, but her mother decided that it was now their turn to leave. The death of her eldest son the prior summer, the harsh winter of 1919–20, the rise in anti-Armenian sentiment in Marsovan, all may have contributed to her decision. In July 1920 Haïganouch sent the family on ahead to Samsun to join her brothers while she stayed behind "to sell all that could be sold and find a tenant for the house." Maritsa describes her mother's plans: "My mother decided we had to leave the country. She said that, as soon as we had saved the money required, we would go down to the Black Sea coast and take the first ship available." Haïganouch and Garo soon joined her children in Samsun.

Unfortunately this attempt failed. Again no explanation is given, but the cost of emigrating and increasing restrictions on travel may have contributed. The family decided to stay, at least temporarily, in Samsun. With her brother's help, Haïganouch found employment as a weaver in the orphanage.

91. Orphans and teachers doing embroidery, sewing, and weaving. Samsun, c.1920.

Yet soon Haïganouch had a change of heart and the family returned to Marsovan:

> However, in Samsun, which is located in a swampy area, the unhealthy air defeated us. My sister, then me, then Aram, then my gallant mother, got sick.
>
> We decided to go back to Marsovan, but Garo stayed in uncle Aram's orphanage in Samsun. Without lingering over the technicalities, I must say that we had a lot of trouble obtaining the authorization to go back to Marsovan. We traveled back in company with a Miss Papazian Annig who had been appointed to teach Armenian at the American College. As an inhabitant of the capital city, she had not known what had been going on in the provinces, in the deep Anatolian country, the ordeals we had endured, our continuous wavering from hope to despair.

The year ahead would move inexorably toward despair.

Anatolia College's second post-war academic year of 1920–1 began without incident. Humayag, Jiraïr and Ara enrolled again in the college with their aunt Haïganouch keeping a watchful eye on them for her brother Tsolag. The threats that had driven Tsolag to Samsun had not gone away. Mariam, not Tsolag, had accompanied her sons back to Marsovan to register them again in the college. Maritsa and her siblings would join them: "My mother was positive that we had to continue our schooling, all four of us. But the money? My aunt Mariam, who always professed the slogan 'study and work,' had registered us with the College together with her sons ... thinking that we would pay our fees by taking professional jobs or discharging duties in the College."

Unlike Aram's many happy memories of his life at Anatolia College, Maritsa conveys a diametrically opposed description of her life as a boarding student:

> That year, snow started as soon as October. We were boarders and slept in a large dormitory under the roof. The windows and doors had to remain open. Our thin blankets were insufficient to protect our bodies that had hardly recovered from illness.
>
> My sister and I each had to each take care of a large table in the refectory: we had to serve, clear away, liaison between the kitchen and the tables. We were the last ones to eat, and we had often to do the dish-washing and sweep the refectory by ourselves or with an occasional help.
>
> We also had to wash every week the wooden floor of the two dormitories. We had to wash our linen in the wash house where, by the time we arrived, there was no more hot water. On Saturdays, we had thirty minutes to have a bath, but Kandi Agha, who was in charge, delivered either too hot or too cold water to make us leave quickly.

Maritsa's work duties were made more burdensome by the illness of her sister and mother:

> This did not last long. My sister got sick and had to keep in bed ... My mother was still convalescent. When I came back home on Sundays, I could see how weak she was. Each morning, I ran back home to light a good fire. Meanwhile in the College, my workload had been increased for I had now to light two huge wood-burning stoves. But this task, normally not so heavy, was made harder by the difficulty to find wood, paper, matches. It was quite a feat ...
>
> Under such conditions, my actual schoolwork was turning into an impossible task. Sometimes, I was called right in the middle of a lesson because one stove or another was not drawing well.

Maritsa finally informed her mother that the situation was impossible. Haïganouch brought her daughters home, and the siblings continued their education by commuting the short distance from their home to campus. At home, the children could all contribute to the textile work that was now the family's chief source of income. Yet despite the appearance of some semblance of normalcy, the fear and loss that marked the worst days of 1915 were returning. Maritsa laments: "We also had reasons for sadness: the death of my brother Haïgouni, of my cousin Hratchia, our Marsovan devastated, and above all, an uncertain existence with that constant fear creeping in everywhere."

As was the case in Samsun, the political power in Marsovan had shifted in 1920. The power now lay in Ankara and not Constantinople. George White reports this shift: "As the weeks of the year 1920 came and passed, there was increasing evidence about us of a resurgent and rising tide of Turkish Nationalism … Ottoman officialdom, which had been in the habit of looking to Constantinople for orders, began to take orders from the separatist and military Government of Angora [Ankara]."[9] White drew parallels to what had happened to the Armenians in 1915:

> Early in 1920 the separatist government at Angora began to employ men and measures after the manner that had become familiar during the Armenian deportations half a decade before. Now the Greeks were the chief object of hatred and hostility. Travel was forbidden for the Christians of the country, and our students found difficulty in going to their homes for the summer vacation and getting back again. A new attitude of unfriendliness toward Americans was manifested, not by our local officials, who knew and understood us, but by the Angora authorities and especially by the military men everywhere.[10]

So much for Admiral Bristol's friendly and accommodating "Open Door" policy with the Turkish nationalists.

Both Aram and White comment on the new source of power in Marsovan, a lawyer named Saduk Bey Mehami (or Mauamy in Aram's spelling). Aram describes one possible motivation for his resentment against the Americans of Anatolia College:

> During deportation, two Turkish lawyer brothers, Shaukry and Saduk Mauamy brothers, just came and took possession of Prof. Hagopian's home (next to my brother and Christine's grandmother's little apartment) without paying any rent to the college treasurer who was the mortgage holder. When in 1918, Britishers came, they made them pay the past and present [amount] due. That hurt their feelings so as soon as things started to go their way, they start to take vengeance. They managed to get from Mustafa Kemal Pasha, the office of Commissar over the Americans and the college.

Saduk Mauamy came to power in Marsovan in December 1920. He played a major role in ending the American and Armenian presence in Marsovan. As we will see, he would also plague the Dildilians on their very last day on the soil of their homeland. White comments:

> In December a Turkish lawyer, Saduk Bey Mehami, came and announced that he had been appointed Comisser [sic] of us Americans in Relief work, and also in education. We accepted the former in view of all the circumstances, but

protested the latter for the College and Girls' School had been fully authorized by the Ottoman government for years. Our protest was unavailing. Saduk Bey was notoriously hostile to us. He was commonly quoted as saying that he would not rest till our campus was turned into a barley field again.[11]

As spring arrived, Saduk Bey would take his first steps to carry out his threat.

Well over two years had passed since the Der Haroutiounians had to hide anyone in their home, but this soon changed as a result of Saduk Bey's presence in Marsovan. Mihran Gharabed Hovagimian, one of the original college escapees who had been hidden in Haïganouch's house, had been hired as an assistant in the college's Armenian Department, but soon he again found himself hiding back at the Der Haroutiounian house. The tensions that had grown between the Armenians and the city's Turks take on an interesting twist in the following passage from Maritsa's notebook:

> One day, at the College, during the Friday evening prayer, Mihran, who had been appointed teacher and monitor, orders a Turkifed Armenian student to take off his fez. The student refuses. Mihran raises his voice in a more threatening way. Now, that boy, Ohannig, was the son of Kiremidjian Hadj' Azniv, people who were close to Turks, in particular to the Saduk family and especially their daughter. Finally, Mihran takes the fez off Ohannig's head and puts it in front of the boy.
>
> Had Ohannig felt wounded in his honor? We do not know, but anyway he complained to Turkish authorities. Mihran was arrested and put in jail. He escaped and went to hide at his half-sister's. But he did not stay there long and, one day, here he comes to our place, just as in the times of the deserters. He had not an ounce of sense in his head … neither a penny in his pocket … My mother was weak enough to take him in again. Each time an Armenian was hunted by the police she used to give him refuge, each time suffering the consequences of it. Again, our bread had a salted taste and our water a bitter taste.

Carl Compton, a teacher at the time and the future president of Anatolia College, also comments in his memoir on this incident: "A minor disciplinary action by an Armenian against a Turkish student was reported to the city as an insult against the Turkish nation."[12] Unease among the Armenian and Greek staff resulted in Americans taking over all classes with Turkish students in them. "Insult against the Turkish nation" was codified into Turkish law by the Kemalists and to this day has hindered free expression in the Republic.

Maritsa's passage raises some interesting questions. If she is correct, then it is clear that not all Armenians relinquished their Turkish identities after the Armistice. Garabed Kiremidjian Hadji had played a leading role in the conversions of 1915. There were many Kiremidjians in Marsovan, related and unrelated to Garabed. By this time Garabed himself had left Marsovan for Constantinople.

Though figures are not provided, White comments that the number of Turkish students registered that school year was the greatest in the school's history, many more than the 12 they had the year before. This must have required changes in the manner in which the school was run. "Friday evening prayer" is a reference to the Christian prayers that were part of the college routine for decades. Were the Islamic students expected to attend? Was a distinction made between a Turkish student and a Turkified Armenian student? Could you be Turkified and still be Christian at this point? Was pressure being put on the Islamized Armenians to return to the fold? White had written: "Yet the number of Turkish students registered that year, 1920, was greater than ever before, though officials were increasingly restrictive regarding them and regarding everything we did."[13] The memoirs do not provide any definitive answers to these questions, though it is clear from the writings of White and other missionaries that they were very respectful of the religious practices of their Turkish students.

There is a great irony in the episode of Mihran and the fez. Within five years Mustafa Kemal would ban the wearing of the fez, denouncing it as a sign of Ottoman decadence that his modernizing agenda rejected. He even condemned it as a head covering commonly worn by the Greeks, the enemy the nationalists had just defeated. My mother once mentioned that her father had angered Turkish sensibilities when he removed the fez of an Armenian who had come to the town hall to receive back his Armenian identity after the Armistice. This contributed to the death threats that eventually forced Tsolag to leave Marsovan. If true, I wonder what went through Tsolag's head when in Athens, years later, he read about Atatürk's ban on the fez. Tsolag the modernizing predecessor of Atatürk!

10

Their Days Are Numbered:
No Place in Turkey for the Dildilians

Reliving 1915: The Persecutions of the Armenians and Greeks of Marsovan

The year 1921 was a pivotal year in the story of the Dildilians in their homeland. That year also marked a turning point in the struggle that would give birth to the Republic of Turkey, a birth that would eventually deprive the Dildilians of a home on the soil that had nurtured them for hundreds of years. The year 1921 also saw the end of most missionary work in Marsovan, bringing to an end Anatolia College's 35-year presence on the soil from which it drew its name.

The spark that began the downward spiral that led to the exodus of the Dildilians and the Americans was the murder of a Turkish teacher on the staff of Anatolia College. President George White had long desired to attract more Turkish students and staff to the college. After the restoration of the constitution in 1908, a few local Turkish students had enrolled but quickly withdrew under pressure from more conservative elements in the community. In the two years since the reopening of the college, three Turks had joined the staff, including M. Zeki Ketani, who taught Turkish language and literature. The ethnic groups on campus had a long tradition of forming literary and sports clubs, each with their own periodical publication. Aram comments: "The Armenians had The Shavarshan Club, which had the 'Nor Aick' weekly and the Greeks had the Pontus." The Greek Pontus literary society had discontinued using the name "Pontus" due to political sensitivities after the Armistice. The Turkish students also had a similar literary society. White relates what happened to the society's faculty advisor:

> On the evening of February 12, Zeki Effendi Ketani, our head Turkish teacher, after presiding at a meeting of the Turkish students' literary society, was assassinated in the street on his way home and within twenty-four hours was dead. We had no doubt that his death was caused by Turks who could not bear to have one of their own number happy in helping us to conduct an American and Christian school.[1]

Maritsa gives some further details of the murder that occurred near their home: "The political situation was worsening again at an accelerated rate. One day, the Turkish schoolteacher with Kurdish origins who was a tenant in the Greek minister's house next to ours, was found strangled next to the confectioner's shop across the street."

As reported in the memoirs of White, Compton, Maritsa and Aram, the college and its staff and students were increasingly viewed as collaborating with the Greeks in the Greco-Turkish War. Dildilian photographs would be used as "evidence" for this supposed collaboration. General Jemil Jahid, "one of the inner circle of Kemal Pasha," moved his army division headquarters to Marsovan and placed the whole region under his military control. On March 18, 1921, a large force of soldiers and police took action against the "revolutionaries" operating on the college campus. Maritsa, as a student in the Girls' School, was an eyewitness to these events as they unfolded:

> In March 1921, during the Greek–Turkish war, it was a Friday afternoon, the Turkish police cordoned off the American College. I was reading a composition in English called "A journey in Turkey." ... Somebody then came into the classroom and whispered something to the headmistress and then to Miss Hasford ... We felt that something very serious was going on. However, the lesson continued as if nothing had happened.
>
> Other compositions were read after mine. But the atmosphere was tense, poisoned. And suddenly soldiers enter into the classroom. They tell us to go on. How are we to go on under such conditions? The Turkish forces searched thoroughly all the classrooms and every nook and corner in all the buildings. Then, all the day-pupils were instructed to go home. So we, my sister and I and our cousins Humayag, Jiraïr, Ara, Adriné and Meliné, went to my uncle's.

George White reports the threefold purpose behind the search of the campus: "The aim was to seek evidence regarding the assassination of the Turkish teacher, to discover arms and ammunition if there were any, and to find any possible evidence of 'political' activity inimical to the Turkish Government."[2] No evidence regarding the murder was found, nor were any arms and ammunition discovered.

Though unsuccessful in finding anything on the first two counts, they still fabricated incriminating evidence regarding subversive "political activity." In doing so the Dildilians were caught up in this nationalist "witch hunt." Carl Compton reports that three incriminating items were found:

> One was a map of St. Paul's missionary journeys on which that area of Asia Minor was labeled Pontus, an area occupied by Greeks in Biblical times. A second item was the list of officers in the Anatolia College Greek Literary Society. A third was a picture of a soccer team in which the players wore striped shirts. Although the

92. Photo of the Anatolia College Pontus Athletic Club, c.1910.

picture was black and white, the investigators claimed that the shirts were blue and white, the Greek national colors.[3]

The photo of the soccer team was taken by my grandfather, as were all the photographs of the clubs on campus. Little did he know when he took the photo that it would be used to condemn innocent men and boys to death. Based on the list of officers and the photographic evidence, many Greeks on campus were arrested, including two of the esteemed professors of the college: Dimitrios Theocharides, Professor of Greek, and Pavlos Pavlides, Professor of Religion. Three other teachers and two students were also arrested and eventually hanged after a show trial in Amasia.

Greeks and some Armenians were being arrested all across the vilayets of Trebizond and Sivas. While some of them may well have been aiding the Greek guerrillas, most were being singled out for collective punishment based on flimsy manufactured evidence. An American lawyer from the U.S. High Commission sent from Constantinople examined the evidence against the Greeks of the college and deemed it "ridiculous."[4] Aram gives a report of the exchanges in the trial or what he called the "Kangaroo Court" in Amasia:

> I would like to tell about two more persons who are well known to our circle, that is, Rev. Pavlos Pavlides, a fine young minister, a graduate of Marsovan Theological Seminary. They ask his name and occupation "I am a minister of the Gospel." "Who pays your salary?" "The congregation." "You mean to say the American

301

missionaries?" "No, the Church." "We know very well you were paid by the American missions so that you would go to Turkish villages, catch hold of the Mohammedan children, claiming that they are Armenian and put them in the Orphanage to make them Christians." Then the speaker [of the court] addresses the crowd, "You brethren, hear this pretentious minister lie openly, yet we know for sure that he has worked as an agent to American Mission to gather as many Mohammedan children as he could and we know that they are in the American N.E.R. orphanage. Now what should we do with him?" "Hang him! Hang him!" Next, one of the Anatolia College Greek teachers, Prof. Theocharides. "What is your occupation?" "Teacher, judge." "Oh! you live in this country, yet you teach Greek young men to revolt and help to occupy the Pontus for the Greeks?" The crowd cries, "Hang him! Hang him!" With the same style they hanged more than 2,000 outstanding Greeks from Samsun and with them they hang a couple dozen Armenians who were able to survive the deportation.

These arrests would soon directly affect the Dildilian family.

The arrests of the teachers and students of Anatolia College were not limited to the Greeks but soon affected the Armenians. My uncle Humayag was arrested and the cause would be another Dildilian photograph. I knew my uncle well and had a great fondness for him. Weeks of our childhood summer holidays were spent visiting his home in Newington, Connecticut. Like the visits to my uncle Ara in upstate New York, visits to Humayag's home felt like a trip to the countryside. The remnant of a farm next door gave the home a rural feeling, though even then the countryside was fast receding as suburbia expanded. Humayag had followed in the footsteps of his father and had become an accomplished photographer. He often talked to me about the art of photography and showed me his darkroom. Much later in life he talked about his past, his life in Greece and his sojourn to Paris for medical treatment that would include a taste of "la belle vie" of Paris in the 1920s. Yet he spoke little about his life in Marsovan and never mentioned his imprisonment in Amasia. My mother told me that his imprisonment was traumatic and when he was finally released he was a changed person. It is not surprising then that he would not talk about those dark days.

Both Aram and Maritsa provide an account of the circumstances of Humayag's arrest. Aram briefly describes what happened: "Because they [the Turkish authorities] did not find any guns [on campus], they were furious and went to other houses to search, especially my brother's house. There they did find a few Armenian history books so they took my nephew, Humayag, to jail with the rest of the Greeks and transferred them to Amasia to be tried by the Kangaroo Court." Maritsa claims that my grandfather's house was specifically targeted for a search because of the Greek tenant who resided downstairs. With most of the family relocated to Samsun, my grandfather had rented out a portion of the house, since only his three sons lived there while his two orphaned nieces boarded at the Girls' School:

> On the ground floor of my uncle Tsolag's house, there was a Greek tenant, a female schoolteacher who lived there with her mother. She was engaged to Tchakaloff – a Russian or a Greek of Russian origin – who was a teacher-monitor at the boys' College. He came often to see his fiancée.
>
> All the people who counted within the Greek community were arrested as having formed a revolutionary organization called *Bondos* [Pontus]. Supposedly compromising documents had been found by the Turks when they had searched the College.
>
> So the police searched the fiancée's lodgings and in so doing they also found Armenian books that my cousin Humayag had concealed there. These were not revolutionary books but, since they had been concealed, the police turned suspicious about their owner. They asked who it was, Humayag said the books were his, and he was arrested and taken away.

Owning of Armenian history books was deemed a subversive act that could lead to imprisonment. The dangerous nature of book ownership was highlighted again for me in 2011 when I first visited my grandfather's house in Merzifon. The current owner, Kemal, explained the changes that had been made to the house. In 1943 there had been a major earthquake in the region that caused an internal wall to collapse in the studio room. Kemal told us that hidden in the wall were five Armenian books and a gun. At what point my grandfather hid these items I do not know, but I can well understand the necessity to do so given what I have read in the memoirs. The dangers of writing, publishing, and reading the "wrong" books has continued to characterize the state of free speech right up until today in Turkey.

When word was brought to Haïganouch that Humayag had been arrested, she sought the assistance of "two Jewish lawyers from Salonika who were members of the Young Turk organization" and happened to be neighbors of Tsolag. I can only assume that these were the Mehami brothers mentioned earlier by George White and Aram. Needless to say, Haïganouch would not receive a sympathetic hearing from them. Maritsa describes what happened and what they learned subsequently about these characters:

> With all her efforts fruitless, my mother applied to one of these lawyers. After long and unsuccessful talking, my mother came back with no solution in hand. But she had however learned two lessons. The first one was what that dog [the Mehami lawyer] had told her: "We, when we want to debase someone, we make him rise first before making him fall so that his fall and decay are even more terrible." In spite of the fact that my uncle had invited them, as neighbors, to his brother Aram's wedding, they did not help my mother …

Later we learned that that man had taken part in the atrocities committed by the *chetes* against the Peynirian family, especially against the two women, the mother and the daughter (Beatrice, a charming girl of my age), atrocities which the pen is unable to describe.

The atrocities referred to here would take place in the upcoming summer when Topal Osman terrorized Marsovan. The mother referred to here was the daughter of Tsolag's next door neighbors, the Djizmedjians. The family had moved to Bulgaria and rented their house to one of the Mehami brothers, who allowed the Djizmedjian's daughter access to the house as she wished. With Seduk Bey living next door in the Hagopian house to the north and his brother, Saléh (or Shaukry according to Aram) living in the Djizmedjian house to their south, my grandfather's house must have been a very uncomfortable place to live in 1921. Tsolag had wisely moved to Samsun the year before.

As I indicated earlier, Dildilian photographs were used as evidence for the revolutionary activities centered on the Anatolia College campus. The photo of the soccer team played a part in the arrest of the Greek staff and students, but yet another photo would result in the arrest of some of the Armenian students, including my uncle Humayag. After the arrest of my uncle, more evidence was brought forth that identified him – a 17-year-old – as a hardened revolutionary guerrilla. Maritsa tells the story of how a good-natured college prank would place my uncle's life in jeopardy:

So Humayag the photographer, a young boy, accused of being a member of "that-great-Greek-revolutionary-organization" Bondos, was thrown into jail. And together with him five other Armenians who had carelessly let them be pictured. The picture was found on Dr. White's desk at the time of the College search. Here is the story.

One day, an American, Miss Tupper, called Garo in. She told him that the Americans were going to celebrate their Independence Day and asked him if he could prepare some surprise for the occasion. Garo, then, imagined something that would make the Americans understand what the ways of the Turks were, what the life of the Armenians was …

He convinced his companions. They all dressed up as *chetes* and, at a moment arranged beforehand, they burst into the hall where the Americans were celebrating, and shouted: "Hands up!" Garo, as leader of the gang, commands that money and jewels be given. A young man who refused is hit, lightly, and he gives his money. "So you are celebrating, ha? cries Garo. You surely have good things to eat. Let's see." He requests all sort of things from the kitchen, and he and his companions have a bite at every dish. Miss Tupper, who had been informed of the game, did not say anything. Then the false brigands walk out, ordering people not to move and leaving a "confederate" as rear guard with a gun in his hand. Then, after ten minutes, they all come back without their disguises and headgears. Everyone is flabbergasted!

After some polite laughs, the Americans say to the fake *chetes* that a picture of them should be taken, and each one of them will have a copy. However, that photograph was found by the Turks when they searched the College, and except for Garo, who was in Samsun, all the others were arrested and put in jail with Humayag.

What had been a school prank just a year before, now became a life and death crisis. After Haïganouch failed to get help from the Mehami lawyer, she wrote to her brothers in Samsun informing them of the situation.

Haïganouch visited Humayag before he was transferred to prison in Amasia:

The Americans did only one good thing, they gave money to the prison warden so that these boys would not be put together with the common law criminals. They were put in the wardens' room.

Three days after, we learned that they were going to be transferred to Amasia for trial. This meant death, or at best life sentence. We begged to obtain permission to visit and it was granted. Shackles were already prepared, next to the prisoners, but had not been put on them. Even the Turks realized that they did not deserve such a treatment, but what's to be done, anyway.

As the family struggled to find a way to save the life of Humayag, the pressures against the college finally reached their inevitable end. Anatolia College was ordered to close. President George White describes the circumstances:

On Friday, March 18th [1921], the Mutessarif of Amasia, the ranking civil official of our region, and General Jemal Jahid, who was the Military Commander of our region, were lodged in the house of Saduk Bey, our "Comisser," and Dr. Marden and I met them by appointment there. We were coldly received, and soon were given a fateful message to carry to our associates ... There was a sense of impending crisis in the air ... Our Americans were ordered to leave in two days (subsequently extended by favor to three days); the College would be closed and all teachers and students scattered to their homes; two of the younger Americans ... would be selected to remain and feed but not teach the orphan children on the Near East Relief basis ... We were forbidden to telegraph either to Constantinople or to Angora, either to Turkish or to American officials ... Ultimately, Mr. Compton with his wife and Mr. Donald M. Hosford, a short term college teacher from Cleveland, were the ones chosen [to stay] from us Americans and accepted by the Turkish officials. It was no light responsibility that confronted our associates who stayed.[5]

Those "approved" to remain behind were least fluent in Turkish, further isolating what remained of the American presence in Marsovan. Yet the fact that these three Americans remained on campus was the crucial factor that saved the lives of the remaining Dildilians later that summer.

White describes the frantic efforts to buy more time while they packed up some of their belongings in preparation for departure. He comments that he, along with many of his American companions, believed that this would be a temporary exile, concluding, "We liked and sympathized with all the people, without ill-will toward any, but as the event turned out we were never to return. We had lived in Merzifon and labored in love and good will there more than thirty years. The people were our friends and our home was there."[6] Thus ended the first chapter of Anatolia College's story. The college would be reborn in Thessaloniki, Greece, but retained its name in honor of its birthplace in Anatolia.

The deported Americans arrived in Samsun in late March and were housed in the U.S. Consulate next to Aram's house while they waited for transportation to Constantinople.

> When Garo learned that the Americans from Marsovan had come to Samsun and were going to board a ship, he went to see them but the policeman on guard did not let him through. As everywhere, bribing was necessary if you had not a pass. So he paid and went in. Dr. White sees him and cries: "You are still here? All your companions were arrested and are in jail, for the Turks saw on my desk the picture of that famous day when you played *chetes*."
>
> My mother also had written to Garo to inform him. So Garo closed his workshop and stayed in hiding in my uncle's house, being once again a fugitive.

The situation for the Dildilians suddenly resembled what they had gone through back in the summer of 1915. Haïganouch was hiding Mihran in her house, Aram and Tsolag were hiding Garo in their house, men were being arrested and executed, travel and communication were restricted, and a war was raging around them.

Humayag's imprisonment did not end in tragedy, and yet again a photograph would play an important role in the story. My mother, who by this time was 11 years old, often told me the story of the photograph that saved her brother's life. This time it was not a photograph taken by one of the Dildilian brothers but a photograph taken in Constantinople in 1919 of Mustafa Kemal before his departure for Samsun. My mother told me that her father made an enlargement of a photograph they had obtained of Kemal. After enlarging it, they colored the photograph, framed it and sent it off to Kemal in Ankara with a plea for clemency. A slightly different version is given by Maritsa:

> Garo went to see his Turkish friends, and one of them told him: "Go tell your uncle to make an enlargement of a picture representing Mustafa Kemal and

306

bring it." When they have the picture, they wrap it up carefully and send it to Mustafa Kemal together, of course, with a telegram explaining why they are applying to him (to free a child). So Humayag was placed under forced residence in Amasia, whereas the others were placed in forced residence in Bitlis but saved their necks.

Whether this gesture had its intended effect, we will never know. I have often wondered whether this photograph and telegram are somewhere in the Atatürk archive.

When it came to freeing Humayag from house arrest, another Turkish friend came to the assistance of the family. Aram tells this part of the story:

93. Mustafa Kemal Pasha, *c.*1919.

> When the sad news came to us in Samsun that our house was searched and Humayag taken to jail in Amasia, we felt awfully bad and did not know what to do! That day, a Turkish friend, a military officer of the Censor[ship] department, came to see me. In the past, I had done him some good and showed some friendship to him … he became a real friend to me, so much so that once sister Nevart wrote me a long letter from America and he brought that letter to me and said, "I can't let you have this letter but while I am here you can read it and write a few lines in it as I must send it back to her …" That day he noticed that something was wrong so he asked me why I was so sad. When I told him what had happened to my nephew, he said, "Do not worry, just give me his name and age and I will write to my father-in-law who is one of the members of the Kangaroo Court." So I gave Humayag's name and details. A few days later his father-in-law calls Humayag to the court and asked about the accusation against him. When they said that he was a revolutionist and they have found Armenian books in his house … the judge got mad and said, "Why, he is a kid, how could he be a revolutionist?" He orders them to release him and send him to his parents.

Thus Humayag's life was saved by the efforts and advice of a sympathetic, or should I say, a righteous Turk.

Maritsa concludes the last of her memoir entries in her notebook with a description of Humayag's return to Marsovan in the late summer of 1921:

When he heard while he was in Amasia that the *chetes* (true *chetes*, this time) had come to Marsovan and large-scale massacres were being committed, he decided – under peril to his life – to come back to Marsovan on foot. He found us in the College. Hungry, exhausted, moved to tears, he threw himself tenderly in the arms of my mother, then mine, then my sister's. Then he noticed that my brothers were absent, and he lamented: "Aram! Haïgaz!" We calmed him down, they were alive. Some little orphans of the borough immediately went to get my brothers, found them, and then brothers were there ... their very selves!

In an interesting footnote to the story of Humayag's imprisonment, Aram notes that when he finally returned to Samsun he was arrested again. In Marsovan Humayag met Mihran who had been hiding for all this time in the underground hiding places, first in Haïganouch's house, and then in Tsolag's house. They traveled together to Samsun, but soon were spotted by a policeman. According to recorded oral testimony of my uncle Ara, a policeman attempted to arrest Mihran who fled, so Humayag was arrested. Restrictions on travel were so severe at the time that any movement between cities came under suspicion, especially when your identity papers did not record you as a resident of Samsun. Fortunately, Humayag managed to slip a note out to his father who came to the police station and verified his son's identity and residency. Humayag was finally released and was returned to the loving care of his family. My uncle's arrival in Samsun thus marked the end of his saga of arrests and

94. Photograph of Humayag Dildilian taken shortly after his release from prison in Amasia, August 1921.

imprisonment. He was never to see Marsovan, the home of his childhood, again. A photo of a haggard-looking and emaciated young Humayag rests in our family photo album as a grim reminder of this frightful episode.

The Crimes of Topal Osman:
The Dildilian Roots in Marsovan Are Severed Forever

With all but three of the Americans gone from Marsovan, the pressure on the Greeks and Armenians increased as spring turned into summer. Relief work with the orphans continued, but with the college closed all schooling stopped for the family. Travel was restricted and very dangerous. Fighting in the countryside between irregular forces of Greeks and Turks made travel perilous. The orphanage still had well over 300 orphans to care for, and the three remaining Americans ably organized their charges with assistance from the few Armenians and Greeks still left on their staff. In mid-June, two additional N.E.R. workers, Gertrude Anthony and Sarah Corning, were allowed to return to augment the staff. By July 1921, a disquieting calm had settled on the campus and the city, a calm that shattered with Topal Osman Agha's arrival on July 24.

Aram devotes a lengthy chapter in his memoir to Topal Osman. Surprisingly there is no mention of Topal Osman by name in Maritsa's notebooks. Aside from the comment quoted in the last section about Humayag rushing to Marsovan after his release because he heard that "large-scale massacres were being committed," there is no mention of the ordeals Maritsa and her family experienced that July. Aram was in Samsun and heard first-hand reports from survivors of the massacres that were taking place throughout the Black Sea coast as Topal Osman and his irregular militia attacked countless towns and villages. Topal Osman already had dirty hands from his early activities during the massacres and deportations of 1915. Aram refers to him as "that terrible hatchet man of Mustafa Kemal Pasha" who was charged with the task of annihilating "all the Greeks and Christians ... of the Pontus region." Osman "started his dirty work in Kerason [Giresun]" killing all the surviving Armenians and Greeks in the towns and villages as he headed west:

> Then they came to Ordu, Ounia [Ünye], Fatsa and Charshamba, ruthlessly killing, killing, killing the people, men, women, and children. We could see plainly at night from our house the red glow and the smoke in every valley and dale and hillside as he was nearing Samsun. Though we were in great fear as he was coming nearer to Samsun, he bypassed Samsun and went to Bafra, Alacham up to Kuzul Ermak [Kızılmark] (Alice River) openly killing, burning and destroying everything that was Greek.

Aram lived next door to the U.S. Consulate. He reports that he often complained to the Consul and the naval officers who gathered there that wholesale massacres were taking place and that the U.S. should do something to stop the carnage. He attributes the lack of action to Admiral Bristol and the Assistant Secretary of the Navy Franklin Delano Roosevelt, who effectively blocked information from reaching the President and his cabinet and the wider American public.[7]

After wreaking carnage along the Black Sea coast, Topal Osman finally arrived in Samsun. But this time he did not get his way. In Samsun a fascinating confrontation occurred between Topal Osman and one of the leading Turks of the city:

But fortunately, a wealthy Turkish merchant, Yousouff Zeddin Bey went to Topal Osman and asked him what he intends to do and who authorized him to do what he aims to do? He said Mustafa Kemal Pasha authorized him and gave the order to wipe out and eliminate all the Christians. Yousouff Zeddin Bey says, "No, you can't do that here, we can't sit still and let you do such an irresponsible thing like that and then we be held to give account for your killings. You better go where you came from; we can't let an outsider come over and do such killings. We can and are able to take care of our city so you better move on and be quick about it." But Topal Osman gets mad at him and slaps him and threatens bodily harm. At once, their bodyguards on both sides intervene and separated each other ... At once, Yousouff Zeddin Bey goes to the telegraph station and wires to Mustafa Kemal Pasha, call that madman back with his hordes. Sure enough, next morning, there was no more Topal Osman.

95. Topal Osman and his two guards, c.1915.

While the bulk of Topal Osman's Laz irregulars were kept out of Samsun, many entered in small numbers and carried on a campaign of assassinations and terror.

Aram reports that Osman and his men, numbering close to 1,000, proceeded toward Ankara, killing Greeks and Armenians in the towns of Kavak, Havza, and then arriving in Marsovan, which he had bypassed on his first sweep of the region. Osman's men arrived on July 23, while Osman himself arrived on the afternoon of July 24. Unlike in Samsun, resistance by the local authorities was minimal. In fact, Saduk Bey and the gendarmes often cooperated in the terror campaign that ensued:

In Marsovan, the mayor (kaimakam) when he finds out about his coming and his intentions, he refuses to cooperate and forbids him to carry on his proposed killings and orders him out ... But Topal Osman was a furious and fear-inspiring man, in anger attacks the mayor and threatens to kill him. So he goes and hides himself for safety in his friend's house at the south side of the town. So the killer Topal Osman had a picnic of his own. He orders his men to rob, rape, kill and do anything else to their hearts' content.

Many of the horrors that Aram goes on to describe were reported to him by his sister Haïganouch once she and the remaining members of the family had escaped to Samsun later in the summer of 1921. His nephews and nieces who also experienced the events in Marsovan corroborated the account.

Immediately upon the arrival of the forces of Topal Osman, violence began. Haïganouch is warned by the most unlikely of individuals:

That morning, my sister Haïganouch, knowing nothing about what is going on, starts to go down town for shopping. On her way, the Germege vineyards' watchman, Hasan Agha, who was a hatchet man and killed many Armenians seven years ago, in a trembling voice said to sister, "Where are you going Haïganouch hanum. I beg you do not go down town, the *chetes* are killing right and left. I just saw one right there at 'Akkash Cami.' I did not dare to go any farther, I am scared! Could you loan me a loaf of bread?" Sister gives him some. Before he departs he said "Haïganouch hanum, do not stay here. Take the children to the college compound as soon as you can." So sister takes some of the most essentials and takes the children to the college main gate but they refuse to open it and one of the Turkish guards said, "I will open the door if you give your daughter to me as wife." Naturally, sister gets very mad at him and gives him a proper answer and comes down to try Pampish Prapion's door. There the doorman was Kanty, he refused to take them in too. So she came up again to try the professor's door across from brother's house. She, in great anxiety, pushes the door with a supreme effort and the door opened by itself. Imagine, that door was never used from the time the teachers were deported. "God's ways are wonderful." That was a real miracle. At once she takes the children to the girls' school in safety and she turns back to arrange for Mihran (who was hiding at her home again). Sister while she was going back home hears some screams and voices of agony from her neighbor's house. At once she pushed open the door and sees four of Topal Osman's *chetes* who were raping and torturing the two young girls, survivors of deportation with their little brother! At once she grabs a big stick (a tzagh avel) from the corner and rushes in with a harsh and commanding voice, she orders them out saying, "How dare you to do that to an apostate family …" Imagine, they were armed yet like scared dogs they run away. So sister took the girls to the college compound through the same door and she rushes back home in great excitement. She gives some food to Mihran and told him, "you do anything you can to save yourself," and rushes back to her children in the college through the same door. She closes the door and piles up lots of big rocks against it. As soon as she goes in she started to make herself useful with Mr. Compton and the big orphan boys. They organized some groups of guards to watch the gates and walls … Some of the boys saw a chete near the cemetery wall. At once they send for Mr. Compton to come over. When he came over and sees the chete, he orders him out and not to come back. When the chete tries to go to the gate, he said, no, just go out where you come in from. Finally he had to climb the wall to the ridicule of the boys. My sister kept watch all night long on the girls' school side. In the morning before dawn, she sees a figure in the Zizangizian garden. She wanted to be sure what she sees was a girl almost nude, so at once she goes and takes a blanket and brings two women along. She puts a stepladder and goes over, covers her and brings her up the wall and puts her in bed and attends her till she was quite well of her shocks and exhaustion. She was one of the daughters of well-known Khatchig Varbed. The *chetes* came into their home at night, in front of the parents they did molest the two daughters and then they killed Khatchig Varbed and his wife. Just then this girl managed to escape to the roof and then from roof to roof was able to come up to that garden and was saved.

Aram tells us that he found it difficult to write about the horrors but believed that he had a moral obligation to do so because little had been written about these events in the region around the Black Sea. When he arrived in the United States he discovered that there was an almost total ignorance of what had happened. People may have been aware of the population exchange between Greece and Turkey that was codified in the Lausanne Treaty, but the violent ethnic cleansing that preceded it was little known. The Pontic Greek Genocide is an episode in history that has only gained attention in the last decade. The destruction of the surviving Armenian population of Anatolia was only a footnote to 1915. For economic and geo-political reasons the United States and its Western allies did much to downplay these events and to facilitate the denialist stance that soon characterized the Republic of Turkey's official history. Even in Armenian historiography, the fact that there were a significant number of surviving Armenians who had returned to Anatolia is not often acknowledged. Aram highlights the figures for Marsovan:

After the deportation there were left in Marsovan not more than 200 Armenians as apostates, but soon after the Armistice, because of the American Missions and because news went around that the British soldiers are coming over to protect the Armenians, soon people, the surviving Armenians came to Marsovan so there was more than 3,000 Armenians gathered there … Out of that 3,000, not more than a few hundred were saved, and those thanks to the College premises. They were saved, all the rest were killed. Killed ruthlessly and killed constantly. It is sickening what I wrote so far and will write some more because as I know, no one ever wrote about those devilish activities in Marsovan. So I better write for the sake of record to show how low man (so-called humans) could go down! The killings lasted several days. They went around to every house in search of Armenians. They even perforated with gun shots the ceilings and walls, with the idea that some Armenians might be hiding around.

The total figures that Aram cites are corroborated in other sources, though the figure of 200 apostates (converts) is too low given the numbers in the official municipal Ottoman registry and other written accounts.

Topal Osman made the Kiremidjian hotel his official headquarters during his visit to Marsovan. Garabed Kiremedjian at this point had left Turkey, but his mother and father still resided in the family mansion. They were both killed by Osman's men. Others who had survived the genocide were also killed, including one of the Anatolia students who was hidden by Aram and Haïganouch: "Few days later, the town crier told the public, saying all those who have been robbed or anything taken away, can put a demand at the Kiremidjian Hotel, the headquarters of Topal Osman … Two of our friends, one of whom I had kept, Hovhanness Sivaslian, go over to demand his horse and the other his lost cow. They both were killed on the spot. They had tortured Hovhanness to death."

Many local Turks participated in the killings and many more in the pillage of the houses that followed. Other local Turks did what they could to rescue their Armenian and Greek neighbors. Aram tells a story about one survivor who was both harmed and helped by locals. Though long, the story is worthy of retelling because it highlights the good and the evil found in humankind:

A carpenter, Hagop Agha and another young man were hiding in an attic for 4 days, no one knew about them. But a former Turkish army officer who had lost an eye in the battle on the front with the Armenian volunteers, had vowed to himself to kill as many Armenians as he could, so he considers this a good opportunity. He goes around and searches for Armenians in empty houses. By chance he goes to the same house where the two were hiding. He cries, "Anybody home?" Poor things, they thought that must be a friend calling. They hide a revolver that they had with them under the tile of the roof and come down. When he sees them, he express[es] sympathy and tells them, "You stay here till dark and then I will come and take you to a safe place …" Later he comes and lets them out and tells them to go down to the street towards the river to the tannery. Then he orders them to undress and kneel down, one blow to each of them with the "yataghan" (big knife). They fall on top of each other. Towards dawn, Hagop Agha comes to himself but he could not raise his head up and feels very cold. He feels with his hands around him and notices that one of the bodies is quite warm so he cuddles himself to keep warm. When it was real light, he sees two Turks passing by so he calls for help. One of them says, "Oh! that gavoor is not dead, let us kill him!" The other said, "No, don't do that, he had enough ..." Then Hagop pleads [with] them to cut a tree branch for him, they do that ... He gets up holding his head up with one hand and leaning heavily on the stick with the other.

In the meantime, the mayor of the city who was hiding in his friend's house from fear of Topal Osman, disturbed and sleepless, was sitting at the window of his friend's parlor. He sees some one coming up the street like a ghost in white underwear. So at once he tells his servant jandarma to meet and bring him up to him. When he finds out what has happened to him, he sympathizes with him and makes him dress up with a suit of clothes and sends him to the municipal pharmacy to be taken care of ... His assassin, the Keor Binbashi, who had a grocery store across the street of the drugstore comes in the morning to open his store, he sees the carpenter inside the drugstore and in anger grabs his pound weight iron and throws it at Hagop's chest crying with a swear word saying "you gavoor infidel, are you alive yet!" Poor Hagop, he falls down on the floor as he was weak, hungry, and had no strength left in him ... Those around him lift him up in pity and sit him in his chair ... Finally, the druggist comes along, dressed his wounds and takes him to an empty house nearby, gives him a cup of hot tea and made him lie down on the floor. Next day when he came to change his wounds, he asked him if he had a sister. He said, "Yes, but I don't know where is she ..." Next morning the druggist brings his sister along. One can well understand their joy and excitement. That man is well and alive now; the neck is broken but he works and is making his living in Paris, France. His sister was miraculously alive and survived too.

Aram concludes the story by explaining how the municipal druggist located Hagop's sister. We see in what he writes that the local military was complicit in the massacre. There are also eyewitness accounts by the Americans that corroborate this complicity. Aram writes:

After the killings were over, the Government, as I said the civilian government, was rendered helpless ... So the military gathered together all the scattered surviving Armenians and put them in the mess hall of the Catholic Jesuit school and was planning what to do with them. One of the officers on the ground conceives a devilish idea. He orders his men to pile some wood in front of all the windows and the doors and put kerosene and matches to it. Just about that moment the young but higher ranked officer who was away comes back to the spot. He sees what is going on. He

314

could not stand the cries and struggle of the poor victims so at once breaks open the door and saves them from burning alive and ordered his man to take them to the big famous stone barracks and give them a loaf of bread each. Some were wounded and some were sick so the municipal pharmacist goes to take care of them. It was among those that he finds the sister of that Hagop Agha. Thanks to God, there are good people everywhere like that young Army officer and the druggist who do good and wipe away our tears.

The incident in the Catholic Jesuit school is recorded in separate reports written by three of the Americans on the campus that confirm the military's complicity in these crimes. Donald Hosford describes in chilling detail what transpired within the school before it was set on fire. Several of the Armenian N.E.R. workers were among those confined to the school and were able to tell their stories. Sexual violence dominated the crimes taking place there and in other locations around Marsovan. The fire that consumed the Jesuit school was not the only fire that broke out that day. Fires were deliberately set in two to four other locations, mostly in the Armenian quarter. Over 400 houses were burned to the ground, mostly those of Armenians but a few owned by Turks. Residents who hid in their homes were shot or hacked to death as they tried to flee the fires. Some were thrown back into the flames and burned alive. The bodies of those who were not incinerated were buried in mass graves and one of the American witnesses confirmed that some victims were buried alive.[8]

The direct killing and pillaging by Osman and his men ended on Wednesday, July 27 though many locals and the military carried on the carnage until July 31. Aram relates one last story about Topal Osman. After his dirty work, it was time for a bath:

> After his destruction of the souls and bodies of the poor survivors was accomplished, he [Topal Osman] goes to the Turkish bath, the Zuloom Hamami (torture bath) it was called because it was built by forced labor. He goes at night to take a bath with his top men. He orders them to bring some Christian girls and women to satisfy their devilish lust and animal instinct … So his men by force and persuasion and trickery were able to round up several women and took them over to the bath house. In the meantime an elderly lady, a simple, fine Christian lady, a well-known friend of ours, the mother of a very fine friend of mine now in New York … She, in pity to those women, volunteers herself to go with them to protect them and be an encouragement to them, without knowing exactly what was to confront the poor souls and herself. After untold satanic actions … and feast … he orders his men to throw them into the fiery furnace of the bath house so that he and his men would enjoy the bath in water heated by the poor souls' body heat … Unbelievable? Yes, no one believes, no one could believe such a devilish action, but this thing actually had taken place. My sister, Haïganouch has seen and has heard all from eye witnesses.

A full account of what happened during that last week in July has never been written but there certainly is enough documentation to do so. In the future, I just may revisit this horrible chapter, however reluctantly. Aram would be pleased.

Needless to say the events of July 1921 were the final culminating horror that ended any hope that Haïganouch and the Dildilian children could still remain in Marsovan. As soon as she secured safe passage, Haïganouch moved the remaining members of the family to Samsun. Aram found a house for her near his studio and for a brief time an uneasy peace returned to the family.

Thus ended the 30 years of Dildilian life in Marsovan. No member of the family would set foot in the city again until the start of the new millennium, when Aram's eldest son Armen and his wife Margaret, in search of the family home, made a brief visit in 2000. The same year, Haïk Der Haroutiounian, Haïganouch's grandson, visited on the first of many trips in search of the family's roots. Given the horrors that the family experienced during the seven-year period from 1914 to 1921, horrors often discussed within the family, one can understand why most members of the family would find such a journey home traumatic. When I first visited Marsovan in 2011 in search of my mother's home, I had no expectation of the warm welcome that I would receive. As I walked the streets of my ancestors, I felt the weight of a history of suffering, one whose full dimensions I was still learning as I prepared to lay the groundwork for this book and an exhibition of the Dildilian Brothers' photography – an exhibition that I would eventually take to my mother's hometown.

The Last Year in our Homeland

The family was now reunited in Samsun but the dangers still remained. The pressures of the local Turkish officials on Aram and the orphanage were increasing. While the explosive violence and pillaging that took place in Marsovan was not repeated in Samsun, the Turkish irregulars often infiltrated the city and harassed and killed Christians. The Greek population was slowly disappearing either through deportations, arrests and executions, or if they were lucky, by emigration.

The initial cooperative attitude of the local Turkish authorities had changed dramatically. The nationalists were now in control and were intent on Turkifying the Armenian remnant. Young orphans were prime candidates for such Turkification. Aram describes two examples of such attempts:

> Twice the Chief of Police called me to his headquarters and demanded some Turkish girls that (supposedly) I am holding in my orphanage as Armenians! I assured him that we had not one single Turkish child in the orphanage. He called me a second time and demanded 9 Turkish girls that are in your orphanage, "We

have proof and you must turn them over to us." When I said, "Positively no, we have no Turkish girls or girls taken out of Turkish homes," he, with an angry and dirty mouth, started to lash me with his hard whip saying, "I will make your good leg lame like the other one" with a very insulting tongue ... He did not know that the lame leg of mine was wooden and was caused by another fanatic Turk like him when I was but a little innocent child.

A few days later, three young Turks came to my office all nicely dressed up. After some sweet and polite conversation, they came out openly and asked if it was possible for them to get married with our orphan girls ... and one of them said, "if at least you could give us some of those girls you have taken from Turkish village people because you Armenians know how to educate and train children." I said, "We have no Turkish girls in this orphanage and our girls are too young to get married. Besides, I have no authority to arrange marriages – that is up to the American Board." They departed displeased.

Aram comments that these two incidents were related. The authorities were trying to gather evidence in order to shut down the orphanage and possibly arrest its Armenian staff. The Rev. Pavlides, acting as the American Mission Agent in Marsovan, had been accused of kidnapping Turkish children from villages and placing them in the orphanage at the college. He was subsequently hanged. As we know today, many young women and boys were forcibly assimilated during this period. Many people today in Turkey are discovering that one of their grandparents was Armenian.

Besides the official threats, there was always the danger of the guerrillas turning up and abducting young women. On a number of occasions Aram had to call for help from the N.E.R. director, since calling the police would only compound the threat. Aram himself was put under surveillance and searches were made looking for incriminating evidence of his subversive activities:

One afternoon, the Mutasarrıf came to our orphanage. The minute I heard about his coming, I rushed to greet him and invited him to my office. He refused to come to my office in a very cold manner and said he wanted to see a few of our buildings and the school room. I said, I would gladly take him over but I added that we have had no school for the last year and a half ... Now all we do is teach the children housework, needlework, sewing, shoe making, carpentry, and feed them. He never showed any interest whatsoever in what I said or showed him. He wanted to see the school room, so I led him over ... Then he asked me some personal questions. He asked me how I knew the English language, how it happens that I was directing this orphanage, and why I walk lame ... He started to go to his Landau and I asked him once more to come in for refreshments but he refused ... A few days later they made a search of my photographic studio and took along all books and pictures. Five days later they sent them all back. A few days later, the Chief of Police calls a friend of ours and asked him, "What do you know about that Dildilian?" He added, "We were given a list of dangerous Armenians, his name is the first. We have put detectives after him for more than a month. All we have seen is that he goes to the Americans, to his brother's and back to the orphanage. We did not find anything wrong with him."

In addition to pressures experienced by Aram, the N.E.R. itself was being pressured by the Ankara authorities. The war with Greece was raging on and supplies were needed for the army. Aram comments that the Turks often requisitioned N.E.R. fuel and supplies. The nationalists were now also aided by their one-time enemies, the Russians, in this case, the Bolsheviks:

> Every other week systematically, a Russian side-wheeler steamer used to come into Samsun harbor and unloaded all sorts of war goods, airplanes, guns, rifles, ammunition and other war supplies ... It was strange that as soon as that side-wheeler was gone, without fail the Greek warships would come over, but they missed the boat always. Something else, each time the Greek warships showed themselves, the U.S. destroyer would go out to parley and send the Greeks off ... the Turks had friends in the Red Russians, Americans, and British ... that way they became stronger and stronger.

We know that the Kemalist forces were aided materially and financially by the Soviets but British or American aid is more questionable. We now know that assistance was also given by the French and the Italians because of their rivalry with the British.

The front lines of the war were far away, but on one occasion the war came directly to Samsun. The Greek and Allied navies dominated the waters of the Black Sea. The Greeks conducted a limited number of naval bombardments of seaports on the coast. Samsun was hit on one occasion, June 7, 1922. Aram reports that the orphanage was hit, while there was no damage to ammunition stores that were the intended target:

> News came to me that the Greek warships were coming over to bombard. On such occasions we knew what to do. First we were told to put up a Red Cross flag and later the sailors will come over to protect the orphans. But later we were told to protect the orphans the best possible way we can ... Every one of our buildings had big basements with heavy stone walls. We had water, and bread, and first-aid kits stored in each house and had appointed two big boys as protectors and as helping hands. At once I sent word to the teachers to take the children down in their respective basements. Before we had a chance to go down with the children in our building, the bombardment started and three shells burst up in the backyard

of our house ... Once we were down, we felt quite safe but [the] constant boom of the big guns was frightful to all of us. My little Margaret huddled her little head in my chest and said, "Turks boom, boom" while the cannonading was going on by both sides as [the] Turks had two big guns on top of the hill just above our house, the guns that the Russians brought in, real long-barreled ones. The Greeks had the "Averoff" [flagship of the Royal Hellenic Navy] ... We heard some commotion out in the street. At once, we went out to see what is wrong. We saw the children from the 4th building across the street. All 6- and 7-year-olds are out in the street running all around crying, "Father, Father." We brought them to our building for safety. It was a real miracle as shrapnel burst up on the main floor in a big closet where we had 12 sewing machines. All were smashed into small pieces, the ceiling, the walls, and the floor boards were perforated just like sieves and all those children were underneath but thanks to God, not one child was hurt or had a scratch on them. They were just scared and ran out into the street. When everything was over, we find out that the kerosene warehouse is still burning, and when we went up to our sitting room, a piece of shell had pierced the wall and fell on the rug ... The bombardment lasted about one hour. The Government building was hit many times but it did not do much damage. A good many houses were hit and damaged but no one was killed except an Armenian girl in the Greek quarters. It is queer that out of thousands of Turks and Greeks, an Armenian will be killed out of a few survivors of the deportation.

The *New York Times* reported that the government building was destroyed along with 40 houses. Slight damage was done to the American Tobacco Company's warehouse and the Standard Oil Company's fuel storage facility was destroyed, but the Turkish army munitions dump was not hit. Ankara reported four dead and five injured.[9]

Aram reports that he often begged the Near East Relief director, Mr. J. E. VanToor, to arrange for an evacuation of the orphans to either Constantinople or Armenia. A fleet of U.S. destroyers operated in the Black Sea and often called into port in Samsun. Aram argued that it would have been easy for the Americans to transport the orphans, but his requests were rejected. On one occasion the captain of the U.S.S. *Sands*, a Captain Robert Ghormley, asked Aram to help arrange for a Protestant funeral for one of his sailors. With no minister available at the time, my grandfather Tsolag, who was a deacon in his church back in Marsovan, officiated. The sailor was buried in a grave near the gravesite of Tsolag's eldest son, my uncle Hratchia. The family helped the American navy but received no assistance in return.

The stalemate in the Greco-Turkish War broke in the summer of 1922. The Greek army was in a rapid retreat by the end of August. Given the wartime restrictions, news of the war was limited. Aram reports receiving conflicting accounts of victory and defeat. As Ottoman citizens, Aram and the family had to show outward loyalty to the Turkish side in this war. After eight years of often violent persecution, it was hard to show any loyalty to a state that had tried to eradicate them from the face of the earth, yet a pretense of loyalty had to be maintained in order to avoid the fate of many of their ethnic Armenian brethren. Aram reports a conversation with a Turkish army doctor:

> In conversation, he gave us the only authentic news we ever had. He told that really we were almost defeated. The Greeks were about to capture Ankara. But we do not know what happen[ed]! Everything changed, the Greeks are on the run, not retreating but running, leaving everything behind and are running ... It was an awkward position for us. Inwardly we were sorry, very sorry about the news as all our hopes once more were shattered, yet on the other hand we had to pretend we were happy about the good news ... Oh! how often these last eight years we had to pretend and show or express things we did not feel and did not believe ... At the time of our deportation, we had three British civilian prisoners in our house, given by the Turkish government. One most critical day I asked one "what should we do about those never-ending pretendings?" He said, "Keep on doing what you are doing because you have not a government to take account for you, while I, I will not stand a minute those degradations. If I am killed, there stands Great Britain to call account for me. But you have no one but yourselves."

"You have no one but yourselves" – that seems to have been the fate of the Dildilian family and the Armenians in general. Despite assurances from various friends around the world, at the worst of times our family had to rely on its own ingenuity and courage to survive. This proved again to be the case once it was clear that it was time to leave their homeland.

The Final Exile: No Home for Armenians in their Homeland

The motto "Turkey for the Turks" finally came true for the Dildilian and Haroutiounian families in November 1922. The Armenian Question would be no more, for, in principle, there would no longer be Armenians on Turkish soil. Aram describes the Kemalist government's decision:

> The town crier announced that all the Christians, Greeks, and Armenians should get out of the country, up to or on November 1, 1922. All those who do not get out of the country will be considered Turks. There was no other alternative ... I had to think about the orphans, about my sister and brother's families. I went to the N.E.R. office to discuss the matter. I was assured that they will have a chartered boat for the orphans, orphanage help, and my family ... I suggested

making Armenian dried bread, basmet, and cheese, but they said the chartered boat will come over with plenty of provisions.

The family thus began to prepare for their departure, but it remained unclear where their destination would be. My mother has testified that Tsolag thought that a relocation to Constantinople was possible. According to the terms of the yet to be negotiated Lausanne Treaty, the city would be exempt from the population exchange and still retained a significant Armenian community.

What transpired in the course of the next few days is not specifically detailed in Aram's memoir, while Tsolag and Maritsa's accounts are completely silent about the family's departure from Turkey. In oral accounts by my mother and uncle Ara, November is confirmed as the month of departure. Soon after the proclamation of the expulsion of "non-Turks" from the country was made, the family began preparations for their eventual departure. When the actual time came for them to leave, very little notice was provided. From Aram's account the family had been given less than a 12-hour notice to pack and board the ship. He writes:

> Mr. J. H. Crutcher, the new N.E.R. manager, came to my house late at night and said, "Though we had planned for your orphanage a special transportation, the British steamer Belgravia, has come for the Greek orphanage and we figured there is room enough for your orphanage too, so round up all your people and try to be on board the ship at 8 a.m. So I told my wife and mother-in-law to take care of our belongings and pack up as much as you can and forget the rest ... At once, I sent the news to my brother and sister to pack up everything and be on board the Belgravia at 8 a.m.

I cannot imagine being told to pack up one's belongings in the course of one night, knowing full well that this will probably be the final time one will be on the soil of Anatolia. I do not know how much in the way of household belongings they packed, but they did pack many photographs and negatives in addition to their cameras. I find it remarkable that I possess boxes of glass negatives that they must have packed that night. They weigh a considerable amount and only a few are broken despite a journey from Marsovan to Samsun by carriage, Samsun to Athens by steamer, and Athens to the United States by ocean liner.

For Aram the first priority was the orphans. The N.E.R. officials did not make his job any easier:

> I went to each one of our orphanage buildings and made all the necessary arrangements. I had already given a complete list of my group but in the morning Mr. Crutcher sent me word demanding a new list in triple copies. So I had to do that and take care of every detail in each building. We made sure that each child

would have a change of underwear, a blanket, and some cheese and bread in his bag. In the meantime, I sent word to a couple of boys who were discharged to come back and join the group, and added a few more names of orphanage help. I made sure that every single one is at the pier on time with their teachers. I went around once more to each building with our watchman, Osman Agha, to be sure of everything, and left the building and the furniture in his charge. And, for the last time, I went back home to pack up a few more things of our belongings... I was sleepless, hungry, and tired, and was trying to pack up a few more of my belongings when a lady N.E.R. worker came and forced me to let everything go and come to the pier and make one more list of my group ... for what, no one knows as I had already submitted more than seven lists.

Just when Aram thought all was clear for him to board the ship, an old nemesis from Marsovan made his appearance. This was Saduk Bey, the commissar whose aim in life was to rid Anatolia of all but the Turks. He had collaborated with Topal Osman the year before to destroy the Armenians and Greeks of Marsovan. It seems that he had made a discovery about his traitorous neighbors the Dildilians:

Well, I left at 2 p.m. and went to the pier. Just as I was entering the gate of the custom house, I saw one of the Mauamy brothers, Saduk, coming after me. When I saw him coming, a sharp chill passed through my body. As soon as I entered [the pier], I went zig-zag in back of the big bales ... As I have mentioned before, he was our neighbor during the war days at Prof. Hagopian's house and during the war days we had dug an underground hiding place from brother's house to Hagopian's yard. We had in our front yard, two big cherry trees and one wet day, a stormy wind toppled down one of those big trees and opened wide the hiding place ... We were told that he was to come over to Samsun to put us under arrest ... Well it was a miracle that I saw him coming up the street. He should have [been able] to see me, if not by anything else, my walking should have betrayed me, but evidently he missed me, thanks to God ... I sat on one of the bales and started to write one more list of orphans as I was asked to. While I was writing, a policeman came by and was watching me write with my fountain pen. He was surprised that I wrote continuously without dipping the pen in any ink well, so he asked me if I would let him have it. I said, "I will, but after I write this for the 'American boss.'" Finally, when I finished my writing, the policeman was gone and I did not have to give my pen away. The name "American" had some magic effect on Turks. In the past, each time the Greek warships showed up on the horizon, the U.S. destroyer would go for a parley. Turks never worried. They used to say, "Our American (Amerikhali) friends are going out to chase them away." They were so sure and right ...

Finally I gave the list to Osman Agha, tipped him, bid him goodbye, and went into the rowboat to take me to the S.S. Belgravia.

This would be the last encounter that Aram would have with a Turk in a position of authority who could determine whether he was to live or die. The desire on the policeman's part to have Aram's fountain pen is laughable in light of all that had been taken from the family over the prior decade – homes, businesses, household possessions, books, brothers, sisters, nieces, nephews, uncles, aunts, cousins, friends, a whole way of life taken away and never to be returned. What could not be taken away were their memories of a homeland; memories captured in photographs, drawings, paintings and stories passed on orally and on the written page to future generations, to me.

The Odyssey of the Exiles

Tsolag and Haïganouch and their families had boarded the ship earlier in the day. Aram was the last to be rowed out to the *Belgravia*: "I was out on the open sea free from sudden and certain death ... I was tired, exhausted, and excited and hardly able to climb the long steps of the steamer. I fell down on the top platform unconscious. I do not know [for] how long or what they did to revive me."

The family was now on the open seas but the freedom they felt was soon to be accompanied by miserable conditions on board the overcrowded S.S. *Belgravia*. What a great irony to have this ship named the *Belgravia*. I had first encountered this name when I visited London as a college student in 1970. Experiencing London for the first time, I explored the very posh neighborhood of Belgravia, a corner of that great metropolis whose understated elegance and wealth continues to this day. This is a far cry from what the family faced on that ship with the same name in 1922:

> As I said before, "The Belgravia" was hired for the Greek orphanage so naturally, the Greek children and Greek teachers were well located in good and proper quarters, and my children and the teachers were put down below the portholes with no air. There were no cabins left for us. We were left in the open on a crowded deck with more than 1,200 children and people. Especially my family was left in the open, in a nook 2x6 [feet], on top of the upper deck and it was about to rain, too. I noticed my darling Margaret, 2-1/2 years old, shivering from the cold wind and so was my wife, who was pregnant. No one, the captain, or anyone else cared. A good thing my brother was able to hire the cabin of the ship's first engineer for $40, and we all huddled in that big room and tried to be as comfortable as we could, about 15 or 16 of us. I was sick and weak, and was much worried about my wife ... yet no one cared for us.

Having lived in the United States for over three years starting in 1904, Aram should have been prepared for the kind of prejudice against "Orientals" that was soon to be displayed against the family:

Two young American men and a young girl dressed in Georgian style, a whip in her hand, came to our cabin and ordered us out saying, "What right have you got to occupy this room?" The Greek sailors put us out by carrying our stuff out. Soon, we found the engineer from whom we hired the room and told him what happened. He was very mad and said, "It is my room and I have the right to do anything with it, no one can interfere with me." So we moved back again, but we paid him $10 extra in gratitude ... We were at the stern of the ship. I was helplessly sick, but thanks to my brother and nephews, they took charge of our orphans and did everything to make them comfortable and safe.

Despite all the responsibilities of taking care of the orphans, Tsolag found the time to document the family's exodus. He took about a dozen photographs shipboard on their odyssey. These are some of the most extraordinary photographs in the collection:

96. Aram's wife, Christine, and my grandmother, Mariam,
on the S.S. *Belgravia* leaving Samsun harbor, November 1922.

These photographs were taken under the most trying circumstances for besides the overcrowded conditions and a lack of adequate provisions, a storm soon ravaged the ship. The N.E.R. officials had not adequately prepared for the enormous task of moving two large orphanages:

97. Orphans on the deck of the S.S. *Belgravia*. My grandmother Mariam on the ladder in the distance pointing to the life preserver, November 1922.

I had suggested a good many things but none were accepted, none were done. There was no food or any arrangement for food. We had plenty of bread but all was moldy and impossible to eat. We could get along for a few days but, unfortunately, the first night we had a terrible storm at sea ... The captain, instead of trying to find shelter in Sinop, which had the only natural and safe harbor, tried to go to Odessa for safety. On the way, the storm broke the front top mast. By the time we arrived in Odessa, the storm was quieted down so we had to turn back to Constantinople. The journey that would have taken two days, took us more than five days. We did not have any water closets (only one for the officers) so the poor children had to use the open deck and it was up to my boys to clean the deck three or four times each day. There was little drinking water – we had it rationed. My boys had to pump the water into a dirty olive oil barrel. First the Greeks would drink and then my children had to drink whatever was left in the bottom after so many hundreds of dirty hands and rusty milk cans had plunged in and out of the same barrel!

The *Belgravia* finally reached Constantinople after what had been a harrowing journey, but the worst was still to come. As she dropped anchor in Sereye-Bournou [Sarayburnu], the Dildilian family still did not know its ultimate fate.

Constantinople was in turmoil. An armistice had been declared in the war between the Greeks and the Turks in mid-October. The British still controlled the city, but their days were numbered. The city was overrun with refugees and the fate of the Greek and Armenian minorities was still to be negotiated. The ship was scheduled to continue on to Piraeus with all the orphans. The Armenian orphans could no longer stay in Turkey. Tsolag still may have harbored thoughts of staying. My mother reported that her father and older brother Humayag disembarked to investigate the possibility of resettling in the city. They soon returned to the boat highly discouraged. Friends advised them that conditions were not good for Armenians and that wherever the ship was going, they should stay on it and go there.

The ship was provisioned and preparations made for the outward journey to Greece. Aram describes the next hurdle that they would need to overcome:

We were anchored in between two big lumber steamers and an ocean liner "New York." I was sick and weak and was sitting on the deck and getting fresh air and sunshine and my wife was standing on the steps. We noticed the lumber boat was coming toward us and soon we were squeezed in between the two big boats with a big crash that shook us violently. We did not know what was happening. The children around us were excited and started crying, "Hayrig, Hayrig" (father), "We are sinking!" Just then, my wife fell down the steps from the terrible jolt. At once, my nephews lifted her up and carried her in to her bed. Thanks to God, nothing happened to her. Later, we found out that the lumber boat had lost its

326

anchor and drifted toward our boat and smashed us in between the ocean liner. Well, this time we had a cracked side and the water started leaking into the hold. My boys were ordered to put the water out by the pailful, day and night, till we arrived in Piraeus Athens.

The absurdity of this situation is beyond belief. Despite the damage, the ship was expected to continue on. Aram begged the N.E.R. officials in Constantinople to find a new boat, but after three days in anchorage, they were forced to sail on to Greece with the orphan boys taking shifts to keep the vessel afloat. Despite the fact that both Greek and Armenian orphan boys were on the ship, the Greeks were not required to help in bailing out the water. Aram reports that the Greek boys were often unsupervised and caused trouble. He had not seen the Greek orphanage director during the eight days on the ship.

I had always been curious as to why there were few postcards in the family collection of images from their homeland. The Dildilian Brothers studio had many of their photographs made into postcards in the years prior to the First World War. I have often seen these postcards in auctions and they fetch the highest bids. I have purchased some for as much as 250 euros each. One explanation as to their rarity in the family inheritance is explained by the following remark by Aram:

> I could not understand why and who ordered my boys only to do all those hard and dirty tasks while the Greek boys were loitering around and stealing goods. They had opened one of my crates and taken away my collection of fine prints and post cards. By the time I was told and sent my nephews, they had thrown them into the sea.

When Aram complained to the N.E.R. representative on the ship, he was told that all orphans are to be treated the same since there would soon no longer be such an identity as Armenian. Mr. Bates, the representative, stated the following:

> "Well you should know that henceforth Armenians are no more to be a nation or a community. They will be a part of the people wherever and whatever country they are to be located. Those who stay in Turkey will become Turks, and those who do not care to stay in Turkey are free to go to any country whose doors are open to them" (unfortunately, those open doors were very few and were not very wide open either ...). About N.E.R. orphans he said, "There are no Armenian or Greek orphans. We will treat them all equal. As soon as they are of age they will be discharged and put on farms, gardens or in any other occupations they are fitted for, and the girls they will be put in Greek homes as house maids or go to find husbands of their own ..." It was useless for me to keep up a conversation with that heartless and cold man who created in me a tempest, a sudden storm in my heart

and mind so that I was about to burst ... who was he, and what authority had he or for that matter how dare he pronounce such a verdict or a death warrant to a nation which had a glorious past and present?

As the ship steamed away from Constantinople, Aram gathered all the orphans and teachers together on the stern of the ship and addressed them. His short speech was his rebuttal to what the N.E.R. official had told him. He believed that accepting such an assimilationist view was tantamount to complicity with what the Young Turks had tried to do to the Armenians in 1915. He summarizes his remarks:

> We will be separated one from another, our Armenian orphanage will not be left a separate unit and "you will be put with the Greek orphans and when you are big enough, you will be sent to Greek villages or Greek houses as housemaids or servants. Maybe you will be forced to get married with Greeks or other people, or you may be left out in the street on your own ... There was a time when all of you had your own father and mother and your own homes. But the Turks have killed your parents and thousands of others. You were uprooted and were left orphans, yet you were fortunate that you were left alive while thousands were killed. I, with your teachers, worked hard to make you happy and tried to make you forget that you were orphans. Now things are changed, we won't be able to help you but let me tell you, no matter wherever you may be or in whatsoever state you are subjected to, first go to your loving heavenly Father in prayer. Second, do not forget that you are Armenians, descendants of the oldest Christian nation. Yes, we are just a few survivors of a great little nation, we are neglected now and are downtrodden but now we have a homeland. The new Armenia is a small country and has no friends ... but we hope and believe some sweet day it will grow to be big and will be able to provide room enough for her roaming and scattered children ... no matter wherever you are, do not forget that you are Armenians."

Aram was well aware that the fledgling Republic of Armenia had succumbed to Soviet and Turkish military assaults in late 1920 and that this "new Armenia" was now part of the Soviet Union. Yet Aram wanted to instill in these children the hope for the future rebirth of their homeland.

Finally the ship arrived in the port of Piraeus. According to my uncle Ara's oral testimony, the ship had encountered another storm and was listing badly when it arrived. He claims that they had been journeying for 20 days. The Greek orphans were allowed to disembark, but the Armenians were prevented from doing so. A new ordeal was to begin:

> The next morning we arrived in Piraeus, the port of Athens. At once they took out all the Greek children, we don't know where, and then they put us all into two big

328

barges and took us to a small island, Ayos Yorios. There were no civilians, but a small military guardhouse, a big metal hangar, a few soldiers and one commander in charge, a real kind-hearted man ... Again the same thing was repeated. Why did they take us to that island? Who was the one who gave the order and arranged the thing? Why did they take the Greeks out into Athens and take us to that island? I was not informed or consulted at all, and why not?

I cannot be certain as to the date that the S.S. *Belgravia* finally reached Piraeus but the journey from Constantinople at that time usually took no more than two days. The family and the orphans were on the quarantine island for about a week before Aram was finally given permission to leave and make arrangements for the orphans in Athens. While on the island he heard a volley of gunshots that marked the execution of the six government ministers and generals who were held responsible for the defeat in the Greco-Turkish War, often referred to as the "Great Asia Minor Catastrophe." These executions took place on November 28, 1922. My family must have arrived in Greece, albeit on this isolated little island, sometime the week before.

Conditions throughout Greece at this time were horrendous. The small country of 5 million people had to absorb between 1.2 and 1.5 million refugees. These refugees had been pouring into Greece for well over a year before the Convention Concerning the Exchange of Greek and Turkish Populations was signed between Greece and Turkey on January 30, 1923. This convention would be incorporated into the Lausanne Treaty ratified later in August that would formally codify the exchange, establish the Turkish Republic's borders, and bring to a final conclusion the conflict that had begun with the First World War. Turkey was also facing huge Muslim refugee flows that had begun well over a decade earlier. The family faced great challenges upon its arrival in Athens. At first they, along with all of the orphans, were housed inside the neoclassical Zappeion Palace that had functioned as a museum before the arrival of the refugees. Many public buildings and spaces were used to house the refugees. My uncle Ara humorously remarks that his first night sleeping on the Greek mainland was under the legs of a large dinosaur skeleton. Aram's frustrations with N.E.R. continued to grow as his recommendations were ignored and his wards were put into unsanitary and dangerous conditions. The orphans were finally moved to an abandoned airfield outside of the city where the conditions were even more difficult than at the Zappeion Palace. Finally out of frustration Aram resigned his position as director of the orphanage. A N.E.R. official had told him that they could provide him and his pregnant wife a private room but that their child Margaret would have to sleep with the rest of the orphans. As he states bluntly in his memoir: "That did it! I had to go out voluntarily."

Tsolag was soon able to rent a half-finished house in which the family lived together for a few months. Tsolag would build a make-shift photography studio in the midst of the refugee camp which was quickly turning into a small town.

Aram and Haïganouch and their families soon joined him. Because of the threat of typhus, smallpox and cholera, Tsolag moved his family to a farm in the countryside and supplemented their meager earnings by living off the land. My mother had some happy memories of farm life in the summer of 1923.

The months ahead would see both joy and sorrow for the three remaining heads of the family, Aram, Tsolag, and Haïganouch. Aram would see the birth of his first son, Armen in January 1923, but in May he was devastated by the death of his daughter Margaret. The struggles that the Dildilian and Der Haroutiounian families faced in Greece and beyond are not directly part of the journey I have taken you on in this book, but I will say just a few more words. By June of 1923, the three siblings' paths would irrevocably be parted.

After the loss of his daughter, Aram decided to return to the United States and convinced the United States consul to grant his family a visa, but they still needed to come under that year's immigration quota. They departed Greece on June 9, 1923 and raced across the Atlantic Ocean, arriving in New York harbor just in time to beat the closure of that year's allocation.

Unable to find a way to enter the United States in order to reunite with her sister Nevart, Haïganouch and her family emigrated to Marseille, France, arriving there June 20, 1923. Garabed Médaksian had been engaged to Maritsa, our storyteller, in Samsun and they would soon marry after reaching France.

My grandfather Tsolag, unable to bring his family to the United States, would settle in the neighborhood of Nikea between Athens and the port of Piraeus. He opened a highly successful photography studio and brought his son Humayag and later his daughter Alice into the business. His son Jiraïr would succumb to the dreaded tuberculosis that had earlier taken the life of his eldest, Hratchia. His son Ara would finish his education in the reopened Anatolia College in Thessaloniki and then at Northeastern University in Boston, marrying and settling in New England.

I began this story with my grandmother Mariam, who lived the last few years of her life in that little bedroom next to mine. After my grandfather Tsolag had died and that other great war had ended, my grandmother and mother emigrated to the United States. With the marriage of my mother, soon my brother and I were born.

I end my story in 1923. That year marks the end of a journey that began so long ago with a blacksmith in the city of Sivas in central Anatolia. As I write these last words, I stare up at a large family portrait that hangs on the wall of my study. It is a photograph taken late in 1922 just prior to my family's exile from their homeland. Captured in this photograph are all 18 of the surviving members of my family who had experienced the genocide and its aftermath in Anatolia. This was the last group photograph taken of the family before their journeys would take them to distant parts of the world. It is a Dildilian photograph, expertly posed and highly evocative. My grandfather stares proudly and confidently into the camera, while my grandmother's eyes reflect a hidden yet deep sorrow that

98. Last group portrait of the Dildilian, Der Haroutiounian,
and Nakkashian families, Samsun, late 1922.

will remain with her throughout her life. My mother Alice sits on the floor in the foreground of the image. She has a sweet, almost impish smile on her face. She will live a long and happy life, a life with good memories, some of which will take her back to her early childhood days in the midst of her warm and loving family in Marsovan. I must end my story here and leave you, my readers, with all these memories – memories that in the course of writing this book have now become my own.

NOTES

Chapter 1: The Dildilians of Sivas

1   The Turkish word for pony is "*midilli*." *Ege Midillisi* is the fast-moving horse referred to here. In English this ancient breed is called the Mytilene or Aegean Pony. They were selectively bred by the Ottoman Turks using the smallest type of Anadolu Pony to develop an animal small enough to stand under trees for the purpose of collecting hazelnuts and olives. They have a "rahvan gait (very fast running-walk)" and "can carry a large load and travel long distances." "Mytilene," in Bonnie L. Hendricks and Anthony A. Dent, eds., *International Encyclopedia of Horse Breeds*, Oklahoma City: University of Oklahoma Press, 2007, pp. 303–4.
2   *The Times*, March 31, 1875, London, p. 5.

Chapter 2: Prosperity and Loss Soon to be Captured in the Dildilian Camera Lens

1   The reference to Dr. Jewett, the U.S. Consul, could be a reference to Dr. Milo Augustus Jewett, (1857–1921) who served as Consul in Sivas between the years 1892 and 1905, although this reference may also refer to his predecessor, his older brother, Henry M. Jewett, who served from 1886–91. While the reference could be to both Jewetts, the latter, Henry M., is never identified as a doctor. The Jewetts were born in Sivas to missionary parents and were fluent in Turkish and Armenian. "Mr. Hubbard" is clearly a reference to the American missionary, Albert Wells Hubbard (1841–99), who along with his wife, Emma, was a missionary for the American Board of Commissioners for Foreign Missions (A.B.C.F.M.) in Sivas between 1873 and 1899. Albert and Emma were well loved by the Armenian community and were influential in drawing some of the Dildilians to Protestantism.
2   Selim Aslantaş and A. Teyfur Erdoğdu, "Mehmed Memdüh," in C. Kafadar, H. Karateke, C. Fleischer, eds., *Historians of the Ottoman Empire*, 2006. http://www.ottomanhistorians.com/database/html/mmemduh_en.html. Accessed September 11, 2012.
3   Kemal H. Karpat, *Studies on Ottoman Social and Political History: Selected Articles and Essays*, Leiden: Brill, 2002, p. 76.
4   Robert H. Hewson, "Armenia on the Halys River: Lesser Armenia and Sebastia," in Richard G. Hovannisian, ed., *Armenian Sebastia/Sivas and Lesser Armenia*, Costa Mesa, CA: Mazda, 2004, p. 69. Hewson writes that more than ten schools for boys were maintained by the Apostolic Church, including the Targmanchants, Nersesian, Sahakian, Aramian, Rubinian, Torgomian, Prkichian, Surb Minas, Mhkitarian, and Vardanian. There were also four girls' schools: Gayaniants, Hrimpsimian, Lusinian, and Bezikian. Other sources have a slight variation in numbers and names.
5   A. Haverkort, *Potato Production in Turkey, and its Improvement in the Gudalan Valley*, International Potato Center (Region IV), and The Turkish National Potato Research and Training Programme,

Menemem, Turkey, 1981. p. 35. Cited in the "World Potato Atlas," https://research.cip.cgiar.org/confluence/display/wpa/Turkey.

6　S. Aslihan Gürbüzel, "Hamidian Policy in Eastern Anatolia, 1878–1890," Masters Thesis, Department of History, Bilkent University, Ankara, July 2008. http://www.belgeler.com/blg/1ca4/hamidian-policy-in-eastern-anatolia-1878-1890-ii-abdlhamid-dnemi-dou-anadolu-politikasi-1878-1890. Accessed August 10, 2012.

7　United States Public Health Service, *Weekly Abstracts of Sanitary Reports*, 9 (34) (August 24, 1894), p. 691.

8　"Woe unto him that giveth his neighbor drink, that puttest thy bottle to him, and makest him drunken also, that thou mayest look on his nakedness!" Habakkuk 2:15, *The 21st Century King James Version of the Holy Bible*. http://www.biblegateway.com/passage/?search=Habakkuk%20 2:15&version=KJ21.

Chapter 3: The Childhood Recollections of Aram Dildilian

1　Arak'el N. Patrik, *Patmagirkʻ hushamatean Sebastioy ew gawaṛi Hayutʻean*, New York: Hratarakutʻiwn Hamasebastahay Verashinatsʻ Miutʻean (Pan Sebastia Rehabilitation Union), 1974–83.

2　Robert H. Hewson, "Armenia on the Halys River: Lesser Armenia and Sebastia," in Richard G. Hovannisian, ed., *Armenian Sebastia/Sivas and Lesser Armenia*, Costa Mesa, CA: Mazda, 2004, p. 70.

Chapter 4: The Hamidian Massacres of 1894–96 and their Aftermath

1　Sultan Mahmud II was the sultan who actually put an end to the Janissaries in the 1826 "Auspicious Incident" (*Vaka-i Hayriye*). Sultan Abdülaziz (reigned June 25, 1861–May 30, 1876) was the son of Mahmud II. He was responsible for continuing the Tanzimat reforms begun during the reign of his brother, Abdülmecid. An Armenian cultural renaissance had begun in this period, especially in Constantinople.

2　In an article by Rev. Earnest C. Partridge in the *Missionary Herald*, Reshid Pasa is identified as an honest and incorruptible reformer who brought a degree of peace and security to the minorities of the vilayet of Sivas. See "A Turkish Reformer," *Missionary Herald*, 105 (5) (May 1909) pp. 196–7.

3　US Archives, RG59, General Records of the Department of State, Dispatches from the U.S. Consuls in Sivas, 1886–1906, no. 67, November 16, 1895.

Chapter 5: The Dildilians Begin their Separate Paths

1　George E. White, *Charles Chapin Tracy*, Boston: Pilgrim Press, 1918, pp. 35–6.

2　Robert H. Hewson, "Armenia on the Halys River: Lesser Armenia and Sebastia," in Richard G. Hovannisian, ed., *Armenian Sebastia/Sivas and Lesser Armenia*, Costa Mesa, CA: Mazda, 2004, p. 60.

3　There are a number of references to Armenians being buried alive: "At Sivas [Timur] buried alive '4,000 Armenians placed in rows of ten in large trenches, their heads tied to their thighs. A roof covered with earth was placed on these trenches, in order to make the death of these victims as frightful as possible.'" *Corpus Scriptorum. History of Byzantium*, Ducas I, XV, pp. 59–60 cited in Vazkène Aykouni, "A Brief Sketch of Armenian History," *Armenian Affairs*, I/I Winter 1949–50, p. 16.

4　Murad A. Meneshian, "Rural Sebastia: The Village of Govdun," in Richard G. Hovannisian, ed., *Armenian Sebastia/Sivas and Lesser Armenia*, Costa Mesa, CA: Mazda, 2004, p. 326.

5   "Darius, King of Persia," in L. W. King, R. Campell Thompson, Sir E. A. Wallis Budge, eds. and translators, *The Sculptures and Inscription of Darius the Great on the Rock of Behistûn in Persia*, London: British Museum, 1907.

6   Edward W. Martin, *The Hubbards of Sivas: A Chronicle of Love and Faith*, Santa Barbara: Fithian Press, 1991.

Chapter 6: The End of a Century and New Beginnings

1   *The Report and Catalogue of Anatolia College and the Girls' Boarding School, Marsovan, Turkey*, Marsovan, 1901, p. 11.

2   Maritsa's reference here is unclear. The Armenian alphabet was created in A.D. 405. Tsorig was born in 1911 so the date Maritsa recalls is mostly likely 1913 or possibly 1914. 1914 was marked by Jubilee celebrations for the 50th anniversary of Anatolia Girls' Boarding School.

3   Given the events described in this account, the wedding was earlier in the summer, probably early July 1908. The reference to the "proclamation of the constitution" refers to the restoration of the 1876 Constitution by Sultan Abdul Hamid II in response to the Young Turk revolution. The constitution was restored on July 24, 1908, so the wedding occurred before that date.

4   The Arvanites or, as Maritsa calls them, Arnavouts were Christian Orthodox who had migrated south in Greece and Ottoman lands. The reference here to Arvanites may be incorrect given the fact that Maritsa identifies them as Muslims.

Chapter 7: The Prosperity and Premonitions of the Pre-War Years

1   Alan Strachan, "Homecoming of the Hear," the 2010 Commencement address given at Haigazian University in Beirut, Lebanon. http://www.haigazian.edu.lb/NewsEvents/Pages/default.aspx?NewsID=293. Dr. Alan Stachan is the grandson of Armenag Haigazian.

2   "50th Anniversary's First Event: Founders' Day," Haigazian University, Beirut, Lebanon. http://www.haigazian.edu.lb/NewsEvents/Pages/default.aspx?NewsID=1.

3   A harrowing first-hand account of his murder is found in Grigoris Balakian, *Armenian Golgatha: A Memoir of the Armenian Genocide, 1915–1918*, trans. Peter Balakian and Aris Sevag, New York: Knopf, 2009, pp. 100–2.

4   Eddie Arnavoudian, "Daniel Varoujean: Keeper of the Faith in the Human Dream," Part 2, Armenian News Network / Groong, December 27, 2003. http://www.groong.org/tcc/tcc-20031227.html.

5   Daniel Varoujan, "The Carts," translated by Tatul Sonentz, from *The Song of Bread*. http://poetrytranslations.blogspot.com/2011/08/daniel-varoujan-carts.html, 2011.

6   Raymond Kévorkian, *The Armenian Genocide: A Complete History*, London: I.B.Tauris, 2011, p. 431.

7   The song was written by the Armenian folk musician (*gusan*), Sheram (born Grigor Talian, 1857–1938).

8   *Anatolia College, Library-Museum Building* (booklet), February 1914, ABC 16.5, reel 506, no. 579–80.

9   *The Anatolian*, Marsovan, January 1913, p. 23.

Chapter 8: The Clouds of War and Catastrophe

1   "This payment, called *bedel-i nakdi* (cash payment-in-lieu) in the sources, should not be confused with the – much lower – sums paid by non-Muslims until 1909. Those who had bought their exemption, like those who drew a lucky lot, were declared reservists, until a change in the law in 1914, which stipulated that they should serve for six months with the active army and only then be classified

as reservists. The same law of May 1914 also made the bedel applicable in peacetime only, but it seems doubtful that the Ottoman government, always hungry for money, actually suspended the practice during World War I." Erik-Jan Zürcher, "The Ottoman Conscription System In Theory And Practice, 1844–1918," *International Review of Social History*, 43 (3) (1998), pp. 437–49.

2   *The Anatolian. Bulletin for the Year 1914–'15. Anatolia College. Anatolia Girls' School*, Marsovan, Turkey, March 31, 1915, pp. 7–8.

3   Erik-Jan Zürcher, "Between Death and Desertion. The Ottoman Army in World War I," *Turcica* 28 (1996), pp. 235–58.

4   Bertha B. Morley, *Marsovan 1915: The Diaries of Bertha Morley*, ed. Hilmar Kaiser, Ann Arbor, Michigan: Gomidas Institute, 2000. Morley's diary provides a good chronology of the events taking place in Marsovan.

5   Raymond Kévorkian, *The Armenian Genocide: A Complete History*, London: I.B. Tauris, 2011, p. 452.

6   Morley, *Marsovan 1915*, p. 4.

7   Morley, p. 6.

8   Talât Paşa, *Ermeni vahşeti* (1916), Istanbul: Örgün Yayinevi, 2005.

9   Morley, p. 8.

10   Morley, p. 8, cites the lower figure while Professor Theodore A. Elmer of Anatolia College cites the higher. (See James Bryce, Arnold Toynbee, *The Treatment of Armenians in the Ottoman Empire, 1915–1916*, ed. Ara Sarafian, 2nd ed., Princeton: Gomidas Institute, 2005, p. 362.) The latter figure agrees with the number given in the unpublished manuscript by Garabed Kiremidjian, "The Life of the Kiremidjian Family," trans. and ed. David Kiremidjian, 2007, personal collection, p. 64.

11   Morley, pp. 10–11.

12   "Statement by George E. White," p. 78.

13   Morley, p. 11.

14   "Statement by George E. White," p. 78.

15   Garabed Kiremidjian, "The Life of the Kiremidjian Family," p. 65.

16   Kiremidjian, p. 65. "[Marsovan]: Letter, Dated New York City, 30th December 1915, From Professor {J. P. Xenidhis}, of the College at {Marsovan}, To an Armenian Professor Resident Beyond the Ottoman Frontier," in James Bryce, Arnold Toynbee, *The Treatment of Armenians in the Ottoman Empire, 1915–1916*, p. 389.

17   Kiremidjian, p. 66.

18   Morley, p. 14.

19   Morley, p. 15.

20   Morley, p. 29.

21   Morley writes in her diary: "We received a wire from the Ambassador to Peter, American Consular Agent, dated August 5. 'Urgent. Minister of War promised me today to telegraph, authorization all professors with their families, nurses, pupils, etc. connected with Americans to remain at Marsovan unmolested.' The Consul sent his vesika to the Kaimakam, which the latter seems to recognize. He sent back a reply, 'Unless orders come from Constantinople, all must go on sefkiat.'" Morley, p. 50.

22   Taner Akçam, *The Young Turks' Crime Against Humanity: The Armenian Genocide and Ethnic Cleansing in the Ottoman Empire*. Princeton: Princeton University Press, 2013, *passim*.

23   Kiremidjian, p. 65.

24   Morley, p. 76.

25   Carl Compton, *The Morning Cometh: 45 Years with Anatolia College*, Thessaloniki: Anatolia College Board of Trustees, 2008, pp. 69–70.

26   Haïg Der Haroutiounian, *Polyphonies anatoliennes: Chronique de l'itinéraire d'une famille arménienne à la fin de l'empire ottoman, Yozgat-Sivas-Marzevan, 1872–1922*, Mémoire présenté en vue diplôme de l'EHESS, Paris 2007, p. 8.

27 These young men are referred to as "deserters" in the memoirs though they never served in the army. They escaped the deportations and conscription into the army.

28 Der Haroutiounian, *Polyphonies anatoliennes*, p. 157.

29 The photograph of the Geneva flag was taken by Haïk Der Haroutiounian and reproduced in *Polyphonies anatoliennes*. He describes the flag thus: "Le fanion, à droite, a été photographié par l'auteur à la Maison de la Culture Arménienne d'Alfortville avec l'aimable autorisation de Mme Hasmig Nadirian-Kévonian. On notera les six étoiles, qui symbolisent sans doute les six provinces à fort pourcentage de population arménienne, appelées en turc «Ermenistan» jusu'en 1864: Erzeroum, Van, Bitlis, Kharpert, Diyarbekir et Sivas." [The flag, right, was photographed by the author in the House of Armenian Culture Alfortville courtesy of Ms. Hasmig Nadirian-Kévonian. Note the six stars, which probably symbolize the six provinces with a high percentage of Armenian population, called in Turkish "Ermenistan" until 1864, Erzurum, Van, Bitlis, Kharpert, Diyarbekir and Sivas.], p. 157.

30 According to Kiremidjian many of these Armenians converted and were allowed to return to Marsovan: "According to the deportation order, the Protestant and Armenian Catholics were exempt from arrest and were not deported. Of their own will, the Protestants went to the neighboring village, Osmanjouk [Osmanoglu, today], and the Catholics went to another Armenian village, Yeni-jeh [Yenice, today], where my friend Momjian Hovhannes lived. The Kaymakam sent Momjian a message to come to Marsovan, but Momjian and the peasants did not return, saying that they did not want to be converted and hence were deported. The Protestants however did accept Mohammedanism, returned to Marsovan, gave the required bribes, and accepted the *hockdin* ('this is the real religion')." Kiremidjian, pp. 65–6.

31 Morley, p. 33.

32 Morley's diary reveals that Professor Xenidhis (Xenides) was given permission to take his family to Constantinople and then on to Greece. He departed Marsovan on August 3 (Morley, p. 47). He provides testimony to the Bryce & Toynbee report to the British Parliamentary investigation of the Turkish atrocities. See *The Treatment of Armenians in the Ottoman Empire, 1915–1916*, pp. 388–91.

33 Kiremidjian describes how he was able to set up this factory employing young Armenian soldiers: "All those under 45 years among the Armenians who were not deported were required to go into the military; they were to serve without arms, as laborers. This suited us well as we did not want to become regulars. For the uniforms of the soldiers, the military administration commandeered from the Armenian merchants various fabrics, flannels, cottons, and so forth; instead of money they gave notes. We knew that they needed fabrics for the soldiers very badly. All the converted women had looms, and we bought the wool, which we gave them for spinning thread, and from this they wove the cloth, put it through the fulling process, and the readymade sample was sent to the Commandant of the Sixth Army, advising them, if they approved the sample, that we could produce it for the army. They approved it and wanted to help us in any way they could; we therefore founded a society of 40 persons with a capital of 10,000 liras. We began to produce the finished fabric, delivered it to the army and cashed its value." Kiremidjian, p. 66.

34 According to Kiremidjian's own memoir the figure cited was 50 Turkish liras each. He goes on to mention that 3,000 of the 12,000 Armenians in the city initially agreed to convert, which would have meant a profit of 150,000 TL, a tidy sum of money. As a result of an order restricting the number of Armenians who could remain to 5 percent of the town's population, the 3,000 figure was reduced to 1,200. The Ottoman records indicate that only 307 were officially registered as remaining, which would be statistically much smaller than the 5 percent rule would allow since the city's population was somewhere between 25,000 and

30,000. The *vali* of Sivas, the kaimakam's superior, demanded that the numbers of Armenians allowed to stay be reduced. I assume that no refunds were provided for those who had paid and were subsequently deported (Kiremidjian, p. 65). See also, Hasan Babacan, "Tehcir Kanununun Uygulanmasinda Merzifon'da Muaf Tutulan Bir Kisim Ermeniler," in Hasan Babacan, ed., *Geçmişten Günümüze Merzifon*, Ankara: 2010, pp. 365–82. His cited document lists 307 names including my grandfather and his immediate family. The Der Haroutiounians are not included in this list, which may account for the kind of discrepancy that contributed to the difference between 1,200 and the 307 figures. The authorities were probably keeping a double set of books.

35 Kiremidjian, p. 67.

36 Morley describes these events in her diary, Morley, pp. 75–8. She reports that on September 11, "30 or more households … all turned Armenians" were deported.

Chapter 9: The Years after the Great War: Rebuilding their Shattered Lives

1 Author: Ray Palmer (1830). Tune: Lowell Mason (1830). Source: Baptist Hymnal 2008 #509. The hymn can be found on many websites, e.g., http://www.hymnal.net/hymn.php/h/429.

2 George E. White, *Adventuring with Anatolia College*, Grinnell, IA: Herald-Register Pub. Co., 1940, p. 95.

3 White, p. 95.

4 White, p. 95.

5 White, p. 104.

6 White, p. 96.

7 White, p. 97.

8 White, p. 98.

9 White, p. 105.

10 White, p. 106.

11 White, p. 104.

12 Carl C. Compton, *The Morning Cometh: 45 Years with Anatolia College*, Thessaloniki: Anatolia College Board of Trustees, 2008, p. 89.

13 White, p. 106.

Chapter 10: Their Days Are Numbered: No Place in Turkey for the Dildilians

1 George E. White, *Adventuring with Anatolia College*, Grinnell, IA: Herald-Register Pub. Co., 1940, p. 107.

2 White, p. 107.

3 Carl C. Compton, *The Morning Cometh: 45 Years with Anatolia College*, Thessaloniki: Anatolia College Board of Trustees, 2008, p. 90.

4 Compton, p. 90.

5 White, p. 109.

6 White, p. 110.

7 A memo I have seen from a staff member, initials H. G. D., in the Division of Near Eastern Affairs of the U.S. Department of State, bemoans the fact that Admiral Bristol did not pass on reports of massacres of Armenians and Greeks to the Secretary of State at the time.

8 A chilling eyewitness account of these atrocities was given by a Near East Relief worker, A. Gertrude Anthony, the niece of Susan B. Anthony, who was on the Anatolia College grounds during Topal Osman's rampage in Marsovan. She wrote a 15-page report to Mark L. Bristol, the

American High Commissioner to Turkey on November 1, 1921. Admiral Bristol did not pass it on to the Secretary of State. A second version was directly delivered to the State Department in mid-December. The report was declassified on May 5, 1961 and is available in the U.S. State Department archives.

9 "90 Casualties in Samsun," *New York Times*, June 12, 1922.

LIST OF ILLUSTRATIONS

INDEX

Aram Dildilian, Haïganouch Der Haroutiounian, and Maritsa Médaksian,
as the chief narrators of the story, are generally not indexed.
Indexed illustrations are indicated in italics.